Democratization and Islamic Law

Johannes Harnischfeger, Dr. phil., Dr. rer. pol., studied Philosophy, German Literature, Ethnology and Political Science. He has taught at universities in Kenya, Nigeria and South Africa.

Johannes Harnischfeger

Democratization and Islamic Law

The Sharia Conflict in Nigeria

Campus Verlag
Frankfurt/New York

Distribution throughout the world except Germany, Austria and Switzerland by

The University of Chicago Press
1427 East 60th Street
Chicago, IL 60637

Bibliographic Information published by the Deutsche Nationalbibliothek.
Die Deutsche Nationalbibliothek lists this publication in the Deutsche Nationalbibliografie;
detailed bibliographic data are available in the Internet at http://dnb.d-nb.de.
ISBN 978-3-593-38256-2

For further information:
www.campus.de
www.press.uchicago.edu

Contents

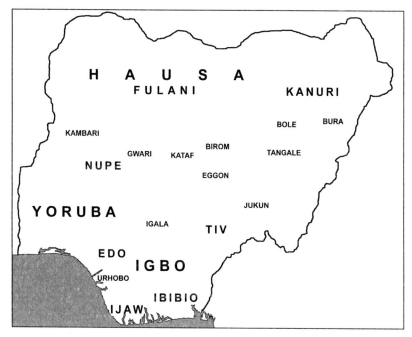

Map 1. Nigeria: Ethic Groups

Map 2. Nigeria: 36 States

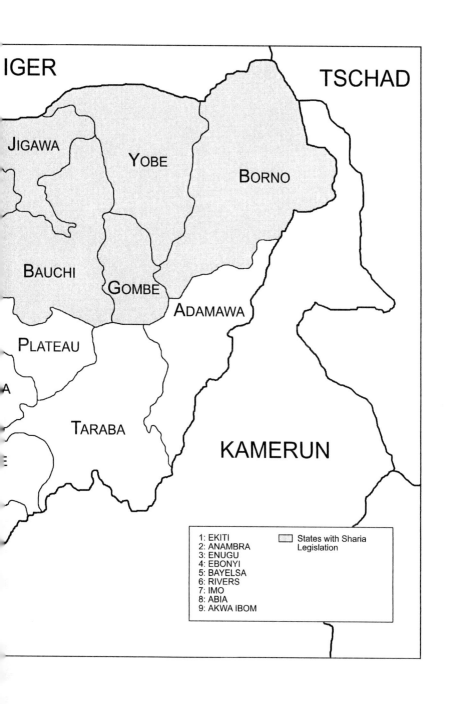

IGER

TSCHAD

JIGAWA

YOBE

BORNO

BAUCHI

GOMBE

ADAMAWA

PLATEAU

A

TARABA

KAMERUN

1: EKITI
2: ANAMBRA
3: ENUGU
4: EBONYI
5: BAYELSA
6: RIVERS
7: IMO
8: ABIA
9: AKWA IBOM

States with Sharia
Legislation

Acknowledgments

I am grateful to Aurel Croissant, Umar Danfulani, Joseph Kenny, Isaac Laudarji and Wolfgang Merkel who commented on earlier versions of this book, and to Jeremy Gaines, Conor McNamara and Jena Gaines who helped in the translation. I would also like to thank the German Research Foundation for funding part of my research in Nigeria.

Introduction

»This Sharia crisis is just a question of [...] who owns the country.«[1]

The Return of Religion into Politics

The transition to democracy, in early 1999, had unexpected consequences. In some states of Northern Nigeria, dominated by Islamic ethnic groups, especially the Hausa-Fulani, the newly-elected parliaments introduced an Islamic penal code and other Sharia laws. Supporters of Sharia, apparently a large majority among Muslims, argued that they were only asserting their right to self-determination. They simply wanted to organize their lives according to the tenets of their faith, without forcing their beliefs on others. This is why Christians and so-called Traditionalists were expressly exempted from the harsh penalties for theft and adultery. When non-Muslims are involved in a legal dispute, whether civil or criminal, they have the right to be heard before a secular court.

Nonetheless, the Muslims' call for autonomy flies in the face of Nigeria's moderately secular tradition. The constitution makes provision for Sharia courts where Muslims can settle family affairs, but only if all parties to a dispute agree to have their case decided by Islamic law. Such courts have operated in most states of the Muslim North for decades. However, no state government has introduced ›full Sharia‹, which includes Islamic criminal law and a strict gender separation. The constitution does not allow elevating any religion to a state religion. Yet this principle is violated when governors in the North use state authority to Islamize public life. In Zamfara, the first state to introduce a strict form of Sharia, the government claimed that its religious reform was bringing about major changes: »all spheres of public life are being transformed into Islamic oriented institu-

---

1 Ex-Brigadier Benjamin Adekunle, in *Tell*, 27 March 2000, p. 17.

tions.«[2] This state-sponsored Islamization affected non-Muslims as well, as they were subjected to some Sharia proscriptions like the ban on alcohol and gender separation in hotels and restaurants, in buses and taxis. In Zamfara's state schools, boys and girls were separated without regard to their faith. In addition, all girls and young women were forced to conform to the Islamic dress code.

Critics of Sharia accused the new legislation of violating basic human rights: Muslims and non-Muslims, men and women are not treated equally, even though Nigeria's Western-oriented constitution forbids discrimination on the basis of religion or gender. Moreover, punishments such as flogging, stoning and amputation are to be regarded as torture or at least as »inhuman or degrading treatment«, which is prohibited by the constitution.[3] Representatives of Christian churches and human rights organizations have thus called for Sharia to be banned. Yet in the South of Nigeria, where Christians are in the majority, human dignity is not always respected, either. In most states, the authorities have supported ethnic militias or vigilantes that hunt down criminals. Anyone suspected of having committed a violent crime must reckon with a quick trial. The militiamen drag the condemned to some street corner and execute them with machetes, gasoline and car tires. Given this widespread use of summary justice, one cannot accuse the Sharia courts of being particularly cruel.[4] In any event, the harsh *hudud* punishments have only been applied very hesitantly. In the first three years of Sharia, the courts sentenced more than 60 thieves to amputation, but only three cases became known in which the sentence was actually carried out.[5] A more dangerous aspect of Sharia, in my opinion, is that it contributes to the decline of the state:

- By declaring the will of God the highest authority, Sharia politicians have given believers permission to disregard all man-made laws and agreements that are at variance with Islam. This undermined the legitimacy of the Christian president, and it also threatens the authority of the emirs and other representatives of the Islamic establishment.

---

2 From a government press statement, in *Hotline*, 4 June 2000, p. 24. – In an interview with *The News* (25 October 1999, p. 27), the Governor of Zamfara claimed: »we are a Muslim state.«

3 Federal Republic of Nigeria, *Constitution 1999*, Section 34 (1).

4 Walles, *Shari'a*, p. 653; Human Rights Watch, *Political Shari'a?*, p. 6; Pérouse de Montclos, *Nigeria*, p. 161.

5 Human Rights Watch, *Political Shari'a?*, pp. 36–37.

- The call to shape state and society through the rules of Islam has increased antagonism between Muslims and members of other faiths. Christians and Traditionalists are worried that Islamic law may spread to other parts of Nigeria and that it may pervade more spheres of social life. Where Sharia becomes dominant, non-Muslims are excluded, to a large extent, from political participation, and their social environment is determined by the laws of an alien religion.

Naturally, Sharia advocates have a different assessment of the consequences of their religious commitment. Their aim was to purge the corrupt state of all immoral practices and, in so doing, to imbue it with new legitimacy: »Shari'a is [...] bringing absolute sanity over the decadent land.«[6] Moreover, Sharia activists denied that their reform policy endangered the peaceful coexistence between the religious communities. They justified the return to their own separate laws by invoking, vis-à-vis non-Muslims, the model of multi-culturalism: »the stability of this country is going to be derived from [...] recognising our cultural diversity.«[7] They maintained that Christians and Traditionalists should recognize that Nigeria is a pluralist society in which every religious community has the right to live according to its own rules. As a means of »cultural self-determination«, Sharia helps to preserve Northern Nigeria's »authentic« culture.[8] In addition, it contributes to legal pluralism, providing an alternative to Western, secular ideas of law, which had been forced on Africans by the colonial power: »Shariacracy [is] a defense against unwanted cultural globalization [...] an alternative to the Western constitutional and legal inheritance.«[9] However, Muslim citizens who are now subject to the draconian Islamic punishments for theft and adultery have not won additional options for self-determination. In case of legal disputes, they cannot choose whether they will stand before a religious or a secular judge. At the behest of the authorities, they are subject to the laws of God in all legal matters. Muslim self-determination does not strengthen the rights of the individual, but empowers the Islamic community, or more accurately, its leaders, who decide in the name of Islam how their brothers in faith have to live: »Muslims have been able to

---

6 *Hotline*, 19 March 2000, p. 25.

7 Ahmed Sani Yerima, Governor of Zamfara State, in *Tell*, 8 September 2003, p. 39; cf. Tabiu, *Sharia*, p. 2; Supreme Council for Sharia, *Plot*, p. 27.

8 Mazrui, *Shariacracy*, pp. 2, 4, 8.

9 *Ibid.*, p. 8, Mazrui, *Two Africas*, pp. 152–154, 164.

take their destiny in their own hands. [...] They are content to submit totally to the Will of Allah.«[10]

Sharia politicians who try to enforce an orthodox way of life are not sincerely interested in cultural diversity. The Sharia Penal Code, which was adopted in Zamfara and other states, contains the death penalty for Muslims who participate in ›pagan‹ rites.[11] It is unlikely that Islamic judges will resort to such drastic punishments, but there are clear tendencies to restrict non-Islamic forms of worship. Non-Muslims have reason to fear that they will become »second-class citizens.«[12] So they observed with trepidation how the Sharia campaign took hold of more and more states. Right at the beginning, in September 1999, when the parliament of Zamfara passed a Sharia law, it had met with little protest, because more than 90 percent of the local population in the far North, on the edge of the Sahel, are Muslims. But then eleven more states followed suit, some of which are home to large Christian minorities. When the Governor of Kaduna announced the introduction of Sharia, although non-Muslims form almost half of the population, violence erupted, leaving more than 1,000 people dead.[13] Following these first ›Sharia clashes‹, Nigeria's president, a Christian Yoruba from the Southwest, invited the governors of the North to the capital city, Abuja, and tried to persuade them to suspend their Sharia plans. But they would not be moved, and so new conflicts broke out in Kaduna, Kano and Jos, claiming the lives of about 5,000 citizens.[14] Since then, non-Muslims have resigned themselves to the fact that Sharia remains in force, at least officially. To rebel against it would only endanger the position of the Christian minority: »the more non-Muslims react negatively to the Sharia, the worse the situation is likely to get.«[15] Christians and Muslims are far from reaching an amicable solution. They may negotiate arrangements on a local level, but as the local balance of power is constantly shifting, the rival parties cannot reach a stable compromise. The constant striving for dominance generates tensions and anxieties, which often erupt in violence. In most cases, religious antagonisms are interwoven with ethnic conflicts, with disputes over scarce land resources, and with rivalries in local markets.

---

10 Yadudu, *Benefits of Shariah*, p. 11.

11 Zamfara State of Nigeria, *Shariah Penal Code*, Section 405, 406.

12 Ilesanmi, *Constitutional Treatment*, p. 547; An-Na'im, *Future of Shari'ah*, p. 329.

13 Danfulani, *Sharia Issue*, pp. 15–22, Boer, *Nigeria*, pp. 62–79; *The News*, 13 March 2000, p. 15.

14 Danfulani/Fwatshak, *Jos*, p. 243; Higazi, *Violence*, p. 83; *Tell*, 18 September 2000, p. 40.

15 Kukah, *Human Rights*, p. 27.

On the Jos Plateau, where the ›indigenous‹ Christian population sees its numerical dominance threatened by Muslim migrants from the North, both sides have tried to expel each other from their territory. After an estimated 54,000 people had died,[16] the central government declared a state of emergency in May 2004, which placed the entire state under the administration of a retired army general for half a year.[17]

Observers in Europe and North America paid little attention to the political implications of Sharia. They were mainly concerned with the severe punishments, the ›unfair‹ trials and the discrimination against women.[18] Given these grievances, Western critics demanded that Islamic authorities comply with ›international‹ standards of human rights, but they showed little interest in other controversial issues, such as what Sharia means for the cohesion of a multi-religious state. Some commentators thought it completely legitimate that Muslims govern their community according to their own religious laws, claimung that in a federation like Nigeria, the 36 states should be allowed to go their separate ways, even when it comes to criminal legislation. Muslim attempts to realize, as much as possible, their own ideas of law and morality are thus seen as part of a healthy democratic competition and therefore »entirely politically correct.«[19] Some critics of secularism even argued that the politicization of religion brings advantages, because it enriches public debates with new ideas on how to organize society. By defending their right to be different, Muslims challenge the »monological« view of human rights organizations and suggest alternatives to it.[20] Therefore it would be disastrous to outlaw Islam's different concepts of law and try to impose the Western separation of state and religion.

Islamic reservations about secularism are shared by some authors in Europe and the USA:

»Although Islam has led in the opposition to secularism, Christians should stand shoulder to shoulder with their Muslim brothers and sisters [...]. It is better to

---

16 According to an official report, cf. Economist Intelligence Unit, *Country Profile Nigeria 2007*, p. 15.

17 Human Rights Watch, *Revenge in the Name of Religion*, pp. 1–2, 40.

18 Kogelmann, *Islamisches Recht*, p. 1.

19 Ostien, *Ten Good Things*, p. 167.

20 Upendra Baxi, in Hackett, *Role of Religion*, p. 92.

make some concessions to accommodate Muslim convictions [...] than to lose our religious soul to the godless forces of political correctness and secularism.«[21]

Breaking with secularism is not only the concern of conservative religious circles; postmodern theories can lead to similar consequences. They can deconstruct the secular order as a power relationship which suppresses religion and expels it from public life. Politically ambitious religions are no longer seen as a major threat; rather they appear as »victims« that are reclaiming their rightful place in society after a long time in »exile.«[22] The present religious renaissance is greeted as a liberating force, because it challenges the intolerance and hegemony of secularism. Those who stick to the old secular dogmas, derived from the ideology of eighteenth century Enlightenment, only provoke unnecessary conflict, especially with Muslims, who are »humiliated« by a secular legal system.[23]

In Nigeria, the debate about secularism has taken a similar turn. A growing number of Christians see the exclusion of religion from politics as a mistake: »The separation of the state from religion, part of the Western democratic tradition, is fast becoming old-fashioned [...] a secularised view of the world devoid of ›true religion‹ can only produce misery, conflict and war.«[24] Although representatives of the major churches still defend the secular elements of the constitution, they do this less out of religious conviction than for pragmatic-political reasons. For them, in a multi-religious country, state authorities should not interfere in religious matters, lest they become embroiled in destructive disputes.[25] However, secular principles that had been brought to the country by Christian missionaries and the colonial administration have remained foreign to most Nigerians. In precolonial times, political power was always based on an alliance with spiritual forces. Every clan, every village and every town community gathered around a shrine to receive strength through the alliance with ancestors or local deities. When enemy groups waged war against each other, their spiritual allies fought with them. Thus the warring parties had no qualms about destroying their opponent's places of worship or stealing their sacred objects. With the Africanization of Christianity, ideas of spiritual warfare have been revived, so that religious and worldly power appear inseparable.

---

21 McCain, *Shari'ah Controversy*, p. 15.
22 Hatzopoulos/Petito, *Return from Exile*, p. 1.
23 Keane, *Limits of Secularism*, pp. 36–7.
24 Gwamna, *Commentary*, pp. 321, 325.
25 Sanneh, *Shari'ah Sanctions*, p. 241; Nwabueze, *Unconstitutionality of Sharia*, p. 3.

Another factor in the growing rejection of secular principles could be the failure of the state. Bureaucratic institutions cannot stop the social and political disintegration, so the only means to control people's behavior and restore some social order seems to be religion.[26] Ideas of right or wrong are increasingly formulated in light of religious principles, so people's faith becomes more relevant for profane, ›extra-religious‹ affairs. In an intensely religious social environment, political systems may only gain stability when they are in accord with religious norms. Since trust in secular state authorities has broken down, a growing number of Christian intellectuals put their hope in religion. They are of the opinion that a decadent and disoriented society can only find a way out of its crisis, if it turns to a transcendent authority that is not contaminated by the general decline: »If Christians and Muslims in Nigeria live the life of their Bible and Koran, there will be harmony.«[27]

Religion and Democracy

Nigeria's dispute over the political role of religion is part of a global debate that questions a basic consensus of liberal democracies. In this debate, the dividing lines do not simply run between the major world religions. Attempts to »unmodernize«[28] faith and liberate it from secular restrictions are also gaining influence within Christianity: »experiments with secularized religion have generally failed; religious movements with beliefs and practices dripping with reactionary supernaturalism [...] have widely succeeded.«[29] A large proportion of American citizens describe themselves as ›fundamentalists‹.[30] This does not mean that they would reject their country's constitution. In contrast to Islamic ›fundamentalists‹, evangelical or charismatic Protestants adhere to secular principles. However, the term ›secular‹ does not mean much more than state neutrality.[31] Most Christian

---

26 Ellis/ter Haar, *Worlds of Power*, pp. 172, 191–2.

27 Nzeh, *Dialogue of Religions*, p. 381.

28 Hatzopoulos/Petito, *Return from Exile*, p. 14.

29 Berger, *Desecularization*, p. 4; cf, Jenkins, *Next Christendom*, pp. 191–209; Roy, *Globalised Islam*, p. 330.

30 *Die Zeit*, 7 October 2004, p. 46.

31 Since many different phenomena are defined as ›secular‹, some writers have suggested a terminological distinction. The state's benevolent neutrality toward religious communi-

groups in the USA would agree that the state is not permitted to favor any of the numerous churches or to discriminate against them, yet claim that public life should be shaped by Christian values, and the state should promote the social activities of faith-based organizations: »Christianity is not to be separated from the world [...]. [It] affects the totality of our being and must be practised twenty-four hours a day, even when we are in public.«[32] State authorities, from the president to the courts, have followed this trend of reversing the separation between church and state: »over the last fifteen years the US Supreme Court has abandoned much of its earlier separationism. [...] public religion must be as free as private religion.«[33]

The claim to follow one's religious convictions in the private as in the public sphere is usually justified in the name of religious freedom. Recent interpretations tend to define this basic right in a very broad sense. It includes not only the right »to profess a faith or to engage in cultic-religious activities«, but also the right »to live out one's faith in all areas of life.«[34] In keeping with this generous interpretation of religious freedom, the parliament of Ontario, Canada, discussed plans to allow a limited form of Sharia, so that Muslim citizens can choose at least in family and inheritance disputes, whether they want to be subject to secular or religious authorities. In Europe, a growing number of legal experts and politicians are pleading to recognize group rights, especially the rights of religious minorities, because »religion could [...] be important in strengthening the cultural resources and bonds of migrant communities.«[35] Yet if religious authorities are empowered to administer their own laws and control people's behavior, important achievements of modernity, such as equality before the law, will be lost. The rights of citizens will be determined according to their faith, and the observation of these rights becomes an internal matter from which ›unbelievers‹ are excluded. Through this exclusivity, religious communities have the opportunity to build up internal

---

ties is called secularity, while the attempt to push back religious influence and make it politically harmless is referred to as secularism. Nigeria's Catholic bishops have recently expressed their support for secularity, but not for secularism (cf. Nwobi, *Sharia*, pp. 72–75). Hans Küng (*Islam*, p. 768) presents a similar argument: It was a »fundamental mistake of modernity to assume that religion can be permanently suppressed, ignored or privatized.« As a result, a legitimate and »sensible secularization changed into a less sensible atheist-agnostic secularism with many negative consequences.«

32 McCain, *Shari'ah Controversy*, p. 14.
33 Hackett, *Role of Religion*, pp. 82–83.
34 Volkmann, *Rechtsordnung*, p. 8.
35 Nolte, *Rückkehr der Religion*, p. 10.

power structures and to confer on their leaders an authority that evades public control. Members with dissenting opinions are put under pressure, and particularly women and children face oppression, because their constitutional rights, which the state should guarantee, are protected partially at best.[36]

There is a growing tendency in multi-religious societies to allow parts of public life to be regulated by religious norms. Yet there is also considerable opposition to it. Influential political thinkers argue that the emergence of religiously diverse Christian-Muslim societies in Europe and other parts of the world makes it all the more necessary to preserve the secular order and shield the political system from religious competition. With the increasing variety of religious persuasions, citizens no longer share basic assumptions about law and morality, so the danger of deep divisions and irreconcilable conflicts rises. Compromises are hard to find, because political demands motivated by religious convictions often pose absolute and hence non-negotiable claims for validity.[37] As ideas about justice and human dignity diverge greatly, it becomes difficult to formulate and realize ideas of the public good. What binds Christians, Muslims and irreligious people together is not much more than the common interest in ensuring that everybody can realize his or her own ideas of a good life: »citizens [...] agree to disagree about many fundamental matters.«[38] If society cannot reach a consensus on how a just and humane social order should look, then the state should refrain from transforming society according to such ideals. It would be unreasonable to use the public's political power to enforce a religious vision »about which citizens [...] are bound to differ uncompromisingly.«[39] Instead, government should »be neutral on the question of good life, [...] respecting persons as free and independent selves, unencumbered by moral ties antecedent to choice.«[40] Following this maxim, democracy would develop into a procedural republic, with greatly reduced social functions. Its main aim would be to guarantee the conditions under which Christians and Muslims, believers and non-believers can live side by side, without disturbing each other.

---

36 Habermas, *Cultures*, pp. 6, 18–20; Kepel, *Revenge of God*, p. 201.
37 Habermas, *Cultures*, p. 25.
38 Barnhart, *Overlapping Consensus*, p. 259.
39 Rawls, *Political Liberalism*, p. 138.
40 Sandel, *Religious Liberty*, p. 73.

When citizens pursue increasingly different ways of life, it becomes all the more important that they feel bound to a minimum of constitutional rules. In a liberal state that rejects despotism, citizens have to accept the laws of the state voluntarily and acknowledge them as their own: »Democratic legitimacy requires that the laws we live under in some sense result from our collective decisions.«[41] Despite their diversity, people have to see themselves as a political unit that deliberates on common issues and decides them on behalf of all its members. However, in religiously divided societies, the idea of an overarching democratic community fades, and its decisions lose legitimacy. How can the state ensure that Muslims, Christians and agnostics feel bound to majority decisions? An open debate and common decisions are only possible if political institutions are not framed by principles which derive from one of the rival religions, to the exclusion of others:

»secularism in some form is a necessity for the democratic life of religiously diverse societies. Both the sense of mutual bonding and the crucial reference points of the political debate that flow from it have to be accessible to citizens of different confessional allegiances, or of none. If the people in this sense were to be confessionally defined, then in fact, non-members would be excluded from full participation in self-rule.«[42]

When Muslims in Northern Nigeria decide to shape their penal code in accordance with their own religious tradition, they exclude non-Muslims from an important aspect of public legislation. As the introduction of Sharia demonstrates, the transition to democracy is not a protection against religious conflicts; it only strengthens the politics of exclusion. The right of self-determination appeals to people who feel united by common values and traditions; it is claimed for one's own religious or ethnic group, not for the Nigerian people as a whole.

»The exclusion is a by-product [...] of the need, in self-governing societies, of a high degree of cohesion. [...] Democracy obliges much more solidarity and much more commitment to one another in the joint political project than was demanded by the hierarchical and authoritarian societies of yesteryear. [...] To form a state, in the democratic era, a society is forced to undertake the difficult and never-to-be-completed task of defining its collective identity.«[43]

---

41 Taylor, *Modes of Secularism*, p. 45.
42 *Ibid.*, p. 46; Habermas, *Religion*, pp. 101–104.
43 Taylor, *Democracy*, pp. 181, 183–184; Taylor, *Religion und Identitätskämpfe*, pp. 362–364.

By defining self-determination in religious terms, the Muslim majority in Northern Nigeria is marginalizing the Christian minority and forcing them to accept the conditions imposed by a rival religious community. According to this exclusive understanding of democracy, citizens have to acknowledge that Zamfara, Kano and Sokoto are »Muslim states that wish to see their state apparatus organized in conformity with their faith.«[44] In such states, non-believers cannot expect to stand at the head of government; they are relegated to the position of a permanent minority. Thus one of the conditions for a functioning democracy ceases to exist: the possibility of changing majorities.

However, Sharia is not to blame for the failure of Nigeria's Fourth Republic. Democracy has never worked in Nigeria. When the Northern People's Congress, a Hausa-Fulani dominated party, took over Nigeria's first independent government in 1960, its leaders asserted their hegemony by whatever means. They rigged elections, falsified census figures, and crushed opposition with military force. Those who lost out could not rely on the protection of democratic institutions. This has not changed with the present Fourth Republic, which was proclaimed in May 1999, after fifteen years of military rule. Its first president, Olusegun Obasanjo, did not come to office through fair elections, but through the machinations of some power brokers in the North. Under his rule, the state introduced some economic reforms, and it improved on its abysmal human rights record. The press is now largely free, the regions enjoy much autonomy, and there is intense political competition. However, core institutions of a democratic state, like the parliament and the judiciary, are not working, and the elections have not become freer or more transparent. When Obasanjo was voted into office in early 1999, rigging was rampant and not more than 20 percent of the electorate had cast their vote.[45] Nevertheless, international election monitors gave the winner a clean bill, because they did not want to jeopardize the transition from a military to a civilian government. The exit of the generals went smoothly, but the ›democratization‹ process did not consolidate democracy. In the 2003 elections, Obasanjo and his People's Democratic Party (PDP) tightened their grip on power. They were able to increase their number of senators from 67 to 73 (out of a total of 109), and their number of congressmen from 212 to 221 (out of 360). Of the 36 states, they won 28 (up from 21), though in some states elections had vir-

---

44 Tabiu, *Sharia*, p. 10.
45 Greiter/Jockers/Rohde, *Wahlbeobachtung 1999*, pp. 344–348; Kew, *Monitoring*, p. 31.

tually not taken place.[46] Before the elections in April 2007, observers speculated that the ruling party »will probably have to steal a lot more votes than in 2003« in order to stay in power.[47] Yet the PDP succeeded again. President Obasanjo, who had to give up power after two terms in office, had picked a successor and rigged the elections in his favor, relying on the help of the police, the State Security Service and the Independent National Electoral Commission, whose chairman he had appointed.

Since voters have little influence on the outcome of elections, one could call Nigeria's Fourth Republic a ›defective‹ or ›hybrid‹ democracy. Popular participation is a central requirement of democracy; when it is not secured, it might even be more appropriate to say that there is no democracy at all.[48] Democracy requires a high degree of trust. Ruling elites will only accept electoral defeat and leave office, if they can trust their rivals, once in government, to give them a fair chance to regain power. In Nigeria, where military and civilian regimes were afraid of giving up power, they have weakened or destroyed all democratic institutions which could have mediated between rival elite factions. Without rules that regulate the exercise of power, politicians had to resort to informal bargaining. However, informal agreements between elites that do not trust each other are unreliable; they have to be backed up by the threat of force. In order to put pressure on their rivals, politicians have mobilized their ethnic and religious followers, with devastating results: »It is estimated that at least 50,000 people have been killed in various incidents of ethnic, religious and communal violence since the return to civilian rule.«[49] Violence, as we shall see, is not just manipulated by elites. It is also fueled by popular movements which are highly critical of the political establishment. Nigeria's ›civil society‹, which ought to act as a counter-weight to corrupt state authorities, is deeply divided along ethnic and religious lines. And its organizations have developed little democratic structures internally. Nonetheless, some Nigerian intellectuals contend that ethnic militias and other self-determination groups form a genuine part of civil society, as they fight with »other progressive social forces« for the liberation of all oppressed peoples: »ethnic militancy is a contribution to democracy and diversity.«[50] Others argue that

---

46 Economist Intelligence Unit, *Country Profile Nigeria 2007*, p. 10; Jockers/Peters/Rhode, *Wahlen 2003*, p. 91.

47 *Economist*, 23 December 2006, p. 69.

48 Fawole, *Voting without Choosing*, p. 167; cf. Merkel/Croissant, *Demokratien*, pp. 7, 10.

49 Economist Intelligence Unit, *Country Profile Nigeria 2005*, p. 13.

50 Douglas/Ola, *Nourishing Democracy*, pp. 47, 42.

the prospects for democracy are gloomy, because the rise of ethnic and religious self-determination groups aggravates the uncivil character of Nigerian society: »the phrase ›civil society‹ [...] mistakenly assumes that there is a section of society that is predominantly civil.«[51]

As in other African countries, Nigeria's transition to democracy upset the balance of power and aggravated ethnic-religious tensions.[52] Nevertheless, the Obasanjo regime has also contributed to stabilizing the country. The conflict in the Niger Delta, over ownership of the oil resources, is still out of control, but elsewhere conflicts have simmered down. Politicians in Yoruba-, Igbo- and Hausaland have lost interest in ethnic and religious mobilization. Thanks to the high prices of crude oil, they are profiting from Nigeria's oil rents like never before. The opportunity to embezzle billions of dollars each year has generated a strong interest in stabilizing the federation.[53] Under military rule, large sections of the elites felt excluded from the wealth of the nation, whereas today no major region or ethnic elite is left out. President Obasanjo made sure to distribute state resources more or less evenly throughout the country. Thus he balanced out ethnoreligious interests. However, there are no democratic mechanisms which could ensure that political power and access to oil money are shared fairly. Under a president who strongly favors a certain section of society at the expense of others, there could be a resurgence of ethnic and religious agitation. Obasanjo did his best, when leaving office, to assuage religious antagonisms. Though a Christian from the South, he picked as his successor a Muslim from the North. Umaru Yar'Adua was the governor of one of the Sharia states, but not a religious hardliner.

Democratic forms of power sharing could only be institutionalized, if all parties acceded to common rules which they can agree are just and fair. Yet the chance to reach a consensus decreases, when some of the actors bind themselves to their separate religious laws: »the development of a strong Islamist movement in the north [...] is destroying the basis on which any generally accepted and democratic state could be constructed.«[54] Sharia activists who declare that God's law is supreme are not obliged to follow any secular rules. They may sign treaties with non-Muslims, but legal and constitutional concessions to infidels will not bind them, so

---

51 Adekson, *Civil Society*, p. 137.
52 Ottaway, *Ethnic Politics*, pp. 310–316.
53 Fourchard, *Nigeria sous Obasanjo*, pp. 25–26.
54 Clapham, *Decay*, p. 11.

agreements with them cannot be trusted. Instead of a consensus, Muslims and Christians can reach at best a modus vivendi, i.e., a compromise between people who have fundamentally different opinions.[55] Muslims may accept restrictions on their religious self-determination, as long as they do not have the power to enforce their ideas of divine justice. But there are no inner convictions that would stop them from reneging, if the balance of forces were shifting in their favor and they did not have to fear reprisals from breaking their promise.

Religious doctrines that hinder a peaceful coexistence between the faiths could, of course, be reinterpreted to make them more compatible with democracy. In a modernized, more liberal form, Islamic law could adopt a catalogue of human rights. Some liberal Muslims even claim that rediscovering Sharia in its pristine form is the best way of arriving at a modern understanding of human rights. Objectionable features of Islamic societies, like the subordination of women, are not derived from Islamic principles but from pre-Islamic patriarchal traditions: »It is a settled fact that *shari'ah* provides women full human, social, and economic rights [...]. However, local customs, laws, and negative value systems continue to encroach upon the implementation of the pure principles of *shari'ah*.«[56] Such attempts to present one's liberal ideas as authentically Islamic are not convincing. The most prominent modernizer among Nigeria's Muslims, S. L. Sanusi, warns that this strategy is counterproductive. Feminists and other progressive Muslims who claim that they are reviving an original form of Islam are only making themselves untrustworthy: »progressive Muslims make untenable claims of unsubstantiated authenticity for their ontology of equality.« »the concept of justice and equality that is held by progressive Muslims originates in a tradition of Western scholarship since the Enlightenment.«[57] According to Sanusi, many Muslims »do not accept the egalitarian conceptions of Western society«, and their understanding of a divinely ordained hierarchy between men and women, believers and infidels is supported by their religious heritage: »In this, the Muslim tradition is no different from most other pre-modern systems of thought. [...] As for the inferiority of the non-Muslim to the Muslim, this was, a fortiori, taken

---

55 Rawls, *Political Liberalism*, pp. 147–148; Barry, *Social Justice*, p. 37; Habermas, *Cultures*, p. 26.

56 Mahdi, *Women's Rights*, p. 4.

57 Sanusi, *The West*, p. 257; cf. Brumberg, *Islam*, pp. 100–101.

for granted.«[58] Therefore, a liberal reinterpretation of Sharia would have to move away from its roots.

A similar view is taken by Gerrie ter Haar, who reminds us that the Koran and other sacred texts which distinguish believers from non-believers, stem from a time when a »humane world view«, as it is understood in the West, did not exist: »In those days the use of violence was commonly accepted and even encouraged in certain circumstances, while peace and tolerance were usually limited to a particular circle of people. [...] All this makes the reinterpretation of sacred traditions in their present context an absolute necessity.«[59] In order to defuse religiously-motivated conflicts and protect the rights of citizens, religious leaders should pick out those elements from holy scripts that allow people to live together peacefully and as equals: »shari'a law could be made compatible with international views of human rights.«[60] The question is, however, how far modernizers can go without compromising their religious identity. The best option for democracy, namely a secular order, is apparently not feasible. Even resolute modernizers like Sanusi emphasize that a reformation of Islam must not result in a »capitulation« to Western values: »any call on Muslims to abandon religious law in the name of secularism, will fail.«[61] Where Muslims want to preserve at least parts of their religious inheritance, secular principles are »untenable«: »advocates of secularism will appear to be calling on their own societies to abandon their Islamic cultural and religious foundations.«[62] Adherents of Sharia are motivated by very different interests and aspirations, however, ideas of tolerance and human rights are not prominent among them. Many Muslims would see human rights as an obstacle in their fight against crime. And they have little interest in equality between men and women, or between believers and infidels. What makes Sharia attractive is, in many cases, its ability to polarize and mobilize the faithful effectively against a common enemy. This is one of the reasons why Sharia conflicts often overlap with ethnic rivalries.

---

58 Sanusi, *The West*, p. 260.
59 ter Haar, *Religion*, pp. 312–313.
60 Ellis/ter Haar, *Worlds of Power*, p. 191.
61 Sanusi, *The West*, pp. 261, 264, 270, 272.
62 An-Na'im, *Political Islam*, p. 119.

Religious and Political Motives

In this study I would like to reconstruct some of the reasons that led to the Sharia campaign. As a social scientist, I am interested, above all, in how religious demands are linked with political interests. It is important, however, to bear in mind that religious commitment is not just a means of furthering political ambitions. Many Sharia activists are inspired by genuine religious motives. After decades of economic and moral decline, it has become more important for both Muslims and Christians to reconsider their religious values and to follow the teachings of their faith. Few Nigerians still believe that democracy, human rights and a free market economy are a way out of the present crisis. Given the failure of Western modernization strategies, it is reasonable for Nigeria's Muslims to reevaluate their traditions. Believers who turn to the teachings of the Koran are not looking for instructions on how to transform their society according to liberal, enlightened principles. The renewed interest in Sharia has grown out of the experience that Western concepts of development have led to a dead end. To get out of it, Nigerians have to find a new sense of direction. Their endeavor to re-model state and society can only be successful, if they are united by a common purpose. They have to agree on ethical standards which nobody can change to suit personal or political interest. Sharia, which is seen by most believers as the immutable law of God, seems best suited for this purpose. God will lead his creatures out of their misery, if only they follow him and his commands. This pious understanding of Sharia is at odds with the attempts by liberal Muslims to submit the legacy of Islam to a historical-critical debate. Liberal authors like Abdullahi An-Na'im point out that »certain aspects of shari'ah are simply inconsistent with basic constitutional government altogether.«[63] If modern Muslims want to free themselves of these outdated restrictions, they will have to break with Islamic jurisprudence as it has hitherto been practiced.[64] This would include abolishing some of the divine commandments, even though they are explicitly stated in the Koran. Thus the modernizers are suggesting that Muslims rise above the holy scriptures and decide – on the basis of political, not religious criteria – which elements of Sharia are worth keeping. Of course, so much human autonomy is unacceptable to orthodox scholars, who remind their opponents that the Koran does not allow revi-

---

63 An-Na'im, *Future of Shari'ah*, p. 330.
64 *Ibid.*, pp. 353–354.

sions: »It is not for any believer, man or woman, when God and His Messenger have decreed a matter, to have the choice in the affair. Whosoever disobeys God and His Messenger has gone astray into manifest error.«[65]

As it is not possible to organize a complex, functionally differentiated society according to a »medieval religious law«[66], pragmatic solutions will prevail. Most Islamic politicians are not interested in submitting to the rigor of Sharia, but it is unlikely that they will abolish the new legislation. A governor who renounced the divine law would be denounced by most religious authorities as an apostate. Nigeria's Islamic elite will continue to live with a high degree of hypocrisy and double standards. Despite calls for a total application of Sharia, divine justice has not materialized, so the mass of the faithful feel betrayed. Most of them had greeted the proclamation of Sharia with enthusiasm; today they defy many of its laws. The official gender separation is ignored in most places, alcoholic drinks are readily available, and the usual vices are back, though relegated to some hidden corners. Sharia monitors can still be seen in the streets, but they often serve as traffic wardens.[67] Muslims in the North have regained much of their freedom by silently ignoring the instructions of the authorities. This does not mean, however, that their basic rights are institutionally guaranteed. Sharia has created legal insecurity; its criminal laws, dress codes and dietary taboos cover a wide area of social activities, but they are enforced only sporadically and arbitrarily.

A British journal described the halfhearted application of Islamic laws as »Sharia lite.«[68] Spectacular punishments are no longer carried out, and the Governor of Zamfara has lamented that »the atmosphere conducive for amputations is not there.«[69] The laws, however, remain in place, and Sharia courts are still applying them so that a large number of convicts are languishing in jail, waiting for the authorities to decide their fate. In Bauchi State, the Sharia Commission urged the newly elected governor in June 2007 to ratify 43 amputations and death penalties (for adultery, sodomy and the like), which had been passed by the state's Sharia courts since 2003.[70] As long as Nigeria's Supreme Court has not decided on the constitutionality of Sharia, governors are reluctant to approve the contro-

---

65 *Koran* 33: 36, p. 431; cf. Oloyede, *Commentary*, p. 302.
66 Küng, *Islam*, pp. 681–682; Schluchter, *Kampf der Kulturen?*, pp. 27, 40–41.
67 U.S. Department of State, *Nigeria 2006*, p. 11.
68 *Economist*, 3 February 2007, p. 42.
69 Quoted in Human Rights Watch, *Political Shari'a?*, p. 39.
70 *Vanguard*, 15 June 2007.

versial punishments, but they may tighten other aspects of Sharia. Whether disputes over Sharia will rise again, depends on changing political constellations: on the policy of the federal government which controls Nigeria's police and army, and on local conflicts and intrigues. In Kano, the largest state in the North, the government had hesitated to enforce its religious laws, but in 2004 and 2005, a wave of Sharia activism swept the state, after a new governor had been elected on a pro-Sharia ticket. Insecurity has grown, above all, for the Christian minority. The state governments, elected by the Muslim majority, appear more hostile or partisan than before 1999. They have asserted the Islamic identity of schools, radio stations and other public institutions, so non-Muslims see themselves more than ever as outsiders. Since religious divisions have hardened, there is not much reason to expect that in the long run Sharia »will strengthen rather than weaken democracy.«[71]

With the rejection of Western constitutional principles, Muslims and Christians no longer have a set of common rules which can regulate their coexistence. This does not preclude them from finding some other common ground for political cooperation. However, possible areas of agreement do not lie where Western observers wish they did. From a Muslim perspective, followers of both religions could converge on the basis of Sharia principles, in particular on the tough punishments for criminals. Some Muslims argue that Christians have nothing to fear from the new penal code, because Islamic justice is guided by laws which are shared by both Abrahamic religions. The Mosaic law of the Old Testament prescribes the most severe punishments for theft and adultery: »the Bible is in total agreement with what the Shari'ah stipulates. [...] Christians who oppose Shari'ah are opposing the Bible for all the laws of the Shari'ah which they oppose are clearly stated in the Bible.«[72] Many Christians grant that they are not all too different from Muslims when it comes to fighting sexual permissiveness. Nor do they want to speak out against the Sharia ban on alcohol. In their struggle against moral decline, even Catholic clergymen do not rule out a partial cooperation: »Muslims and Christians face the same real enemies namely a secular view of life, worship of wealth,

---

71 Sakah Saidu Mahmud, *Islamism*, p. 92; cf. Fuller, *Political Islam*, pp. 51–59; David, *Islam*, pp. 8–10. – Statistical data from other African and Asian countries suggest that Islamic societies are »extremely resistant« to democratic reforms. Of 47 Islamic states, in 2000 only Mali could be termed a constitutional democracy (Merkel, *Religion*, pp. 102–104; Bruce, *Politics and Religion*, pp. 206–207).

72 Oloyede, *Shari'ah*, pp. 135–136.

corruption and oppression.« Dialogue »can combat the evil of secularism and materialism.«[73] Attitudes toward Muslims are fluid. Whether Catholics discover theological similarities or whether they emphasize what separates them, does not only depend on religious considerations. Political interests play a major role, yet one cannot discuss them in isolation. They are shaped by questions of faith and religious identity, so that social scientists cannot leave theological aspects of the Sharia controversy out of consideration.[74]

There are further reasons that make it difficult to reconstruct the reasons for the Sharia conflict. Muslims do not debate the issue openly. Those politicians who initiated the religious campaign and who stuck to it despite violent conflicts with Christians, have not named the reasons for their commitment. They simply insisted that their faith obliged them to live according to God's instructions. But why did this pious view only start to spread after a Christian Yoruba was elected to the presidency? For almost 40 years, the Islamic elite of Northern Nigeria had dominated the political scene, without a government making efforts to introduce an Islamic penal code. The former president Shehu Shagari, for example, who suddenly emerged as a champion of Sharia, had never tried to pass new criminal laws while he was in office. Muhammadu Buhari, a former military dictator, took a similar stance. With the dawn of democracy, he joined the Sharia activists and assured his coreligionists: »I can die for the cause of Islam.«[75] Non-Muslims were unimpressed by this godly pathos: »Why was Sharia criminal law not so desirable when they were both in power? [...] Have they ›suddenly seen the light‹ and become ›born-again‹ Muslims?«[76] During the election campaign in early 1999, Sharia had barely played a role. Only Ahmed Sani Yerima, who was running for the governorship in Zamfara, had promised voters that he would Islamize the law. But even Sani, who was later celebrated as the »apostle of Sharia«[77], had not been known for his piety. He had been an Abacha Boy, a follower of the military leader Abacha who died in 1998. Thanks to his loyalty to the generals, he had obtained a leading position in the central bank, which, as he later acknowledged, gave him the opportunity to embezzle large sums of money.[78] How-

---

73 Nzeh, *Dialogue of Religions*, p. 362.
74 Hasenclever/Rittberger, *Religion*, pp. 113–115; Thomas, *Religious Pluralism*, p. 32.
75 *Tell*, 29 October 2001, p. 36.
76 Fani-Kayode, *Sharia*, p. 48.
77 *Hotline*, 4 June 2000, p. 24.
78 Maier, *This House*, p. 186.

ever, since the beginning of democracy he has been a changed man. He has grown a full beard and only wears Islamic robes.

Nobody expected Ahmed Sani and his allies to talk candidly about their motives. The religious discourse which they use does not permit the sober weighing up of the advantages and disadvantages of Sharia. Whoever acts in the name of God, must not give the impression that he manipulates sacred law for mundane political purposes. Of course, behind the scenes there was bitter controversy over the benefit of the religious project; but non-Muslims were excluded from this debate. Church representatives and Christian politicians assured me that they did not know the aims of the other side. They argued that they could only speculate why Muslim politicians had initiated the campaign, and therefore could not predict how far their adversaries would take their confrontation strategy: Was Ahmed Sani serious when he announced that he wanted to introduce Sharia throughout the country? »Zamfara is ready to contribute whatever it will cost to spread Sharia in the Southern part of Nigeria.«[79] Of course, Nigerian politicians of all religious persuasions are accustomed to discussing with each other, but what really moves them is negotiated in small, exclusive circles. This segregation did not come about because of the Sharia campaign. Among Nigeria's fragmented elites, trust has always been missing. Processes of self-reflection only take place within one's religious or ethnic group, since members of other groups are seen as potential enemies and traitors.[80]

While Sharia politicians protested that they were led only by religious motives, their critics presumed the opposite. President Obasanjo alleged that Sharia served as a political »instrument.«[81] Yet it was a matter of dispute what the purpose of this instrument was. A Catholic observer speculated that Sharia was meant »to cause anarchy and then send their military guys.«[82] Yet this is unlikely, as Islamic politicians lost control of the army, after Obasanjo assumed power. So they might not have profited from an overthrow of democracy. Other critics of Sharia like Anthony Okogie, the Catholic Archbishop of Lagos, supposed that Muslims wanted to replace the Christian president with another civilian politician. However, the assumption that Sharia was a »weapon« to »pull down«[83] Obasanjo, is not

79 Gouverneur Sani, in *Tell*, 6 March 2000, p. 23.
80 Cf. Rothchild, *Ethnic Insecurity*, p. 327; Berman, *Ethnicity*, pp. 47–50.
81 *The News*, 10 April 2000, p. 15.
82 Odey, *Sharia*, p. 95.
83 Archbishop Okogie, in *The News*, 10 April 2000, p. 21.

convincing either. Whatever the aims, I do not believe, unlike many Christian observers, that the Sharia campaign was thoroughly planned. In summer 1999, when Governor Sani presented his Sharia plans, he presumably had not consulted the ruling circles of Northern Nigeria. It was only when Sharia found great approval among ordinary Muslims, that leading politicians recognized the advantages of »religious populism.«[84] Another important factor that may explain the sudden religious enthusiasm of the political class was the conflict with President Obasanjo, who had broken with his patrons in the North and built a power base of his own. There is much evidence that Sharia was used, above all, to exert pressure on the president and other politicians from the South: »Sharia was dusted up to challenge him, intimidate him, to force him to back down and play things their way.«[85]

Since Sharia politicians and their Christian opponents manipulated ethnic-religious tensions for their own interests, it appeared as if the mass of believers were willing pawns in a cynical power play: »the dominant classes among Muslims and Christians appropriate large numbers of the deprived as cannon-fodder in their competition for political and economic space.«[86] Yet at times, the masses played a very active role. When Islamic politicians hesitated to jump on the Sharia bandwagon, they were pressured by demonstrators, sometimes intimidated and even assaulted. For the solemn proclamation of the new legislation, more than a million faithful gathered in Kano,[87] and many of them expressed ideas about Islamic justice that sounded like threats to the emirs and politicians. While the ruling circles used Sharia as a means of political intrigue, the mass of believers tried to use the divine law to set limits on the reckless behavior of the rich and mighty.

We cannot determine precisely what people expected from the introduction of Sharia. Talking to Muslims was the best way for me to learn about their motives for supporting or rejecting the religious reform project, yet what I found could not be verified in empirical studies. I do not know of surveys which provide reliable data about attitudes to Sharia among

---

84 Kalu, *Safiyya*, p. 391.
85 Kukah, *Beyond Sharia*, p. 3; Fayemi, *Religion*, p. 150; Hauwa Mustapha, *Islamic Legal System*, p. 114; Mazrui, *Shariacracy*, p. 2.
86 Sanusi, *Shari'a Debate*, p. 1.
87 *Financial Times*, 13 June 2002.

various parts of the population.[88] It is not even possible to get a clear idea of how popular Sharia was and is. A political scientist at the Bayero University in Kano told me in March 2001 that the majority of Muslims do not want Sharia, neither in Kano, the biggest city of the North, nor elsewhere. Yet most observers had the impression that the Sharia campaign enjoyed widespread support. Murray Last wrote in early 2000: »Parmi tous les musulmans, un consensus se fait autour de l'idée, que la charia est juste.«[89] Four years later Human Rights Watch reported that most Muslims were disillusioned. Yet their disappointment was not directed at Sharia itself, but rather at the way in which politicians had implemented it: »People want Shari'a but are not satisfied with what they're getting.«[90] A cow thief and two other petty criminals had their right hand amputated, but the politicians continued to embezzle billions of dollars.

To capture the mood among Muslims, the Human Rights Watch report quotes representatives of human rights« groups and other non-governmental organizations that identify the Islamic jurisdiction with the corrupt authorities: »Most Shari'a trials are stage-managed [...] to terrorize people and to manipulate gullible subjects.«[91] It is difficult to say how many Muslims in Nigeria would agree with this view. A reliable survey of public

---

88 Attitudes toward democracy are better explored. In an essay on *Islam, Democracy and Public Opinion in Africa* (pp. 494, 501), Michael Bratton reports on comparative surveys conducted in four African countries between 1999 and 2001. Nigeria's Muslims showed the weakest support for democracy, but it was not much below the average figure of 71 percent. A follow-up study in September 2003 found that a majority of Nigerians, both Muslims and Christians, still preferred democracy to an autocratic regime, yet »confidence in the new democratic dispensation« had »rapidly declined«: »The 50-point collapse in mass satisfaction with democracy over four years in Nigeria was larger and more rapid than anywhere else in Africa« (Bratton/Lewis, *Durability*, pp 9–10, 34). According to Bratton, Mattes and Gyimah-Boadi (*Public Opinion*, p. 85), »support for democracy may well be shallow. [...] In Africa, prodemocracy sentiments may be a veneer beneath which lasting democratic commitments, behaviours, and habits have yet to take root.« My impression is that among Nigerians democracy does not mean much more than majority rule.

89 Last, *Charia*, p. 143. – A poll, conducted by Afrobarometer in August 2001, found that Sharia was supported by 65 percent of Muslims in the North and 38 percent in the South (Lewis/Alemika/Bratton, *Down to Earth*, p. 47).

90 An »activist« in Kano, in Human Rights Watch, *Political Shari'a?*, p. 90; cf. O'Brien, *Charia*, p. 57.

91 An anonymous employee of a non-governmental organization in Kaduna, in Human Rights Watch, *Political Shari'a?*, p. 91.

opinion is not possible, because people are afraid to express their opinions openly:

»Human Rights Watch researchers observed a form of self-censorship among critics – including academics, human rights activists, members of women's organizations, lawyers and others – who were willing to express strong reservations about Shari'a in private conversations, but not in public. They claimed it was not possible, or too dangerous, to express such views in public. Very few Muslims in northern Nigeria – however strong their criticisms of Shari'a – are willing to take the risk.«[92]

Even in academic circles there is no open debate. When Professor An-Na'im, a Sudanese living in the USA, gave a lecture at a Sharia conference at the University of Jos, in January 2004, between 200 and 300 Muslim attendees left the hall.[93]

The lack of statistical data also means that we cannot evaluate how strictly Sharia laws have been applied in the twelve states. It is almost impossible to access court files, and the authorities do not provide reliable information. In Kano, the archivist of the Sharia Court of Appeal stated that no one in his state had been sentenced to an amputation. Yet representatives of Human Rights Watch investigated ten such cases in Kano.[94] While it is hard to assess the activities of the Sharia courts, the religious conflicts that accompanied the introduction of Sharia are better documented. Nigeria's newspapers and magazines reported in much detail and very controversially on the events.[95] While journalists in the South generally argued against Sharia law, their colleagues in the North defended it. Given the passionate antagonisms, reports by Muslims and Christians differed widely. Each party blamed the other for the conflict, and exaggerated the number of their own victims. Even official information was not reliable. When a wave of clashes swept Jos and its surroundings in September 2001, the accounts of the security forces contradicted each other.

---

92 *Ibid.*, p. 88. – Given the risks, I have decided to protect the anonymity of informants who spoke with me about Sharia. In the course of my research in Northern Nigeria I was arrested and questioned by the State Security Service four times.

93 Harneit-Sievers, *Debate about Sharia*, p. 5; Ado-Kurawa, *Jos International Conference*, pp. 20–23.

94 Human Rights Watch, *Political Shari'a?*, pp. 36–37, 2, 57–58.

95 Even under military rule, Nigeria's journalists reported more openly and critically than I could observe in other African countries. The weekly magazine Newswatch won the Commonwealth Media Award in 1997, during the Abacha dictatorship, for its excellent coverage (*Newswatch*, 4 May 1998, p. 34).

The police, who had hesitated to advance on the armed demonstrators, talked of 500 dead, while military officers, whose troops eventually suppressed the unrest, declared that 5,000 people had been killed.

Despite the shaky information base, I have provided figures to indicate how many people died or were expelled in local clashes. My intention was only to give a rough idea about the magnitude of individual conflicts. In trying to estimate which press information is more accurate, I could rely on personal experiences, since I visited many of the places where religious clashes had occurred.[96] My understanding of the events has been shaped, above all, by conversations with informants. However, for readers of this study I have tried to illustrate the political and religious convictions of the main players by quoting from newspapers, weekly magazines, religious tracts and academic articles. These references to current sources also provide a chronology of the major events. However, readers should bear in mind that a part of the data, for example, on the ethnic and religious composition of the population, cannot be exact. I suppose that about half of the people in Nigeria are Muslims, yet this is disputed. Both Muslims and Christians maintain that they outnumber their rivals.[97] Opinions of foreign experts are likewise divergent. According to the World Christian Encyclopedia, Christians form the largest religious community, while reports by the Economist and the CIA place the Muslims in front, with 50 percent of Nigeria's population against 40 percent Christians.[98] The remaining ten

---

96 From 1993 to 1996, while I was a lecturer at the University of Nigeria in Nsukka, in Southeast Nigeria, my university was mostly closed by strikes. This gave me ample opportunity for research. After my work contract expired, I returned to Nigeria five times. My visits in 2001 and 2002, both times from January to April, were part of a University of Frankfurt research project. The last visit was from November 2006 to January 2007. My research since 1993 brought me into a number of towns and villages, in which (ethno-)religious clashes had erupted since the early 1980s. Among the places I visited were Bambam, Barakin Ladi, Bauchi, Biliri, Gombe, Ilorin, Jalingo, Jimeta, Jos, Kachia, Kaduna, Kafanchan, Kaltungo, Kano, Langtang, Maiduguri, Mavo, Numen, Pankshin, Potiskum, Tafawa Balewa, Vom, Wase, Yola, Zangon Kataf, Zaria, Zonkwa.

97 Kenny, *Sharia*, p. 360.

98 Barrett/Kurian/Johnson, *Encyclopedia*, p. 549; Miles, *Religious Pluralism*, p. 221; Economist Intelligence Unit, *Country Profile Nigeria 2005*, p. 16; Freedom House, *Talibanization*, p. 64. – There are not even reliable figures about the total population of Nigeria. In its census of 1991, the National Population Commission discovered that earlier data on the population development had overestimated the number of inhabitants by more than 30 million people (Fricke/Malchau, *Volkszählung*, p. 163). The census of March 2006 set the total population at 140 million, but many Nigerians claimed that they had not been counted (*Newswatch*, 22 January 2007, p. 21). The census forms did not include questions

percent are followers of African religions. They are generally called ›traditionalists‹, though the old religions have greatly changed under the influence of Islam and Christianity.

The difficulties of gathering important data extend to other areas as well. It would improve our understanding of the Sharia conflict, if we had more inside information about Muslim organizations. Inner-Islamic rivalries certainly contributed to the rise of the Sharia campaign. There are indications that some religious leaders used the common fight for Sharia as a means to settle the bitter divisions within the Islamic camp. Violent clashes, mostly between conservative and progressive Muslims or between rival brotherhoods, date back to the late colonial period. Around 1980, the conflicts escalated when many university students and intellectuals began to push for radical reforms. The reformers were divided from the very beginning, inspired by Wahabi theories from Saudi Arabia or by the Shiite Revolution in Iran. And they were both in conflict with the old-established brotherhoods. The best way to push these intractable disputes into the background was to focus on the »core of Islam«[99], that corpus of Sharia laws that is not much disputed between the different schools of Islamic law, not even between Shiites and Sunnis. However, I will not go into great detail, when referring to these controversies. My own insights are very limited here, and I could not present much more than the results of some English-language studies, most of which were written before the Sharia crisis.[100]

Finally, there is another important aspect of the Sharia conflict which falls outside the scope of this book. What looks like a national conflict that splits the 140 million Nigerians into two camps, appears, on closer inspection, as a series of local conflicts, in which very different actors are involved. In Kano and other cities of the far North, Christian migrants from the South, mostly Igbo and Yoruba, have clashed with Muslim

---

about ethnic and religious affiliation. However, the ethnic composition has not changed much since colonial times, so one can refer to the census of 1952/53 which is considered the most reliable. (Its main results were reprinted in Diamond, *Nigeria*, p. 420) According to these figures, the Yoruba comprised 17, Igbo 18, Hausa 18 and Fulani 10 percent of the population. Ethnic identifications are, of course, fluid (cf. Harnischfeger, *Islamisation and Ethnic Conversion in Nigeria*).

99 Schacht, *Islamic Law*, p. 1; Tabiu, *Sharia*, p. 3; Crone, *Islamic Political Thought*, p. 8.

100 The organization that spearheaded the Sharia campaign, the Yan Izala, is currently being studied by a scholar who has better access to Islamic circles, Ramzi Ben Amara of the University of Bayreuth.

Hausa-Fulani, who use the Islamization campaign to assert their ancestral rights over the economically successful ›settlers‹. Further south in the Middle Belt, an intermediate zone between the Muslim North and the Christian South of Nigeria, the power structure is very different. Here, the Hausa-Fulani are often migrants who left the dry, over-populated Sahel zone to an area where they encountered small ethnic groups, the so-called minorities which are predominantly Christian. The ›settlers‹ from the North, who compete with the ›indigenous‹ population for the few remaining land resources, have not only taken land and set up their own separate villages; they have also demanded political control in their new homeland. The call for Sharia was popular among them, as it provided them with a divine mission. The migrants strived to assert supremacy over the local non-Muslim population in order to remodel public institutions according to the will of God.[101] Yet my aim in this study is not to talk about local conflicts with their diverse origins. Rather, I limit myself to the question of how Sharia is related to Nigeria's democratization, or to be more precise, to the failure of democratization. Within this framework, I cannot discuss all the causes of the Sharia campaign. The main topics that will come up in this book appear in the synopsis below, which summarizes the following six chapters:

1. The revival of precolonial legal traditions evokes the idea of a new golden age, of an Islamic empire like the Caliphate of Sokoto, which was founded in the early nineteenth century and which extended into much of today's Northern Nigeria. Sharia advocates argue that only the unifying force of religion can transcend ethnic antagonisms and bring peace to a deeply divided country with hundreds of ethnic groups that have little in common: »all Muslims, irrespective of race, language or nationality, must constitute a single brotherhood, one Umma. [...] the Umma, from one end of the world to the other, is but one single nation, its diverse peoples sharing but one faith, one law, one culture and one destiny.«[102] However, the jihad that established the Sokoto Caliphate, went hand in hand with ethnic hegemony right from the start. While spreading the rule of Islam, it established the dominance of a Fulani aristocracy and their Hausa allies. When the British occupied the area around 1900, they concluded an alliance with the Fulani rulers and supported their religious authority, including their law courts. As Sharia remained in force in the emirate territories,

---

101 Harnischfeger, *Control over Territory.*
102 Ibraheem Sulaiman, *Islam*, p. 11.

English common law never gained dominance, as it did in the rest of the country. The juxtaposition of several legal systems is one of the reasons why Nigerians, despite a series of constitutional experiments, could never agree on a legal order that would be acceptable to both Christians and Muslims. The dispute over the proper role of Sharia is linked to political competition between elites in the North and the South. Therefore, the majority of Christians in addition to many Muslims in Southern Nigeria interpreted the attempt to entrench Sharia as an »ethnic plot by the Hausa-Fulani.«[103] The mistrust between politicians in the North and the South dated from colonial times, yet it was exacerbated by a traumatic event in 1993, which put an abrupt end to the transition to Nigeria's Third Republic. The country was set on a course of disintegration, when General Babangida, a ruler from the North, annulled the presidential election of June 12, 1993, which a Southerner had won.

2. Under the military, which ran a centralist regime, no state could proclaim its own legal system. It was only with the transition to democracy and federalism, that Muslims gained the opportunity to assert their religious autonomy. For many of them, Sharia was their »dividend from democracy«,[104] the most important achievement of their re-won freedom. Self-determination is not practiced by the Nigerian people, but by a religious community which uses its legislative power to distinguish its members from the adherents of other religions. Like an ethnic group or nation, it demands control over a territory where its laws shall be enforced. The claim to rule ›Muslim states‹ by religious principles relegates non-Muslims to the position of outsiders, so the Sharia campaign provoked bitter resentment. In states like Zamfara, where the Christian minority is numerically insignificant, they had to accept a considerable Islamization of public life. In other states, where the position of Christians was more entrenched, the application of Sharia was severely limited from the beginning. The way Muslims and Christians arrange their coexistence is determined by local compromises which reflect shifting balances of power. Such pacts or informal agreements are fragile; they do not bring lasting peace, because they are not based on and guarded by common legal or moral principles. Neither the law of God nor the constitution is in force.

---

103 *Tell*, 27 March 2000, p. 20.
104 Dr. Lateef Adegbite, Secretary General of the Supreme Council for Islamic Affairs, in *Vanguard*, 24 March 2002, p. 21.

3. Nigeria's ›democratic‹ president Obasanjo came to office through an agreement between some military and civilian politicians. Such informal deals do not establish an enduring political order, because there is no neutral authority, beyond ethnic and religious disputes, which could compel the rival parties to keep their promises. The agreement before the 1999 elections had envisioned that presidential power would pass temporarily to a Southern candidate, but when Obasanjo assumed office, he did not uphold his part of the bargain. He antagonized his patrons in the North, so they feared they would be marginalized, losing access to state resources, above all, to Nigeria's oil revenues. As they could not rely on the protection of democratic institutions, they had to protect their interests by other means, resorting to a dangerous weapon: the religious mobilization of the population. By threatening to fuel the Sharia crisis in Kano, Kaduna and other urban centers of the North, they turned members of the Christian minority, many of whom were migrants from the South, into hostages who could become victims of religious clashes at any time. The threat was directed against Yoruba politicians and other Southerners who had profited from the power-shift under Obasanjo's rule. In case they used their new positions too recklessly, they would have to watch their kin in the North become the victims of looting, killing, and ethnic-religious cleansing.

4. The Sharia crisis indicated that Nigeria's fragmented elites could not settle their conflicts by democratic means. Yet Sharia was a symptom of the failure of democracy from another angle, too. Citizens have not succeeded in using democratic institutions to subject their elites to public control. As in the years of military rule, a small stratum of politicians, business people and (retired) army officers are the ones to decide who gets what office. Since Western models of liberal democracy were incapable of checking the excesses of the ruling class, many Muslims set their hopes on Sharia. The immutable law of God should become the yardstick by which both rich and poor, were measured. The devout campaign, launched by members of the elite, could thus be turned against its instigators. As long as Sharia activists were able to mobilize the mass of the faithful, they could indeed, to some extent, intimidate the rich and powerful. However, the religious movement did not create institutions that were able to establish a permanent and effective control of political office-holders. The attempt to conduct politics according to religious laws did not make the administration transparent, predictable, and responsive to the needs of the people;

rather it contributed to the decline of state authorities. Because the call to obey God, not men, empowers any individual or group that knows God on their side to take the law into their own hands.

5. The last two chapters do not focus on further causes of the Sharia campaign, but on the controversies which it generated. Most politicians who pledged allegiance to divine justice, had no genuine interest in maintaining a strictly Islamic regime, yet they could not come out openly against Sharia. The politicization of religion has created a counter-elite of religious experts that has an interest in defending orthodoxy. Muslim intellectuals, human rights campaigners and women's rights activists who rejected central elements of the new legislation had to argue from within the Islamic tradition. While acknowledging the validity of Sharia in principle, they advocated a modern, progressive interpretation of the law that rejected the letter of the divine revelation and claimed to follow its spirit.

6. When religious obligations gain importance, it becomes harder for Muslims to reach an understanding with Christians. Both sides speak the language of human rights, democracy and religious freedom, but these terms have very different meanings. Muslim scholars and politicians call for collective rights which can be used to impose conformity on members of the *umma*, the community of the faithful. How they treat offenders is perceived as their own affair, from which infidels, with their deviant ideas about law and morality, are excluded: »Islam and shari'a are inseparable. No amount of blackmail […] will stop Muslims from the pursuit of their fundamental human rights to practice their religion in full, without dictation, as to which aspect of their faith should or should not be observed.«[105] Freedom of religion, which empowers the Muslim community to follow its divine laws without restrictions, means that its members have no choice but to obey these laws. Christians still reject the idea that religious obligations should be enforced by the state, yet their understanding of the political role of religion is also changing.

---

105 Southern Council for Islamic Affairs, in Ilesanmi, *Constitutional Treatment*, p. 544.

Religious and Ethnic Supremacy

The Caliphate of Sokoto

In Africa south of the Sahara, in contrast to other regions of Africa and Asia, Islam was not initially spread by force. Arab warriors who conquered the north of Africa in the seventh century, also pushed across the Nile Valley to the south, threatening Christian Nubia and Ethiopia. Otherwise, however, the Sahara acted as a barrier and prevented warring campaigns from entering the south. It was extremely difficult to move armies along the caravan routes through the desert, and such a military venture would not have made much sense, because little tribute could have been extorted from the subsistence farmers in the Sahel zone. The month-long, dangerous journey was profitable only for merchants. Some of them settled in Timbuktu and other West-African towns, though they did so in their own quarters cut off from the remaining population. Local rulers who sought to monopolize the trade with the caravans of the Arabs and Berber protected these small Islamic communities. Indeed in the eleventh century the kings of Ghana, Mali and Kanem-Bornu converted to Islam, and from the fifteenth century onwards the rulers of the Hausa kingdoms in present-day Northern Nigeria followed suit. Of course, Islam remained a courtly religion that managed to gain a few urban followers, but had little appeal for the peasant population with their fertility cults.[1] It was not until 1804 when Usman dan Fodio, a Fulani preacher, called on people to wage a holy war against infidels that Islam spread across Northern Nigeria.

Many Muslims still view the jihad as a model of religious revival, but even in the nineteenth century the struggle against infidels served to assert the supremacy of an ethnic group. The Fulani, to whom Usman dan Fodio belonged, were originally cattle nomads, who migrated from present-day Senegal and, from the fifteenth century onwards, penetrated Hausaland.

---

1 Adeleke, *Islam and Hausa Culture*, p. 107.

An educated minority that had acquired great learning from its contact with Islamic culture, settled in the residences of the Hausa kings and rose to important positions. As preachers and advisors to the kings or as their secretaries and tax collectors »they gained influence and authority out of all proportion to their numbers.«[2] They resided in their own quarters on the outskirts of large towns, or established religious enclaves in the country, as did Usman dan Fodio and other scholars, who were keen to secure independence from the rulers. It was these outsiders who had made Islam their profession that started the rebellion against the ›ungodly‹ Hausa kings.

The rebellion by the warrior-scholars would have been rapidly put down had they not found support in other sections of the population. Their most important allies were the Fulani nomads who lived apart from the peasant population. As most of the Fulani pastoralists were not Muslims, they lacked the religious ethos of the jihadists, but they did suffer under the despotism of the Hausa kings, and this prompted them to heed the call for a holy war.[3] Some peasants and merchants were similarly drawn to the teachings of the jihadists, since Usman dan Fodio vigorously condemned the rulers' corruption and tyranny: »Whomsoever they wish to kill or exile or violate his honour or devour his wealth they do so in pursuit of their lusts, without any right in the Shari'a!«[4] Kings who followed Islam were not allowed to take their subjects prisoner at will or enslave them. Moreover, the laws of Sharia forbade them to oppress the peasants with high tributes or to impose arbitrary taxes on the cattle breeders. By citing the word of God, the jihadists established a yardstick of criticism that had equal currency across ethnic and social borders for all sections of the population.

Their reference to Sharia was also important for another reason. Since Islamic orthodoxy forbids war against fellow Muslims, Usman dan Fodio could only proclaim a jihad, if he declared his opponents to be apostates who had turned away from the principles of Islam. Thus, social criticism combined with religious rigor. The kings were accused of tolerating ›heathen‹ cults, indeed of participating in them. Music, dance and alcohol were not banned, and women could move about freely without wearing a veil.[5]

---

2 Hogben, *History*, p. 53; I. M. Lewis, *Introduction*, pp. 30–31.

3 M. G. Smith, *Jihad*, pp. 222–223; Hiskett, *Sword of Truth*, pp. 79–80; Osswald, *Sokoto-Kalifat*, pp. 11–113, 123–125.

4 Isichei, *History of Nigeria*, p. 203.

5 Doi, *Islam*, pp. 35–38; Last, *Sokoto Caliphate*, pp. LXVIII–LXX; Falola/Adebayo, *Pre-Colonial Nigeria*, pp. 81–82; King, *State and Ethnicity*, pp. 17–19; M. G. Smith, *Jihad*, pp.

Since the Hausa kings ruled over a largely ›pagan‹ population they had indeed failed to insist on compliance with Islamic laws. But some of those who were ostracized by Usman dan Fodio, considered themselves to be devout Muslims. For instance, the official sources of the jihad acknowledge that the king of Gobir remained true to his faith even in moments of great distress. Although he was being pursued by the Fulani warriors, this did not prevent him from pausing during his flight in order to perform the prescribed prayers.[6]

Within five years the Hausa kings had been driven out, but the feudal social order remained. The old aristocracy was simply replaced by ›royal‹ Fulani families. Thus the jihad leaders practiced precisely what Usman dan Fodio had condemned, namely »that appointments to sensitive posts were being made not on the basis of merit but of blood relationship.«[7] Dan Fodio's brother Abdullahi, who turned away from the jihadists out of disappointment, wrote of the new upper class that most of them were hypocrites, »whose purpose is the ruling of countries [...] and the collecting of concubines, and fine clothes.«[8] As people often suffered more under the taxes and raids of the new rulers than they had previously, there were repeated revolts against the Fulani leaders even in the early stages of the jihad.[9] Their supremacy might have been quickly eroded owing to ethnic differences, if they had not directed the internal aggression against the ›infidels‹ outside the empire. So the armies of the Fulani and their allies did not stop at the borders of the Hausa territory, but penetrated farther eastwards toward Bauchi (the ›Land of the Slaves‹), and southwards to the Nupe and into Yoruba territory. In the course of the nineteenth century, emirates evolved in these conquered regions, which depended on the leader of the faithful, the Caliph in Sokoto.

The only means of uniting the subdued peoples and holding the disparate empire together was Islam. Religion alone created a feeling of belonging that could transcend ethnic loyalties. In order to gain legitimacy the emirs had no other choice than to set up a theocratic rule. As custodians of the true faith they were intent on asserting the external manifestations of

218–219; Christelow, *Islamic Law in Africa*, p. 379; Sodiq, *History*, pp. 89–90; Sulaiman, *Revolution*, pp. 69–72, 79–80, 96, 104–105.

6 Isichei, *History of Nigeria*, p. 205.

7 Sulaiman, *Revolution*, pp. 96, 118; Sodiq, *History*, p. 94.

8 Quoted in Last, *Sokoto Caliphate*, p. 66; cf. Hiskett, *Sword of Truth*, pp. 106–109, 112.

9 Hiskett, *Jihads*, p. 148; Last, *Sokoto Caliphate*, pp. 34, 67–71; Osswald, *Sokoto-Kalifat*, pp. 112–121; Weiss, *Hausaland*, pp. 136–143.

the new religion, like Ramadan, Friday prayers and other rites that were suitable for disseminating a uniform culture. In areas where they sought to establish a lasting state order, as in Hausaland or amongst the Nupe and Yoruba, the subdued population was pushed to adopt its conquerors' faith. Yet conversion to Islam did not result in the converted seeing themselves as equals to their fellow Muslims. Rather, being a Muslim meant recognizing the emirs' religious and political authority and accepting one's place in a stratified social system. Islam established an enduring structure of subjugation, which safeguarded the conquest of ›heathen‹ societies: »Praying to Allah mean[t] praying to the God of the powerful.«[10] For example, those Nupe who converted to Islam, were generally also prepared to serve the foreign invaders. Their ethnic loyalties changed, and they were perceived by their ›pagan‹ brothers as part of the new ruling class: »Of such men the Nupe say not ›they become Mohammedans‹ but [...] ›they become Fulani‹.«[11]

Nonetheless, in most regions only a loose form of dependence prevailed. Village communities or ethnic groups had to pay the emirs tributes to avoid being ransacked by troops from the capital, but otherwise they preserved much autonomy. Despite its wars of conquest, Islam remained on the whole an urban religion.[12] Especially on the margins of the empire, where hundreds of ethnic groups lived, people attempted to evade the Fulani's claim to power – and consequently that of Islam. In these areas, the jihad resembled a looting expedition, as the warriors were more intent on taking slaves than spreading their religion. European explorers, who crossed the border regions of the Fulani Empire in the middle of the nineteenth century, reported of constant wars and predatory attacks that depopulated entire swathes of land.[13] In contrast, the center of the caliphate was densely populated, and there were millions of slaves, most of whom worked on the plantations.[14] Considerable prosperity developed in

---

10 Nadel, *Black Byzantium*, p. 142.

11 *Ibid.*, p. 143.

12 King, *State and Ethnicity*, p. 20.

13 Weiss, *Hausaland*, pp. 123–173; Gleave/Prothero, *Population Density*, pp. 320–321; Mason, *Population Density*, pp. 559–561.

14 At the end of the nineteenth century, slaves comprised between 25 and 50 percent of the total population, and in the center of the caliphate, around Sokoto and Gwandu, the percentage was much higher (Lovejoy, *Slave Control*, p. 240; King, *State and Ethnicity*, p. 24). As a consequence of the jihad, the number of slaves had risen »dramatically« (Lovejoy, *Slave Control*, p. 240); yet slavery had been widespread long before (Emmer, *Sklave*, p. 12; Iliffe, *Africans*, pp. 50–51, 151–152). When the first Arab travellers from

the cities thanks to the plantations; the transport routes were relatively safe, and trade flourished. But the constant demand for cheap labor meant that the periphery of the empire remained insecure: »Fula[ni] power was most brutal in frontier regions like Adamawa, but even in wealthy and sophisticated Kano City the Fula generally went armed, while Habe were forbidden the use of arms and horses and were required to remove their shoes on entering the Fula quarter.«[15] Emirates such as Kontagora, which were surrounded by unconquered, ›heathen‹ territory, financed themselves solely through the slave trade.[16] Presumably the frequent slave hunts explained why large sections of the North were not Islamized. After all, converting to Islam could not save people from being enslaved.[17] In some border regions such as Adamawa, the Fulani even prevented the subjugated population from converting to Islam: »Until the end of the 1950s, those locals who tried to convert to Islam (and those Fulbe who proselytized) were beaten and jailed by the Sultans.«[18] The foreign conquerors, who claimed all power for themselves, had no interest in assimilation, and therefore employed their religion in order to distinguish themselves from the ›primitive‹ indigenous population.

In an attempt to escape the raids by the slave hunters, people took refuge in the Jos Plateau, the Muri Mountains and other impassable regions that were difficult for the Fulani horsemen to navigate. Most of the areas

---

North Africa crossed the Sahara, about a thousand years ago, they met slaves in many parts of the Sahel zone (cf. Levtzion/Hopkins, *Corpus of Early Arabic Sources for West African History*).

15 Iliffe, *Honour*, p. 42.

16 Crowder, *Nigeria*, p. 172.

17 Fisher, *Slavery*, pp. 18–32; King, *State and Ethnicity*, pp. 25–26; Last, *History*, p. 44.

18 Gausset, *Spread of Islam*, p. 169. – This exclusive connection between religion and ethnicity recalls the beginnings of Islam, when Arab warriors conquered large parts of North Africa and Asia. As the ruling stratum of a new empire, they jealously preserved their separate identity and tried to keep their religion for themselves: »It was the mission of the community to bring God's true ways into all the world; hence the *rule* of the Muslim community [not their creed – J.H.] should be extended over all infidels.« »Islam [...] should guide those in command among men, and these should be the Arabs, to whom Islam was properly given« (Hodgson, *Islam*, pp. 322, 226). In the course of the eighth and ninth centuries, when the foreign rulers turned into an indigenous aristocracy, they began to share their religion with others, though converts were not granted the same rights: »to be a Muslim in the full political sense, a convert had to become associated, as a client [...], with one or other of the Muslim Arab tribes; as such, he and his descendants were socially inferior to the original members of the tribe, but shared its allegiances« (*ibid.*, p. 229).

they retreated to were in Nigeria's Middle Belt, a vast stretch of savannah that separates the semi-arid north from the tropical, humid south. Even today hundreds of minority peoples, who have largely maintained their independence, live in this intermediate zone. However, farther north in the center of the caliphate assimilation took place. The Warji, Pa'a and other small groups that converted to Islam, gradually assumed the identity of the majority population, the Hausa. Even the politically dominant ethnic group, the Fulani, adopted the language and often also the culture of the Hausa, which is why people today mostly speak of the Hausa-Fulani. That said, the nomadic ›Bush Fulani‹, who live from cattle breeding, have retained their traditional way of life. And even many sedentary Fulani (especially in the Northeast of Nigeria, where they did not settle under the Hausa, but under diverse minority peoples) still see themselves as a distinct ethnic group with their own language and separate settlements. There are other areas in which old rivalries between Hausa and Fulani emerge, for instance in the officer corps of the army.[19] It is in any case difficult to talk of a shared Hausa-Fulani culture, as the Hausa exhibit strong local differences. Up until the era of the jihad they formed a »hotch-potch of peoples«[20], and consequently, there was only a weak sense of solidarity. It is true that the people in Kano, Katsina or Zaria spoke dialects of the same language, but their identity was shaped regionally by their affiliation with one of the kingdoms, which had been in conflict with each other for centuries.[21]

Islam was a major element in the creation of a common Hausa-Fulani identity. The shared religion made it easier for the noble Fulani families to minimize ethnic antagonisms; at the same time it did not compel them to

---

19 The magazine *Tell* claimed: »in the army, there are Hausa officers, and there are Fulani officers, but there are no Hausa-Fulani officers« (15 July 1996, p. 13).

20 Meek, *Northern Tribes*, p. 27.

21 King, *State and Ethnicity*, pp. 9–10, 25–26. – With reference to early history, it is problematic to talk of a Hausa people. »The term Hausa referred only to the mother tongue of the inhabitants of the territory: it appeared as the ethnic name for the people of this territory in the written Arabic sources only in the sixteenth and seventeenth centuries. Until that time, these peoples were known by the names of their particular cities or kingdoms« (*ibid.*, p. 10). In the case of the Yoruba, Igbo and most other peoples in today's Nigeria, their ethnic identities are even more recent: »the very ethnic category ›Yoruba‹, in its modern connotation, was the product of missionary ›invention‹.« Before the end of the nineteenth century, »the speakers of ›Yoruba‹ dialects [...] knew themselves as Egba, Ijesha, or Awori, or else just by the name of their *ilu*, or ›town‹« (J. D. Y. Peel, *Religious Encounter*, pp. 278, 28, 283–286; Falola, *Ethnicity*, pp. 151–157).

renounce their privileges as rulers. Consequently, religion assumed a paradoxical function: It enabled the foreign conquerors to integrate into the majority society, while retaining their exclusive status. Today a few Fulani families still have the right to decide who should ascend to the throne of Sokoto. By taking the title ›Caliph‹ the emperors aspired to be representatives of the Prophet Mohammed. After the British conquest, when they had to swear loyalty to the British king, they contented themselves with the title ›Sultan‹, but this office still had to devolve to a direct descendent of Usman dan Fodio. The same principle applied to other high offices, which had been made over to a handful of Fulani families since the early nineteenth century. Even in a town like Ilorin, where the vast majority of the population has been Yoruba, the emir has, for generations, been chosen from one of the royal Fulani dynasties. His claim to rule was based on the jihad, so it was important to preserve this religious tradition. The Fulani aristocracy had to present themselves as guardians of a pure, strict Islam and stressed their descent from Usman dan Fodio and his companions. Later descendents of the caliphs' family even claimed to stand in a direct line to the Prophet Mohammed.[22] These remote yet distinguished origins fit in well with the fact that the Fulani, like the Tuareg, were originally lighter-skinned than other inhabitants of the Sahel zone. They often bragged that their descendents were Arabs, but it is more likely they originated from Berbers who mixed with black African peoples such as the Wolof and Serer in today's Senegal.[23] At any rate, there were several reasons for their sense of superiority. In addition to the pride that Islam lent them, they had a code of honor based on their nomadic traditions. It imbued them with a feeling of freedom and independence not shared by the hoe cultivators around them.[24]

22 Bello, *My Life*, p. 239; Paden, *Ahmadu Bello*, pp. 309, 574–575.

23 Salamone, *Ethnic Identities*, p. 47; Olorunfemi, *Fulani Jihad*, p. 125.

24 Vereecke, *Ethnic Change*, pp. 94–99; Gausset, *Spread of Islam*, pp. 169–170, 173. – In this respect, the Fulani resembled the Arabs, Mongols and other groups of conquerors who ruled in the name of Islam, but marked their superiority by more exclusive criteria: their noble nomadic descent (Manz, *Multi-Ethnic Empires*, pp. 76–90). However, only the ›Bush Fulani‹ have kept to their separate, endogamous way of life, while the sedentary Fulani have mixed, so that many of them can no longer be distinguished by their physical appearance from the Hausa, Kanuri, Nupe or Bole. Nevertheless, the old racial attitudes still matter, as they classify themselves as ›black‹, ›red‹ and ›white‹ Fulani. A relative of the Emir of Gombe, Bappayo Bappah, told me that these different types are ranked as in the case of cattle: A white cow fetches a higher price, and so a ›white‹ bride is more expensive than others.

As proponents of a strict form of Islam, the caliphate leaders sometimes applied rigorous force in suppressing ›pagan‹ customs.[25] But their efforts to purge society of all non-Islamic practices repeatedly failed in the face of indifference or the silent resistance of large sections of the population. Despite some initial success, reform movements always ran out of steam: »The spirit is willing but the social flesh is weak.«[26] Nonetheless, toward the end of the nineteenth century, shortly before the British conquest, life in the towns was strongly influenced by Islam, and the authorities made an effort to enforce at least some Sharia laws. For instance, thieves often had a hand cut off, and draconian punishments were meted out for non-observance of ritual duties.[27] In the aristocrats' palaces the wives, concubines and occasionally the unmarried princesses were clad in Islamic garments and closely watched, but other women were not required to be veiled and enjoyed »great liberties.«[28] Particularly in rural areas and amongst the poorer urban classes, people resisted religious regimentation, so Islam was practiced at best in traditional, syncretistic forms.

However, the dependent sections of the population did not just form an apathetic, reluctant mass that frustrated the efforts of religious reformers. Dissatisfied peasants or fugitive slaves sometimes could be mobilized to support Islamic demands, if they fell under the influence of charismatic leaders. Many militant preachers and rebel leaders, including Fulani princes who had been passed over as successors to the throne, opposed the oppressive regime of the emirs and their courtiers. As many insurgencies in the second half of the nineteenth century show, Islam did not only help to consolidate political rule but also inspired resistance against it. In this respect, the Sokoto Caliphate resembled other empires in which Islam, though spread by the upper classes, captured the political imagination of the masses: »the great radical movements in the Islamic empire were all movements within Islam and not against it.«[29] Once the subjugated population had appropriated the foreign conqueror's religion, it could turn the divine message against its original carriers. Islamic authorities found it difficult to control the political use of religion, because theological texts, rites and symbols were not administered by institutions like a

---

25 Hiskett, *Jihads*, p. 143; Trimingham, *Influence of Islam*, p. 39.

26 Gellner, *Postmodernism*, p. 13.

27 Lugard, *Northern Nigeria*, p. 21; Staudinger, *Haussaländer*, p. 568; Christelow, *Islamic Law and Judicial Practice*, pp. 187–190.

28 Staudinger, *Haussaländer*, p. 559; Callaway/Creevey, *Islam*, p. 31.

29 Bernard Lewis, *Middle East*, p. 73.

church and an ordained clergy. Every believer who succeeded in gathering enough adherents could follow in the footsteps of Usman dan Fodio and declare his own jihad. This is why the caliphate, like other Muslim societies, developed »an enormous potential for mass movements and mass outbreaks.«[30] Yet the religious mobilization of the population did not give rise to institutions that could be used to domesticate state power. Neither the caliph nor the emirs could be legally deposed.[31] Rebellion against their autocratic rule did not lead to democratic control; it simply replaced one despot with another. Religiously-inspired warlords often succeeded in driving away the Fulani aristocracy, but they could not establish more legitimate authority. Toward the end of the nineteenth century, many towns and villages, particularly at the eastern margins of the empire, had been devastated by revolts of self-appointed Mahdis.[32]

Islam as Support of the Colonial System

In 1902/03 when British troops occupied the North of Nigeria, they met with little resistance. Even in Sokoto, the center of the Fulani Empire, the population did not defend the Islamic authorities. It did not take long for the caliph and a few defiant emirs to be expelled. Yet the British did not think it advisable to break the power of the ruling families, as the colonial power lacked the staff to administer the conquered territories. In the centers of the Fulani emirates, the British found a functioning administration. At least in the towns, the people were accustomed to paying taxes and obeying the authorities. Furthermore, the British met with a judicial system, which they could take over without many modifications. Muslim law was relatively easy to integrate into the colonial administration, as many of its regulations already existed in written form. So Sharia remained the recognized law in the emirates until the end of the colonial era. The only practices that were abolished were those which the new rulers viewed as inhumane, namely torture and mutilation.

Nor did the British tolerate slavery: They had, after all, justified their conquest of Sokoto by arguing that they wanted to stop the slave trade.

---

30 Eisenstadt, *Öffentlichkeit*, p. 319.
31 Whitaker, *Politics of Tradition*, pp. 260–261.
32 Clarke/Linden, *Islam*, pp. 109–118; Low, *Nigerian Emirates*, pp. 166–175.

However, once the colonial government was established it adopted a pragmatic attitude. The British banned public slave markets, and it was no longer possible to conduct large-scale slave raids. That said, excessively strict measures would have threatened the economic position of the Fulani rulers. Some of them, like the Emir of Kontagora, were quick to declare that they would defy any ban: »Can you stop a cat from mousing? I shall die with a slave in my mouth.«[33] It made more sense for the British governors to put aside moral scruples and make allowances for their allies' interests. It was not until 1936 that a decree was passed under which all citizens of Nigeria were born free. However, slavery continued to be tolerated in modified form; at the royal courts in particular, it survived the colonial era.[34]

The alliance between the British and the Fulani aristocracy gave birth to the system of ›indirect rule‹. Though sovereignty lay with the British crown, the ›native authorities‹ remained in direct control of the population. The emirs also retained the right to distribute land, and they levied poll and animal taxes. Furthermore, together with the sultan they were the highest judicial authorities. Not only did they appoint professional judges (called *alkali* after the Hausa word for *al kadi*), they also presided over the court in their palaces. They were allowed to intervene at will in ongoing trials, take charge of lawsuits and even reverse rulings.[35] For the colonial administration it was a relief that they did not have to engage in the Africans' way of life. However, the British were not the only ones who profited from this power-sharing arrangement. So did the Fulani, who could extend their sphere of influence. After all, it was only thanks to the colonial army that it became possible to pacify the ›warrior tribes‹ of the uplands and other peripheral regions. Ethnic groups who had succeeded in defending their independence during the entire nineteenth century were now subjugated to Islamic authorities at the behest of the British governor.[36] The Kataf, for instance, and a dozen related ethnic groups came under the rule of the Emir of Zaria, with the result that for decades every post in the district administration from judge to messenger was filled with Hausa and Fulani.[37]

---

33 Quoted in Crowder, *Nigeria*, p. 173.
34 Lovejoy/Hogendorn, *Slavery*, p. 30; Schacht, *Islam in Northern Nigeria*, pp. 139–142.
35 Whitaker, *Politics of Tradition*, pp. 269–270.
36 Ballard, *Pagan Administration*, pp. 4–12; Perham, *Native Administration*, pp. 134–139; Schacht, *Islam in Northern Nigeria*, pp. 126–127; Yahya, *Shari'ah*, p. 8.
37 Abdul Raufu Mustapha, *Minority Identities*, p. 92.

In all those regions of the Middle Belt, which were not formally incorporated into the emirates, native administrations were established to apply local customary law, not Sharia. Councils of elders, chiefs and village heads, who worked to the satisfaction of the British district officer, were authorized to mete out justice as they saw fit, but only when it involved minor crimes or disputes. More serious cases were tried by the provincial courts, presided over by British judges. They were instructed, however, not to pass sentence according to foreign, European legal principles. English criminal law, which had been introduced in 1904, only applied to Europeans, Levantines, Indians and Africans from other colonies. Otherwise, the judges at the Magistrate Courts and the High Court (later Supreme Court) passed sentence according to the prevailing customary law. That said, the British lacked the money, staff and communication to control the ›pagan‹ regions effectively, so they often relied on administrative staff they had recruited under the Hausa and Fulani.[38] After all, it was often impossible to find chiefs or other people in authority amongst the populations in the minority areas, and even when they did encounter traditional rulers, the latter were often reluctant to cooperate with colonial officials: »each petty chief [is] a passive resister, and not one with sufficient power over his people to be able to enforce my orders.«[39] For the British, it was often easier to engage ›friendly‹ Fulani as district and village heads. Communicating with them was easier, both sides held similar colonial attitudes, and it appeared that the Fulani – like the British – had been destined to rule: »We feel that the Fulani and the English races have much in common. Both have had a long experience and special aptitude for administering their own and other people's affairs.«[40]

Until the end of the colonial era, Sharia applied in all regions subjugated to the emirate system. Even where the majority of the population was ›pagan‹, civil and criminal proceedings had to be heard by Islamic judges. In keeping with the traditions of Sharia, political and judicial power

38 Perham, *Native Administration*, p. 150. – When the first British High Commissioner assumed the administration of Northern Nigeria on January 1, 1900, he had eight political or administrative officers at his disposal (Lugard, *Northern Nigeria*, p. 6). Eleven years later, a total of 1000 British officials were deployed in the whole of Nigeria, and in 1938, when Nigeria's population had reached about 30 million, the number was 2001 (Coleman, *Nigeria*, p. 33).

39 H. L. Norton-Traill, 1911, in Ballard, *Pagan Administration*, pp. 5–6.

40 Lt. Colonel Beddington, 1934, in Omolewa, *Colonial Legacy*, p. 11; cf. Turaki, *Colonial Legacy*, pp. 186–190.

were not divided; the sultan and some of the important emirs retained the right to pass the death sentence on their subjects. Moreover, as in the past they used their authority to fill almost all the judges' positions with members of allied Fulani families.[41] From a European perspective such extensive power was problematic. In order to prevent the emirs from misusing their office, the administration of justice was placed under the supervision of British judges and district officers. Death sentences were only effective if the governor confirmed them, and even in the case of longer prison sentences, the government could reverse rulings or transfer trials to other courts.[42] In addition, the colonial administration reserved the right to modify Sharia itself. Anything that was deemed »repugnant to natural justice and humanity« could be forbidden.[43] Until today many Muslims consider it presumptuous and insulting that the Europeans claimed to teach others what is humane and just. However, only rarely did the colonial regime exercise its right to overrule ›repugnant‹ sections of the Sharia.[44] With the exception of amputations and other harsh physical punishments, the British administrators tolerated most Islamic legal practices even when they were at odds with European concepts of justice. For example, Sharia judges could sentence suspects to death without sufficient evidence, if male relatives of the victim swore 50 oaths against the accused.[45] The colonial government also accepted that non-Muslims suffered massive discrimination. In 1958, for example, a government commission established that some of the Fulani judges – in accordance with Sharia – did not allow nonbelievers to testify against Muslims.[46] Moreover, the punishment depended on the religion of the accused. When a Muslim was murdered, the killer faced the death sentence, or if agreement was reached on the payment of compensation, he or she had to pay the full amount of blood money. In contrast, a Muslim who murdered an infidel only received one hundred strokes of the cane and was sentenced to one year in prison. In cases of compensation, the victim's family was entitled to only a fraction of the full

---

41 Schacht, *Islam in Northern Nigeria*, p. 126; Abun-Nasr, *Islamisches Recht*, pp. 203, 207–209.

42 Keay/Richardson, *Native Courts*, pp. 21–27, 39–44; Anderson, *Islamic Law*, p. 175; Sa'ad Abubakar, *Northern Provinces*, p. 455; Abun-Nasr, *Islamisches Recht*, pp. 205, 209.

43 Keay/Richardson, *Native Courts*, p. 22; Milner, *Sentencing in Nigeria*, pp. 263–264.

44 Muhammad Sani Umar, *Islam and Colonialism*, p. 42.

45 Anderson, *Islamic Law*, p. 202.

46 Willink Commission, *Fears of Minorities*, p. 126; Essien, *Penal Code*, p. 89.

amount of blood money: Christians received half, while heathens received just one fifteenth.[47]

By upholding these Sharia provisions, the colonial administration institutionalized the inferior status of non-Muslims in the emirate areas. Even in those regions of the Middle Belt that had not been made over to the emirs, it was obvious that the British treated Fulani officials in the local administration with more respect than the old-established local dignitaries. Consequently, traditional big men emulated the behavior and speech of the Fulani, or they adopted their dress and occasionally their religion.[48] The aristocracy in the centers of the Fulani Empire soon learned that it could assert its religious and political influence more quickly in alliance with the British than during the times of jihad, and it fully appreciated this preferential treatment by the colonial administration. Ahmadu Bello, the political leader of the Northern Region, noted that the British were »the instruments of destiny«, and that their conquest of Nigeria was »fulfilling the will of God.«[49] And indeed, colonialism was a blessing for the spreading of Islam, not only in Nigeria, but also in other parts of West Africa: »in half a century of European colonization Islam progressed more widely and more profoundly than in ten centuries of precolonial history.«[50]

Immediately after the conquest of the Fulani Empire, the British High Commissioner had promised that the new administration would not interfere with the Muslims' religion.[51] The intention was to prevent the outbreak of religious unrest, such as the British had experienced several years previously during the 1884 Mahdi revolt in the Sudan. Moreover, the British had to accept the fact that their new allies, the Fulani rulers, maintained their position by virtue of their religious authority. As *defensores fidei* the emirs could not permit their Muslim subjects to defect from true religion.[52] Consequently the colonial administration ordered the emirate regions to be closed to Christian missionaries. Missions were even barred from the Sabon Gari (foreign quarters) of Sokoto or Kano, where Christian immi-

---

47 Anderson, *Islamic Law*, pp. 200–201, 221; Perham, *Native Administration*, pp. 139–140; Peters, *Islamic Criminal Law*, pp. 3, 11, 26.
48 Crampton, *Christianity*, p. 53; Schacht, *Islam in Northern Nigeria*, p. 129.
49 Quoted in Logams, *Colonial Forces*, p. 46.
50 Froelich, *Islamisation*, p. 166; I. M. Lewis, *Introduction*, p. 82; Levtzion/Pouwels, *Islamization*, p. 14. – Under Belgian rule, which favored Christianity, Islam was not able to spread (I. M. Lewis, *Introduction*, p. 77).
51 Lugard, *Northern Nigeria*, p. 24; Hamza, *Lugard*, pp. 121, 123.
52 Kukah, *Religion*, p. 4.

grants from the South had settled. Church representatives vehemently protested this obstruction of their work, but the colonial ministry declared it was unwilling to make any concessions in this matter: »Whatever threatened the Muhammedan religion threatened the authority of the Emirs and so imperilled the organization of ›Indirect Rule‹.«[53] Only in 1931 were Christians allowed to preach in ›quiet places‹; and priests could visit people's homes, if they had been invited.[54] Even today many cities of the North relegate the construction of churches to outlying areas.

For decades the missions' activities concentrated on the South, which is now largely Christian. Only in some Yoruba towns such as Ilorin or Ibadan, which had an Islamic influence that predated the colonial era, do Muslims make up the majority of the population. In contrast, in the Southeast of the country, under the Igbo and the ethnic minorities on the coast, European missions asserted themselves. Christianity also appealed to the ›pagan‹ minorities in the North. In order to distance themselves from the advancing Hausa-Fulani culture, many of them converted to Christianity. In this manner they acquired a ›respectable‹ modern identity that made it easier for them to maintain their independence.

Since missions were accompanied by schools and hospitals, they resulted in the emergence of a Western lifestyle in the country's South and in parts of the Middle Belt. In contrast, the Islamic North remained protected from the influences of Western modernity, and this explains in part why the regions around Sokoto, Katsina and Bauchi are still among the poorest and least developed regions in Africa. In 1957, only 185,000 children in Northern Nigeria attended primary school; in the South however the number stood at 2,300,000.[55] Reservations about the European education system persist in postcolonial Nigeria, because the highest authorities such as the Sultan of Sokoto warn parents about its corrupting influence: »Western education destroys our culture.«[56] The majority of the people in the North are still illiterate because parents refuse to send their children to

---

53 Statement of the Colonial Office, 1917, in Crampton, *Christianity*, p. 60. – In response to the »unchristian« colonial policy in Africa, an Anglican missionary predicted: »The British official may one day see that all this subservience to the Muslim and neglect of his own faith gains him neither the respect, gratitude nor affection of the people, but the very reverse« (Temple Gairdner, quoted in Walls, *Africa*, p. 59).

54 Crampton, *Christianity*, p. 64.

55 Okeke, *Hausa-Fulani Hegemony*, p. 23; Coleman, *Nigeria*, p. 134.

56 *Guardian*, 24 May 1994.

school or because they prefer Koran schools, where the pupils memorize holy verses, but do not learn to read and write.[57]

The stark contrasts between North and South were produced, in part, by the policy of the colonial power. Its system of indirect rule reinforced differences not only between regions, but also between ethnic groups that lived in proximity. In Kano and other cities of the North, the administration created foreign quarters for traders and administrative officials from the South, who had settled in Northern Nigeria in large numbers after the construction of the railway. Admittedly, the practice of ethnic and religious segregation predated the colonial era. The old town of Kano had been reserved for the Hausa and Fulani, with other ethnic groups being forced to settle outside the city walls: The Arabs were in Durimin Turawa, the Tuareg in Agadasawa, and there were also special quarters for non-Muslims.[58] Laws had restricted the contact among these groups; for instance, Sharia had forbidden non-Muslims to marry Muslim women. This ban was upheld under British rule.[59]

The decision to administer Nigeria by a system of indirect rule was a pragmatic one. However, the fact that in doing so the British favored the Fulani aristocracy was motivated by personal preferences. The Fulani's courtly culture and their religion seemed to the conquerors from Victorian England to be evidence of a noble civilization. Members of the colonial oligarchy such as Lady Lugard also noted with appreciation the lighter skin color of the Fulani and their almost European features: »the high nose, thin lips and deep set eye, the Aristocratic thin hand [...]; the ruling classes in the North are deserving in every way of the name of cultivated Gentlemen; [...] there are races which are born to conquer and others to persist in conquest.«[60] British officials who served in Nigeria, applied to be posted to the residential towns of the emirs where living conditions were more pleasant and their own work conferred greater prestige.[61] Moreover, in their dealings with the Fulani aristocracy they could be sure that their prejudices against the »uncivilised pagan tribes«[62] were shared. The Emir of Zaria, for example, responded to the call for autonomy by those peoples

57 Awofeso/Ritchie/Degeling, *Almajiri*, pp. 313–314; Schacht, *Islam in Northern Nigeria*, p. 130.

58 Osaghae, *Migrant Organizations*, pp. 27–28; cf. Nnoli, *Ethnic Politics*, pp.115–116.

59 Osaghae, *Migrant Organizations*, p. 31.

60 Quoted in Logams, *Colonial Forces*, p. 48.

61 Ballard, *Pagan Administration*, pp. 4–6.

62 Lugard, in Ballard, *Pagan Administration*, p. 3.

whom his ancestors had seen as a pool of slaves by saying that he could not see how »people who ate dogs and whose women wore little but a bunch of leaves should be led to believe that they could administer themselves.«[63] Lugard made similarly derogatory comments on the tribes which were difficult to rule and persisted »in the lowest stage of primitive savagery.«[64] Islam, in contrast, seemed to have achieved a transition to a higher form of civilization. Some of the colonial officials considered it highly advantageous that since the start of British rule many ›pagan‹ peoples had come under the influence of Islamic authorities. Following the end of the slave hunts it was believed that the religious-political culture of the emirs would exert a positive influence, especially on those newly conquered peoples, who first had to learn to obey state authority: »Islam is the best religion for Africans.«[65] Others, however, pointed out that Islam with its proud insistence on god-given rules of conduct would ultimately hinder the transition to a modern way of life.

The fact that large numbers of the ›pagan‹ population in the South converted to Christianity did not necessarily lend them more respectability in the eyes of the British. Many colonial officials did not disguise their contempt for the ›semi-civilized mission boys‹, who tried to imitate the behavior of the whites.[66] While the large majority of the Muslim population were subservient and willing to cooperate, the Christian converts were often perceived as tiresome competition. They were anxious to appropriate the knowledge of the Europeans, but with the intention of taking over their privileged positions. Consequently, the mission schools were seen as breeding grounds for African nationalism. It was here that the modern elite which later revolted against the foreign rule of the whites, evolved.[67]

---

63 Quoted in Kukah, *Religion*, p. 49.
64 Quoted in Ballard, *Pagan Administration*, p. 6.
65 Perham, *Native Administration*, p. 142; Barnes, *Evangelization*, pp. 427–428; Walls, *Africa*, pp. 55–59.
66 Barnes, *Evangelization*, pp. 413–427; Barnes, *Christianity*, pp. 282–283; Enwerem, *Dangerous Awakening*, pp. 28–29.
67 Kastfelt, *Christianity*, pp. 195–196.

Transition to Independence

As early as the 1940s it became apparent that the colonial system was becoming untenable. This meant the British administration had to begin preparing for the gradual hand-over of power to the Africans. But to which Africans? In a nation with 500 ethno-linguistic groups[68] it would have been impossible to restore the precolonial power structures. Local princes and emirs could not expect to regain their former autonomy. In a »world of nation-states«[69] which was geared toward Western standards, there seemed to be no place for chieftainships or segmentary societies. Rather, the African colonies had to embark on the same route already taken by the former colonies in Asia and Latin America. With their arbitrarily drawn borders, which forced together a large number of ethnic and religious communities, they had apparently no other choice but to transform themselves into modern territorial states.

The ›native authorities‹, on whom indirect rule had been based, were poorly equipped for taking over a Western-type administration. They not only lacked the democratic legitimacy but often the necessary expertise.[70] In particular, the Islamic rulers in the North were aware that they would likely end up as the losers when the process of decolonization was completed. Executive positions in the state machinery, which would need to be filled anew following the colonial officials' departure, could only be occupied by an ›educated‹ elite. And it looked as if European criteria alone would define ›educated‹. Young Nigerians, who had learned English in the mission schools, now held the key to success, while all forms of Islamic learning had been devalued.

The Igbo and Yoruba from the South had taken early advantage of their lead in the education sector by accepting positions in the colonial administration. Once the British withdrew, they could reckon on taking control of the state machinery. In 1960, less than two percent of the employees working in the ministries of the capital Lagos and in other federal authorities had come from the North.[71] As such, the Fulani aristocracy feared that with independence they would lose their influence. Under the British protectorate the political elite of the North had felt, by and large,

---

68 Crozier/Blench, *Index of Nigerian Languages.*
69 Coleman, *Nationalism*, p. 422.
70 Flint, *Decolonization*, p. 395.
71 Loimeier, *Islamische Erneuerung*, p. 103.

fairly treated; but they could not expect to receive favorable treatment from their black brothers in the South. Ahmadu Bello, who in 1954 was elected first Prime Minister of the Northern Region, openly expressed this mistrust of the ›nationalist‹ politicians from the South: »what had we to hope from an African Administration, probably in the hands of a hostile party. The answer to our minds was, quite simply, just nothing.«[72] In the House of Representatives in Lagos, which united delegates from the North and South, there was a confrontation as early as 1953. When a representative of the Action Group presented a motion that Nigeria should be made independent within three years, he was voted down by politicians from the North.[73]

Though the colonial administration did not have the power to halt the move toward independence, it was influential enough to set the course for the future. Those radical politicians, who had campaigned on anti-imperialist slogans for an independent Nigeria, were not to profit from the fruits of independence. From the British point of view, the conservative elite of the North, which had formed the Northern Peoples' Congress (NPC) in 1951, was much better suited to maintaining stability in a time of transition.[74] In order to ensure that Hausa and Fulani politicians would inherit colonial power, the governor-general was willing to meet the NPC's key demands. In 1954, the protectorate received a federal constitution, which established an African government with extensive powers for each of the three regions. This meant that NPC politicians could entrench their influence in the administrative centers of the North without much interference from the federal capital. Moreover, the Northern Region remained a single political unit, notwithstanding the embittered resistance of the non-Muslim minorities. Consequently, the NPC, whose primacy in the North was based on the dominance of the Muslim population, also had the opportunity to bring the minority regions of the Middle Belt under its control.

As early as 1939, the South of Nigeria had been divided into Western and Eastern provinces, while the North remained a single administrative unit even though it encompassed three-quarters of Nigeria's territory. Likewise, in terms of total population, the Northern Region appeared to have a slight edge on the South according to the 1952/53 census. As a

---

72 Bello, *My Life*, p. 111.
73 Sklar, *Political Parties*, pp. 125–128.
74 Diamond, *Nigeria*, p. 421; Kukah/Falola, *Religious Militancy*, pp. 50–51; Hiskett, *Islam*, p. 121.

result, the North was granted more seats than the West and East combined, when the first independent federal parliament was elected in 1959. Any party that succeeded in bringing the Northern Region under its control was in a good position to secure power in Lagos. Indeed, this was the only chance for the old elite of the Fulani to prevent its lapse into insignificance. Deprived of the means of controlling the government of independent Nigeria, the entire North would have been further marginalized. After all, not only the education gap between Christians and Muslims favored the South. In terms of economic development, the Northern Region lagged hopelessly behind. Its decisive handicap, however, was that the enormous oil resources, which had been tapped as recently as the 1950s, lay far away in the Niger Delta. If the North were to profit from this wealth, its elite had to secure its political dominance.

Presenting itself as a regional party, the Northern Peoples' Congress did not win a single seat in the West or East in the decisive elections for independence.[75] Its motto »One North: One People Irrespective of Religion, Rank or Tribe«[76] called on the people of their own region to unite against the impending hegemony of the South. However, the ethnic groups in Northern Nigeria did not see themselves as ›one people‹, nor did the NPC come close to representing all social and ethnic groups equally. Rather, the party apparatus was firmly in the hands of the Fulani aristocracy. The fact that the old elite succeeded in manipulating the modern party system in its favor had to do with certain features of colonial policy. According to British plans, the transition to democracy was conceived as a gradual process that was to start at the local level, based on the existing native authorities, which were authorized in 1946 to send delegates to a Regional House of Assembly. While the members of the first regional parliament were appointed by the emirs and other traditional authorities, in 1951 and 1956 they were elected, albeit by an indirect electoral process that favored the local notables.[77] As a result, the Fulani elite were able to consolidate their influence to the extent that after independence, when the regional parliament was elected by direct vote, they emerged as the dominant force: 40 percent of the members elected in 1961 were members of

---

75 Ngou, *Elections*, p. 100; Paden, *Ahmadu Bello*, p. 159.
76 Sklar, *Political Parties*, p. XIII.
77 *Ibid.*, p. 321; Paden, *Ahmadu Bello*, pp. 164–169; Coleman, *Nigeria*, pp. 271–281.

royal families, a further 28 percent belonged to other noble families, and only two percent were descended from slaves.[78]

Representatives of the Christian minorities, who had never felt themselves part of the Fulani Empire, founded their own party, the United Middle Belt Congress. Their primary goal was to split off the Northern Region in order to gain autonomy through a region of their own. With the support of Christian politicians from the South, they forced the colonial government to set up a commission to investigate the idea. However, the commission came out against autonomy, and thus the Christian-traditionalist minorities remained under the authority of the NPC government in the Northern Region. Prime Minister Ahmadu Bello repeatedly assured them that his government was committed to the interests of all citizens: Northerners should forget their religious differences and work for the unity of their region. »Here in Northern Nigeria ... we have people of many different races, tribes and religions who are knit together by common history, common interests and common ideals. [...] we have no intention of favouring one religion at the expense of another. [...] Let us forget the difference in our religions and, remember [...] the common brotherhood before God.«[79] Needless to say, the colonial government was not placated by such assurances. It was prepared to favor the Fulani elite when handing over power, but made this subject to conditions. Against the Muslims' resistance it insisted on granting all (male) citizens, including non-Muslims, the same voting rights.[80] And it demanded that they all forego using Sharia, at least its penal code. The leaders of the Northern Peoples' Congress bowed to the pressure of the colonial power, and thus the parliament of the Northern Region voted to restrict the scope of the Islamic courts. From October 1, 1960, their jurisdiction was limited to civil proceedings involving questions of Islamic personal law, like marriage and divorce, family status, guardianship, religious endowments, and the disposition of estates. Other areas of civil law, in particular commercial law and questions of tort, were however excluded.[81]

The jurisdiction of the Sharia courts had already been pruned on earlier occasions. In 1947, the West African Court of Appeal had annulled a judgment by the Emir of Gwandu, although under existing Islamic law it

---

78 Whitaker, *Politics of Tradition*, p. 322.

79 Ahmadu Bello, in Paden, *Ahmadu Bello*, p. 305.

80 Hiskett, *Islam*, pp. 121, 126.

81 Ostien, *Opportunity*, pp. 223, 228; Ajetunmobi, *Reorganisation*, pp. 98–101.

was quite correct. The British judges ruled that it was not justifiable to sentence the accused to death for murder, because a secular court, using English common law, which distinguished premeditated murder from homicide, would only have passed a prison sentence in this case. As illustrated by this case, the decision over life and death depended on whether a religious or secular court declared itself to be responsible. In order to avoid such unequal treatment in the future, the Sharia judges were instructed not to hand down harsher sentences than those that secular judges, finding according to English law, would do in comparable cases.[82] The intention of this decree was to standardize the competing legal systems. The British acted in the conviction that a »medieval« law such as the Sharia was destined to give way to modern law anyway.[83] In an independent and democratic Nigeria, all citizens would enjoy the same rights. A uniform body of ›modern‹ law also appeared necessary in order to foster trust among foreign investors.[84] In the negotiations with the NPC leadership, however, they could not agree on a common law code, not even in the field of criminal justice. Instead of adopting the Criminal Code, derived from the British legal system and installed as the sole criminal code in the two Southern provinces, the Northern legislators passed their own Penal Code. It also drew heavily on the English criminal code and was thus suited for secular courts, yet it preserved a few elements of the Islamic penal system. Adultery and the consumption of alcohol remained forbidden, but only for the Muslim part of the population, and the penalties were not as strict as envisaged by Sharia.[85]

In an effort to clear the obstacles out of the path to a modern, democratic Nigeria, the colonial government endeavored to push through another reform: to reduce the influence of traditional authorities and thus sever the ties between judicial and political power. When the British governor announced in 1959 that the sultan and the emirs would also have to bow to

---

82 Abun-Nasr, *Islamisches Recht*, pp. 209–211; Christelow, *Islamic Law and Judicial Practice*, p. 193; Keay/Richardson, *Native Courts*, pp. 46–52; Muhammad Sani Umar, *Islam and Colonialism*, pp. 53–54.

83 Hiskett, *Islam*, p. 116. – Until the 1960s, Western experts assumed that Islamic societies were subject to a process of secularization and would abolish Islamic law (Prof. Ruud Peters at a Sharia Conference in Bayreuth, 11 July 2003; cf. I. M. Lewis, *Introduction*, p. 91; Park, *Nigerian Law*, pp. 139–143).

84 Keay/Richardson, *Native Courts*, p. 62.

85 Essien, *Penal Code*, pp. 94–96; Ajetunmobi, *Reorganisation*, pp. 99–101.

ministerial decrees, the persons in question were »shocked.«[86] In the system of indirect rule, they had been incorporated into the hierarchy of the colonial administration, along with all the staff members of their native administrations, meaning that they no longer lived from payments of tribute and instead received government salaries. However, they had not been prevented from filling key positions in the judiciary and administration with their followers and family members.[87] Shortly before independence, they were stripped of the power to appoint and discipline Islamic judges. They could still continue holding court in their palaces (a right they did not lose until 1967 under military rule), but as of 1957 their judgments could be overturned by a higher Islamic court, the newly instituted Muslim Court of Appeal.[88]

The gradual loss of power by the Islamic aristocracy came about only because the Prime Minister of the North supported this process. Ahmadu Bello, who had the title of Sardauna (crown prince), was himself of royal blood and had no interest in abolishing the institution of the emirates. He did, however, have an interest in bringing the emirs to heel. In 1963, he had criminal proceedings for embezzlement of tax revenue initiated against the proudest and least compliant of them: the Emir of Kano.[89] While the power of the traditional notables decayed, the influence of politicians from the non-aristocratic Hausa and Fulani families increased, and they were now integrated into the ruling stratum of society. Many of them had received a Western education, for example in the administrative colleges in Katsina and Kaduna, where British lecturers had trained a modern Islamic elite.

The elite that had received Western training did not necessarily espouse principles of democratic rule. As long as the colonial government supervised the transition to democracy, at least the elections were largely free and fair.[90] But after independence the NPC leadership showed little restraint in using the state's monopoly on power to secure its still fragile

---

86 Paden, *Ahmadu Bello*, p. 170.

87 Sklar, *Political Parties*, p. 323; Paden, *Ahmadu Bello*, pp. 450, 457; Schacht, *Islam in Northern Nigeria*, p. 126.

88 Keay/Richardson, *Native Courts*, p. 70; Paden, *Ahmadu Bello*, pp. 208–209, 211; Christelow, *Islamic Law and Judicial Practice*, p. 195; Kukah/Falola, *Religious Militancy*, p. 16.

89 Paden, *Ahmadu Bello*, pp. 440–448, 463; Whitaker, *Politics of Tradition*, pp. 279–282.

90 A former colonial officer in Nigeria, Harold Smith, alleged decades later that »the British Government interfered with the elections so as to achieve Northern domination of Nigeria« (*Tell*, 21 February 2005, p. 61).

dominance. Thanks to the federal constitution, the Premier of the Northern Region had far-reaching powers. He decided on the allocation of state resources and access to public offices; he also controlled the police and later the regional radio and TV stations. Ethnic minorities therefore found that it did not pay off for them to support opposition parties, as in doing so they risked exclusion from development projects and other state blessings. If they openly opposed the dictates of the regional government, as did the predominantly Christian and traditionalist Tiv, their revolt was put down by the army.

Opposition politicians who defected to the government party were rewarded with lucrative posts and public contracts. However, those who were not prepared to take the victors' side had to live in fear of financial ruin or imprisonment. Three years after independence, the opposition was largely inactive, and North Nigeria had almost been turned into a one-party state.[91] The victims of the repression not only included Christian groups, but also Muslim opposition parties, especially the Northern Elements Progressive Union (NEPU), a left-wing populist party which opposed the political and religious hegemony of the royal family of Sokoto, and the Bornu Youth Movement (BYM), a regional party of the Kanuri minority in Northeast Nigeria. Charges against members of NEPU and BYM were, as long as Islamic criminal law was in force, brought in the name of Sharia. This gave judges the chance of harking back to a set of very broad discretionary rights, *siyasa*.[92] In cases where the violation of public order was tried, the testimony of two Muslim witnesses was enough to secure a conviction; the judges did not have to give reasons for their decision, and attorneys were not allowed to argue before Islamic courts.[93] To prevent the colonial government from intervening in political court cases, the judges were mostly content with imposing lighter punishments. Defendants were given twelve lashes, or were imprisoned for three months.[94] If they were

---

91 Dudley, *Parties*, p. 190.

92 Reynolds, *Time of Politics*, p. 65; Anderson, *Islamic Law*, pp. 195, 200; Bosworth, *Siyasa*, p. 694.

93 Sklar, *Political Parties*, p. 360; Reynolds, *Time of Politics*, pp. 70, 95.

94 Reynolds, *Time of Politics*, pp. 73, 93. – The colonial administration had no objections to corporal punishments like lashing and flogging. In the Islamic North, *haddi* lashing has been widely used since precolonial times, though in a mild form. The person carrying out the punishment had to hold an object under his arm which prevented him from inflicting severe pain (Anderson, *Islamic Law*, p. 197). When the British codified Sharia punishments, they made this lenient variant the only legal one, and it has remained the legal norm until today. However, a government commission doubted already in colonial

not cowed when released, they could be locked up for a few more months.[95] As a rule, punishments were carried out as soon as the sentence was passed, so no appeal was possible. In any case, appeals against the judgments would have failed, because with such minor penalties, the appellate procedures went no further than the nearest emir's court of law. Appeal courts with European members only accepted cases in which the appellant had received a prison sentence of more than six months or a fine of more than 25 pounds.[96] Thus aside from a few exceptions, opposition politicians were only tried by Islamic judges, who had close ties to the ruling party and local authorities: »The police were in the hands of the chief, the prison was in the hands of the chief, and the court was in the hands of the chief, and the chief was an NPC member.«[97] »It is notorious that in the rural districts, the district heads and the Alkalis together wield virtually absolute political power over the peasantry. Collusive political intolerance on their part renders opposition party activity extremely difficult if not hazardous.«[98]

Opposition politicians in the North had formed alliances with the major parties of the South in the 1950s, because such alliances were their only hope of breaking the supremacy of the Fulani elite. However, the Northern Peoples' Congress mobilized popular resentment against ›the people from the South‹ who had occupied important administrative posts, not only in Lagos but also in the cities of the North. The indigenous population often had no chance against migrants from the South, who, thanks to their better education, had established themselves in all modern sectors of the administration and economy. Thus in 1954, with the approval of the British governor, the government of the Northern Region adopted a policy of positive discrimination. Applicants from the North were given preference for all positions in the regional and local administration. If there were no suitable candidates available, Europeans were allowed to retain their posts where possible, otherwise Southerners were hired on fixed-term contracts.[99] This led to the dismissal of thousands of Igbo and Yoruba. Even if they had been born or lived in the North for

times that the courts strictly adhered to this prescription (Willink Commission, *Fears of Minorities*, p. 130).

95 Gumi, *Where I Stand*, pp. 100–101; Reynolds, *Time of Politics*, pp. 72–73, 92–93.

96 Keay/Richardson, *Native Courts*, p. 67; Reynolds, *Time of Politics*, pp. 61–62, 72, 87.

97 Malam Lawan Danbazau, a legal adviser for NEPU, in Reynolds, *Time of Politics*, p. 63.

98 Sklar, *Political Parties*, p. 363.

99 Ujo, *Manipulation Strategies*, p. 96.

decades, they had no claim to equal treatment. For the policy of North-ernization was meant to defend the privileges of the ›indigenous‹ popula-tion, so it classified citizens of other ethnic groups as ›strangers‹. Since then, it has become customary, in other parts of Nigeria as well, to give preferential treatment to members of ›autochthonous‹ groups: in filling administrative posts and teaching positions in schools, in granting scholar-ships and free education, in allocating housing and agricultural land.[100] Right up to the present, ethnic (and religious) groups have continued to claim the political-administrative control of their ancestral lands. Therefore most Nigerians see it as legitimate that state and local governments favor the indigenous part of their population. Even the current democratic con-stitution does not insist that Nigerians enjoy full rights of citizenship in all parts of the country. Like the constitutions of 1979 and 1989, it acknowl-edges the popular notion that only those residents properly »belong« to a state whose parents or grandparents come from an »indigenous« commu-nity.[101] All the others who live there are given the status of non-indigenes.

Many Igbo and Yoruba, who lost their public positions, did not return to the South, but established themselves in their new homeland as traders and craftsmen. Their success in the private sector also caused resentment, of course, so the Prime Minister of the North promised his countrymen to dislodge the »strangers« from their economic positions:

»The Northernization policy does not only apply to Clerks, Administrative Offi-cers, Doctors and others. We do not want to go to [Lake] Chad and meet strangers (i.e., southern Nigerians) catching our fish in the water, and taking them away to leave us with nothing. We do not want to go to Sokoto and find a carpenter who is a stranger nailing our houses. I do not want to go to the Sabon-gari Kano and find strangers making the body of a lorry, or to go to the market and see butchers who are not Northerners.«[102]

It was not only the Hausa-Fulani who benefited from the Northernization policy, but to an even greater extent, so did the Christians from the Middle Belt. Thanks to their education in the mission schools, they often had the formal qualification to occupy positions becoming vacant. For many of them it looked, as though it were more advantageous to bank on the soli-

---

100 Bach, *Indigeneity*, pp. 337–342.
101 Federal Republic of Nigeria, *Constitution 1999*, Section 318 (1).
102 House of Chiefs Debates (mimeo), 19 March 1965, p. 55, in Albert, *Religious Conflicts*, p. 73.

darity of the North than to ally with the South on the basis of a common religion.[103]

When Nigeria became independent, relations between the North and the South of the country were already extremely tense. Thus one could have expected that the parties of the South would join forces to form the central government with opposition groups from the North. Yet this option failed because of the rivalry between the two dominant ethnic groups in the South. Although the Igbo suffered the most under the NPC's Northernization campaign, they considered the Yoruba their real rivals, who had established themselves with similar success in the colonial administration. In a joint government with the Yoruba, they would have to share civil service posts, while a coalition with the backward North had the potential to bring a significant portion of the state apparatus under their control. However, the Igbo leaders underestimated the NPC's assertiveness. As the dominant power in the first independent government, the NPC ministers lowered the entry qualifications for Northerners applying for jobs in the civil service. Their own followers were given positions over others and were promoted more quickly. In addition, they resorted to emergency laws and military action to silence their political adversaries. In 1963 in the Southwest of Nigeria, they had the political leader of the Yoruba, Awolowo, thrown into prison for high treason, and imposed his rival Akintola as Premier of the Western Region.[104] Shortly afterwards, the political repression turned on their own coalition partner from Igboland. At the end of the first legislative period it became apparent that the NPC leaders were not prepared to surrender power. They intimidated their opponents so blatantly that in many electoral districts no opposition candidates stepped forward at all.[105] In addition, they used yet another instrument to cement their control: religion.

Hegemony of the North

Violence alone was not enough to create a cohesive Northern Nigeria. The policy of Northernization therefore aimed at propagating a joint culture for

103 Kukah, *Religion*, p. 51.
104 Diamond, *Class, Ethnicity*, pp. 103–112.
105 Post/Vickers, *Structure and Conflict*, pp. 170–171.

the many heterogeneous peoples. Civil servants were expected to speak Hausa, and anyone wishing to make a career came under pressure to convert to Islam: »Advancement or even retention within the civil service was seen as a matter of embracing orthodoxy.«[106] As the only means to eclipse ethnic differences, the dominant religious culture was meant to be visible everywhere. The regional government decreed that public buildings be erected in an Islamic style.[107] With state money and donations from Arab countries, the Premier of the Northern Region launched a conversion campaign among the inhabitants of the Middle Belt, first among the ›pagans‹ and later among Christians too.[108] In the process, he relied on local chiefs and village heads who were answerable to his administration. For example, the chief of Kuta declared that the inhabitants of his town had collectively decided to adopt Islam. In order to sever the links to their traditional faith once and for all, he had the old »idols« burned.[109] The prime minister personally attended the conversion ceremony, at which 1,357 inhabitants of Kuta embraced Islam. As with other mass conversions, the occasion was organized as a public festival at which the new converts received small gifts or honorary titles from the premier's hand. In 1964, Ahmadu Bello boasted before the Muslim World League that in only five months he had converted 60,000 infidels. His efforts in Northern Nigeria – so he assured his audience – were but the first step to spread Islam in other regions as well: »I hope when we clean Nigeria we will go further afield in Africa.«[110] Following his successes in the Northern Region, the decision was taken at the end of 1965 to extend the campaign to the South.[111]

The prime minister's Islamization campaign was not just informed by political considerations but also by personal ambition. As a direct descendant of Usman dan Fodio, he had attempted in vain to assume the throne of Sokoto in 1938. Having seen his ambitions dashed, he used the office of prime minister to continue the religious project of his famous ancestor: »the work of salvation for all the people which he so nobly undertook has

---

106 D. J. Muffet, a British colonial officer, in Kukah/Falola, *Religious Militancy*, p. 108.

107 Zabadi, *Kaduna Mafia*, p. 117.

108 Paden, *Ahmadu Bello*, pp. 566–578; Gilliland, *African Religion*, pp. 150–171; Falola, *Violence in Nigeria*, pp. 70–73; Hiskett, *Islam*, pp. 119–120.

109 Paden, *Ahmadu Bello*, pp. 567, 570, 573.

110 Quoted in Paden, *Ahmadu Bello*, p. 541.

111 *Ibid.*, p. 569.

now been handed to me. I dedicate myself totally to its completion.«[112] In public addresses, the premier often used the imagery of the jihad and emphasized the continuity between the NPC-government and the old caliphate.[113] However, his references to the nineteenth century merely planted fears of renewed »colonialism«[114] by the Hausa-Fulani. The state-driven Islamization did not forge closer bonds between the Muslim elite and the ethnic minorities, but rather increased mutual distrust. When in early 1966 the news broke that Ahmadu Bello had been killed during a military coup, impromptu celebrations were held in the minority regions. Many of the Muslims who had only converted at the behest of the government buried their religious paraphernalia and reverted to their old faiths.[115] Yet it was not only in the Middle Belt that the coup was welcomed as liberation. The NPC government had become so hated throughout the country that the premier's fall was even greeted in Muslim cities.

A notably large number of Igbo officers were among the organizers of the coup, swiftly kindling speculation that the army's intervention was actually an Igbo coup. In particular the North had cause for concern because among the immigrants from the South who lived in the cities' Christian ghettos, the coup was hailed as a victory for the Igbo. Posters that appeared on the streets in Kano showed an Igbo soldier sitting atop the fallen prime minister.[116] The new president could easily have dispelled the population's fears. In order to get the minorities in Northern Nigeria on his side, all he needed to do was to declare parts of the Middle Belt or the Kanuri region as provinces in their own right. But General Ironsi took the opposite approach. On May 24, 1966, he dissolved the federal constitution and created a centralized administration. Every observer immediately knew that this would give the Igbo the opportunity to regain their former positions in the regional administration of the North. Thus only a few days after the announcement of the decree, Igbo were massacred in

---

112 Quoted in Crampton, *Christianity*, p. 89. – Close confidents of Ahmadu Bello reported that his conversion campaign was also meant to gain support from Arab politicians: »it was [...] to convince his Muslim Arab brothers that he was really helping Islamize Nigeria. [...] The Sardauna needed money, and the Arabs poured money when he was with them« (Paden, *Ahmadu Bello*, p. 577). I will not dwell on the role of Saudi Arabia, Libya and Iran in the attempt to Islamize Nigeria. For further information, see Hunwick, *Africa*, pp. 37–52; Taheri, *Iran and Saudi Arabia*; Bunza, *Muslims*, pp. 54–59).

113 Reynolds, *Politics of History*, p. 56–60.

114 Tyoden, *Middle Belt*, p. 4.

115 Kukah, *Religion*, p. 37; Gilliland, *African Religion*, pp. 170–171.

116 Osaghae, *Migrant Organizations*, p. 39.

Northern Nigeria, and two months later General Ironsi was ousted by a counter-coup.

The two coups in 1966 marked the beginning of a series of military governments. Only once, during the Second Republic (1979-1983), did civil politicians have the chance to form a democratically elected government. Otherwise, the army directed Nigeria's fortunes until the end of the century, and the army was, since colonial days, under the sway of ethnic groups of the North. About three-quarters of the soldiers had been recruited from the North, most of them from the Middle Belt.[117] When the military seized power in 1966, the future of the country depended on which side the minorities from the Middle Belt supported. Under the rule of the Northern Peoples' Congress, the minorities had never been permitted to rule themselves, but an Igbo-led central government seemed just as unwilling to compromise. The fact that in such a setting the officers of the Middle Belt resolved to ally with the Muslim North and overthrow the Christian president can be explained mainly by pragmatic considerations. During secret negotiations, the leaders of the North had promised to accept a new federal constitution that would grant the minorities far-reaching autonomy.[118]

In May 1967, under General Gowon as the new head of state, twelve states were in fact founded, but the transition to a federal system did not prevent the ethno-religious conflicts from escalating. General Ojukwu and other Igbo leaders opted for secession and declared the Republic of Biafra, because they could not trust their opponents in the federal government: In September 1966 the state radio in Kaduna, the administrative capital of the North, had falsely reported that numerous Hausa had been murdered in Igboland. The response in the cities of the North was an Igbo witch hunt.[119] Thousands were killed and more than a million fled back to their home country. Since General Gowon's government was either incapable or unwilling to protect the Igbo, secession seemed to be their best option.

The Biafran war of secession (1967-1970) ended with the defeat of the Igbo, enabling the North to expand its domination. The victorious generals remained allies of the Hausa-Fulani leaders, meaning that the influence of Christian politicians decreased. Citing the multi-ethnic ›federal character‹ of the country, the rulers from the North introduced quota regulations to

---

117 Okeke, *Hausa-Fulani Hegemony*, p. 62.
118 Ayu, *Solution*, pp. 130–132.
119 Kukah, *Religion*, p. 200.

entrench their power. Whenever positions were to be filled in the public administration, in state-run enterprises or in the oil industry, applicants from Northern Nigeria claimed preferential treatment. Officially speaking, the quota arithmetic was designed to even out ethnic and regional imbalances. However, instead of inculcating a »sense of belonging« and »national unity«, it did the opposite, generating mistrust and resentment.[120] In the field of education, for instance, the definition of quotas had severe consequences. In order to promote students from the primarily Muslim states, the authorities paid them scholarships and favored them in gaining entrance to the universities, while applicants from the South who had performed far better in the entrance exams were often refused admission, even to universities in their home region. From the viewpoint of these unsuccessful applicants, it seemed as if study slots and exam certificates had turned into the booty that rival ethnic groups fought over: The ›people from the North‹ were not content with occupying key positions in the army; they used their political dominance to gain control of all walks of public life.

The creation of quotas for employment and educational opportunities would have been more acceptable if the state had endeavored to be fairer in other areas. In order to curb the influence of the churches, Christian missionary schools and hospitals were nationalized. At the same time, the government supported pilgrimages to Mecca by establishing a National Pilgrimage Board that organized the trips and subsidized the participants' travel expenses. The scale of the subsidies was later cut back, owing to the treasury's depleted coffers. However, around 1980, when as many as 100,000 pilgrims were being supported each year, Nigeria boasted that it was sending more people to the holy sites than any other country in the world.[121] Additional money from the government flowed into building mosques and into paying Imams' salaries, into Islamic radio and TV programs. The government newspaper New Nigerian, financed with tax money, felt itself destined to champion Islamic interests, or in the words of its editor-in-chief: »we [will] continue to fight for the introduction of Sharia, the application of quota system or federal character in all spheres of national life.«[122]

---

120 Ekeh, *Federal Character*, pp. 32–35; Bach, *Nigerian Federalism*, pp. 226, 235, 240.
121 Loimeier, *Pilgrimage Scheme*, p. 213.
122 Quoted in Kukah, *Religion*, p. 78.

Under General Murtala Mohammed, who came to power in 1975 in yet another coup, a major decision was taken. Instead of the old capital city of Lagos, located on the south coast in Yorubaland, a completely new metropolis was to be established further north. The planners envisaged the future center of the country having an Islamic face, with major town gates in the Arabic style.[123] The town gates were never built and instead, with money from government and donations from the Gulf States, a ›national mosque‹ arose in the heart of Abuja. In contrast, no land was initially allocated for the building of churches which were to be erected by private funds in downtown Abuja.[124] The state did not set out to preserve its neutrality but presented itself, especially in Northern Nigeria, as an Islamic power. The Christian minorities could never rely on the authorities being above party interest, while Islamic activists felt encouraged in their efforts. When in the 1980s religious conflicts escalated and thousands were killed in Kano, Kafanchan and other cities of the North, many Muslim zealots acted in the conviction that, in the last resort, they could rely on the support of the government.

Instead of strengthening the elements of a shared ›national‹ culture, political and spiritual leaders appealed to the solidarity of their co-religionists. Abubakar Gumi, who was religious adviser to several presidents, admonished the faithful to be aware that the conflict lines would in future run between the religious communities: »It will not be South against North but it will be Islam against Christianity. […] Once you are a muslim, you cannot accept to choose a non-muslim to be your leader.«[125] Representatives of Islamic orthodoxy thus strengthened the trend among ethno-religious communities to set themselves off from one another. For example, the Muslim inhabitants of Ilorin set out to block the incursion of non-Muslims by declaring their old town an alcohol-free zone. Female Muslim students at Queen Amina College in Kaduna called for a separate building to ensure they did not have to share a roof with Christian students.[126] In another college in the North, students demanded their own drinking water, insisting that they would be polluted if they used the same water containers as the Christians.[127]

---

123 Kukah/Falola, *Religious Militancy*, p. 61.
124 Kukah, *Religion*, pp. 162–165.
125 Quoted in Odey, *Sharia*, pp 52–53; vgl. Loimeier, *Islamische Erneuerung*, p. 137.
126 Loimeier/Reichmuth, *Bemühungen*, pp. 75, 78.
127 National Institute, *Religious Disturbances*, p. 29.

The intensification of religious conflicts coincided with the transition to Nigeria's Second Republic. Sharia emerged as the most controversial issue at the constitutional conference in 1977/78, which deliberated on the institutional structure for the future democracy. The call to give Islamic law greater importance came from Hausa-Fulani politicians, namely those who had formed the National Party of Nigeria (NPN), a kind of successor to the NPC. In the South, the NPN put on a moderate face as it set out to win Christian politicians over to its cause, while in the North the party leader and later President Shehu Shagari (who comes from a royal Fulani family) called on the electorate not to cast their vote for the infidels.[128] These warnings against infidels were directed not only at Christians, but were intended to discredit those Muslim politicians who had joined left-wing populist parties. During the NPN election campaign, these ›progressive‹ Muslims were depicted as heretics who had allied with politicians from the South in order to establish a godless secular state. One pernicious myth circulating was that Waziri Ibrahim, one of the leaders of the oppositional UPN, had had a church built in the Southeast.[129]

The focus on Sharia also served to paper over internal differences in the Muslim camp. During the 1970s, rival Muslim organizations had clashed violently on several occasions. These intra-Islamic hostilities had been fuelled, among others things, by the military's policies. Their press censorship and prohibition on political parties shifted the site of political debate to the mosques and churches.[130] The disputes among religious groups thus reflected ethnic and regional tensions. Sokoto, the old heart of the Fulani Empire, was traditionally dominated by the Qadiriyya, whereas the rival brotherhood, the Tijaniyya, had gained the upper hand in Kano. When the Emir of Kano switched allegiance to the Tijaniyya, he did so deliberately in order to gain his independence from Sokoto.[131] In the prayers of the Tijaniyya, resentment of the sultan's claim to power was voiced openly: »O Lord, destroy the Amir of Hausa [...]/ Destroy his house and hasten the one/ who will announce his death.«[132] As early as 1956, there had been deaths in religious clashes, when followers of the

128 Enwerem, *Dangerous Awakening*, p. 143.
129 Ujo, *Manipulation Strategies*, p. 106.
130 Falola, *Violence in Nigeria*, pp. 227–246.
131 Stewart, *Islam*, p. 210; Paden, *Kano*, p. 69.
132 Kukah, *Religion*, p. 45.

Tijaniyya had tried to prevent their opponents from performing evening prayers.[133]

The most traumatic religious conflict occurred in December 1980. It was not triggered, however, by the traditional brotherhoods, but by an obscure preacher by the name of Maitatsine, a migrant from Cameroon. He had gained many disciples in the poor districts of Kano when castigating the depravity of the unbelievers. His criticism was leveled not so much at the Christian minorities as at hypocritical Islamic dignitaries who pretended to be guardians of the faith while basking in Western luxury. Along with the bigotry of the ruling elites, he denounced Western consumer goods that his impoverished listeners could not afford anyway: elegant dresses, watches and cars. He is even said to have forbidden his followers from attending schools and reading books (with the exception of the Koran). Despite his inflammatory speeches against the decadence of the rich, Maitatsine nonetheless cultivated relationships with segments of the establishment. Some of his confidants had even received invitations to the governor's residence, where they prayed with Governor Rimi.[134] It only came to a confrontation with the state authorities when members of the sect tried to take over the Friday Mosque in the city center. The police who were called to the scene proved incapable of keeping the attackers back. Protected by amulets and magic sand that they used to shield themselves against bullets from the police guns, Maitatsine's supporters resisted for days, until army units were finally sent into the city. When the tanks retreated, 4,177 people were dead, according to official statistics.[135] Hundreds of Maitatsine supporters were arrested, but were granted an amnesty by President Shagari as early as 1982. Soon afterwards the group reformed, and further protests flared up in other regions of Northern Nigeria. In October 1982, 3,350 people died in street fights in Maiduguri, and one and a half years later in Yola, between 700 and 1000 were killed.[136]

To unite Nigeria's Muslims, in 1978 Abubakar Gumi, the country's most prominent Islamic scholar, acting with Saudi Arabian support, founded Izala, the ›Society for the eradication of [un-Islamic] innovations, and the establishment of the Sunna‹. Religious unanimity could only be

---

133 Paden, *Ahmadu Bello*, p. 306.

134 Kukah, *Religion*, p. 155.

135 Aniagolu-Tribunal, *Maitatsine Riot*; Lubeck, *Islamic Protest*; Hock, *Prophezeiung*, pp. 211–219.

136 Isichei, *Maitatsine*, pp. 194, 197, 199.

achieved – according to the doctrine, inspired by Wahabi'ism – if Muslims based their faith on the immutable word of God. Calling for a purification of Islam, Gumi opposed the mysticism and the belief in miracles on the part of the Sufi brotherhoods, especially the Tijaniyya. Whoever adopted the prayer posture and the recitations of this group made himself an unbeliever, someone whom anyone was allowed to kill.[137] Izala members were forbidden from eating the meat of animals that had been slaughtered by Tijaniyya members. Further, Izala reformers resisted the idea that ›heretics‹ were allowed to lead righteous Muslims in public prayers. So they sought to drive the Tijaniyya out of their traditional mosques, with violence if necessary.[138]

The Izala's efforts to enforce a correct interpretation of Islam failed to overcome the rifts among Muslims. The controversies over sacred rites and symbols have been shaped by a centuries-old tradition of religious disputes, which no authority can solve. The only way to achieve unity was to return to the fundamentals, the divine laws that no one could contest. As the Sharia gives very clear, unequivocal commandments, it seemed the best instrument to bridge the gap between believers: »We [...] limit our struggle to [...] the full implementation of the Sharia, because it is only through the Sharia that Muslims can be united; they can never unite on theological issues.«[139] In a state which is home to roughly as many Christians as Muslims, divine law could not be implemented single-handedly. In the debates over the future constitution, Islamic delegates initially demanded just a modest innovation: a Sharia Court of Appeal on the federal level. The vehemence displayed in the fight for such a court seems strange, at first glance, for Islamic traditions made no provision for a right of appeal. This right was first introduced in Northern Nigeria by the colonial rulers.[140] Nevertheless, it is understandable that Muslims called for a Federal Sharia Court of Appeal with limited jurisdiction. It was to be confined to deciding civil litigations involving matters of personal status and family relations, i.e. cases that were routinely dealt with by Sharia courts in most parts of the North. There had been a Sharia Court of Appeal in the capital of the Northern Region until 1967, as the top appellate body for all

---

137 Loimeier, *Religiöse Unruhen*, p. 65; Muhammad Sani Umar, *Islamic Identity*, p. 166; Loimeier, *Islamic Reform*, p. 298.

138 Kane, *Muslim Modernity*, pp. 136, 88–90, 162–165, 209–210, 243

139 S. U. Utere, Ahmadu Bello University, Zaria, in Byang, *Sharia*, p. 33.

140 Abun-Nasr, *Islamisches Recht*, pp. 209, 221; Keay/Richardson, *Native Courts*, p. 26; Laitin, *Sharia Debate*, pp. 413–414.

local Sharia courts. Its judgments had been final so it could unify Islamic jurisdiction throughout the North. Yet when the Northern Region was divided into six and later into ten states, this court ceased to exist. The state governments established their own Sharia Courts of Appeal, but there was no longer a supreme Islamic court that could have guaranteed a standard interpretation of Sharia.[141] When judgments by the State Sharia Courts of Appeal were challenged, the matter went, in a last instance, to the secular Supreme Court. Thus the Islamic judicial system was no longer autonomous, not even in the limited domain of civil law. With the help of the Supreme Court, which stood guard over the federal constitution, non-Muslims were able to influence how Sharia judges dispensed justice: »that [...] means [...] putting the fate of Muslims in the hands of pagans, atheists and Christians.«[142]

The Christian delegates at the constitutional conference were not prepared to accommodate the Muslims' wishes; they feared that the introduction of a Federal Sharia Court of Appeal would not permanently settle the conflict between the religious communities. What was to stop Muslims making further demands in the name of religion? Concessions would only clear the way for a »creeping« Islamization.«[143] Christian fears were heightened by the demand by Hausa-Fulani politicians to introduce Sharia courts in all parts of the country. Opposition to this spread toward the South was voiced even by some Muslim delegates at the constitutional conference, particularly by Yoruba Muslims from Southwest Nigeria. Their reluctance to ally with their fellow believers from the North was primarily motivated by ethnic loyalties. Among the Yoruba there are as many Christians as Muslims, and the line separating them runs through the middle of many families.[144] If Sharia supporters were to insist that Muslims are governed by their own religious rules, they would see bitter family disputes in matters of divorce and inheritance. According to Islamic law, non-Muslims have no right to inherit from a Muslim, and vice versa; thus making close familial cooperation problematic.[145] It is for this reason that many Yoruba Muslims

---

141 Abun-Nasr, *Islamisches Recht*, p. 220; Ostien, *Opportunity*, pp. 229, 234.
142 Muslim Students' Society, *Press Release*, p. 168.
143 Suberu, *Religion and Politics*, p. 405.
144 Laitin, *Sharia Debate*, p. 425.
145 Anderson, *Islamic Law*, pp. 217, 221–223; Ransome-Kuti, *Sharia*, p. 1. – These rules of inheritance were intended, right from their inception in the time of the Prophet, to sever the links with non-Muslim family members so that the Islamic community could be organized »wholly independent« of its pagan environment (Hodgson, *Islam*, p. 176).

did not want to advocate the introduction of Sharia courts, as the juxta-position of rival judicial systems would only lead to »disunity.« »what good can that do if there is one court for Muslims and one for Christians«?[146] In the precolonial period, when Muslims formed a small minority, there were no Sharia courts in the Yoruba kingdoms.[147] The colonial administration did not want to change that, and even today, in independent Nigeria, democratically-elected Yoruba governors have always refused to establish religious courts. A secular compromise seems to offer the best protection of Yoruba interests. This is consistent with the opinion of many Yoruba Muslims that Sharia is a »northern thing«: »it is not Nigerian law, it is Arabic law.«[148]

Sharia critics at the constitutional conference also raised *fundamental* objections to religious courts. As soon as the government paid judges who only applied the laws of one religion, that religion would receive preferential treatment. Therefore, Christian delegates called for a strict separation of state and religion. And this call was supported by the major churches: »laws of any religion [...] should be a matter for personal conviction, and the administration of such religious laws should remain within the responsibilities of various religious groups.«[149] They maintained that it was not the responsibility of the government to build churches and mosques or to finance pilgrimages. Thus it should be stated in the constitution of the Second Republic that no state authority may use tax money to promote any religion.[150]

The suggestion that Nigeria be defined as a secular state was not to be realized. Yet the attempt to establish a Federal Sharia Court of Appeal also failed. As the wrangling parties could not agree, the military leadership had to intervene. The constitutional assembly was denied the right to discuss the status of Sharia, and General Obasanjo decreed a compromise that satisfied none of the parties. The word ›secular‹ that had been used in the first draft of the constitution was deleted. It was replaced by an ambiguous phrase which set limitations on the religious activities of the state, but only

---

146 Interview with a Muslim in Ijebu-Ode, in Clarke/Linden, *Islam*, pp. 84–85.
147 Sayed Malik (*Shari'ah*, p. 160) mentions two exceptions: a Sharia court in Ede, another one in Iwo (cf. Doi, *Islam*, p. 213).
148 Interview with an Imam in South Nigeria, in Clarke/Linden, *Islam*, p. 85.
149 Memorandum of the Catholic Bishops, 1988, in Nzeh, *Dialogue of Religions*, pp. 137–138.
150 With the transitions to Nigeria's Third and Fourth Republics, when the constitution was revised again, the churches confirmed this position (Ngwoke, *Islam*, p. 30; Ilesanmi, *Religious Pluralism*, pp. 176–179, 191; Rasmussen, *Christian-Muslim Relations*, pp. 62–67).

vaguely defined them: »The Government of the Federation or of a State shall not adopt any religion as State Religion.«[151] The month-long debates had only made it clear that no constitution could be drawn up that would be acceptable to both Christians and Muslims. When the constitution came under renewed discussion during the transition to the Third Republic, ten years later, the negotiations again threatened to founder on the Sharia question.[152] This time around too, the Armed Forces Ruling Council had to end the discussions and force a compromise on the squabbling parties: No concessions were made to the Sharia advocates who called for an Islamic court of appeal at the federal level, but the Christian politicians' wish to define Nigeria as a secular republic also fell on deaf ears. The constitution of 1989 simply adopted the regulations of 1978, and this unsatisfactory compromise was, at the generals' command, also inserted into the constitution of the Fourth Republic.[153] Despite this unresolved dispute, Christian politicians and intellectuals have maintained, right up to the current debate on the constitutionality of Sharia, that Nigeria is a secular state: »the constitutional prohibition of the establishment of a state religion does import the secularity of the state in the fullest sense of the term.«[154] Against this arbitrary interpretation, Muslim jurists have rightly pointed out that a constitution which provides for state-financed Sharia courts cannot be secular.[155] Secular principles were only adopted in a diluted form.

According to Islamic scholars and politicians, a secular state would not be neutral toward the different religions; rather, it would seal the dominance of a foreign civilization. While Islamic culture is to be pushed into the private sphere, it is taken for granted that European influences have penetrated all sectors of society. It is not the Islamic calendar that is used in public life, but the Gregorian calendar. It is not Friday that is a public holiday, but Sunday. State hospitals do not display a red crescent, but a red cross.[156] Islamic scholars called for a break from these relics of the colonial

---

151 Constitution 1979, Section 10, in Iwobi, *Sharia Controversy*, p. 115; cf. Usman, *Religion*, p. 31.

152 Suberu, *Continuity*, p. 209.

153 Iwobi, *Sharia Controversy*, pp. 114–120.

154 B. O. Nwabueze, in Iwobi, *Sharia Controversy*, p. 129; Agbakoba/Obeagu, *Sharia*, p. 2; Nwanaju, *Christian-Muslim Relations*, p. 193. – The former President of the Catholic Bishops' Conference, Cardinal Okogie, also insisted: »Nigeria is a secular nation« (*The News*, 10. April 2000, p. 21; cf. Freedom House, *Talibanization*, p. 56).

155 Tabiu, *Sharia*, p. 8; Sada, *Sharia in Nigeria*, p. 6; Pérouse de Montclos, *Vertus*, p. 546.

156 Kenny, *Sharia*, p. 354; Falola, *Violence in Nigeria*, p. 90; Jama'atu Nasril Islam, *Memorandum*, p. 81; Oloyede, *Shari'ah*, pp. 144–146.

era. Judges should not wear robes which originated from »monks and Christian choirs.«[157] The military should not lay wreaths at remembrance ceremonies, as this is a Christian custom.[158] Moreover, they insisted that the national anthem, with its »Christian melody«, be replaced.[159] Some of these practices have actually been changed in recent years. In Zamfara State, Sunday is now a workday, and on Fridays public life comes to a standstill.[160] In addition, during the other weekdays all businesses, including the Christian ones, have to remain closed during the five daily prayers.[161] This state-enforced revalidation of religious traditions allows Muslims to assert their cultural hegemony. Many activists consider this a key function of Sharia. They are not so much interested in strictly Islamizing all domains of life, but in »increas[ing] the symbolic presence of Islam in the state.«[162] In religiously and ethnically divided societies, it becomes important to occupy public space in order to institutionalize one's supremacy: »groups [...] derive ›prestige and self-respect‹ from the harmony ›between‹ their norms and those which achieve dominance in the society.‹ [...] Politics thus constitutes one of the important ›rituals by which status is determined.«[163]

The struggle over the religious thrust of the state was refueled in early 1986, when the news spread that Nigeria had joined the Organization of the Islamic Conference (OIC). According to the statutes of the OIC, every member state is obliged to promote Islam – something that is incompatible with Nigeria's constitutional tradition. The president was, of course, aware that Christians would not have accepted joining the OIC, so he did not bother to seek a consensus on the issue. He simply sent a secret delegation, made up solely of Muslim ministers and permanent secretaries, to the OIC conference in Morocco, which was to decide on Nigeria's application. The Christian members of the cabinet, as well as Christian officers in the Armed Forces Ruling Council, knew nothing of the president's plans.

---

157 Kenny, *Sharia*, pp. 354–355; Falola, *Violence in Nigeria*, p. 90.

158 Kenny, *Sharia*, p. 355.

159 Ibrahim, *Ethno-Religious Mobilisation*, p. 101; Ilesanmi, *Religious Pluralism*, p. 184.

160 Danfulani/Ludwig/Ostien, *Sharia Controversy*, p. 90.

161 Ebeku, *Human Rights*, pp. 160–161.

162 Alli, *Commentary*, p. 66. – Compromises are difficult to find, because public prayers and other rituals are intended to highlight religious differences. The faithful are called upon to distinguish themselves from infidels day by day in a highly visible manner (cf. *Koran* 2: 143–150, pp. 18–19).

163 Horowitz, *Ethnic Groups*, p. 217.

Nigeria's accession to the OIC would hardly have become public, had not journalists from the Guardian read of it from a report by the French press agency.[164]

The Christian Association of Nigeria (CAN), to which almost all churches in the country belong, spoke out resolutely against membership in the OIC. But otherwise it supported General Babangida and his Transition Program, which was intended to lead to a new, democratically-elected government. During the build-up to the Third Republic, representatives of the churches tried to prevent religious squabbling from again taking center stage in political debate. Their de-escalation strategy can best be illustrated by looking at the presidential election in June 1993. The military government had decreed that only two political parties could register for the election, and in both Muslims were nominated as presidential candidates. Bashir Tofa, the NRC's nominee, chose a Christian candidate for vice president for reasons of proportionality. His rival from the SDP, Moshood Abiola, likewise found himself under pressure to name a Christian running mate. In this tense situation, with religious antagonisms threatening to hang over party politics, the Chairman of the Christian Association of Nigeria issued a remarkable statement. He said that it was not important for the churches whether the future president and his running mate were Muslims or Christians. What was decisive, he claimed, was whether they had the necessary expertise and moral competence for the job.[165] Moshood Abiola, a Yoruba from the Southwest, was thus free to nominate a Muslim from the North as his running mate, and with such a Muslim-Muslim ticket, collected more votes, even among the Christian population, than his rival Tofa.

As soon as it became clear that Abiola was well ahead in the count, General Babangida had the election declared void. The churches could easily have tolerated the decision, as Abiola was a fierce proponent of Islamic interests. During the debate on the constitution for the Third Republic no other politician from the South had so vociferously called for the dissemination of Sharia in all parts of the country.[166] Nevertheless, the spokesmen of all the major churches agreed to insist on Abiola's claim to become president. Since the elections had been surprisingly free and fair,

---

164 Byang, *Sharia*, p. 65; Falola, *Violence in Nigeria*, pp. 93–102; Sanneh, *Piety and Power*, pp. 129–132.

165 *The News*, 14 November 1994, p. 18.

166 Kukah, *Religion*, pp. 128, 135, 143; Suberu, *Religion and Politics*, p. 411.

General Babangida had no right, they said, not to heed the will of the electorate. However, Abiola did not find nearly as much support among his Islamic allies in the North. The Sultan of Sokoto told the faithful that it had been the will of Allah to annul the election.[167] No one had any illusions why there was this fault line within the Islamic camp. Abiola was Vice President of the Nigerian Supreme Council for Islamic Affairs, but since he was born a Yoruba in the South, he was not trusted by the power-brokers in the North. On earlier occasions, Hausa-Fulani politicians had openly stated that the North would commit »political suicide« if it gave the presidency over to a politician from the South.[168] Muslims in Yorubaland were shocked by the ›treason‹ of their co-religionists. Some even called for the Southern Muslims to quit the Supreme Council for Islamic Affairs and set up a new umbrella association in the South: »[The sultan has been] unmasked and exposed as an ethnic demagogue indecently committed to the political interest of the northern Hausa/Fulani Muslims.«[169]

The Abiola affair shows how Nigeria's churches envisaged a balance between the religious groups: In political elections and in awarding public offices, confessional ties were not to play a role. This Western secular model only functions, however, if all involved keep to the rules of the game. Any attempt to conquer political positions in order to use them for religious ends triggers a vicious circle of mistrust that forces the opposite side to likewise opt for a power play. As long as Christians have to fear that under a Muslim governor they will not have the same rights, it would be folly not to struggle to place their own applicants in the highest offices.

---

167 *The Week*, 17 October 1994, p. 11; *Tell*, 17 October 1994, p. 11; Kalu, *Religious Dimension*, pp. 671, 681, 683; Maier, *This House*, p 159.
168 Okeke, *Hausa-Fulani Hegemony*, p. 114; cf. Bergstresser, *Militärherrschaft*, p. 79.
169 *The Week*, 17 October 1994, p. 12.

The End of the Secular State

Withdrawal of the Military

The Nigerian people did not attain democracy through their own efforts. Faced with the superiority of the military, which always found plenty of allies among civilian politicians, the pro-democracy movement never had a chance. At most, the regime was at risk from ethnic revolts, which could have led to secession and civil war, like in the late 1960s, when the Igbo in Southeastern Nigeria proclaimed the Republic of Biafra. The transition to democracy was prompted just by chance. In June 1998 the news suddenly spread that Nigeria's strongman, General Sani Abacha, had met a premature death in the arms of two Indian prostitutes, supposedly after having taken poisoned Viagra. It was a stroke of luck that power did not pass to the highest-ranking officer but to General Abubakar, who was prepared to hold free elections within ten months.

A major reason for the return to the barracks was that the military was completely discredited, not only in the eyes of the people, but in their own minds.[1] A career as an officer looked like a means to ascend into government positions and steal public funds. The prospect of such a career was especially attractive to adventurous types: »Youths go into the military [...] with the sole intention of taking part in coups and to be appointed as military administrators.«[2] A consequence of the brutal tussles for power and money was that trust among the soldiers evaporated. It is said that officers who applied for promotion not only submitted their own application papers but also dossiers containing compromising material about their superior officers, whose positions they coveted.[3] Some did not hesitate to implicate their rivals in alleged coup attempts. This was a risky game, as

---

1 Omeje, *Military Rule*, pp. 127–128.
2 President Obasanjo in his inaugural speech, May 1999, in Maier, *This House*, p. 20.
3 *Newswatch*, 2 October 1995, p. 11.

General Abacha, a participant in several coups himself, saw conspirators everywhere. He had dozens of his subordinates arrested, and did not shy away from extracting confessions under torture. Suspects who fell into the clutches of the military secret service, sought to throw the blame on to others until no one felt safe any more. Power gradually shifted to a few confidants of General Abacha, thus undermining the command structures. Even generals had to put up with being ordered around by Major Al-Mustapha, the security advisor in the presidential bunker. According to one of his close associates, the Major with his intelligence dossiers was able to defy any military authority: »the fear of Major Al-Mustapha is the beginning of wisdom. He was powerful, arrogant, brutal and ruthlessly ambitious. Major Al-Mustapha had no regard for anybody then, not even [for] General Diya, the official number two man.«[4]

While individual officers amassed fantastic wealth, the army as a whole degenerated into a rabble of poorly-paid and badly-trained mercenaries. The overcrowded barracks with their shabby camps often looked like the slums surrounding them, thus reflecting the general decline of the country. At the height of the oil boom around 1980, shortly before the military seized power, per capita GDP had been over 1,000 dollars. Fifteen years later it was 200 dollars.[5]

What also contributed to the wretchedness of the Nigerian army was that its generals flouted all of the agreements they had made with civilian politicians. Since the mid-1980s they had given assurances to restore democracy, albeit by a slow, well-planned transition process. In order to avoid the mistakes of the failed First and Second Republics, General Babangida deemed it necessary to draw up a new constitution. Four years passed, before a draft was submitted and, as it turned out, the constitution of 1989 differed from its predecessor only in some details. The General then established two parties by decree – one »a little to the left«, the other »a little to the right« – and had party offices set up for both in more than 500 towns.[6] Further delays occurred when presidential candidates were nominated, because they proved themselves as tribal and corrupt as expected. They consistently gave the regime new pretexts to defer the hand-over of power. Between 1989 and 1992, General Babangida postponed the

---

4 Lieutenant I. S. Umar, Commander of the notorious Strike Force, a death squad of the secret service, in *Tell*, 18 December 2000, p. 27.

5 *Economist*, 15 January 2000, Nigeria Survey, p. 5.

6 Agbese/Kieh, *Military Disengagement*, p. 18; Osaghae, *Crippled Giant*, pp. 219–220.

crucial election four times, until hardly anyone took the president's promises seriously. In the end, many were surprised when elections actually took
place on June 12, 1993. The complex transition program, which had cost
the state billions of Naira, seemed to have paid off despite all skepticism.
So it was all the more perplexing when Babangida annulled the election
eleven days later.[7]

If all the politicians who had taken part in the democratization process
had accepted the election results of June 1993, Babangida would not have
been able to defy the will of the people. However, the common interest in
civil forms of political competition is not well developed among Nigeria's
political elite. Followers of the defeated candidate immediately asked for
the result to be nullified, and even in the party of the victorious candidate
many members, particularly Muslims in the North, supported the decision
of the generals.

Babangida's successor, General Abacha, who staged a coup in November 1993, also promised to return the country to democracy. So he called a
constitutional conference and restarted the whole transition game. The old
parties were dissolved and five new ones founded; elections were
announced and postponed again. After four years of transition to democracy it became clear that the promised elections would merely serve to turn
General Abacha into a civilian president. The only serious resistance to the
dictator's plans came from the Yoruba in Southwest Nigeria, the homeland
of would-be President Abiola. When the government arrested him in June
1994, pro-democracy activists and trade union leaders in Yorubaland
organized a general strike. However, the call to strike nation-wide met with
little support in other parts of the country. Politicians from the North
scoffed that their Yoruba rivals were only harming themselves with their
militant protest: »killings and economic sabotage caused by the south-west
[…] only succeeded in affecting them. Who was killed? Whose houses
were destroyed? Whose economy was destroyed? […] We are thankful to
them for killing themselves and crippling their economy.«[8] Of course,
many people in the North also suffered under the military regime, as no
one was safe from Abacha and his secret police. Even the Sultan of Sokoto
was sent into exile, and his son was put on the wanted list. At the same
time, Abacha sought to ensure the North's supremacy, and in so doing he

---

7 Bergstresser, *Militärherrschaft*, pp. 76–80; Peter M. Lewis, *Endgame*, pp. 326–327.

8 Abubakar Buba Galadima, a minister in the Abacha cabinet, in *TSM. The Sunday Magazine*, 4 December 1994, p. 17.

harnessed his political survival to the fate of the region.[9] Why should Hausa-Fulani politicians work for the downfall of the military regime, if their efforts brought a Yoruba to power? The Igbo in Southeastern Nigeria, among whom I lived between 1993 and 1996, took a similar view. When I asked local government workers why they were not joining the general strike, they replied pragmatically: »Would the Yoruba go on strike for us, if an Igbo had won the presidential election?«

When Abacha died in 1998, the dispute over the annulled election flared up again. Yoruba politicians demanded that Moshood Abiola, who had been imprisoned without trial since 1994, be released from custody and sworn in as the lawful president. However, just a month after Sani Abacha's sudden demise, Abiola was found dead in his cell, supposedly of heart failure. For the more than 20 million Yoruba this was shocking news. For almost four decades, none of them had been given the chance of gaining power through democratic elections. Why should they continue to be part of the Nigerian federation, if they were excluded from ruling it?

While Yorubaland was swept by a wave of secessionist agitation, those in power gained the impression that Nigeria could fall apart, unless someone from the South was made president. The three major parties, which were created with the transformation to Nigeria's Fourth Republic, arrived at an understanding that this time a Yoruba politician should become head of state. So they nominated at their party conventions two Yoruba candidates, who vied for the presidency without contenders from other ethnic groups. It was a risky game for those who had benefited from Northern hegemony. With a Yoruba on top, the power structure could change permanently, so that politicians from the North would no longer have a chance to re-conquer power at the center. Quite a few Yoruba declared openly that the North had plundered the state resources long enough and that now it was their turn. It was feared that Olu Falae, the presidential candidate from the Alliance for Democracy, harbored similar thoughts. He had always seen himself as a Yoruba patriot and champion of ethnic interests. In contrast, his contender Obasanjo had the reputation of being one of the country's few »detribalized«[10] politicians. From 1976 to 1979 he had already ruled Nigeria as the head of a military junta, though this position had fallen to him only because of the death of his superior, General Murtala Mohammed, during a failed coup. Unlike other military rulers

9 Joseph, *Ethnomilitary Rule*, p. 367.
10 *Tell*, 13 November 2000, p. 27.

Obasanjo did not cling to power, but handed it over to civilian politicians after a three-year transition program. Moreover, he did not intervene in the outcome of the election. Instead of favoring a presidential candidate from his own ethnic group, he allowed a Muslim from the North to succeed him as head of state. This unbiased stance won him respect in all parts of the country, except in his native Yoruba region. In the six states of Southwestern Nigeria, which comprise most of Yorubaland, he remained so unpopular that 20 years later, in the 1999 presidential election his rival Olu Falae received between 73 and 88 percent of the vote. In the rest of the country, however, Obasanjo could win all but three states.[11]

It is unusual to find an African statesman who was not elected by his own ethnic group, because he made it clear that he would not favor them in the allocation of public funds and government positions. Obasonjo's credentials as a neutral arbiter facilitated the transition to civilian rule. The transfer of power went smoothly because all parties involved had reason to trust that the future president would not play ethnic politics, as his predecessors had done. And Obasanjo had yet another advantage – he made it easy for the generals to relinquish power, as he was a military man himself who had no interest in damaging the army. This is why his election campaign was financed by (retired) army officers. Apparently Obasanjo only made it to the top because the money and influence of Ibrahim Babangida paved the way for him. Despite this support from military circles nobody doubted his commitment to democracy. Under the Abacha regime he had been in the forefront of attempts to unite politicians in the North and South against military rule. He had been arrested in 1995 and sentenced by a military tribunal to fifteen years in jail. Only Abacha's sudden death sprung him from detention and into the presidential palace.

Muslim Self-Determination

As long as the military was in power, no state would dare to introduce Sharia. It is true that Islamic generals had headed the regime for fifteen years, but they had to consider the Armed Forces Ruling Council which comprised as many Christian as Muslim officers. Military rulers such as Murtalla Mohammed and Muhammadu Buhari, who had tried to Islamize

---

11 Bergstresser, *Demokratiehoffnungen*, p. 142.

Nigeria, did not stay in office for long. General Mohammed was shot dead in 1976, and Buhari was imprisoned following a coup in 1985. His successors still favored the Islamic elite in the North, but they shied away from a religious confrontation that would have split the officer corps. In principle, everyone who profited from military rule had an interest in maintaining the cohesion of the armed forces. Moreover, the federal army saw itself, since its victory over the secessionist Republic of Biafra, as a guarantor of Nigeria's unity. So the officers were anxious to negotiate religious compromises, and they had the power to implement these compromises in all parts of the country, because the states did not enjoy much autonomy. Under the control of the army, with its centralized command structure, Nigeria was a federation only in name. The state governors who were, as a rule, not elected but appointed, followed the instructions from the federal capital, without much consideration of local interests.

The new constitution that came into force with the beginning of the Fourth Republic grants a lot of autonomy to the 36 states. The possibility of regional self-determination was appealing, above all, to Islamic politicians in the North, many of whom belonged to the opposition All People's Party (APP). In the governorship elections in January 1999, the APP had won nine Muslim states, and in 2003, under the name All Nigeria People's Party (ANPP), seven states. Though it was the largest opposition party, it had taken only a quarter of the seats in the National Assembly.[12] Since the Hausa-Fulani elite had lost control over the federal institutions, it is understandable that they wanted to secure supremacy at least in their home region. With the help of Sharia they could evade federal control and rule themselves autonomously. The decision to reject essential elements of the federal constitution was made first in Zamfara State, a rural and very backward region, in which virtually only Muslims live. The breach with Western concepts of law was hugely popular among the people, so Governor Sani, the pioneer of Sharia, was reelected in 2003 by an overwhelming majority.

Zamfara's government challenged critics of Sharia by arguing that the Muslim majority in the North had only asserted its right to self-determination. Why should Christians meddle in the affairs of Muslims and dictate how they should exercise their faith? The constitution gave each citizen the right to practice his or her religion without interference. Moreover, the Sharia laws that now applied in twelve states of the federation had been passed by democratically-elected parliaments with clear majorities. If Christians still called on the federal government to ban Sharia, they would deny their opponents the same democratic rights which they claimed for themselves: »Democracy for Me but not for Thee.«[13] Thus, Zamfara's Minister of Justice called on Christians to respect the rights of others and acknowledge that Nigeria was a pluralist society.[14] Some observers in the West took a similar view, arguing that the Sharia experiment was legitimate because Nigeria's Muslims pursued their religious ideals by democratic means: »This is unique in the modern political development of Islam. [...] Northern Nigerian Muslims are identifying themselves, not only as Muslims, but as democrats.«[15]

However, the citizens whose will the Sharia politicians invoked hardly had an opportunity to influence the outcome of the legislative reform. None of the three political parties which took part in the 1999 elections had mentioned Islamizing the legal order. Only Ahmed Sani, the APP candidate in Zamfara, had promised Sharia to his voters. But not even Sani was eager to open a public debate about what an Islamic legal system should look like. His decision to punish thieves and robbers under draconian Islamic laws, certainly reflected the wishes of the people, though it is less clear whether a majority of Muslims would have voted in favor of stoning adulterers or enforcing a strict gender separation. Governor Sani did not put these questions to the public, instead he appointed, just a few weeks after his inauguration, an 18-member commission to draw up a new penal code. Two months later, in September 1999, a bill was presented to parliament and passed without amendments.[16] No one had consulted the representatives of the Christian minority. Even Islamic authorities such as the sultan and emirs had not been given the opportunity to comment on the proposed reform. According to the Emir of Gwandu, nobody had informed them about the legislative initiative.[17]

Zamfara's Sharia Penal Code was obviously drawn up in a great hurry. It contains omissions and contradictions, incomprehensible formulations and erroneous cross-references. Despite its shortcomings, it was adopted with minor changes by the other eleven Sharia states, with the exception of

---

13 *Hotline*, 9 April 2000, p. 22.

14 Ahmed Bello Mahmud, *Shari'ah*, p. 9.

15 Ludwig, *Religion and Politik*, p. 3; Ostien, *Ten Good Things*, pp. 166, 169.

16 *Hotline*, 4 June 2000, p. 23.

17 *The News*, 24 April 2000, p. 19.

Niger State (therefore, when quoting the Sharia Penal Code, I shall refer to the Zamfara version). Islamic jurists were, of course, aware that the new law code, when assessed from a technical point of view, was of »poor legislative quality.«[18] It needed corrections and clarifications; moreover it was deemed advisable to unify the penal codes in the twelve Sharia states, as this would facilitate the training of judges and give citizens greater legal security. So the Institute for Islamic Legal Studies at the University of Zaria was commissioned to look at the various codes, harmonize them and compile a standard penal code, which would apply in all Sharia states. This revision was again seen as the affair of experts. The only criterion to decide which legal provisions should be adopted was religious orthodoxy.[19] In August 2006, the Institute presented the standardized version of the Sharia Penal Code, but so far, only the parliament of Zamfara has passed it into law.

The reason given for avoiding public debates about the law reform was that Sharia is a complex and comprehensive legal system, which is familiar only to a small group of scholars. There was no point in having laymen discuss what should be regarded as a crime and which penalty should be applied. Instead, Muslims were obliged to accept the divine law in its entirety: »Islam means unconditional submission to the dictates of sharia in all spheres of life, social, political, economic, legal etc.«[20] After the colonial rulers had allowed only a ›truncated‹ and ›corrupted‹ version of Islamic jurisdiction, it was the duty of the faithful to restore the law in its pristine purity. The most explicit way to demonstrate that Muslims had freed themselves from Western prejudices and idiosyncrasies was to re-implement the orthodox penology. The authors of the Sharia Penal Code therefore made sure that they adopted the whole spectrum of classic penalties, with the proviso of course, that these penalties only applied to Muslims. Since then, thieves have to face the amputation of their right hand (and in case of recurrence the left foot, then the left hand, and finally the right foot). Cross amputation (right hand and left foot) is prescribed for robbers,

---

18 Peters, *Islamic Criminal Law*, pp. 14–15; Yadudu, *Sharia Implementation,* pp. 13–14.

19 Professor Sada, the Director of the Institute for Islamic Legal Studies, gave me an example. The parliament of Kano had introduced a clause that embezzlement of public funds should be treated as theft and be punished with amputation. Yet this is at variance with orthodox Sharia, so it was dropped when drafting a unified penal code (personal communication, Zaria, 29 December 2006).

20 M. L. Rafindadi, General Secretary of the Council of Ulama of Nigeria, in Ludwig, *Sharia Controversy,* p. 2.

stoning for adulterers,[21] and crucifixion for robbers who have taken lives. In cases of ordinary murder, which according to Islamic tradition is not subject to criminal law but to civil proceedings, the relatives of the murdered person have a right to retribution. They may either demand blood money or insist that the perpetrator be killed in the same way as his victim. The same applies to grievous bodily harm. On May 26, 2001, a Sharia court in Katsina State ruled that a defendant have his right eye removed. However, the plaintiff was given the option of receiving compensation to the value of 50 camels, in return for which the offender would not be blinded.[22]

Sharia politicians who defended these harsh punishments against massive criticisms by human rights organizations, gave the impression that they were simply adhering to the letter of the law. Governor Sani justified his uncompromising attitude by arguing that he had to follow God's commandments »a hundred per cent.«[23] However, Sharia politicians were prepared to make all sorts of concessions and tactical maneuvers. What the government of Zamfara presented to its citizens as divine law was a concoction of different legal systems. The basis for the Sharia Penal Code with its 409 paragraphs was the old Penal Code for Northern Nigeria, which British jurists had drawn up in the late 1950s. Several paragraphs were dropped from the revised version, but most regulations were adopted, often word for word, with Sharia clauses added and inserted at the appropriate points.[24] Some Sharia provisions that were impossible to implement under present Nigerian conditions, were tacitly put aside and left out of the new penal code. These included regulations which would have discriminated too blatantly against non-Muslims. Some of them had already provoked objections in colonial times. Christians had found it offensive that Islamic judges considered the social status of the victim when deciding cases of murder or assault. If a freeborn Muslim was killed, the murderer faced the death penalty. If the victim was an infidel and therefore of infe-

---

21 Strictly speaking, Islamic law does not recognize adultery as a criminal offence, as a man has the right to keep slaves as concubines (Schacht, *Islamic Law*, p. 179; Hodgson, *Islam*, pp. 183, 341). However, slavery has been banned since colonial times, which means Nigeria's Muslims are no longer able to have sex legally outside of marriage.

22 Peters, *Islamic Criminal Law*, p. 28.

23 *The News*, 28 February 2000, p. 29.

24 Ostien, *Islamic Criminal Law*, p. 3.

rior »worth«, the murderer's life could not be taken, provided he was a Muslim.[25]

Another aspect of Islamic law which had provoked resistance was the provision that in criminal proceedings against Muslims the testimony of infidels was inadmissible.[26] Today, when taking evidence, Sharia judges are supposed to follow the slightly modified rules of the British common law, even though these rules do not fit the Islamic legal system.[27] As Islamic law has been introduced only in a compromised form, some militant Muslims protested this fraud. According to the leader of a Shiite movement, the new legislation does not deserve the designation Sharia.[28] However, the great majority of scholars and politicians preferred not to remind non-Muslims that Sharia in its orthodox form would demand much stronger limitations on the rights of infidels.

There is yet another reason for blending Western and Islamic law. The claim by Sharia campaigners to return to a pure, original form of Islam is difficult to realize, because in Islam's early stages Sharia did not exist.[29] As long as Mohammed, as God's messenger, led the community of the faithful, it was unnecessary to fix a system of Islamic laws. Only after the prophet's death were his revelations compiled in a book. Yet the Koran was never intended to be a code of law, though it is interspersed with passages that state unequivocally what should be done with thieves or robbers.[30] But these instructions remain far too incomplete to constitute a legal system. Therefore, Islamic jurists had to rely on an additional corpus of holy texts, called *hadith*. They contain a copious collection of reports about the life of Mohammed and the early Muslim community. These reports had been handed down orally for generations, before they were put into writing. However, the legal and moral prescriptions contained in these stories and anecdotes were never codified and promulgated into law. It remained a matter of private scholars to interpret the sacred manuscripts

---

25 Peters, *Islamic Criminal Law*, pp. 3, 11, 26; Schacht, *Islamic Law*, pp. 132, 184.

26 Ostien, *Islamic Criminal Law*, p. 2; Schacht, *Islamic Law*, pp. 132, 194.

27 Only Sokoto State has introduced the Islamic law of evidence, thereby defying Nigeria's constitution. Enacting laws of evidence falls into the exclusive legislative competence of the federation. So the Obasanjo Government, whose rights have been infringed, ought to have taken legal action against the Government of Sokoto (Iwobi, *Sharia Controversy*, pp. 153, 161).

28 Ibrahim El-Zakzaky, in *The News*, 12 June 2000, p. 25.

29 Hodgson, *Islam*, pp. 321–322; El-Affendi, *Rationality*, p. 154.

30 *Koran* 5: 33 and 38, pp. 105–106.

and derive coherent legal principles from thousands of details: »Islamic law represents an extreme case of ›jurists' law‹; it was created and developed by private specialists; legal science and not the state plays the part of a legislator, and scholarly handbooks have the force of law.«[31] The classic literature of the four great Sunni law schools discussed a wide range of legal cases with a high degree of sophistication and casuistry. So Islamic judges in West Africa, who have adhered to the Maliki school of law, could refer to clearly defined rules when settling legal disputes. However, when it comes to reforming a modern state system, as in today's Nigeria, the medieval tracts do not provide much guidance. The attempt to construct an Islamic polity by referring to handbooks of the eleventh or twelfth centuries leads to arbitrary and controversial decisions which provoke bitter disputes among Muslims.

Islamization of all Spheres of Life

Sharia encompasses the divine commandments in their entirety – ritual obligations, purity taboos, penal laws and moral provisions, which are supposed to determine every aspect of people's lives, down to the most intimate details. Sharia »deals not only with a Muslim's faith, how he prays, when he prays and where he prays, but with a Muslim's education, health, housing, nutrition, employment, environment, commerce, transportation« and more.[32] Among politicians and jurists, it was not clear which measures were to be taken to Islamize all these areas. Parliaments, ministries and regional authorities in the twelve Sharia states issued a flood of laws and ordinances, which intruded massively in people's private lives. But many of these radical reforms, which initially made headlines, were soon forgotten because they were impossible to enforce. A particularly heavy-handed step toward Islamization was taken by the local government chairman of Talata Mafara, in Zamfara State, who instructed all unmarried and divorced women either to marry or leave the region, as Sharia abhors prostitution.[33]

---

31 Schacht, *Islamic Law*, p. 5.

32 Abubakar D. Muhammad, *Muslim Responses*, p. 15.

33 *Guardian*, 18 November 1999; *Tell*, 27 December 1999, p. 10. – »The only word for an unmarried woman of childbearing age in the Hausa language is *karuwa*, which translates as ›prostitute‹« (Callaway/Creevey, *Islam*, p. 36).

Single women who were employed by the local administration were given an ultimatum to marry within three months or lose their job. Another bizarre innovation, which characterized the beginning of the Sharia era, was Governor Sani's announcement that henceforth only bearded men would be eligible to receive government contracts.[34]

Some core elements of the legislative reform, particularly the harsh punishments for theft and adultery, could not be enforced either. Researchers from Human Rights Watch found more than 60 cases in which thieves had been sentenced to amputation, but only in three known cases was the punishment actually carried out.[35] Without its spectacular punishments, Islamic law lost much of its deterrent effect. Governor Sani had to admit that his state was plagued by a »crime wave«, which he blamed however on »some bad elements from outside the state.«[36]

Carrying out the classic *hudud* punishments was difficult for numerous reasons. One was the constitutional provision that Sharia courts are subject to the supervision of federal courts. A defendant who has been sentenced according to Sharia may appeal against it, first to a higher Sharia court, but eventually, after passing through several instances, to the Supreme Court, which has to ensure that judicial authorities comply with the constitution. In order to avoid this process, the authorities in Zamfara had to obtain the approval of the convicts, before carrying out the amputation. One of the men, a cow thief, who was the first person in Nigeria to lose his right hand under the new law, was offered 25,000 Naira in »rehabilitation assistance.«[37] Several months later, shortly before the second convict, a bicycle thief, was to have his hand amputated, he apparently negotiated the amount of compensation due: »the second amputee […] was actually in Gusau for settlement in a deal allegedly struck with the state government before he accepted to have his limb amputated.«[38] After the sentences were carried out, both offenders were also given jobs by the state government.[39]

There is a further reason why the authorities hesitated to carry out amputations and stonings. The great majority of the faithful were dis-

34 *BBC Focus on Africa*, Jan. – March 2000, p. 18; *Economist*, 6 November 1999, p. 53.

35 Human Rights Watch, *Political Shari'a?*, pp. 36–37.

36 *Tell*, 16 September 2002, p. 68.

37 Bergstresser, *Nigeria 2000*, p. 138.

38 *Tell*, 30 July 2001, p. 71. – The convicted men were also under strong social pressure to accept the penalty (personal communication, Prof. Philip Ostien, University of Jos; Quinn, *Pride*, p. 34).

39 Human Rights Watch, *Political Shari'a?*, pp. 38–39.

appointed at the uneven approach to criminal prosecution. Virtually all those who received harsh penalties were poor, marginal individuals. According to Human Rights Watch, they had not been informed of their rights, and they had no legal representation, even in cases in which the death penalty could be imposed.[40]

It was easier to implement religious reforms in other areas, such as in regulating ritual activities. The government of Zamfara took it upon itself »to ensure that every Muslim worships the way he is supposed to do.«[41] Since then, official events began with praise for Allah, and civil servants were required to attend the congregational prayers during their working hours. According to the commissioner for justice, the state was obliged to encourage all its citizens to observe the daily prayers at the appropriate time.[42] However, enforcing these obligations turned out to be difficult because the police as a federal authority were not trained to supervise compliance with religious rules. Therefore, the Sharia states established their own vigilantes, who patrolled the streets and clamped down on »un-Islamic behavior.«[43] The model of these *hisba* groups were Islamic guards, who had emerged in the eighth century under the Abbaside dynasty. They had controlled the imams and muezzins, supervised trade and industry, ensured that the five daily prayers began punctually and that the faithful participated.[44] Jurists at the time had considered it a misdemeanor to neglect one's ritual duties; however, they did not fix penalties but left it to the discretion of the authorities to impose the appropriate sanctions.[45] Without clear instructions from Sharia textbooks, the governments in Northern Nigeria did not determine what measures *hisba* members should take, if Muslims ignored their prayer obligations. In Kano, the largest city in the North, *hisba* guards set up »roadblocks throughout the city, stopping traffic, and inducing the lukewarm faithful to pray, or at least to cease from driving.«[46]

In a press release, the Government of Zamfara listed among its achievements the funding of Islamiyya schools and the construction of

---

40 *Ibid.*, pp. 2, 23, 36–37, 41.
41 Governor Sani, in *Tell*, 13 March 2000, p. 23.
42 Ahmed Bello Mahmud, *Shari'ah*, p. 8
43 Maier, *This House*, p. 190; Olaniyi, *Vigilantes*, p. 61.
44 Fwatshak, *Shari'a Enforcement*, pp. 2–4.
45 Schacht, *Islamic Law*, p. 187.
46 Miles, *African Islamism*, p. 1; cf. Nouhou, *Islam*, p. 241.

mosques.[47] It also paid the imams' salaries and subsidized pilgrimages to Mecca, but this had started long before the Sharia era.[48] Funds to sponsor religious activities were not envisaged for the Christian minority. Christians did not receive airtime on state radio and TV, and they were not allowed to teach Christian religious knowledge in public schools. Instead, Islamic religious knowledge was made compulsory for all students.[49] There was, however, no standard arrangement that would fix the rights of Muslims and Christians under Sharia. In Kano State, where many Christians from the South have settled, the government regulations were as uncompromising as in Zamfara. Katsina State initially took a more liberal stance, but in August 2006 it removed Christian religious education from the curricula of public schools and made the teaching of Islamic Religious Knowledge compulsory. In Sokoto, Bauchi and some other Sharia states, Christians were allowed to broadcast on state radio and TV.[50]

In all Muslim-dominated regions of Northern Nigeria, the construction of churches has been subject to restrictions. According to Islamic orthodoxy, Christians may practice their faith and hold church services, but they are not allowed to build new churches. Nor can they arrange public processions or display the symbols of their faith.[51] None of the Sharia states would include these openly discriminatory rules in their legislation; instead, they cited the protests of Muslim residents, local traditions or urban development regulations to justify official measures against the building of churches. In Zamfara, for example, it was not the newly created Ministry for Religious Affairs but the Town Planning Board that ordered the razing of some churches. The Evangelical Church of West Africa, for instance, received a note that its church building, constructed sixteen years previously, had been built without a permit.[52] According to the town planners, all churches had to be situated in a special quarter of town. Christians who

---

47 Press release by the Government of Zamfara, in *Hotline*, 4 June 2000, p. 24.

48 Civil Liberties Organization, *Sharia*, pp. 1–2.

49 Christian Association of Nigeria, Zamfara State, *Peace*, pp. 7–9, 14; Marshall, *Nigeria*, p. 120.

50 Committee, *Report*, pp. 18, 19, 21, 25; Christian Solidarity Worldwide, *Findings*, p. 3.

51 Cahen, *Dhimma*, p. 228; Küng, *Islam*, p. 679; Schacht, *Islamic Law*, p. 131.

52 Christian Association of Nigeria, Zamfara State, *Peace*, p. 6. – The report lists a few church buildings that were demolished. In Kano the authorities issued orders to tear down 54 churches whose construction had allegedly violated building regulations. In Katsina 38 churches were to be removed (Freedom House, *Talibanization*, pp. 44–45). However, only a few were actually destroyed.

claimed that they were being treated like »lepers«[53] tried to bypass this ordinance by holding prayer meetings and church services in private houses. However, by making »illegal« use of their residences, they risked eviction.[54]

Muslims are not affected by such restrictions. Many business people and politicians who want to give an impression of Islamic piety, have erected mosques in their private homes. Prayer rooms and small mosques have even been built on the sites of petrol stations, inviting drivers to have a rest and pray. However, Muslims will not usually tolerate churches in their vicinity. In the old town of Kano, no permission to build a church has ever been given. The same applies to the nearby university campus: Just behind the main entrance, visitors will encounter a grand mosque, but Christian students and lecturers have not been allowed to build a chapel. Even in the Christian quarter of Kano, no building permits have been issued since the early 1980s.[55] In this respect, the introduction of Sharia did not fundamentally change government policy. Nonetheless, Christians felt more threatened than ever, because the Muslim majority could now rely, in cases of religious conflict, on the support of its democratically elected government. Militants became confident that state authorities would not prosecute them severely. This may be a reason why churches have been burnt down more frequently since the introduction of Sharia.

Efforts to enforce strict Islamic behavior also affected everyday life. Zamfara's government closed down the only movie theater in the capital Gusau and opened a center for Koranic instruction in its place.[56] Commercial video presentation rooms and beer-halls were closed; as were brothels, although these had already been proscribed by the old penal code. In line with classic Islamic law, Christians should have been allowed to drink alcohol, but several Sharia governments extended the ban to the entire population.[57] *Hisba* groups and Muslim police officers sometimes searched the cars and apartments of non-Muslims in order to confiscate alcoholic drinks. However, the guilty people usually got away with a fine or a bribe, instead of receiving the prescribed 80 lashes.

---

53 Gwamna, *Christian Reactions*, p. 9.

54 Christian Association of Nigeria, Zamfara State, *Meeting*, p. 2; Marshall, *Nigeria*, p. 119.

55 Ibrahim, *Democracy*, p. 18; National Institute, *Religious Disturbances*, pp. 31–32; Danfulani/Ludwig/Ostien, *Sharia Controversy*, pp. 83–84.

56 Finkel, *Crime*, p. 8; *Newswatch*, 17 September 2001, pp. 25–26.

57 Schacht, *Islamic Law*, p. 131; Ladan, *Legal Pluralism*, pp. 21–23; Human Rights Watch, *Political Shari'a?*, p. 17.

Another measure that changed the lives of everyone was the gender separation in hotels and restaurants, schools and public transport. At Zamfara's only polytechnic which lacked the facilities to teach men and women separately, male and female students continued to share seminar rooms, but were no longer allowed to interact.[58] When asked about these rules, Governor Sani had to admit that his original assurances that Sharia would not affect Christians »in any way« were wrong. He added, however, that those regulations only served to raise »the moral standards« of Christians as well: »it does not affect their lives negatively, it affects their lives positively.«[59] Under pressure from Islamic authorities, Christians had to bow at least to some of the rules imposed by the rival religion. They were not reduced to a *dhimmi* status, and they did not have to pay infidels' tax, but Sharia, even in its limited form, compelled them to pay a kind of symbolic tribute, whereby they acknowledged their inferior status vis-à-vis the Muslim majority.

The Islamization campaign had more serious consequences for adherents of traditional religions, yet so-called traditionalists or animists have rarely participated in public debates about Sharia. Unlike members of Christian churches, they are usually not organized beyond their local cults, so they were unable to put up much resistance to the encroachments of militant Muslims. They had suffered from Islamic militancy since the 1960s, when a number of shrines and sacred objects were destroyed.[60] Despite the state-sponsored Islamization drive, many traditional village communities had survived even in the heartland of the emirates. Only in recent years have many Maguzawa – ›pagan‹ Hausa – converted. Their adherence to Islam may only be nominal; nevertheless they are now subject to Sharia, which forbids praying to beings other than Allah: »Whoever [...] takes part in the worship or invocation of any juju [...] shall be punished

58 *Newswatch*, 17 September 2001, p. 24.

59 *Newswatch*, 6 March 2000, pp. 16, 15.

60 An interesting case are the Jukun, an ethnic minority, whose culture and language varieties were studied by colleagues at the University of Frankfurt. The Jukun had once controlled a powerful empire, whereas today they live in isolated settlements, spread across five states. Where Islam has established itself, their old places of worship were destroyed, while Christian Jukun communities have preserved their traditional cults. Much of the iconoclasm occurred in the mid-1960s, when the Prime Minister of the Northern Region began his conversion campaign (cf. Gausset, *Islam or Christianity*, pp. 268–271; Gausset, *Spread of Islam*, pp. 173–174).

with death.«[61] This paragraph is in keeping with orthodox Islam, which only grants toleration to the followers of the other two Abrahamic religions: Christians and Jews.[62] It is unlikely that ›idol worshippers‹ in Nigeria will be executed. However, the official ban on polytheism could give encouragement to those Muslims who are ready to use force in order to remove the relics of ›heathenism‹.

Some of the old cults that had been displaced by the gradual spread of Islam, had retreated into the domestic sphere, so that ›pagan‹ elements were preserved in the innermost part of Hausa society. Memories of the ancient spirits lived on in the women's possession cults, but this ecstatic form of piety has come under threat from the purism of Sharia adherents. The government in Katsina criminalized imported elements of Hausa culture by banning singing, drumming, public dancing and flute-playing.[63] The old cults and festivities cannot be suppressed by administrative prohibitions alone. In rural communities, the state is hardly present, but the call to exorcise one's ›heathen‹ past inspired ordinary people to become active. The pre-Islamic rites, which social anthropologists could still observe at least in remote villages, have been disappearing: »La culture domestique ›traditionelle‹ que j'ai connue il y a trente ans n'existe plus.«[64] What might be referred to as the »de-Africanization of northern Nigeria«[65] is reflected, among others, in the people's appearance. Women who once walked the streets bare-breasted, only appeared veiled.[66] However, despite the religious fervor which swept rural communities, it is difficult to transform a ›pagan‹ or syncretic way of life. For the economic well-being of subsistence farmers it can be more advantageous to have women work the fields, as

---

61 Zamfara State of Nigeria, *Shariah Penal Code*, Section 406. – The term ›juju‹ is defined in Section 405: »»Juju‹ includes the worship or invocation of any object or being other than Allah.«

62 Bernard Lewis, *Middle East*, pp. 230, 234; Hodgson, *Islam*, pp. 289–291, 322, Muhibbu-Din, *Principles*, pp. 164, 171. – When Mecca was conquered, the Prophet is said to have personally smashed hundreds of idols (Hitti, *Arabs*, p. 118; Hodgson, *Islam*, p. 194).

63 Miles, *Shari'a*, p. 63. – For Zamfara see Ahmed Bello Mahmud, *Shari'ah*, p. 5.

64 Last, *Charia*, p. 148. – Susan O'Brien, reporting from Kano, emphasises that spirit possession cults and other elements of ›traditional‹ culture live on in the rites of *rukiyya*, an Islamic exorcism practised by Sufi sheiks (O'Brien, *Charia*, pp. 59–64, 67).

65 Miles, *Shari'a*, p. 65.

66 Miles, *African Islamism*, p. 2.

they did in the past. Therefore, many men were not willing to subject their wives to *purdah* and keep them locked up at home.[67]

Despite the enthusiasm for Sharia, some aspects of the reform policy encountered resistance from the start. In Zamfara and Katsina, the authorities wanted to prevent men and women who were not related by kinship or marriage from having contact with each other.[68] In order to enforce gender segregation, the government of Zamfara announced that it would provide separate buses and taxis for women. But there seems to have been a lack of funds to acquire enough vehicles, which meant that women had a long wait at bus stops and taxi stands. They often had no other choice but to walk, as they were also banned from using motorcycle taxis, which are widely used all over Nigeria.[69] The ordinance that barred women from using motorcycle taxis had not made any exceptions for non-Muslims. But the umbrella organization of Christian churches, the Christian Association of Nigeria, protested on behalf of its female members against this restriction of their freedom of movement and announced that it would defy the ban.[70] To this end CAN had to organize its own taxi service, the Association of Christian Motorcycle Operators, whose members were recognized by the cross on their vehicles. Of course, Muslim women were not allowed to use the Christian taxis, but a compromise was found for them too. They were given permission to share public transport with men, but on condition that they sit at the back of buses and taxis while the men stay up front with the driver. Once the authorities' religious fervor waned, the silent and tenacious resistance of the people eroded government bans even further. In Sharia strongholds like Zamfara, veiled

---

67 Militant Muslims from the city sought to prevent peasant women from working out in the open but had little success (*Tell*, 12 January 2004, p. 26).

68 Ladan, *Legal Pluralism*, p. 26; Peters, *Islamic Criminal Law*, p. 57. – Sokoto, Kebbi and other states opted for more liberal rules. In Zamfara female patients were banned from being examined by male doctors. The government promised to bring in female doctors from Egypt, but failed to keep its promise. Only wealthy men, who invited doctors illegally to their homes, were still able to provide their wives with medical treatment (*Newswatch*, 17 September 2001, p. 26).

69 *Tell*, 13 March 2000, p. 22; *Newswatch*, 17 September 2001, p. 26.

70 Christian Association of Nigeria, Zamfara State, *Peace*, in the appendix: ›Press Conference‹, pp. 1–2 and letter to Governor Sani, p. 1.

women can now be seen flagging down motorcycle taxis and being driven through the city by men to whom they are unrelated.[71]

Several months after the introduction of Sharia, the government of Zamfara boasted that it had »wiped out prostitution, gambling and alcoholism« among its citizens.[72] In fact, these vices had only been pushed into the shadows. When public bars lost their alcohol licenses, beer became available in private homes. Social life in some cities moved to the outskirts, into military barracks, which are administered by the federation, not by state governments. The Governor of Kano insisted that his prohibition applied to army personnel too, but the commanding officer informed him that if anyone was going to confiscate beer at the barracks, they would have to do it by force. In many places, the authorities have given up the fight, and beer is on sale again.

In countries like Nigeria, where the public administration is too weak to discipline society, the enforcement of Islamic law depends to a large extent on the religious enthusiasm of the people. When the religious fervor cools down, the strict laws have only a very limited impact on people's lives. This does not mean that these laws are innocuous. Their arbitrary and unpredictable application undermines legal security. Religious authorities, vigilante groups and police can interfere in people's lives at any time, because Sharia, which lays claim to regulate every aspect of life, provides numerous pretexts to harass people. The holy scriptures do not differentiate public creed from private belief, or law from morality, so that the concept of a legally protected private sphere does not exist.[73] Zamfara's Justice Minister considered it legitimate for the state to regulate the »every day conduct« of its people. Citizens should learn to adhere to *halal* rules (with its many taboos related to diet and hygiene). Furthermore, the state should go »against bad habits like telling lies, back-biting and deceit/cheating in the public and private sectors.«[74] When asked by a journalist, how the *hisba* groups fulfilled their supervisory duties, a spokesman for the Ministry of Religious Affairs said: »We normally have informants who help us catch people.«[75] Against the intrusiveness of this morality police, Islamic law

---

71 *Economist*, 27 September 2003, p. 42; *Tell*, 16 February 2004, p. 24. – In several Sharia states such as Sokoto and Kebbi, the governments did not even make an attempt to prohibit women from using motorcycle taxis (*Newswatch*, 17 September 2001, p. 29).

72 Press release, in *Hotline*, 4 June 2000, p. 24.

73 Hodgson, *Islam*, p. 322; Laitin, *Hegemony*, p. 32.

74 Ahmed Bello Mahmud, *Shari'ah*, p. 8; Maier, *This House*, pp. 181, 190.

75 Maier, *This House*, p. 190.

does not provide legal safeguards. The new penal code even empowers state authorities to punish citizens for offences which are not mentioned in the Sharia Penal Code or in other laws of the state. When a Muslim contravenes divine rules, which are laid down in the Koran, the *hadith* or the ancient texts of the Maliki jurists, then he or she can be punished at a judge's discretion: »Any act or omission which is not specifically mentioned in this Sharia Penal Code but is otherwise declared to be an offence under the Qur'an, Sunnah and Ijtihad of the Maliki school [...] shall be punishable: a) With imprisonment for a term which may extend to 5 years, or b) With caning, or c) With fine which may extend to N 5,000.00.«[76] This aspect of Sharia denies a principle of European law, which has been enshrined in Nigeria's constitution: An individual can only be convicted of an offence, if this offence is clearly defined and if the penalty for it is specified in a formally enacted law.[77]

The discrepancy between the far-reaching claims of religion and the empirical reality is a problem in many Islamic societies: »Sacred law can consistently be neither implemented nor eliminated.« Since people cannot comply with all its prescriptions, »sacred law is an effective weapon in the hands of those who administer it.«[78] Empowering political and religious authorities by an unrestricted divine law is dangerous in a country where violence easily spirals out of control. It enhances the tendency of law enforcement agents to harass people arbitrarily. In Kano, security forces swarmed out on December 24, 2000, and arrested 200 women who had been seen talking to men.[79] The delinquents were chosen at random, and their arrest did little to engender lasting respect for Islamic law. Such raids simply made it unpredictable, as to which aspects of the sacred law will be enforced and which group of culprits will be targeted. Uncertainty has been growing even within the administration. Various departments and their staff developed an uncontrollable life of their own, because they felt entitled to take the law into their own hands. In Kano, Governor Kwankwaso was rather hesitant in applying Sharia, while his deputy sought to stand out as an uncompromising campaigner for Islam. At the head of a *hisba* group, he personally stormed several luxury hotels and had the beer

---

76 Zamfara State of Nigeria, *Shariah Penal Code*, Section 92.
77 Federal Republic of Nigeria, *Constitution 1999*, Section 36 (12); cf. Peters, *Islamic Criminal Law*, pp. 15, 39, 44.
78 Schluchter, *Hindrances to Modernity*, p. 109.
79 Peters, *Islamic Criminal Law*, p. 56.

bottles in the bars smashed to pieces.[80] In some cases it was no longer possible to tell who had authorized a raid. In Gusau, Zamfara's capital, a Christian woman was held in custody for eleven days, after a police officer, a soldier and a local government official burst into her house and discovered a carton of beer in her bedroom.[81]

As the governors implemented their Sharia laws at best half-heartedly, independent *hisba* groups emerged, organized by volunteers who were often linked to radical preachers and imams. In order to place all *hisba* groups under government supervision, the state parliaments passed laws which regulated vigilante activities. However, official *hisba* groups wearing uniforms sometimes existed side by side with informal groups operating without a government mandate. In Kano there was much rivalry between them, until a new governor, elected in 2003 on a pro-Sharia ticket, put the more radical elements on the payroll of the state. 9,000 volunteers were trained and given a wide mandate to prosecute »anti-Islamic behaviour.« They were authorized to arrest thieves and robbers, suppress traditional music and magic, counsel women on marriage issues and stop usury, hoarding, speculation and lending money at interest.[82] Their activities were supervised, at state and local government levels, by *hisba* committees which were manned by Islamic scholars, imams, political office holders and representatives of the police. Nevertheless, relations between Islamic vigilantes and the police have been tense from the beginning. Police officers were accused of sabotaging Sharia by converting their stations into taverns and by providing armed guards for trucks which brought beer into Kano.[83] However, attitudes of the police can change depending on who is in control of the federal government. President Obasanjo had seen to it that police commissioners posted to crisis areas were opposed to Sharia, so the police often acted as a check against *hisba* excesses. In Kano, two *hisba* leaders were arrested in early 2006, though this step was only taken after the Sharia monitors had lost public support. They had tried to stop women from using motorcycle taxis, but had met with fierce resistance from the taxi drivers.[84]

---

80 Fwatshak, *Shari'a Enforcement*, pp. 17–18; *Tell*, 30 April 2001, p. 49.
81 *Tell*, 27 December 1999, p. 10.
82 Olaniyi, *Vigilantes*, pp. 60–63.
83 Peters, *Islamic Criminal Law*, p. 29; Gwarzo, *Civic Associations*, p. 307.
84 O'Brien, *Charia*, p. 66.

Hisba members were not allowed to carry firearms, and they were supposed to hand over suspected criminals to the police, but they often punished them on the spot. Flogging was a common means of dealing with offences, but I did not come across reports that they executed criminals. Since many *hisba* volunteers only felt beholden to the principles of Islamic law, they had little inclination to cooperate with state authorities, and they did not feel bound to political compromises with infidels, which exempted non-Muslims from most Sharia prohibitions. In some cases, *hisba* members seized Christians who had flouted the alcohol ban and flogged them on the street, or they dragged Christian women from motorcycle taxis and beat them.[85] Christians knew that they stirred up resentment among Muslims, when they availed themselves of freedoms that were denied to their fellow citizens. In order not to provoke the Muslim majority, Christian women covered their hair with headscarves or sometimes put on a veil.[86]

In Zamfara, where Christians form just two or three percent of the people, they had to come to terms with the hegemony of Islam. Things were different in Kaduna, a Sharia state further south at the edge of the Middle Belt. Due to the resistance of non-Muslims who make up almost half of the population, Islamization made little progress. Only the north of Kaduna State and some districts of the capital were declared Sharia zones, while the other parts remained under secular laws. This concession jeopardized the entire Sharia project. In a divided city like Kaduna, in which Christians could hold on to their freedoms, it was impossible to impose a strictly Islamic lifestyle on the Muslim section of the population. Any Muslim seeking amusement simply headed for a district where the morality police were not allowed to operate. A German businessman who had lived in Kaduna for many years reported that Muslim men had been accustomed to entertaining themselves as they wished: »After Friday prayers they went straight from the mosque to a bar to drink beer. And there were girls available next door.« With the beginning of a more rigorous Sharia, they simply moved a few blocks further to a neighboring quarter. Thanks to Christians

---

85 Fwatshak, *Shari'a Enforcement*, pp. 16–19; Christian Association of Nigeria, Zamfara State, *Peace*, pp. 4, 8–9; *Vanguard*, 19 January 2001.

86 European women who had lived in Northern Nigeria for years said they had always made sure, when in public, that their body was covered. However, when Sharia was introduced they no longer dared to go out wearing pants, blouses or sweatshirts but instead wore flowing shawls and headscarves. They also mentioned that they were no longer served at some market stalls, if they went shopping without their husband accompanying them.

operating bars and hotels, they found an infrastructure that made it easy to break the laws of their faith. Liquor dealers claimed that most of their sales were to Muslim customers. The more liberal atmosphere of Kaduna also offered considerable latitude to Muslim women. Yoruba women, in particular, dressed as they pleased, in Western clothes or traditional African attire.

Sharia adherents can hardly accept in the long run that some people among them enjoy much more freedom than Muslims. When it is impossible to discipline the entire population, it becomes unpopular among Muslims to submit to Sharia. Drinking alcohol and engaging in other vices are common among all sections of the population. Who would want to risk being flogged for such offences, when others do not have to fear any punishment? And why should infidels, among all people, enjoy a more lenient treatment? For Sharia supporters this was an awkward situation. If they campaigned too vehemently against the vices of their fellow Muslims, many of them would have found it no longer appealing to be a Muslim. The alternative would have been to choose a denomination whose members were exempt from the supervision of Sharia guards. Some Muslims obtained a second ID card with a Christian name in order to be protected from *hisba* groups.[87]

Western Constitutional Principles Rejected

For Christians, who make up almost half of Nigeria's population, it has always been important to live in a state that is impartial in religious matters. But the right to equal treatment was repudiated by Sharia politicians. By using government institutions to Islamize parts of the country, they contravened the constitutional precept that no religion shall be elevated to a state religion.[88] In addition, the attempt to dictate to Muslim citizens how to practice their faith violates the basic right to freedom of religion; and the

---

87 Last, *Charia*, p. 143; Abubakar D. Muhammad, *Muslim Responses*, p. 12.
88 Federal Republic of Nigeria, *Constitution 1999*, Section 10. – Sharia advocates denied that they intended to make Islam a state religion. The Speaker of Zamfara's House of Assembly declared: »the state was not being Islamised, only the people in it« (Civil Liberties Organisation, *Sharia*, p. 3). For the controversy on how to define ›state religion‹ see Durham, *Nigeria*, p. 165; Iwobi, *Sharia Controversy*, pp. 128–134; Ladan, *Legal Pluralism*, p. 30; Yadudu, *Sharia Implementation*, p. 9.

cruel corporal punishments are incompatible with the right to humane treatment.[89] Moreover, the new laws discriminate against women, and they infringe the rights of children, who are subject to amputation and other mutilations as soon as they reach puberty.[90] Muslim judges might well disregard all these violations of the constitution, but there is one judicial problem they cannot ignore, because it could bring down major parts of the legal reform. The Nigerian version of Sharia discriminates against Muslims. Compared with other sections of the population, they receive much harsher punishments merely because of their faith. For a number of crimes, the Sharia Penal Code stipulates the same prison sentences as the civil law, but it adds public flogging. Or it imposes the death sentence in cases in which a Christian or traditionalist would get away with a short prison term. For witchcraft or cannibalism, for example, secular law envisages two years in jail or a fine. Muslim defendants, however, face the death penalty. The tendency to prescribe harsher punishments is most obvious in the case of sexual offences, which Islamic law seeks to eliminate. Adultery or sodomy have to be punished more severely than sex with animals, i.e. with death.[91]

Before the introduction of ›full Sharia‹, when Islamic courts only dealt with fairly innocuous family matters, the parties could decide themselves whether they wished to be heard by a secular or religious judge.[92] Today, all Muslims are led to a Sharia court, without being asked whether they agree with the sacred law and its archaic punishments.[93] Thus, Muslim citizens can no longer determine the laws under which they wish to live. The will of God is above the will of man. Given the superiority of the Law and its custodians, it was not meant so seriously when pro-Sharia activists argued in the name of democracy against their Christian critics. As Governor Sani pointed out, Muslims had no right to reject the laws which his government had enacted: »These are divine rules and regulations. Anybody who says he

---

89 Federal Republic of Nigeria, *Constitution 1999*, Section 38 and 34 (1).

90 An overview of the constitutional principles that have been violated by Sharia is given in the study of Ruud Peters, who investigated Nigeria's Sharia reform on behalf of the European Commission (Peters, *Islamic Criminal Law*, pp. 21, 38–42).

91 Zamfara State of Nigeria, *Shariah Penal Code*, Sections 131, 137, 406, 408.

92 Federal Republic of Nigeria, *Constitution 1999*, Section 277 (2); Civil Liberties Organization, *Sharia*, p. 11; Iwobi, *Sharia Controversy*, p. 135.

93 Some Muslims who had money and influence tried to buy their way out of Islamic justice. By bribing the police or judges they succeeded in having their case heard not by Sharia courts but secular courts (Human Rights Watch, *Political Shari'a?*, pp. 20–21; Thagirisa, *Sharia Project*, p. 492).

doesn't want them is not a Muslim.«[94] This interpretation of Islam was confirmed by the highest spiritual authorities, such as Dr. Lateef Adegbite, General Secretary of the Supreme Council for Islamic Affairs: »Once you reject sharia, you reject Islam. So, any Muslim that protests the application of sharia is virtually declaring himself non-Muslim.«[95] Muslims who did not share this understanding of Islam might have preferred to renounce a faith that comes with so many constraints on their personal freedom. But apostasy is a crime which carries the death penalty, according to Islamic orthodoxy. In Nigeria, political realities did not allow Sharia politicians to include the death penalty for apostasy in the new penal code. Given these official restrictions, Governor Sani called on his citizens to take the law into their own hands and execute the culprits:

>If you change your religion from Islam, the penalty is death. We know it. And we didn't put it in our penal code because it is against the constitutional provision. It is the law of Allah, which now is a culture for the entire society. So if a Muslim changes his faith or religion, it is the duty of the society or family to administer that part of the justice to him.«[96]

The Supreme Council for Islamic Affairs claimed that each state is »completely autonomous« in constituting its penal laws.[97] But the constitution declares the very opposite. In its first paragraph it states that any laws inconsistent with the provisions of the constitution shall be void. In order to remind the Sharia governors of the legal situation, Nigeria's Justice Minister informed them in a letter that the Sharia Penal Code was unconstitutional.[98] Despite this warning, the federal government did not take any steps to protect the rights of its citizens in Zamfara, Sokoto or Kano. It even refused to give legal assistance to women who had been sentenced to death for adultery.[99] As President Obasanjo was not prepared to move against the breach of the constitution, representatives of Christian churches and human rights organizations heaped accusations on him. Some even implied that he tolerated the spread of Sharia, because he was indebted to politicians in the North who had financed his election cam-

---

94 *Newswatch*, 5 March 2000, p. 15.
95 *Vanguard*, 24 March 2002, p. 21.
96 *Newswatch*, 6 March 2000, p. 17; cf. Paden, *Unity with Diversity*, p. 34.
97 *Vanguard*, 24 March 2002, p. 21.
98 Ebeku, *Human Rights*, p. 174; Peters, *Islamic Criminal Law*, p. 31.
99 *Tell*, 9 September 2002, p. 31.

paign.[100] Whatever his personal motives, it seems to me that it was a wise decision not to meddle in the religious conflict. If a Christian president had attempted to outlaw Sharia, this would have stirred up millions of Muslims against the central government.[101] Some human rights activists sought to bring down Sharia by litigation, but their lawsuits against Zamfara's government were dismissed as they had no *locus standi*.[102] According to Nigerian law, lawsuits may only be initiated by injured parties, in this case by persons convicted under Sharia and threatened by amputation, stoning or similar punishments. As Nigeria has no constitutional court, appeals must be filed in state courts and will then slowly go through several instances until they reach the Supreme Court. At the end of this process, which could last more than ten years, the Supreme Court judges would have to determine that it is incompatible with the constitution's principle of equality for an adulteress to be stoned, merely because she belongs to a particular religion.[103]

However, a judicial decision would not settle the Sharia dispute, because Nigeria's constitution is not a suitable basis for an agreement between the contending parties. Why should Muslims feel bound to a body of laws that are derived from European concepts of justice? The catalog of human rights as well as the separation of state and religion are alien to Muslim culture, as Islamic scholars emphasize: »the Constitution [says] that the cutting of hands goes against human rights. The question we Muslims are asking them is who laid down these human rights? We have never been consulted. Why should we wear the cross of America always?«[104] Any attempt to force these constitutional principles on them would only widen

---

100 This argument ignores the fact that Obasanjo had already distanced himself from his patrons. A more plausible explanation might be that he could not afford to antagonize the Muslim majority in the North, as he tried to establish »his own power base« and find new allies (Wan-Tatah, *Shari'ah*, p. 28). Closely related is the speculation that the »Federal government simply maintained a studied silence since the Shari'a issue was obviously a political trap« (Agbu, *Federalism*, p. 41).

101 A former minister of justice, Dr. Onagoruwa (*Sharia*, pp. 316–317), suggested that the federal government should declare a state of emergency and »do away with the State House of Assembly« in Zamfara. There is no consensus among Nigerian academics on how best the Sharia crisis should have been handled. Non-Muslims told me that the president should have used the army to nip Sharia in the bud. This would have saved the lives of thousands who died in the Sharia clashes.

102 Ahmed Bello Mahmud, *Shari'ah*, p. 8; Yadudu, *Benefits of Shariah*, p. 5.

103 Peters, *Islamic Criminal Law*, p. 32.

104 Sheikh Abdulkadir Orire, General Secretary of Jama'atu Nasril Islam, in *Vanguard*, 24 March 2002, p. 21; cf. Ilesanmi, *Constitutional Treatment*, pp. 542–543.

the chasm between Christians and Muslims. The president of the Supreme Council for Sharia even announced that Muslims are prepared to go to war, if Christians deny them the right to live according to the laws of their faith.[105] Forty years after gaining independence it had become obvious that the attempt to rule Nigeria in accordance with Western legal principles had led into a dead end. Thus, many Muslims claimed it was high time that they shook off the colonial heritage and relied on their own legal tradition: »there is nothing legally wrong for any State [...] enacting its Code of Crimes different and distinct from those Codes given to us by our erst-while colonial masters.«[106]

Muslim demands to organize ›their‹ states according to their own religious traditions exclude non-Muslims from political participation and annihilate the concept of a shared public sphere. Muslims want to decide among themselves, based on the tenets of their faith, how to organize their society: »Every community should be free to determine its own legal system.«[107] Sovereignty no longer lies with the Nigerian people but with the community of the faithful, or more precisely, with their God, who is supposed to be the only legislator. For those guided by Allah, the word of infidels carries no weight. Muslims see it as interference in their internal affairs when Christian critics of Sharia raise objections: »Non-Muslims [...] are challenging and vilifying Muslims on sharia. What is their business«?[108] The idea that Christians are no longer part of their political community is often taken for granted, for example, when religious authorities claim that states like Kano are »Muslim states« and that the people living there are »almost 100 per cent Muslims.«[109] Millions of Christians in the North are not regarded as part of the indigenous population, though their migration from the South started generations ago. The government of Zamfara declared, despite the protests of its Christian citizens, that the introduction of Sharia was »the unanimous wish of the people.«[110] All those who did not

---

105 *The News*, 25 September 2000, p. 52. Similarly the Governor of Yobe State: »If necessary, we are prepared to fight another civil war. We cannot be blackmailed into killing Sharia« (Freedom House, *Talibanization*, p. 51).

106 Chukkol, *Application*, p. 29.

107 *Hotline*, 26 March 2000, p. 19.

108 Dr. Lateef Adegbite, General Secretary of the Supreme Council for Islamic Affairs, in *Vanguard*, 24 March 2002, p. 21.

109 Tabiu, *Sharia*, p. 10; Council of Ulama in Zaria, in Suberu, *Federalism*, p. 204; Dr. Datti Ahmed, in *The News*, 15 May 2000, p. 24.

110 *Hotline*, 4 June 2000, p. 23.

belong to the people should accept that the Muslim majority set the terms under which everyone else had to live. Religious minorities who did not like these terms were advised to leave: »If any individual feels too uncomfortable with any set-up established by the majority in any state, he has the right to choose another state.«[111] In Kaduna the Christian minority was strong enough to maintain the rule of secular laws at least in its own settlement areas, whereas in Zamfara, the whole territory was declared a Sharia zone. On behalf of the government, posters were plastered throughout the capital, informing visitors that the constitution had been suspended: »God's Law is Supreme.«[112]

Politicians in the Christian South urged the president to take action against the breach of the constitution and outlaw Sharia. But their claim to act as guardians of the constitution was hypocritical, as they themselves had few inhibitions about infringing the constitutional rights of their citizens. With the tacit or open support of the authorities, militias and armed security services have been formed, meting out »jungle justice.«[113] Robbers have been executed in broad daylight, and people joined the crowds to see how criminals were hacked to pieces or burnt to death with petrol and tires. Among both citizens and politicians, there have been hardly any objections to this lynch law. The Governor of Anambra, a born-again Christian and lay preacher, called himself the »commander-in-chief« of the notorious Bakassi Boys, and his counterpart in Lagos, Governor Tinubu, demanded that the Oodua People's Congress (OPC), a Yoruba militia, be entrusted officially with police functions.[114]

As the judiciary and police were unable to stem the rampant crime, a majority of citizens in all parts of the country agreed that drastic measures had to be taken. However, militias and vigilantes in the South did not fight in the name of religion. The Bakassi Boys, for example, were set up by market traders who gave their security force a very limited mandate. They were not to interfere in the private lives of citizens but only to chase bandits, something they did very effectively. Only a few months after the Bakassi Boys had started their operations, a commission of journalists declared the state of Anambra »the most crime-free state in Nigeria.«[115] As

---

111 Dr. Datti Ahmed, in *Tell*, 10 April 2000, p. 25.

112 Maier, *This House*, p. 180.

113 *The News*, 13 November 2000, p. 23.

114 *Tell*, 26 March 2001, p. 43; *Financial Times*, 23/24 June 2001; Harnischfeger, *Bakassi Boys*, p. 39.

115 *Newswatch*, 14 May 2001, p. 42.

the militias in the South are not meant to impose a religious way of life, they do not care whether men and women are properly dressed or whether they lead a decent family life. Adultery may be a moral offence, but the decision on how to deal with it is left to the people involved.

Most citizens in the South balked at getting drawn into a religious confrontation. Even church leaders, such as the Catholic Archbishop of Lagos, played down the religious aspects of Sharia and emphasized its political function: Hausa-Fulani politicians used Sharia as a »weapon« to bring down the Obasanjo government.[116] As Christians regarded the Sharia campaign as an »ethnic plot«,[117] they did not seek a religious answer to the crisis. Only the parliamentarians in Cross River, one of seventeen Southern states, threatened to declare their territory a »Christian state.«[118] And the Governor of Anambra, Dr. Mbadinuju, announced: »If Zamfara is a Muslim state, allow them to organize their state on that basis. If I'm a Christian state, I organize my state on that basis.«[119] However, this announcement was not meant seriously. It is true that Igbo governors such as Mbadinuju flouted the constitution, but not because they introduced a Christian legal system (which does not exist), but because they used ethnic militias to pursue their political interests.

If we compare how Nigeria's politicians define their role in ethnic and religious disputes, a clear pattern emerges. Muslims in the North, such as the former President Buhari, tend to see themselves as protagonists in a religious confrontation: »I can die for the cause of Islam.«[120] In contrast, politicians in the South, such as Governor Kalu, define their political interests more in ethnic terms: »I belong to a generation of Igbos that is ready to do everything to defend the interest of the Igbo anywhere, anytime.«[121] Ethnic nationalists have no qualms defying the constitution. When hundreds of Igbo were killed in Sharia riots in Kaduna, Governor Kalu announced that people would take the law into their own hands: »If they kill an Igbo man, we will retaliate immediately.«[122] On the following day, armed gangs, led by the Bakassi Boys, erected roadblocks and, within 24

116 *The News*, 10 April 2000, p. 21.
117 *Tell*, 27 March 2000, p. 20; cf. Sanneh, *Sacred Truth*, p. 43.
118 Maier, *This House*, pp. 177.
119 *Tell*, 26 March 2001, p. 43.
120 *Tell*, 29 October 2001, p. 36.
121 *Tell*, 19 February 2001, p. 24.
122 *The News*, 27 March 2000, p. 11.

hours, killed more than 300 Northerners who had been living in various Igbo towns.[123]

---

123 Meagher, *Bakassi Boys*, pp. 100, 102–103.

Sharia as a Means of Political Blackmail

>»The Hausa man is selfish in his quest for power.
Why shouldn't he be? Who will protect him?«[1]

The Rise of Militias

With the transition to democracy, Nigerians expected that a government elected by the people would be in a better position to balance ethnic and religious interests. However, the Nigerian experience confirmed what had been observed in other African countries: »In societies that are still deeply divided by race, religion or ethnicity [...] democratization has the tendency of only reinforcing cleavages that are already very hard to manage. Democratic politics in these countries becomes the politics of identity.«[2] Self-determination was demanded not for the Nigerian people, but for Nigeria's ethnic and religious groups, who used their autonomy to distance themselves from one another. Each of these groups claimed control over its own territory, so conflicts between them were almost inevitable. As long as the military ruled with an iron fist, they were able to suppress most of these conflicts, yet with the end of the Abacha regime, religious and ethnic violence ›exploded‹.[3] Journalists who had always wrangled with the rule of the generals came to realize that the liberation from centralist rule was a mixed blessing: »Nigerians were living in harmony with one another until the exit of the military.«[4]

Immediately after the death of General Abacha, ethnic self-determination groups had formed or resurfaced. In the Southeast, representatives of Ohanaeze, a forum of prominent Igbo politicians, demanded that the Nigerian army be replaced by six »regional armies.«[5] In the Southwest,

---

1 Olisa Agbakoba, President of Civil Liberties Organisation, in *African Guardian*, 2 May 1994, p. 14.

2 Hyden, *Democratisation*, p. 55; Ottaway, *Ethnic Politics*, pp. 310–311.

3 Ukiwo, *Ethno-Religious Conflicts*, p. 115; Agbu, *Ethnic Militias*, pp. 5, 13.

4 *The News*, 15 May 2000, p. 20. – »fewer people died in the entire period of military rule than they have now died in the first two year[s] of our democracy" (Kukah, *Sharia Law*, p. 23).

5 *The News*, 31 August [7 Sept.] 1998, p. 24; Suberu, *Federalism*, p. 191.

ethnic leaders among the Yoruba discussed similar models of decentralization. For Afenifere, a ›socio-cultural‹ organization, which comprised nearly all eminent Yoruba politicians, it was (and still is) a matter of course that only the Yoruba people are entitled to decide the future of their home region. Members of other ethnic groups that have settled in Lagos, Ibadan and other cities of the Southwest, were regarded as »guests« who had to recognize the prerogatives of the indigenous population.[6] As Yoruba leaders saw their nation as being sovereign in their ancestral land, they reserved the right to decide whether the six states of Southwest Nigeria should split from the rest of the federation. In order to prepare for a possible secession, the delegates at the Sixth Pan-Yoruba Congress in 2001 decided to design a national flag and compose a national anthem.[7]

Democracy permits ethnic and religious interest groups to develop almost unimpeded: »Chauvinists in almost every country, if freed from authoritarian constraints, exploit the media and the right to assemble freely, using these opportunities to mobilize their followers.«[8] Nigeria's democracy allowed communal tensions to rise, but it did not provide credible institutions that could have balanced the rival claims. In principle, the federal arrangements of the constitution were meant to defuse ethnic and religious conflicts. However, the right of regional self-determination has strengthened those centrifugal powers that endanger Nigeria's cohesion. State governors seeking the support of the local population acted as representatives of their ethnic groups, demanding more influence and resources on behalf of the Igbo, Yoruba, Ijaw and other nations. Their patriotism blended well with their own political ambitions, because what they demanded in the name of their people, served to extend the competence of their governments and to evade surveillance by the federal authorities. In order to strengthen regional autonomy, they demanded, among other things, the right to have their own police forces. Yet President Obasanjo, who was in command of all police and army units, did not want to relinquish the federal government's monopoly on power, so some of the state governors formed their own armed gangs. Governor Mbadinuju, for example, declared that he needed men who obeyed his commands, no matter whether it was an official state police or the local vigilante group, the Bakassi Boys: »I'll prefer something I'll control, whether

6 Frederick Fasehun, OPC leader, in *Africa Today*, February 2000, p. 28.
7 *The Week*, 19 November 2001, p. 34.
8 Byman, *Constructing*, p. 59; Almond/Appleby/Sivan, *Strong Religion*, p. 195, 206.

you call it police or you call it anything. This is because when I make my own law, I will have somebody to enforce it.«[9] The vigilante group, which was popular among his Igbo people, gave him some independence from the president in distant Abuja, and it helped him intimidate political rivals.[10] The *hisba* vigilante, organized by Governor Sani, assumed a similar function. Its members were personally committed to the governor, so he could deploy them against opposition politicians.[11]

The efforts to turn one's home region into a bastion of power against the federal government show that Nigeria's fragmented elites had no trust in the new democratic institutions. The former rulers from the North who saw themselves as the losers of democracy, had more than others reason to be worried. Their influence on federal politics was waning, so they were faced with the prospect of being increasingly excluded from government jobs and contracts. While politicians and businessmen feared for their traditional privileges, ordinary citizens felt threatened as well. As long as the military had ruled, the Hausa-Fulani diaspora in Southern Nigeria could feel relatively safe, whereas under democracy they were massacred in Lagos, Aba and other cities. Dr. Datti Ahmed, who later presided over the Supreme Council for Sharia, lamented that in the first ten months of the Obasanjo government more Northerners were murdered in the South than in the previous forty years.[12] The organization responsible for most of the attacks was the Oodua People's Congress (OPC), a militia named after the mythical ancestor of the Yoruba people. It enjoyed the support of the six governors in Southwest Nigeria, so it could operate openly in the streets of Lagos and Ibadan. From the perspective of Hausa-Fulani nationalists, the president's people seemed to be on the offensive: »Obasanjo tribesmen are running roughshod over other tribes and killing them like chicken[s].«[13]

The OPC militia had been formed in August 1994, during the struggle against military dictatorship. As the Abacha regime had forced opposition groups into illegality, human rights activists and trade union leaders in Lagos decided to organize their own security service, and founded the OPC as the armed wing of the National Democratic Coalition. Nigeria's pro-democracy movement, whose protests against the Abacha regime

---

9 *Tell*, 26 March 2001, p. 43.
10 Human Rights Watch, *Bakassi Boys*, pp. 20–23.
11 *Tell*, 8 October 2001, p. 20.
12 *The News*, 15 May 2000, p. 25.
13 *Hotline*, 19 November 2000, p. 9.

enjoyed considerable support abroad, was largely run by Yoruba activists. Moshood Abiola, who had won the 1993 election, was a fellow Yoruba, so they had more interest than politicians of other ethnic groups in actualizing his democratic mandate. They even appealed to the international community to impose economic sanctions against Nigeria, until the generals abdicated and the duly elected president was inaugurated. When military rule ended, their commitment to democracy and human rights took a back seat, and the OPC fighters assumed a new mission: the »protection of Yoruba interests anywhere in the world.«[14] So far, OPC units have not operated outside Nigeria; their main area of operation is the Southwest of the country, but here, in their home territory, the struggle for Yoruba interests has gone quite far. When dock workers elected some Igbo as their trade union leaders, an OPC commando stormed the port of Apapa and shot members of the rival faction to ensure that a Yoruba candidate would be head of the organisation. Dr. Fasehun, the leader of the more moderate OPC faction, defended this intervention: »we felt that our fatherland was being taken away from us. The OPC had to invade the ports to show solidarity and assert the rights of the marginalized Yoruba.«[15] OPC gangs also attacked Igbo traders who were accused of having ›monopolized‹ parts of the Alaba electronics market, and they clashed with militias of the Ijaw community in Lagos, but their main targets were members of the Hausa diaspora. The militiamen were not willing to accept that the biggest abattoir in Lagos was managed by Hausa butchers, and they also intervened at the Mile 12 market when Yoruba traders clashed with the Hausa Yam Sellers Association, giving their rivals an ultimatum »to cede control of the market.«[16] Another target was a radio station broadcasting BBC news in Hausa, the lingua franca of the North. The OPC »accused the management of Raypower of cultural imperialism which undermine[s] the culture of Yoruba people«,[17] and »threatened to deal with them if the broadcast were not stopped within two weeks.«[18]

Although OPC fighters had killed hundreds of Hausa, Igbo and Ijaw, no prominent Yoruba politician condemned the militia.[19] The Governor of

14 *Tell*, 13 December 1999, p. 19.

15 Quoted in Adekson, *Civil Society*, p. 122; cf. Akinyele, *Ethnic Militancy*, p. 627; Human Rights Watch, *O'odua People's Congress*, p. 23.

16 Human Rights Watch, *O'odua People's Congress*, pp. 14–16; *Tell*, 13 December 1999, p. 15.

17 Adekson, *Civil Society*, p. 122.

18 Ikelegbe, *State, Ethnic Militias*, p. 500.

19 *Newswatch*, 4 December 2000, p. 10.

Ondo State called the militiamen »freedom fighters«, and his colleague in Lagos, who acted like a »patron« of the OPC, wanted to entrust them with official police functions.[20] Given this acquiescence to large-scale violence, it is understandable that Governor Sani was annoyed by the hypocrisy of most Sharia critics. On the front page of The News, a Lagos-based magazine, he was presented as ›The Butcher of Zamfara‹,[21] whereas the Governor of Lagos, who sponsored the OPC and its war against criminals, was not portrayed in such an insulting manner: »Do people in Lagos not prefer the OPC method of arresting robbers and cutting them to pieces [...]? There was a day when the OPC killed 25 suspected robbers.«[22] Journalists and human rights campaigners in the South got all excited about the »primitive«, »stone-age« methods of Sharia,[23] while calmly accepting the brutality of their own militias. Dr. Beko Ransome-Kuti, for example, who enjoyed much respect in Western human rights circles as chairman of the Campaign for Democracy, was also national treasurer of the OPC.[24] And Gani Fawehinmi, Nigeria's most prominent human rights lawyer, was allied with the more militant Gani Adam's faction, which later became notorious through acid attacks on policemen. When asked about his involvement, he claimed that until 1999 he had not known about violent acts, but had mistaken the organisation for a »human rights group.«[25] Personal ties between the OPC and other segments of civil society may explain why the Civil Liberties Organisation defended the militia against attempts to ban it: »Banning the OPC [...] will lead to an increase in crime rate. The group has instilled fears in the mind of criminals.«[26] Sunday Mbang, Bishop of the Methodist Church and President of the Christian Association of Nigeria, also pleaded against a ban, and Professor Wole Soyinka, the Nobel Laureate, stated that the OPC was a »legitimate organisation.«[27]

20 *Vanguard*, 31 March 2002, p. 21; Reno, *Gier*, p. 297; *Financial Times*, 23/24 June 2001; Human Rights Watch, *O'odua People's Congress*, p. 49.

21 *The News*, 10 April 2000.

22 Ahmed Sani, in Ibrahim, *National Conference*, p. 202.

23 *The News*, 27 March 2000, p. 13; *Tell*, 27 December 1999, p. 10 and 30 September 2002, p. 3.

24 *Newswatch*, 6 November 2000, p. 23.

25 *Tell*, 31 January 2000, pp. 16, 17, 19; *Newswatch*, 6 November 2000, pp. 21, 23.

26 *The News*, 13 November 2000, p. 23.

27 *Tell*, 7 August 2000, p. 33; *Newswatch*, 6 November 2000, p. 23. – According to Dr. Fasehun, the OPC President, Wole Soyinka was a member of OPC's »intellectual vanguard.« (Adekson, *Civil Society*, p. 112) Nigeria's professional associations and trade unions, church organizations and human rights groups are often dominated by ethnic

Some critics in the North accused President Obasanjo of having »licensed« the »ethnic cleansing.«[28] Others blamed him for having failed to protect the Hausa diaspora in the South: »His people in Ogun State massacred our people«, »without Obasanjo raising a finger.«[29] Yet these accusations are unfounded. After the Governor of Lagos failed to curb the violence, Obasanjo declared the OPC illegal and gave the order to shoot at any member who resisted being arrested. In order to enforce the ban, he deployed anti-riot police and army units, which executed their mission with »ruthless« force.[30] Business people suspected of financing the OPC were brutally beaten and their property destroyed in an »orgy of violence.« Scores of OPC members were killed and at least 2000 were detained,[31] yet the security forces were unable to regain control over Lagos with its ten or twelve million inhabitants.

Spokesmen for Afenifere accused the police of taking sides in the ethnic clashes, arresting mostly Yoruba and letting Hausa killers go free. Eyewitnesses reported that soldiers were accompanied by local Hausa youths who »pointed at the houses of perceived adversaries after which the armed men set in to unleash violence.«[32] The OPC leader Gani Adams claimed that the infamous Rapid Response Squad 129 consisted of »bizarre looking Hausa policemen« who were sent, along with other police units, on a »state-sponsored mission to systematically silence the Yoruba race.«[33] From the viewpoint of many Yoruba, the security forces acted like an army of occupation. This lessened scruples among OPC fighters to kill them. Hausa police officers learnt that they ran a high risk in Lagos, thus many of them applied for transfers back to their home region.[34]

---

groups or split along ethnic and religious lines. In his study *The Perverse Manifestation of Civil Society. Evidence from Nigeria* (pp. 1–2, 5, 10) Augustine Ikelegbe criticizes the naive »romanticism« of political observers who see civil society as a democratic force that defends citizens' rights against an oppressive state: »civil society may become so parochial, divisive, divergent and disarticulative that it actually undermines democracy.« According to Ikelegbe, even human rights organizations rarely cooperate, but compete against each other for financial aid from the West (cf. Obadare, *Religious NGOs*, p. 149).

28 *Hotline*, 18 February 2001, p. 14; *Newswatch*, 4 December 2000, p. 19.
29 Dr. Datti Ahmed, in *The News*, 15 May 2000, p. 25.
30 *The News*, 13 November 2000, p. 22.
31 *The News*, 13. November 2000, pp. 22–23 and 4 December 2000, p. 19; *Economist*, 29 January 2000, p. 53; Human Rights Watch, *O'odua People's Congress*, pp. 1, 41, 43–44.
32 *The News*, 13 November 2000, p. 23.
33 *The News*, 31 January 2000, pp. 18–20.
34 *The News*, 4 December 2000, p. 19; Akinyele, *Ethnic Militancy*, p. 627.

The Hausa diaspora could not expect much support from the Lagos police, who consisted of only 12,000 poorly paid and miserably equipped men. Since the state could not guarantee their security, they had to protect themselves by arming young men who guarded streets and quarters where the Hausa ›settlers‹ were concentrated. Given the high demand for security, large numbers of weapons have been smuggled into the country, often by members of the army who had been dispatched to Sierra Leone and Liberia on international peacekeeping missions. At the request of OPC members and other militants, some Yoruba smiths have specialized in making rifles. Moreover, policemen and soldiers kept supplies up on the arms market by selling their service guns to the highest bidder: »people [...] were going from barracks to barracks looking for rifles and ammunition to buy. [...] buyers [are] probably those presently engaged in communal wars, robberies or politicians getting ready for 2003 [elections].«[35]

As soon as armed gangs patrol the streets and defend their territory, any minor incident may trigger a wave of violence. The unrest in Ajegunle, a multi-ethnic slum in Lagos, started when OPC militiamen pursued an alleged thief who happened to be a Hausa. The man on the run grasped his only chance to evade instant justice by hiding among some fellow Hausa, who refused to hand him over to his pursuers. The Yoruba fighters, however, insisted on their right to secure law and order in all parts of their hometown. They called in reinforcement and embarked on a »kill-and-burn operation«[36] against the Hausa. From Ajegunle, the violence spread to other parts of Lagos so that the governor had to call in the army and impose a curfew. After three days of fighting, when journalists could finally inspect the »war zones«, they saw the streets »littered« with corpses.[37]

Leaders of the Hausa community threatened »to ruin Lagos if any Hausa resident is killed again.«[38] Yet as a minority, Hausa fighters had no chance to gain the upper hand. In the North, however, they could strike back *en masse*. So whenever ethnic clashes erupted in the Southwest, the Yoruba minority in the North had to fear for their life. After the killings of Hausa in Sagamu, near Lagos, Yoruba migrants in Kano had to pay. Hundreds of them were killed, and endless convoys of refugees headed south,

---

35 *Tell*, 6 August 2001, pp. 32, 34–35; cf. Ebo, *Small Arms Proliferation*, pp. 19–26.

36 *The Source*, 30 October 2000, p. 11; *Newswatch*, 6 November 2000, p. 23.

37 *Newswatch*, 30 October 2000, p. 22; Human Rights Watch, *O'odua People's Congress*, pp. 16–18.

38 *The News*, 4 December 2000, p. 15.

back to their homeland where they could feel safe.[39] In a press communiqué, the Arewa Consultative Forum (ACF), an association of Northern politicians, announced: »henceforth, attack on northerners in any part of [the] country will not [...] go unavenged.«[40] In order to give credence to this threat, the ACF set up its own militia with the help of Brigadier Akilu, a former Director of Military Intelligence. Its prime aim was »to check Yoruba expansionism«[41] which was seen as the biggest security threat: »The North does not need the hate-race Yoruba to be in power.«[42] Since Obasanjo had been head of state, the »OPC anarchists« had »turned the socio-political landscape into an abattoir.«[43]

Elite Pacts instead of Democracy

In June 2000, a magazine in Northern Nigeria featured a photograph of the president on its front page with the headline »Face of a Betrayer.«[44] The magazine reminded its readers that politicians in the North had trusted Obasanjo to protect their interests. But as soon as he was sworn in, he began to marginalize them. For the Hausa-Fulani elite, this ›betrayal‹ was a serious affront, as Obasanjo owed his presidency solely to their support: »It is very rare in human life to see a people who will surrender power voluntarily [...]. When the north supported General Obasanjo as a presidential candidate, it did so because it had confidence.«[45] When asked why they had made such a generous concession, the standard reply was that they had acted in the interest of the Nigerian nation: »the northerners picked a Yoruba to be the president [...] because we believe in unity, in power sharing.«[46] But had they really intended to share power? Or had it been their plan to install, for as short a period as possible, a proxy, a man like Obasanjo who was regarded by many as a Hausa-Fulani in a Yoruba

---

39 *The News*, 15 May 2000, pp. 18, 20.
40 *Tell*, 20 November 2000, p. 25.
41 *Africa Today*, February 2000, p. 20.
42 *Hotline*, 19 November 2000, p. 28.
43 *Ibid.*, pp. 24, 17.
44 *Hotline*, 4 June 2000.
45 Dr. Datti Ahmed, in *The News*, 15 May 2000, p. 22.
46 Senator Bello Maitama Yusuf, in *Newswatch*, 4 December 2000, p. 14.

skin?[47] Nigeria's press speculated that Obasanjo had only gained the support of ex-President Babangida and other Northern leaders because he had promised to stay in office for just one term. In addition, he had allegedly accepted to fill certain cabinet positions with candidates from the North. When he broke his part of the deal, they looked for ways to put his government under pressure. They had »looked for someone whom they thought could dance to their tune and they [had] found him in Obasanjo. […] But unfortunately, after his inauguration, the very first speech Obasanjo made shocked so many people, especially some bigwigs in the north […]. First, they complained, saying the north was marginalised by this government […]. Then they […] played up sharia and politicised it.«[48] Seen from this perspective, a broken promise lay at the bottom of the Sharia crisis, and the pious campaign was entangled in a web of intrigues and betrayal.

In October 2002, when Northern politicians initiated impeachment proceedings against the president, he disclosed that a secret pact actually existed. The terms of the agreement did not become very clear,[49] but it seems Obasanjo's partners had persuaded him to sign a document that committed him to stay in power for only four years and to be a largely ceremonial president.[50] It is quite possible that he never intended to keep his part of the bargain. His inauguration speech had already perturbed many people, as he announced an uncompromising fight against corruption: »There will be no sacred cows. Nobody, no matter who and where, will be allowed to get away with the breach of the law.«[51] A few days later he dismissed 150 senior army officers, most of whom were from the North. They were »political officers« who had served the military junta in high government offices.[52] Thus it is understandable that they were retired with the beginning of democracy. But it is also understandable that Muslims in the North saw this measure as a kind of »coup.«[53] They were now

---

47 *Tell*, 31 July 1995, p. 12.

48 Anthony Okogie, Catholic Archbishop of Lagos, in *Newswatch*, 12 November 2001, pp. 46–47.

49 Lt.-General Gusau, the former National Security Adviser, gave an interview under the headline: »Why we brought Obasanjo to power« (*Vanguard*, 12 December 2006, p. 5). But he, like Ibrahim Babandida, did not reveal the details of the deal.

50 *The Week*, 19 May 2003, p. 11; *Tell*, 23 December 2002, p. 24; *West Africa*, 18 November 2002, p. 12.

51 Maier, *This House*, p. 20.

52 Bergstresser, *Nigeria 1999*, p. 149.

53 *Hotline*, 4 June 2000, p. 11.

clearly under-represented in the army leadership, so they insisted that some younger Hausa and Fulani officers be promoted over the heads of their superiors. However, Defense Minister Danjuma, a Christian from the North, resisted such a move arguing that politically motivated promotions would undermine the professionalism and morale of the officer corps. The vacant posts were filled strictly according to the rules of merit and seniority, and in this process the leadership of the army, air force and navy went to generals who belonged to the minorities in the Middle Belt.[54] Thanks to the president's ›betrayal‹ the position of the old rulers was decisively weakened within a few days. In case of conflict they could no longer count on the army to intimidate their rivals.

Deals negotiated between elites to share power have an advantage over democratic majority decisions in that they can consider the interests of all ethnic and religious groups involved. In deeply divided societies in which the losers of elections must fear exclusion from state resources, it makes sense to negotiate compromises in order to forestall violent conflicts. Yet these compromises are fragile, as they are not backed by an independent authority that could force all parties to respect the agreements. Nobody can rely on the other side to keep its promises. This uncertainty becomes a serious problem when the balance of forces, which was reflected in the initial settlement, begins to shift. Elite pacts which involve a political transformation from a military to a democratic regime, necessarily produce a shift of power structures, and consequently, the interests of the parties involved also change. Groups whose influence is rising have little incentive to abide by concessions made at an earlier date. Their opponents whose bargaining position is weakening, must reckon with being damnified. Rather than waiting until they get into a hopeless situation, it can be advantageous for them to risk an open confrontation, even if this means accepting high losses.[55]

In Nigeria's case, the transition from military to civilian rule went hand in hand with a shift of power from North to South and from a Muslim to a Christian head of state. This made the position of the former rulers precarious. At the beginning of the transition process, when the Provisional Ruling Council under General Abubakar decided to lead the country back to democracy, they consulted among themselves and with their Northern

---

54 *Tell*, 31 July 2000, pp. 31–32 and 8 April 2002, p. 30.
55 Rothchild, *Ethnic Insecurity*, pp. 330–331; Fearon, *Commitment Problems*, p. 118; Barry, *Social Justice*, pp. 37–40.

allies, while Yoruba and Igbo politicians had little influence on the course of the political transformation. The military refused to organize a constitutional conference at which representatives of all ethnic groups could have negotiated the future of the country. All important decisions were taken in closed circles. The military and their legal advisers devised the constitution of the Fourth Republic, basically a replica of the 1979 constitution, and they selected the head of state. After the inauguration of Obasanjo, the formerly marginalized groups gained influence, but this was, of course, inevitable in the interest of ›national‹ reconciliation. As the Northerners had dominated for decades, it was a matter of fairness to curb their influence. Nevertheless, the aims of the Yoruba president were not clear. Was he laying the foundation for a fair equilibrium? Or was the redistribution of public offices just a first step to sideline the outgoing elite?

There could be no certainty in this issue. In a religiously- or ethnically-divided society, nobody knows the intentions of his opponents. Nor is it possible for the party that gains supremacy to give the weaker side reliable assurances that it will keep earlier promises. After all, as soon as it is strong enough to turn the situation to its advantage, nobody can prevent it from exploiting this opportunity.[56] At any rate, it would have been imprudent for the Hausa-Fulani elite to count on the good intentions of the president. Nor could they rely on the protection of democratic institutions, as Nigeria's elections had always been manipulated. Once Northern politicians had established themselves in power in 1960, they never gave their rivals a chance: »the North simply went berserk in terms of appropriation of government machinery for itself. [...] the head of state and all his principal officers, the military, the parastatals and key organs of government were dominated by the North.«[57] What was to prevent their successors from behaving the same way? There were no institutional safeguards. The transition to the Fourth Republic, with its flawed elections, had not established new rules for a more restrained political competition.

When Obasanjo broke the pact with his backers in the North, they assumed that he would turn to his own ethnic group to build a new power base. Wada Nas, a former minister and close confidant of General Abacha, accused the new president of pursuing an aggressive ethnic strategy: »Marginalisation of the North is part of Yoruba agenda. [...] They have a long-term plan and that plan is how to deal with the Northern part of this

---

56 Fearon, *Commitment Problems*, p. 118.
57 Ahmadu Abubakar, in *The News*, 13 March 2000, p. 17.

country. I warned all of us before the election: don't vote for them, they are our number one enemy. [...] The hatred is deep in their blood.«[58] The allegation that Yoruba politicians sought to ruin their rivals was also made by the governors of the 19 Northern states, who met on November 18, 2000, for a kind of emergency meeting. In a press statement, they accused their counterparts from the South, in particular the Yoruba governors, »of ganging up against the North« and of planning the »economic strangulation« and »political repression« of the North.« Since the federal government under Obasanjo did not defend them, the governors appealed to the leadership of the North to unite and fight for their interests: »ensur[e] that the north gets its due share of the national cake.« The governors' communiqué made specific demands for this purpose: The federal government should finance the construction of a trans-Sahara highway, build more power stations, and resume the dredging of the rivers Niger and Benue, which connect Northern Nigeria with the coast.[59]

Whether the governors' main concern was the country's infrastructure is open to doubt. When politicians from the North had controlled the resources of the federation, they had never cared about the needs of the population. Public schools and health facilities in the North were even less developed than in the rest of the country: »the minister of education was a northerner. His minister of state (education) was a northerner. And all the parastatals under the ministry of education: JAMB, Universities Commission, NPEC, NBTE, NTI, they were all under northerners [...]. And surprisingly, this total control by the North of the ministry of education and its parastatals has not improved the level of education in northern Nigeria.«[60] Obasanjo could not win the support of the Northern elites by introducing a free education scheme. The well-to-do did not send their children to state schools, nor did they depend on the public supply of electricity and potable water. Behind the walls of their compounds, they kept their own water tanks and generators. General Abacha, like his predecessor, had not invested in the development of his home region; instead he had transferred over four billion dollars to his bank accounts abroad.[61] Those Northern power brokers, who protested the marginalization of the North, were

---

58 *Hotline*, 4 June 2000, p. 21.
59 *Newswatch*, 4 December 2000, pp. 12, 11.
60 Col. Abubakar Umar, in *Tell*, 13 November 2000, p. 27.
61 *Financial Times*, 20 August 2003.

mainly interested in securing their ill-gotten wealth. And they succeeded. Obasanjo did not touch them.

Investigations conducted after Abacha's death traced his booty to a global network of 130 banks. Yet Nigeria's government was reluctant to collect the embezzled money. In order to freeze the accounts of the Abacha family in England, it would have been necessary to open criminal proceedings against them. But the president preferred an out-of-court settlement.[62] Maryam Abacha, the dictator's widow, and now in charge of the robbed assets, was allowed to continue living her privileged lifestyle. When the government negotiated with her about a return of the stolen money, she declared that she would not succumb to state »intimidation.«[63] After three months of negotiations, she offered between five and ten percent of her family fortune, in addition to the 800 million dollars which had already been confiscated, because it had been hoarded in the family's private rooms or at local banks.

Mrs. Abacha had good reason to be annoyed, since no action was taken against ex-President Babangida, who had evidently embezzled much more money. A government commission, appointed in 1994, a year after the fall of the dictator, had uncovered spectacular instances of official corruption. In 1990/91, during the Kuwait crisis, when the prices for oil had risen dramatically, he had paid the oil windfall of 12.4 billion dollars into a so-called ›dedicated account‹ from which most of the money disappeared without a trace.[64] Like other military leaders, Babangida was implicated in political murders, but when asked to give evidence before a panel of investigation, which had held public hearings throughout the country since October 2000, he ignored all summones. His refusal to assist in the investigation did not cause any protests in his constituency in the North. For many Muslims, the investigations by the Oputa Panel were merely a show which the new rulers from the South had arranged to discredit their old rivals. A professor of Political Science at a Northern university told me laconically: »Yorubas are always trumpeting human rights.«

The president could have forced the retired generals to testify before the tribunal, but he accepted that most of them kept mute. Obasanjo did not even intervene when the newly-elected governors and their administrations started embezzling money. Six years after he had taken office and

---

62 *Tell*, 24 July 2000, pp. 13–18; *Tell*, 15 December 2003, p. 24.
63 *Tell*, 24 July 2000, p. 18.
64 *Newswatch*, 16 January 1995, pp. 9–14; *Tell*, 9 October 2000, p. 20.

promised an all-out fight against corruption, not a single high-ranking politician had been sentenced under the new Anti-Corruption law.[65] This restraint surprised many Nigerians, as some of Obasanjo's successors had staged a lot of crime-fighting activities. General Buhari, who came to power in 1983, dismissed 50,000 corrupt civil servants, decreed a minimum punishment of 21 years' imprisonment for economic crimes, and made oil smuggling punishable by death.[66] Even Sani Abacha, who scarcely kept account of the money coming into and flowing out of his government, launched a crusade against state mismanagement under the motto: War Against Indiscipline and Corruption. Part of it was a tribunal that investigated shady dealings in the financial sector. However, the main victims of this clean-up were bank managers from Yorubaland.[67]

Obasanjo, who had barely survived his imprisonment under the Abacha regime, had no personal reasons to make allowances for the former rulers. Years before, he had already expressed his disgust with Ibrahim Babangida: »Since independence [...] there is no leader that has been credited with so great a capacity for mischief, for evil like Babangida.«[68] Obasanjo presumably had a similar relationship to his immediate predecessor, General Abubakar, who had led the interim government after Abacha's death. Since Abubakar had handed over power to a civilian government, he had earned a great deal of respect abroad, so the United Nations appointed him a ›special envoy‹. But for him and his followers even the brief, hasty transformation process was a lucrative business. When he left the presidential palace after eleven months, the central bank's foreign currency reserves had fallen within a few weeks from 6.7 to 4 billion dollars.[69] Under his successor, Abubakar did not need to answer any questions. Obasanjo stopped the investigations even though he knew that Abubakar, who had served the Abacha regime as chief of defense staff, shared responsibility for Obasanjo's detention. Thanks to a video which Abacha's security adviser had recorded, it became known that Abubakar had pleaded before the Provisional Ruling Council to execute Obasanjo.[70]

There was widespread speculation why Obasanjo, who had headed the Advisory Council of Transparency International, sabotaged all efforts to

65 Bach, *Country*, pp. 74–75; *Economist*, 29 October 2005, p. 48.

66 Diamond, *Nigeria*, pp. 440–442; Hauck, *Demokratisierung*, pp. 74–75.

67 Reno, *Warlord Politics*, pp. 202–203.

68 *New Impression*, March 2001, p. 11.

69 *Economist*, 15 January 2000, Nigeria Survey, p. 6.

70 *Tell*, 18 December 2000, p. 25.

prosecute the generals and their civilian allies. Was he under the thumb of Babangida and other politicians from the North? Or did he opt for a policy of reconciliation in order to secure a smooth political transition? A wave of proceedings against the beneficiaries of military rule would have destabilized the country. When Obasanjo started some official investigations into corruption and human rights abuses, it was probably meant as a warning to the former rulers. Yet they did not know how far he would go. Parts of the military establishment had never trusted him. When the Provisional Ruling Council decided to adopt Obasanjo as a presidential candidate, some of its members warned that he would use his office to take revenge on those who had put him into prison.[71] A small group of Abacha's henchmen was indeed detained, among them one of the dictator's sons, who was accused of assassination attempts against opposition politicians. Critics of Obasanjo called the trial against Abacha's son a »vendetta.«[72] They rejected all official investigations, arguing that politicians from all parts of the country had lined their pockets under military rule: Targeting Muhammed Abacha and his accomplices was just hypocrisy. »What a selective justice. Every Nigerian is corrupt, in fact corruption runs in our blood.«[73] However, the charge against the seven defendants was murder, not corruption. But even murder cases, it was argued, ought to be forgotten in the interests of »reconciliation.«[74] When, in August 2002, 58 senators supported an impeachment of Obasanjo, he could only avert his fall by releasing the dictator's son from prison.[75]

Migrants as Hostages

The governors in the North had threatened their opponents in the South: »Our restraint must not be mistaken for weakness. There is a limit to patience and tolerance. [...] we cannot tolerate any more killings of our people.«[76] But what could they use as a threat? How could they prevent further marginalization? Under the Abacha regime, with the army on their

---

71 *Tell*, 18 December 2000, p. 26
72 *Hotline*, 4 June 2000, p. 21.
73 *Hotline*, 19 November 2000, p. 9.
74 Wada Nas, in *Weekly Trust*, 23 November 2001, p. 27.
75 *Tell*, 3 February 2003, pp. 34–35.
76 *Newswatch*, 4 December 2000, p. 11.

side, it had been easy to intimidate their rivals. A minister of the Abacha cabinet stated openly that »the North was ready to go to war over the oil reserves down South.«[77] With Obasanjo's purge of Hausa and Fulani officers, the army was neutralized as an instrument of political blackmail. Moreover, Northerners lacked the economic power to exert pressure on their opponents. Compared to the rest of the country, their region was hopelessly backward, a fact which reflected, among others, the education gap between Muslims and Christians. The few industries that foreign investors had set up in Kano or Kaduna, did not work profitably, and many firms have been closed, not least because of the Sharia crisis. To make matters worse, the North did not possess any mineral resources worth speaking of, and its agricultural sector was unproductive. Until the 1970s, it had generated enough surplus for export, whereas today it barely meets the local demand. The ruling classes could not collect taxes or tributes from their impoverished peasants who have been struggling with scarcity of land, ecological degradation and rudimentary farming technology.[78] The wealth of the Islamic elite derived solely from the oil resources, which accounted for 98 percent of Nigeria's export earnings and made up 95 percent of the federal government's income.[79] At the height of the first oil boom, in 1979, Nigeria's president had announced that the country would become »one of the ten leading nations in the world by the end of the century.«[80] Since then industrial production has declined to under five percent of the gross domestic product.[81] Over 60 percent of industrial activity is concentrated in the region around Lagos, which is also the site of West Africa's largest port.[82] The Governor of Lagos State could finance most of the monthly wages of his administration through internally-generated revenues,[83] while his counterpart in Zamfara collected just three mil-

---

77 Muhammadu Gambo, in *Tell*, 15 July 1996, p. 13.
78 Most farms in Nigeria cover less than a hectare (Economist Intelligence Unit, *Country Profile Nigeria 2005*, p. 32).
79 *Economist*, 15 January 2000, Nigeria Survey, p. 5; Economist Intelligence Unit, *Country Profile Nigeria 2003*, p. 41
80 Achebe, *Trouble*, p. 9.
81 De-industrialization progressed under the democratic government (Economist Intelligence Unit, *Country Profile Nigeria 2007*, p. 24). The Manufacturers Association of Nigeria reported that over 1,800 firms have closed down since 1999 (Herskovits, *Nigeria*, p. 119).
82 Economist Intelligence Unit, *Country Profile Nigeria 2007*, p. 37.
83 *Newswatch*, 25 March 2002, p. 27.

lion dollars a year in taxes from his three million citizens.[84] Without the oil money from the federation account, the authorities in the North could not pay the salaries of their teachers and administrative staff; there would be no funds for road construction and other public investments, and the Fulani aristocracy could not keep their palaces bright and shiny. Their rivals in Yoruba- and Igboland, who had suffered long enough under the arrogance of the old rulers, had little interest in financing their opponents' extravagant lifestyle. What was to prevent them from dissolving the federation with the »parasitic«[85] North and secede?

As Hausa-Fulani politicians and traditional rulers were losing control over the means of their existence, they had good reason to feel threatened. The only way to extract concessions from their opponents was to threaten them with massive damage. Sharia was well-suited to this end, because it could have extremely dangerous consequences. When Ahmed Sani and other governors announced that they were introducing an orthodox form of Sharia, everyone realized that this would spark religious riots. Since the early 1980s, clashes between Christians and Muslims in cities of the North had claimed thousands of lives. With the Sharia controversy, these conflicts were rekindled, bringing some of the bloodiest massacres since the Biafra War. Everybody knew that the number of dead could grow if the authorities in the North provoked further clashes. All they needed to do was to insist that the newly-created laws were strictly applied, or worse still, that non-Muslims were subjected to the *hudud* punishments.

People in the South were not directly affected by the Sharia campaign. They could have sat back and watched the North marginalize itself through religious fanaticism, had it not been for the millions of Igbo, Yoruba and other Southerners who had settled there. These minorities would be the first victims if religious conflicts escalated. In the worst-case scenario they would have to flee *en masse*, like the Igbo did in 1966, when thousands were killed and over a million fled to their place of origin in the Southeast. Since their expulsion and the civil war over the secessionist Republic of Biafra, the Igbo have settled once again in the North. As they are, on average, better educated (like other Christians in Nigeria who attended mission schools), they are more successful economically than the majority of the indigenous population. The prospect that they could be forced to abandon

---

84 Civil Liberties Organisation, *Sharia*, p. 2. – Zamfara's only industry, the Gusau Textile Mills, closed down in 2004 (*Tell*, 4 October 2004, p. 63).

85 *Newswatch*, 4 December 2000, p. 11.

all their property and return to the hopelessly over-populated Igbo region is a nightmare, not least for their relatives who have remained at home. Land in the South-east is so scarce that rural areas have turned into net importers of food.[86]

At the height of the crisis, in February and May 2000, refugees fled to the South in droves. Many who no longer felt safe in Kano, Kaduna or Bauchi, sought refuge in Jos, where the Christian population was still in the majority. But even here, riots broke out a year later. A Yoruba, who gave up his business in the North reported: »If you were there, you would never advise Yoruba to return. People were roasted like chicken[s].«[87] Despite this trauma, most refugees have returned, as they could not establish a reasonable existence in Igbo- or Yorubaland. Back in the North, their status has deteriorated. Since the indigenous population has asserted its Islamic identity, non-Muslims are already segregated by their appearance and, in case of violent conflict, marked as potential victims.

By using the threat of religious violence, Hausa-Fulani politicians pursued a risky policy of confrontation. The five governors in the Southeast condemned the »institutionalised kind of violence against the Igbo race«[88] and threatened revenge. A few days after the Sharia riots in Kaduna, when truckloads of corpses arrived in Igboland, the main mosque in Aba went up in flames and hundreds of Hausa-Fulani died in Igbo towns. The massacres were not a spontaneous reaction, but had been carefully planned.[89] In Okigwe, for instance, the transport workers' union made sure that no buses or taxis left the town, lest the local Hausa-Fulani have a chance of escaping their murderers. It was the first time since the lost civil war that non-Igbo were massacred in Igboland. For 30 years, Igbo had exercised restraint, and for good reason. Millions of them are living in cities of the North, while just a few Hausa-Fulani are residing in Igboland. If mutual killings escalated, Igbo would be the losers, like in 1966, before the war broke out. Their defensive attitude had other reasons as well: The Catholic and Anglican churches, which enjoy much influence in Igboland, vouch for the secular tradition of the constitution and advocate equal coexistence. So they urged their followers not to expel adherents of other faiths. For dec-

---

86 See the case study by Malchau, *Einkommensstruktur*, pp. 109–110, 147–151; Horowitz, *Ethnic Groups*, pp. 152–154, 245–250.
87 *The News*, 15 May 2000, p. 27.
88 *The News*, 27 March 2000, p. 12.
89 Meagher, *Bakassi Boys*, p. 102.

ades, Muslims could live safely in Igboland and other parts of the South. However, it is difficult to keep one's supporters from launching attacks, when the opposite side does not exercise the same restraint. Anyone who shrinks away from hitting back, feeds the suspicion that he fears an escalation, and therefore invites the other side to behave even more ruthlessly. Attempts to de-escalate can easily be taken as a sign of weakness, therefore, church representatives emphasized that their appeal not to take revenge should not be misconstrued: »What is holding Christians back at the moment is what we are telling them, it is good to live in peace and not in pieces. But if they [Muslims – J.H.] take that as a weakness, good luck to them.«[90]

Most Igbo I spoke to about the massacres alluded to the murders of the Hausa with pride: »It shows them that an Igbo life is not so cheap.« Of course, no Igbo leader wanted to accept responsibility for the rage of their ›boys‹, but they advised their opponents to take the 300 deaths as a »warning signal.«[91] Their belligerent mood was expressed by the former Biafran leader, ex-General Ojukwu, who is still popular among many Igbo: »there is nothing actually wrong with vengeance. It is the national policy of Israel you know, ours cannot be different. [...] I am a Roman Catholic. Every time, you hear Muslims say we want jihad, we want jihad. When did Jihad start frightening Christians?«[92]

The religious confrontation deepened the mistrust among Nigeria's fragmented elites and made it more difficult to forge alliances. During the First and Second Republics, prominent Igbo politicians had sided with the Muslim North against their Yoruba rivals, but after the Sharia campaign the political landscape changed completely: »The recent killing of Igbo residents in Kaduna over Sharia finally cut the Igbo political link with the North.«[93] Though resentment against ›the Yoruba‹ remained strong among Igbo politicians, it was no longer possible to play them off against each other. The Igbo establishment had supported Obasanjo in the 1999 election, but did not gain much influence over his government and soon felt sidelined by the Yoruba president. Nevertheless, the North could not exploit the rift between them. Members of Ohanaeze Ndigbo rejected a pact with the North: »[It is] unreasonable, for any person to think that the Igbo

---

90 Anthony Okogie, Catholic Archbishop of Lagos, in *Newswatch*, 6 March 2000, p. 13.
91 *The News*, 27 March 2000, p. 16.
92 *Newswatch*, 20 March 2000, p. 16.
93 M. C. K. Ajuluchukwu, member of Ohanaeze's inner circle, in *Tell*, 31 July 2000, p. 26.

will continue to unite with their killers.« [94] Not all Igbo politicians were so categorical in ruling out an alliance. Ahead of the 2003 elections, Governor Kalu and others started negotiations over a joint presidential ticket, but they insisted that the North could no longer be the dominant force in a coalition: »it is our turn to rule Nigeria.«[95] Hausa-Fulani politicians had no interest in assisting a Christian Igbo get into power; they wanted Igbo support for their own candidate and offered their interlocutors only the vice presidency, so the negotiations broke down. The dominant party in the Muslim North, the ANPP, picked its candidate for the presidential election without strong allies in the South. Muhammadu Buhari, a former military ruler and staunch Sharia supporter, found much support among ordinary Muslims in the North where he was able to win ten states. His image as a law-and-order politician who would fight corruption also appealed to Christians, but his role in the religious crisis weighed against him. As the elections were »massively manipulated«, it is impossible to say how much support the candidates truly had.[96] Outside observers assumed that Obasanjo would have won the contest even without vote-rigging.[97] Among the Yoruba, who had rejected him in 1999, his reputation had changed. He was no longer seen as a puppet of the Hausa-Fulani, but as a defender against Northern domination. His challenger Buhari, in contrast, »has always been accused of prosecuting an anti-South agenda when he was military head of state.«[98] For the Igbo and the Christian minorities of the Middle Belt, who had suffered most from the Sharia clashes, it was not appealing to entrust an »Islamic hardliner«[99] with control over the police and the army. At the height of the religious campaign, Buhari had demanded the introduction of Sharia throughout Nigeria.[100] When the 2003 elections came up and he addressed a Muslim audience, he called on them not to vote for a Christian candidate.[101] At the same time he avoided talking about Sharia, as he had to win Christian votes.[102] In the 2007 presi-

---

94 M. C. K. Ajuluchukwu, in *Newswatch*, 10 April 2000, pp. 15, 12.

95 *Tell*, 2 December 2002, pp. 21, 22.

96 Jockers/Peters/Rohde, *Wahlen*, p. 91.

97 Bergstresser, *Zweite Wahl*, p. 45; Economist, *Country Profile Nigeria 2005*, p. 7; *West Africa*, 9 June 2003, p. 12.

98 *Vanguard*, 18 December 2006, p. 43.

99 Bergstresser, *Zweite Wahl*, p. 45; Magbadelo, *Politics of Religion*, pp. 92–94.

100 Peters, *Islamic Criminal Law*, p. 55; *Tell*, 24 September 2001, p. 27.

101 Ukiwo, *Ethno-Religious Conflicts*, p. 123.

102 Kogelmann, *Sharia Factor*, p. 272.

dential election, the Sharia issue was eschewed again, yet Buhari, the most promising opposition candidate, lost a second time.

The Sharia campaign had many unintended consequences, which forced Muslim politicians to reassess its benefit. In a paper for the Arewa Consultative Forum, one of its members suggested that the political class in the North rethink its strategy: »What is the reason for using religion as a political weapon? What are the short/long term benefits? An in depth study is necessary to ensure that the disadvantages do not outweigh the advantages.«[103] The advantages, though not mentioned explicitly, were obvious. The religious violence served as a »brutal reminder of the risks« which Southern politicians faced if they sidelined the North.[104] Furthermore, the religious intimidation helped enforce discipline in one's own camp. After the Hausa-Fulani elite had lost control of the federal government, it had to secure its supremacy in its home region. In the First and Second Republic, federal authorities had interfered massively in states run by opposition parties, in order to deepen internal divisions and ruin their rivals' power base. With a Yoruba on top, Northerners had to close ranks in order to keep the federal influence at bay. With the help of Sharia they could mobilize the Muslim majority against those who collaborated too closely with the new rulers from the South.[105] Under pressure of the faithful, even PDP governors, who worked for the electoral victory of the Christian president, had to swear allegiance to Sharia. In the predominantly Muslim areas of the North, they could not distance themselves from the cause of Islam, as they risked being branded as traitors who sided with the Yoruba rulers: »Let those with whom they [Yoruba] are pleased with among us continue to serve them. [...] No matter how long it takes there must be a day of reckoning.«[106]

While the Sharia campaign enforced loyalty within, it alienated Muslims in the North from other sections of the population. Nigeria's opposition groups did not unite against the Obasanjo government and pursue common democratic interests. During his first term in office, Obasanjo had to struggle to remain on top, as influential personalities within the ruling party, including the vice president, sought to topple him. But in his second term, he gained control over the party apparatus and consolidated his grip

---

103 Mahmoud Ibrahim Attah, in *Hotline*, 19 November 2000, p. 35.
104 Bach, *Charia*, p. 125.
105 *National Review*, Nov./Dec. 2003, p. 40.
106 *Hotline*, 19 November 2000, pp. 27, 28.

on power. After he had asserted his independence from all those who had brought him into office, he was free to embark on a policy of economic reforms. Critics deplored his arrogance and his dictatorial style; as a general accustomed to giving commands, he did not seem willing to listen. Yet he did not damage the interests of the North and its political elites. Despite their anxieties about the ›stubborn‹ Yoruba president, they did not fare badly under him. Since he came to office, more money has flowed into the budgets of the Northern states than before. When the prices of oil and gas began to rise in 1999, federal government revenues rocketed to more than 50 billion dollars in 2006,[107] and this additional money was distributed evenly throughout the country.[108] Under military rule, part of the oil rents was diverted to ›dedicated accounts‹, from which much has disappeared, but under Obasanjo, the money was distributed as prescribed by law: 56 percent went to the federal budget, 24 percent to the 36 states and another 20 percent to the 774 local government administrations.

The distribution of the oil and gas revenues is one of the most controversial issues in Nigerian politics, so the federal government tried to mediate between the ›oil-producing‹ ethnic groups in the Niger Delta, who had much support among their Igbo and Yoruba neighbors, and their opponents in the North. While looking for a compromise, the president took great care not to offend the interests of the North. The debate focused on the so-called ›derivation‹ formula. Since 1999, 13 percent of the oil rents has been paid directly to the states along the oil-producing south coast. The ethnic minorities in the Niger Delta wanted to increase this share to 50 percent. As the ›owners‹ of the oil fields, they also demanded resource control so that they could enter into direct negotiations with international oil companies and market their oil wealth autonomously. Politicians in the North strongly rejected such an arrangement, maintaining that ownership of the oil belonged to the Nigerian nation, and President Obasanjo supported their position. He also sided with them when debating the legal status of the oil fields off the coast. While the Ijaw, Ogoni and other minorities saw the maritime oil fields as belonging to the adjacent Niger

---

107 *Economist*, 28 April 2007, p. 46.
108 The transfers from the federation account to the states rose by almost 400 percent between 1999 and 2001. This includes additional payments to the oil-producing states in the Niger Delta (Economist Intelligence Unit, *Country Profile Nigeria 2003*, p. 29; Bergstresser, *Nigeria 2001*, p. 155).

Delta states, their opponents insisted that these deposits were situated on federal territory.[109]

The president also backed the Hausa-Fulani elite in several local conflicts. When the Yoruba majority in Kwara State wanted to disempower the Emir of Ilorin, a Fulani, Obasanjo sided against his fellow Yoruba and protected the interests of the Fulani aristocracy.[110] In Benue State, the Christian Tiv resisted the sale of their largest industrial plant, a state-owned cement factory, to a Hausa-Fulani businessman who was suspected of having helped finance the Sharia violence in the North. However, the president confirmed the sale of the Benue Cement Company and dismissed his minister of industry, a Christian, who had sought to prevent the deal.[111] In the most severe confrontation between Muslims and Christians: a series of ethno-religious cleansings in Plateau State, Obasanjo was again anxious to calm Northern sensibilities. He did not interfere when Muslims committed massacres in Yelwa and expelled the entire Christian population. But when Christians retaliated, three months later, he sent in the army, declared a state of emergency and suspended the Christian governor.[112]

It is difficult to assess the extent to which the pressure of the Sharia campaign forced such concessions. My impression is that Obasanjo had a genuine interest in strengthening the coherence of the federation by creating a balance between North and South. At the end of his presidency, when he was strong enough to choose his successor, he did not favor a Christian from the South. Thus he demonstrated that power sharing can work. Those who had handed over government eight years before had not ruined themselves, but were given the chance to regain power. However, this chance had not been guaranteed by democratic institutions; it was the result of Obasanjo's personal decision. Until December 15, 2006, the day before the crucial PDP convention, nobody knew whether he would pick a Northern or Southern candidate. His choice of Umaru Yar'Adua helped to de-emphasize religious, ethnic and regional divides, and thus helped to

---

109 Bach, *Country*, pp. 72–73; Bergstresser, *Nigeria 2002*, p. 169; Dibua, *Citizenship*, pp. 20–22; Ejobowah, *Who Owns the Oil?*, p. 40.

110 Another affront to Yoruba (and Igbo) interests was Obasanjo's decision not to cancel the quota regulations which have favoured Northerners who sought admission to universities or applied for government jobs (*Tell*, 15 December 2003, p. 27).

111 *Newswatch*, 29 May 2000, pp. 38–40; *Tell*, 17 December 2001, pp. 31–32.

112 Human Rights Watch, *Revenge in the Name of Religion*, pp. 40–41; Civil Liberties Organisation, *Danger*, pp. 385–404.

defuse the Sharia conflict. Yar'Adua was the governor of a Sharia state, but he had not fought for the introduction of full Sharia, therefore, Islamist organizations did not campaign for him. Izala members and other Sharia activists supported Buhari, hoping that he would create conditions that were favorable for the implementation of Islamic law.[113] However, Obasanjo made sure that Buhari had no chance in the elections. The ballots were clearly rigged against him, yet the political establishment in the North did not rise to defend Buhari's rights. Many politicians did not trust the former general; they feared him as someone unpredictable, rigid and fanatical, while Yar'Adua looked like a more acceptable alternative. If the president had tried to install a Southern Christian as his successor, they might have instigated riots. Yet they could live with the imposition of Yar'Adua, a Fulani aristocrat and moderate Muslim. Yar'Adua was even acceptable to the ordinary people, as he was the only governor in the North who had never been accused of corruption.[114]

Obasanjo handed the president's office back to the North, but he did not allow Northerners to decide who became president. The crucial moment was at the PDP primaries, in December 2006, when Obasanjo presented the little-known Governor of Katsina as a ›consensus candidate‹. Other PDP governors nurtured their own presidential ambitions, but they withdrew from the race when the president threatened to sue them for corruption. If he had played by the rules and let party delegates choose the presidential candidate, the decision would not have been more transparent and democratic, either. The most promising contender had been Vice President Atiku Abubakar, »the principal architect of the election rigging in 2003«,[115] who was allied to some of the most corrupt governors. The other heavyweight had been Ibrahim Babangida, a major financier of the PDP, who would have used his fabulous wealth to buy his way up to the top. Obasanjo did not touch Babangida, Gusau and other former sponsors; they could keep their wealth, yet he did not allow them to stage a political

---

113 Buhari had initially more support from Sufi groups, while most Izala members backed Governor Sani's presidential aspirations. Since Buhari was a member of a traditional ruling family with Sufi connections, he had opposed Izala when he was head of state in 1984/85 (Kane, *Muslim Modernity*, pp. 208–210). Ahmed Sani, in contrast, was closely associated with the Izala (Loimeier, *Nigeria*, p. 69), but is closer now to the Ahl as-Sunna, an organization of former Izala members who stress Islamic unity and de-emphasize antagonisms toward Sufi brotherhoods.

114 *Tell*, 25 December 2006, p. 20.

115 Herskovits, *Nigeria*, p. 122; *Daily Trust*, 27 December 2006, p. 42.

comeback. Babangida abandoned his presidential campaign, after his eldest son was arrested and interrogated by the Economic and Financial Crimes Commission.[116] Among the opposition, intra-party democracy was no better. When delegates of the newly formed Action Congress (AC) met in Lagos, they learnt that there was only one presidential candidate: Vice President Abubakar, who had quit the ruling PDP. Even the members of the party executive were elected unopposed.[117] The other large opposition party ANPP also took its decisions at closed door meetings, when Muhammadu Buhari convinced the other aspirants to step down in his favor. Adherents of Governor Sani, his main rival for the presidential ticket, complained that a large part of the delegates, who wanted to vote for Sani at the party convention, had not been accredited.[118]

The accession of Yar'Adua helped to avert a renewed conflict between North and South. Yet the new president, who only came to office through the machinations of his predecessor, was in a weak position. He had no democratic legitimacy, and he could not count on a consensus among the elites. Within the ruling PDP, rival factions had not reached an agreement on whether power should shift to a Northern president or to a non-Yoruba from the South. Representatives of the Niger Delta argued that Northern politicians had ruled the federation for 34 years and that the Yoruba in the Southwest had had their share under Obanajo.[119] So they said the presidency should rotate to the oil minorities, who had never produced a civilian or military head of state. Igbo leaders in the Southeast voiced a similar claim, as ›they‹ had ruled Nigeria for only six months in 1966. Democratic institutions did not help to end their marginalization, so they were ready to pursue their interests by more effective means. While the Hausa-Fulani elite played the »Sharia card«[120], their rivals in the South pushed for ethnic autonomy, resource control or secession, and they also mobilized the masses. Ethnic self-determination groups like the Ijaw National Congress, Urhobo National Assembly or Movement for the Survival of the Ogoni People were in league with local elites and strengthened their bargaining power. However, the strategies of these groups differed, as

---

116 Economist Intelligence Unit, *Country Report Nigeria 2006*, p. 21.

117 *This Day*, 5 December 2006, pp. 1, 4 and 21 December 2006, p. 1.

118 *This Day*, 21 December 2006, p. 19; *New Nigerian*, 5 January 2007, p. 5.

119 Looking at the ethnic identity of the head of state can be misleading. Obasanjo's tenure as military ruler, 1976 to 1979, cannot count as Yoruba presidency, as he was under strong influence of Hausa-Fulani politicians.

120 *Tell*, 17 April 2000, p. 5.

a comparison of ethnic mobilization in Igboland and in the Niger Delta will show.

The agitation for secession was strongest among the Igbo, but since the Igbo form substantial ›settler‹ communities with massive investments all over Nigeria, they could not risk a violent confrontation. Their most popular liberation group, the Movement for the Actualisation of a Sovereign State of Biafra (MASSOB), tried to avoid clashes with members of other ethnic groups. Its founder, Ralph Uwazuruike, had been a member of the PDP who had supported Obasanjo during his election campaign in 1999, but he was soon disappointed with government policy. The Yoruba president, when making federal appointments, did not give the Igbo their »due«, though they had supported him in the election with 70 percent of their votes.[121] Disillusioned with party politics, Uwazuruike predicted that the Igbo could wait for another 50 years and participate in ›democratic‹ elections, without ever ruling Nigeria.[122] His campaign for secession was not taken seriously at first. It looked like a one-man-show, but when hundreds of Igbo died during Sharia clashes in February 2000, the agitation for Biafra fell on fertile ground.

Uwazuruike has burned his Nigerian passport, but it is not clear whether he really wants to break up the federation. His strategy, so he claimed, was based on Mahatma Gandhi's principles of non-violence and passive resistance. He advocated that the Igbo should gradually opt out of Nigeria and establish their own political structures in a long process passing through 25 stages. MASSOB introduced a new currency, the Biafra Pound, it opened a Biafra House in Washington D.C., and it has been broadcasting news through its radio station, Voice of Biafra. Its activists hoisted the old separatist flag and patrolled the streets in the uniform of the former Biafra police. However they did not carry arms, like the OPC, and they did not attack ›non-indigenes‹ living in Igboland. Separatists parading as Biafra police were a bizarre masquerade, meant to impress politicians from other parts of Nigeria. By displaying more and more symbols of national sovereignty, they were trying to give the impression that Igboland was in fact gravitating toward secession. For Igbo nationalists, this was the only way to compel Hausa-Fulani and Yoruba politicians to pay attention to the plight of the Igbo. Ralph Uwazuruike would probably have stopped the countdown to independence, if his people had been

---

121 *The News*, 17 April 2000, pp. 16, 13.
122 *Insider Weekly*, 20 December 2004, p. 28.

given access to the machinery of government. Before the 2003 elections, MASSOB activists demonstrated under the slogan: »Igbo Presidency 2003 or Biafra.«[123] With one of their politicians on top, Igbo could have secured their piece of the ›national cake‹, yet their campaign for an Igbo president was not just about money. Their most pressing problem was that successive governments had failed to give them security. For those living outside Igboland, discrimination and the threat of massacres have become a regular feature of life: »anytime there is a problem in the north, they begin to kill the Igbo.«[124] When young Muslims protested the caricatures of Mohammed in a Danish newspaper, in February 2006, they vented their anger on Igbo churches and businesses. Whenever they celebrated Jerusalem Day to show solidarity with the Palestinian people, Igbo and other Christians had to fear for their lives.

After the Sharia clashes in Kaduna, the five Igbo governors had warned that they could not »again tolerate any situation where Easterners are killed without any provocation.« Further attacks would compel them to reassess their faith in »the continued existence of Nigeria.«[125] But they did not have the means to put pressure on their opponents. A few kilometres to the south, in the Niger Delta, ethnic militias could blackmail the president in Abuja by blowing up pipelines and other installations belonging to oil companies. Igbo militants, in contrast, could only have destroyed their own infrastructure: government buildings and schools, power lines and bridges. Or they could have attacked targets outside Igboland, but this would have jeopardized their kith and kin in Lagos, Abuja and Kano. Other Nigerians knew that the Igbo would lose massively if Nigeria broke apart, so the campaign for Biafra was often dismissed as an empty threat: »If they think the north will suffer they are making a great mistake because they are land locked. They don't have land for farming, they have erosion all over the place. The land is too small for them to live.«[126] Given this overpopulation, Northerners calculated that the migrants from Igboland could not risk an escalation of violence: »Igbos [...] in the North [...] are most vulnerable to ethnoreligious conflagrations.«[127] Militant Muslims made it quite plain that they would not hesitate to drive out the unpopular migrants: »the general

123 *The News*, 7 February 2005, p. 18 (photo).
124 M. C. K. Ajuluchuku, in *Newswatch*, 10 April 2000, p. 14.
125 *Newswatch*, 23 October 2000, pp. 15–16.
126 Nuhu Kuso, former Justice Minister of Niger State, in *Hotline*, 3 April 2000, p. 19.
127 *Hotline*, 9 April 2000, p. 36.

belief in the North is that ›every Igbo man is a criminal‹.« »I cannot wait to see them carry back with them the only things they brought to us. These are: armed robbery, prostitution, cultism.«[128] Igbo have little bargaining power. They have been the first to be attacked and expelled when communal clashes erupted in the North, but they have always returned. As a Northern magazine put it: »You can kill them easier than send them home. [...] they are essentially parasites. They only serve as middle men, buying from A to sell to B. ›So if they all go home who will buy from whom?‹«[129]

MASSOB's strategy of non-violence has led to a dead end. The federal government did not make any concessions; instead it deployed anti-riot police and army units, which killed hundreds of MASSOB members. The security forces were often used to quell unrest, and their imposing presence could often prevent further eruptions of violence. However, army atrocities like the massacre in Odi, Baylesa State, could backfire and stiffen local resistance. In the Niger Delta, violence cannot be contained. During clashes between Ijaw and Itsekiri militias, the oil corporation Chevron reckoned that production facilities and pipelines worth 500 million dollars were destroyed.[130] In 2006, about 20 percent of Nigeria's oil production capacity was shut down, and in the first half of 2007, over 100 foreign workers were kidnapped.[131] The security forces cannot guard the oil installations and hundreds of kilometers of pipelines, so the militants could cause more disruptions if the federal government and the oil companies refused to compromise.

Since 1956, when oil production in the Delta started, Nigeria's government has earned more than 400 billion dollars in oil revenues, yet most people in the oil-producing areas live in poverty, amid a decaying infrastructure. Peaceful protests did not impress the federal authorities; politicians in Abuja only began to make concessions when militants occupied oil platforms and blew up pipelines. With the beginning of democracy in 1999, the derivation quota was raised from 3 to 13 percent, and the six Delta states have been allotted far more revenues from the federation account, but most of it has been embezzled. The crisis in the Niger Delta cannot be solved by simply pumping in more money. Liberation move-

---

128 *Hotline*, 3 April 2000, pp. 17, 20.

129 *Ibid.*, p. 20.

130 Michael Peel, *Niger Delta*, p. 17.

131 *Economist*, 4 August 2007, p. 12; *Africa Research Bulletin. Economic Series*, 16 May to 15 June 2007, p. 17407B.

ments, despite considerable popular support, were not able to use the new democratic institutions to bring their governors and local government chairmen to book. Billions of dollars in additional payments have only intensified the relentless struggle for a share of the oil rents. Fighting for their oil wealth has pitted the indigenes against each other, creating bitter divisions between villages, clans and ethnic groups. Far more people have died in communal feuds than in clashes with the police and the army. The dominant actors are local gangs, called ›cults‹, which form fragile alliances with local politicians, government officials and oil companies.

The escalation of violence may force Shell and other international companies to abandon their investments in Nigeria, but their withdrawal would benefit no one. Many militants, it seems, know that their rebellion is out of control, so there are attempts to curtail the use of violence. The Movement for the Emancipation of the Niger Delta (MEND), which started operations in early 2006, has condemned all commercial forms of hostage taking and sabotage. Oil installations must not be vandalized to extort a few jobs and some money from oil managers. Violence is only legitimate if it helps the Niger Delta people to negotiate a political solution, i.e. to extract concessions which improve the living conditions of all inhabitants. Yet it is unlikely that MEND and allied groups can establish a monopoly of violence and turn into reliable bargaining partners with the federal government and oil companies. As long as the living conditions in the Delta do not improve, local gangs like the Icelanders, Vultures or Ku Klux Klan cannot be stopped from extorting money. Something drastic must happen. Self-determination groups in the Delta and other areas of the South suggested organizing a (Sovereign) National Conference to restructure the federation. They recommended that a new constitution should be designed that guarantees ethnic autonomy, resource control, and rotational presidency. Some militants went even further and rejected all compromises with the federal authorities. If Asari Dokubo, an Ijaw warlord, had his way, there would be only one topic on the agenda of a Sovereign National Conference: secession. In his words, »Nigeria […] only exists in the imagination of the bandits.«[132]

---

132 *Tell*, 1 August 2005, p. 49 and 18 October 2004, p. 17.

Restructuring the Federation

The call for ethnic autonomy or secession had been an effective means of mobilizing the Yoruba and other Southerners against military rule. When the generals and their Hausa-Fulani allies accepted a »power shift« and »allocated the presidency to the Yoruba«,[133] interest in secession or a looser form of federation waned. With the introduction of full Sharia, however, the unity of Nigeria was again on the political agenda. The governors of all 17 Southern states met for the first time and called for a National Conference in order to redesign the federal system. Since the Sharia states had rejected essential elements of the constitution, there was no more legal basis on which to regulate Muslim-Christian coexistence. Nigeria needed a new constitution which acknowledged the fact that the members of the federation were drifting apart. The introduction of an Islamic legal system demonstrated that Nigeria's citizens no longer aspired to live under common laws, so the project of nation-building had come to an end.

The political establishment in Abuja showed little interest in drafting a constitution which decentralised power. Initiatives to restructure the political system came from regional forces, from ethnic militias and other self-determination groups, supported by intellectuals and human rights activists. After the Sharia crisis could not be settled amicably, the campaign for ›true federation‹ or confederation was backed by most politicians in the South and in the Christian parts of the Middle Belt. In Southwest Nigeria, eminent Yoruba from all walks of life signed the Yoruba Agenda, a position paper meant as a common platform for negotiation with other ethnic groups. It contained the blueprint of a new constitution which established ›Yorubaland‹ as one of six geo-political zones within a very loose federation. Secession was not ruled out, but viewed as a last resort, in case the Yoruba could not realise self-determination within a Nigerian state.

Politicians, intellectuals and social activists from across the South agreed that the members of the federation should have more autonomy, and this autonomy was defined in ethnic, not religious terms: »What is vital is to recognise our social pluralism, to recognise that from now, Nigeria is a federation of ethnicities and nationalities, nothing else.«[134] Starting from this premise, Nigerians should design a new type of federalism which was

---

133 Ibrahim, *Dividends of Democracy*, p. 3.
134 Claude Ake, in *The News*, 25 November 1996, quoted in Douglas/Ola, *Nourishing Democracy*, p. 41.

no longer based on geographical units like the present 36 states, but took autonomous ethnic groups as its constituent units: »The Ethnic Nationalities shall be the building blocks of the Federation, with the right to self-determination.«[135] Legal experts suggested reconstituting Nigeria as a (con)federation of ethnic republics or of six geo-political zones which would be free to decide internally how to distribute power between their component ethnic (and religious) units. However, before the technicalities of a new constitution could be worked out, Nigerians would have to take a fundamental decision: How much sovereignty should be left with the central government? Self-determination groups saw three options: a federal system with greatly reduced powers at the centre, a confederal arrangement in which the individual units could nullify decisions by the central government, or a complete break-up.[136]

Ethnic elites in Southern Nigeria had very divergent ideas about a future constitution, but they agreed to convene a National Conference where representatives of all ethnic nationalities would sit together, air their grievances and discuss how they wanted to be associated in future. Such an inter-ethnic dialogue, where all options could be presented, would give Nigerians the opportunity for a fresh start. A new social contract agreed by all groups might be the only chance to stop the descent into violence. The six constitutional conferences which Nigerians had held since 1950 had never established an acceptable legal order. The proposed National Conference was intended to break with these traditions by using an organizational model which better reflected social realities. Those coming together to reconstitute Nigeria should not be representatives of the Nigerian people but of ethnic nationalities. As such, they would not be elected by citizens of ethnically mixed constituencies, but would have to be nominated by their ethnic groups. Since these groups were considered autonomous, it was their internal affair to decide how they selected their spokespersons. A coalition of ethnic leaders that submitted a bill to convene a National Conference suggested that the delegates should be nominated by ethnic associations like Afenifere representing Yoruba elders, or Ohanaeze, its Igbo counterpart.[137] This model of representation marks a clear break with liberal-democratic principles of constitutionalism. Ethnic groups become

---

135 Campaign for Democracy, 1998, in Ibrahim, *National Conference*, p. 203; cf. Adekson, *Civil Society*, p. 66; Ejobowah, *Who Owns the Oil?*, p. 31; Sagay, *Nigerian Federalism*, p. 95.
136 Ben Nwabueze, in *Newswatch*, 23 October 2000, p. 12; Sklar, *Unity or Regionalism*, p. 46.
137 The Patriots, *National Conference*, p. 3; Sklar, *Unity or Regionalism*, p. 46.

the crucial rights-bearing entities. They have a will, they take decisions, and they enter into contractual relationships with each other.

Most of Nigeria's 500 ethno-linguistic groups are too small to establish their own state; but their leaders also claimed some form of control over their territory, arguing that each nationality was »entitled to a space on the map of Nigeria.«[138] Smaller groups might be forced to join an autonomous geo-political zone or region where they would have to share power with neighbouring ethnic groups; nevertheless each of them could have its separate constitution and administration.[139] Recognizing such claims for autonomy would have severe consequences; it would lead to a »pluralist idea of citizenship«[140] which divided the population into two broad categories and accorded full citizenship rights only to the ›original‹ inhabitants of a place. Indigenes living on their ancestral land would be regarded as the rightful owners with the power to decide how their territory is governed, whereas members of other ethnic groups that ›did not belong‹ to that area would be relegated to the status of settlers who had to accept the hegemony of the ›sons of the soil‹.[141]

Relationships between ethnic nationalities which enjoy much autonomy are difficult to manage. Common institutions can only work if the political actors can trust their rivals to abide by the rules, even when it is not in their immediate interest to do so. Legal principles ought to be valued in themselves, as a means of achieving justice for all. However, the ethnic and religious groups which were lumped together in the Nigerian federation have not developed common values and convictions. Their common history is short and overshadowed by traumatic events; it does not promote a feeling of unity but engenders resentment and mistrust. The collective memory of the Igbo, for instance, is shaped by the experience of discrimination, mass expulsions, and the hunger blockade imposed by federal troops during the Biafra War. Most likely, Nigeria would have split years ago, were it not for the oil fields in the Niger Delta, from which everyone wants to profit. However, peaceful coexistence cannot be founded on purely material interests. The wish to appropriate the oil wealth, which

---

138 Dr. Joshua Maina, Leader of the Middle Belt Movement in Gombe State, in *Our Vision. A Pan Middle-Belt News Magazine*, January 2002, p. 23.

139 Sagay, *Nigerian Federalism*, p. 95.

140 Ejobowah, *Who Owns the Oil?*, p. 32; Jinadu, *Ethnic Conflict*, p. 15; Bach, *Indigeneity*; Nwachukwu, *Local Citizenship*, pp. 236, 239–242, 255–259.

141 Among the Yoruba, the »sovereignty of the original indigenes of the land« is so widely accepted that it was included in the *Yoruba Agenda*, p. 8.

holds the North and the South together, has driven them into brutal competition. In order to gain access to the state resources, politicians enter into all sorts of alliances, but these marriages of convenience are incalculable and determined by the intention of gaining advantages over their partners. Without a sense of mutual obligations, Nigerians will not learn to trust in joint institutions:

»Rules in African political systems are usually the result of [...] opportunistic deals that have little durability because they have been entered into not to abandon the principle of self-interest, but to guard it. There is little scope in such systems for impartial justice, according to which rules are ends in themselves.«[142]

A conference of ethnic nationalities would face a difficult, if not impossible task: »to organize a cultural hodgepodge into a workable polity.«[143] In the long term it would be in everyone's interest to stick to rules which restrain the contest for power and facilitate accommodation. However, the chance to build mutual trust sinks as soon as one section of the polity commits itself to its separate religious rules. If the will of God is decisive in political matters, it supersedes all laws and contracts which Muslims reach with infidels. Non-Muslims cannot trust such agreements; they must assume that concessions to unbelievers are only valid as long as they are opportune. The most important concession is that strange arrangement which exempts non-Muslims from the severe *hudud* punishments. It is at variance with sacred law, so in principle, infidels have no right to it.[144] Professor Sada, whose institute was responsible for drawing up a uniform Sharia penal code, explained: »this exemption of non-Muslims from the application of the Sharia Penal Codes is seen as a very generous concession.«[145] The question is simply what motivated Nigeria's Muslims to be so generous. Do they have reasons that still apply when Christians are too weak to defend their liberties?

For Muslims who are interested in the spread of Islam, it cannot be desirable to make the legal position of non-Muslims more attractive than their own. The fate of infidels should not appear to be worthwhile. In a state whose constitution was truly based on Sharia, Christians would be

---

142 Hyden, *Governance*, p. 191; Berman, *Ethnicity*, pp. 49–50.
143 Ilesanmi, *Religious Pluralism*, p. 163.
144 Schacht, *Islamic Law*, p. 132.
145 Sada, *Commentary*, p. 177.

subject to many legal restrictions.[146] As ›protected‹ citizens who have to obey Islamic authority, they would not even be in a position to negotiate their social status. They would be assigned rights and duties by the true believers whom Allah has appointed to lead society.[147]

Of course, Nigeria's Muslims are pragmatic enough not to insist on the full application of the divine regulations: »an Islamic State [...] is not attainable in Nigeria, given the present realities of the country.«[148] If it is futile to fight for a strict Islamic order, then Islamic orthodoxy allows believers to depart from God's commands and to enter into extensive compromises with non-believers. But such covenants cannot form the basis of a lasting peace, they are only temporary expedients: »The interruption of hostilities, [...] according to strict shari'a doctrine could only be a truce, a brief interlude in the otherwise perpetual struggle to Islamize the world.«[149] Islamic organizations in Nigeria are aware that the divine order cannot be realized as long as the political power of non-Muslims remains unbroken: »Sharia [...] can only be fully implemented in an Islamic state.«[150] According to the investigations by T. H. Gwarzo in Kano, all Muslim organizations, from the conservative brotherhoods to the radical ›Shiites‹, seek to establish an Islamic state. They differ mainly in their methods. The Shiite-inspired Islamic Movement and other militants want to overthrow the political order, because under present leaders, who have to make deals with their Christian partners in the South, a pure form of the Sharia is not feasible: »there can never be real sharia without shedding of blood [...]. Nigeria must be made an Islamic State completely before sharia could be implemented.«[151] Against this militant posture, other organizations assume that Sharia can be implemented gradually by participating in the political system and transforming it from within. In this reformist strategy, Sharia is not a distant goal, but an essential instrument for pushing forward the Islamization of state and society.[152]

---

146 Cahen, *Dhimma*, pp. 227–228; Schacht, *Islamic Law*, p. 131; Kohlhammer, *Islam und Toleranz*, pp. 598–599.

147 Hodgson, *Islam*, pp. 317, 322.

148 Adegbite, *Muslim Leaders*, p. 172.

149 Bernard Lewis, *Middle East*, p. 235; Johnson, *Holy War*, p. 63.

150 Gwarzo, *Civic Associations*, p. 312.

151 Abubakar D. Muhammad, *Muslim Responses*, p. 14.

152 Gwarzo, *Civic Associations*, pp. 312–313; Bunza, *Muslims*, pp. 61, 63. – Murray Last (*Charia*, p. 147) also emphasizes that support for Sharia is not a matter of Islamic radicalism or ›fundamentalism‹: »ceux qui soutiennent l'application de la charia ne sont pas des radicaux, mais plutôt des musulmans modérés.« (cf. O'Brien, *Charia*, p. 48).

When trying to establish Islamic law at least in a limited form, it is not advisable for Muslims to remind their antagonists that Sharia requires the submission of non-Muslims. No religious or political leader has demanded that Christians be relegated to a *dhimmi* status. Instead Islamic dignitaries asserted that Islam does not approve of force when dealing with other faiths: »all practicing Muslims know that God has said that there is no compulsion in religion. Therefore Shari'a will not be forced on anybody. It will only be forced on the Muslims.«[153] Since the Koran forbids religious compulsion, it was argued that there was no reason for Christians to be concerned, that indeed, it was incomprehensible why they protested so vehemently, when Muslims turned to the tenets of their faith: »[It is a] historical fact that Shari'a has never had anything to do with non-Muslims.«[154] The authors of these statements know better, of course. Every year Islamic politicians and business people set out by the thousands on pilgrimages to Saudi Arabia, where they can observe that the strict regulations apply to adherents of all religions. The scope of Islamic law can also be studied in the Sudan, where the government's attempt to force Sharia on Christians and ›Animists‹ in the South pushed the country into civil war. The majority of those 180 amputations which Islamic judges have ordered since 1984 were performed on non-Muslims.[155] If Nigeria's Muslims were really content with a diluted form of Sharia that exempts infidels, they would have to name the ethical principles they consider more important than the commands of God. What should otherwise prevent them from altering their opinion and following religious leaders who do not feel bound to earlier agreements with Christians? Under changing circumstances, the faithful might be drawn to leaders who advocate a more consistent Islamization: »a jihad is necessary until Shari'a is established as the governing law in Nigeria.«[156] As long as Muslims do not state for what reasons and according to which criteria they wish to restrict Sharia, nobody

---

153 Muhammadu Buhari, in *Hotline*, 19 March 2000, p. 12. Similarly Sheikh Ahmed Lemu, formerly Grand Kahdi of Niger State, in *Vanguard*, 24 March 2002, p. 20.

154 *Hotline*, 19 March 2000, p. 25.

155 Personal communication, Prof. Sean O'Fahey, Northwestern University, Evanston, 14 May 2003.

156 Malam Ture Muhammad, in Birai, *Tajdid*, p. 197. – As Rothchild (*Power-Sharing*, 161) observed in the case of ethnic and regional conflicts: »Since one set of leaders cannot bind their successors, the next set of leaders may not feel committed to the peace arrangement. Consequently, should the balance of power between the negotiating parties shift, previously enforceable contracts may become unenforceable.«

can know where they will draw the line. It will be risky for Christians to grant concessions when they cannot anticipate how far their rivals will seek to take Islamization: »Christian Nigerians would fairly and reasonably think that Muslims are being tactical by demanding now only what they think they can get, until they are able to demand and get more later on.«[157] What gives rise to mistrust is precisely the claim that non-Muslims have nothing to fear from Sharia: »They expected Christians to be ignorant of the status of non-Muslims according to the classical treatises on an Islamic state.«[158]

When debating with Christians, Islamic politicians often quote a sentence in the Koran that promises protection to non-Muslims: »A whole verse of the Quran says there is no compulsion in Religion.«[159] What they did not mention is the context of this verse which relates to (forced) conversions and not to religious compulsion in general. »[The verse] was usually interpreted to mean that those who profess a monotheist religion and revere scriptures recognised by Islam as earlier stages of divine revelation may be permitted to practice their religions under the conditions imposed by the Islamic state and law.«[160] While polytheists and ›idol-worshippers‹ only have the choice between conversion and death, Christians and Jews are granted the right to retain their faith. Their life and property are protected, yet they have to submit to restrictions which are prescribed by Sharia. Where they live in their own communities apart from Muslims, they may administer themselves with their own judges and political authorities. But if they offend the Islamic order or if they commit violent crimes, Sharia prescribes the *hudud* punishments for them too.[161] Nigeria's Christians have to reckon that the present, diluted form of Sharia is just one step on the road to Islamization, at least for politicians like Ahmed Sani, who propagate a »pure Islamic law.«[162] In an interview, Governor Sani intimated that the current regulation which exempts non-believers from severe punishments such as amputation, needs to be modified. His reasoning: The Muslims in Zamfara would not accept over the long term that a Christian

157 An-Na'im, *Future of Shari'ah*, p. 330; Danfulani, *Commentary*, pp. 278–279; Kenny, *Commentary*, p. 137.

158 Kenny, *Sharia*, p. 347; Oyelade, *Shari'a*, pp. 39–43; Idowu-Fearon, *Shari'a*, pp. 22–23.

159 Dr. Lateef Adegbite, in *Tell*, 31 July 2000, p. 30; cf. *Koran* 2: 256, p. 37.

160 Bernard Lewis, *Middle East*, p. 57.

161 Cahen, *Dhimma*, p. 228; An-Na'im, *Islamic Reformation*, p. 89; Hodgson, *Islam*, pp. 206, 317; Schacht, *Islamic Law*, pp. 132–133.

162 *The Week*, 13 September 1999, p. 17.

thief is treated more leniently.[163] The same applies to the ban on blasphemy. When a controversy broke out over staging the Miss World competition in Nigeria, a journalist quipped that the Prophet, had he been alive, might have chosen a wife from among the beauties. In response, the government of Zamfara demanded that Islamic law be applied and the Christian journalist be beheaded.[164]

The extent to which Christians become subject to Sharia depends on their ability to defend their liberty – if need be by violent means. They cannot count on the protection of Islamic authorities, because Islamic law does not grant them those civil rights they enjoy under the largely secular constitution. Their rights as Nigerian citizens are only protected, as long as they are strong enough to prevent the spread of Islamic law. A theocracy cannot be established against the resistance of 60 million Christians, so Sharia adherents have to make concessions, but from the perspective of their faith they are not bound to them. As soon as the opportunity arises to impose a purer form of Sharia, they are authorized by divine law to renege on their promises: »All debates, communiqués, resolutions, agreements, treaties which are done by Muslims with non-Muslims outside of an Islamic theocracy, are at best temporal, imperfect and non-binding before Islam. Islam reserves the absolute right of finality.«[165]

Although Islamic politicians dismissed important principles of the constitution, they were not eager to negotiate a new one. The Arewa Consultative Forum, which brings together a significant portion of Northern politicians, rejected the call for a sovereign National Conference as »a coup against the North.«[166] When self-determination groups in the South made a

---

163 Maier, *This House*, pp. 184–185. – The same position was taken by Prof. Sada, Director of the Institute for Islamic Legal Studies, Ahmadu Bello University, Zaria, at a conference in Bayreuth on ›The Shari'a Debate in Northern Nigeria‹, July 11–12, 2003.

164 *Tell*, 9 December 2002, p. 30; *The News*, 2 December 2002, p. 70.

165 Turaki, *Shari'a Debate*, p. 28. – Discussing the validity of constitutional agreements Dr. Adegbite, the General Secretary of the Supreme Council for Islamic Affairs, pointed out that in Sura 9: 4 (p. 179) the Koran acknowledges temporary agreements with non-believers, and that it urges Muslims to keep them until their term has expired: »pacts between the believers and idol worshippers (who are accursed) have to be observed to the letter provided they the idol worshippers or hypocrites continue to honour the spirit and letter of any pact« (Adegbite, *Muslim Leaders*, p. 172). The decision on whether the other side is abiding by the spirit and letter of a pact is down to the Muslims. In a country like Nigeria, with its long history of sectarian violence, they will always find ample opportunity to complain about broken covenants.

166 *Tell*, 6 August 2001, p. 55.

first attempt to organize such a conference in April 2006, only a few Northerners attended, and they made it clear that they would rather defend the status quo than risk a radical restructuring.[167] Transforming Nigeria into a looser federation might be a first step toward a complete disintegration which would end the flow of oil money to the North. Moreover, Hausa-Fulani politicians reject the principle of ethnic self-determination, as they do not want to negotiate with representatives of other ethnic groups on the basis of mutual autonomy. As they have »transregional aims and interests based on both precolonial history and religious culture«,[168] they want to stifle autonomist tendencies and incorporate the minorities of the Middle Belt and the Northeast into a wider, religiously-defined North. At the headquarters of the Arewa Consultative Forum, I was told that Islamization helps to »homogenize« the population.[169] In this context of religious politics it is disturbing that Southerners want to assert the secular elements of the Nigerian federation. The Yoruba Agenda, which reflects a wide consensus of politicians, traditional rulers and intellectuals in Yorubaland, insists that »Nigeria must remain a secular state.«[170] As the project of a National Conference was obviously meant, among others, to contain the religious autonomy of the Muslim North, some Northern politicians complained that it »is targeted at destroying the Sharia legal system.«[171] Religious and political authorities in the Muslim North have no interest in a constitutional debate which may set limits for the implementation of divine law. The current practice of simply ignoring undesirable constitutional restraints is preferable to a legal compromise, as it gives Muslim politicians wide latitude to choose between strategies of confrontation or cooperation. Depending on the local balance of forces, they can decide pragmatically in each state, to what extent believers and non-believers shall be subjected to the dictates of Sharia. In Zamfara, they hardly considered Christian interests, while they granted liberal concessions in Kaduna. And in the Christian

---

167 *Tell*, 17 April 2006, p. 35.

168 Sklar, *Unity or Regionalism*, p. 43.

169 Many if not most Hausa-Fulani Muslims still regard the jihad of Usman dan Fodio as a religious ideal whose attractiveness lies, among others, in its imperialist achievements. A spokesperson for Governor Sani declared that Sharia served to restore a »new caliphatic order« (quoted in Abdul Raufu Mustapha, *Ethnicity*, p. 270). According to Loimeier (*Nigeria*, p. 62), a younger generation of intellectuals who want to overcome the »old Sufi–Izala dichotomies« and unite Muslims on the basis of Sharia »stress the legacy of the Sokoto jihad as a model for Nigeria's Islamic revolution.«

170 *Yoruba Agenda*, p. 8.

171 *The Week*, 21 February 2005, p. 17.

South, where the authorities adhere to secular principles, the Muslim minority claimed the right to be treated equally, to practice their religion and build mosques without hindrance. However, the unregulated coexistence of competing legal systems is a constant source of friction.

A National Conference to restructure the federation only makes sense if all participate. As it was unrealistic to expect that North and South would agree on a new constitution, the federal government advocated a pragmatic approach: keep the present constitution and discuss, if there are any modifications all parties can agree upon. In order to debate possible amendments to the constitution, the president convened a National Political Reforms Conference, which started in February 2005. Representatives of the Muslim North participated because they had been assured that the conference had only a limited mandate. The continued existence of Nigeria, its presidential system and a few other given facts were not to be questioned. In addition, care was taken to exclude from among the participants the more militant and uncompromising elements of civil society. Most delegates were nominated by the president and the governors, so militia leaders, human rights campaigners and other social activists played just a minor role. The Sharia issue was largely avoided; instead the debate focused on less intractable problems like the derivation formula and rotational presidency. Two participants of the Reform Conference told me that an agreement on these topics was within reach, but the conference derailed when the president tried to manipulate the constitutional reform to create the legal basis for a third term in office.[172] In July 2005, the talks ended without solutions to Nigeria's most pressing problems. It had been the best chance to reach at least a partial settlement, but Nigeria's elites could not even agree on how to react to the greatest threat: the insurgency in the Niger Delta.

Government critics like Wole Soyinka had rejected the president's conference project from the start, claimung that a conference had to be able to decide autonomously, without government interference, and that it needed popular participation. All ethnic nationalities should be represented, supplemented by delegates from trade unions, women's groups and professional organizations. To such critics, taking ethnic autonomy as a starting point was a solid basis for a peaceful federation: »if an ethnic group is treated justly and democratically, it does not usually contemplate seces-

---

172 Prof. Nnoli, Enugu, 14 January 2007; Dr. Ezeife, Abuja, 22 January 2007.

sion.«[173] Niger Delta activists, for instance, suggested solving the controversy over oil resources fairly and »democratically.«[174] However, when dealing with autonomous ethnic and religious groups, democratic solutions do not work. The inhabitants of the Delta states constitute less than 20 percent of Nigeria's population. If a referendum were held, their demand that half of the oil revenues should be remitted to the oil producing areas would be voted down. When they presented their case at Obasanjo's National Political Reform Conference, a majority of the delegates rejected the 50 percent quota. In protest, the representatives of the Delta people staged a walk out, and when the conference ended, some Delta politicians approached Asari Dokubo, leader of the Niger Delta People's Volunteer Force, with a request to resume the armed struggle.[175] Violence is an essential element in their bargaining strategy. To gain concessions, they have to convince the majority groups that it will be too costly for them to disregard the interests of the oil minorities.

Nigeria's fractured elites are in an unenviable position. They cannot settle their conflicts through the present democratic institutions, but taking ethnic autonomy as the basis for a new constitution is not a realistic alternative. It narrows the scope for compromises and makes agreements even more difficult. If ethnic nationalities are free to decide how they want to associate with others, they cannot be expected to accept majority decisions. Why should they submit to the will of other peoples? A new social contract which stipulates the rights and duties of autonomous groups could only be entered on the basis of voluntary decisions: »if Nigeria is desirable, it has to be negotiated, not imposed.«[176] Delegates of a National Conference would have to design a political order acceptable to all, but this is not achievable. Splitting the federation, as some militants have suggested, would not solve the problems either. With the dissolution of a common state, the Igbo, Yoruba and Hausa-Fulani would still face the same controversies: What is the legal status of settlers? Who will protect ethnic diasporas or communities of infidels? Who controls natural resources and trade routes? Furthermore, ethnic republics would not necessarily be more stable. Yoruba and Igbo nationalists assume that democracy, which did not work on an interethnic level, stands a better chance when it is rooted in smaller, ethnically

---

173 Douglas/Ola, *Nourishing Democracy*, pp. 46–47.
174 Douglas/Ola, *Defending Nature*, p. 337.
175 This is what Asari Dokubo claimed, in *Tell*, 26 September 2005, p. 28.
176 Agbu, *Ethnic Militias*, p. 33.

homogeneous societies, bound by common traditions and ties of moral obligations. However, the Igbo never had a strong common tradition. What is today labelled a nation was in precolonial times just an agglomeration of autonomous village groups, without any overarching religious or political institutions.[177] Among the Yoruba, cultural unity played a greater role, yet Yoruba society is rife with sectional rivalries.[178] Critics of ethnic nationalism predicted that an autonomous Yorubaland would be destabilized by the same centrifugal forces which have been tearing the Nigerian federation apart: »the Yoruba [...] have seeming unity in a united Nigeria because, of course, they have rivals, the Igbo and particularly the Hausa-Fulani. Now without these people, the Yoruba will go back into a state that also the whitemen met them. You remember the Yoruba wars. They were involved in internecine warfare, the area was totally ungovernable.«[179]

For the minorities of the Delta states, political independence could also trigger a wave of violence. While a few militias claim to fight for a Niger Delta Republic, most minorities fear that such a republic would be dominated by the Ijaw, the largest ethnic group in the region. Ken Saro-Wiwa, the Ogoni leader, who was one of the first to call for a National Conference, rejected the idea of a common Delta Republic. All ethnic groups should administer themselves, though under the auspices of a loose Nigerian federation: »The only law to be in Nigeria is: You are free to rule yourself [...] nobody should take care of the other; let everyone care for himself. [...] I would like to see [...] one Hausa state, one Tiv state, Idoma state, Ijaw state, one Ogoni state.«[180] However, the right of ethnic nationalities to be autonomous does not necessarily lead to a peaceful and equitable coexistence. With the failure of democratic institutions, the question arises as to the mechanisms for regulating possible conflicts. How can ethnic and religious groups that are not subject to the control of a central power, coexist peacefully and as equals? In the precolonial tradition there are no models for an order that would protect the rights of minorities. The only political systems to which one could have recourse in order to create stability for larger regions are imperial edifices such as the

---

177 Harneit-Sievers, *Constructions*, pp. 2, 16, 30, 39.

178 The most violent clashes, between the Ife and Modakeke communities in Osun State have claimed approximately 2,000 lives since 1997 (Ogbara, *Ife-Modakeke*, p. 44).

179 Colonel Abubakar Umar, in *Tell*, 13 November 2000, p. 25. – Before the British conquest, the Yoruba-speaking peoples had indeed experienced a century of warfare (Ajayi/Smith, *Yoruba Warfare*, p. 9; J. D. Y. Peel, *Religious Encounter*, pp. 27–46).

180 Saro-Wiwa, *Our Oil*, pp. 355, 356, 357.

Caliphate of Sokoto or its ›heathen‹ equivalents, the Kingdoms of Benin, Oyo or Kwararafa. Minority leaders insist that all ethnic groups, no matter how small, must enjoy the same rights. But who shall guarantee these rights, if power is decentralized? Without protection from the federation, the small Ogoni nation might learn that 15 or 20 million Igbo living north of them would not treat them on the basis of equality. Signs of future conflicts are already on the horizon. While campaigning for Igbo secession, MASSOB members circulated maps of a future Biafra Republic which encompassed five of the six Delta states. Representatives of the minorities warned Igbo nationalists not to include any Ijaw or Ibibio villages in their Biafra project, but MASSOB leader Uwazuruike insisted, at least initially, on his annexation plan: His organization is going to liberate not only the Igbo but also the coastal people.[181]

Playing with the Biafra option does not mean that Igbo politicians are working toward secession. Since the Igbo are major actors in a commercial network that stretches all over Nigeria, the dismemberment of the federation would be a disaster. Despite the inflammatory speeches against the ›religious fanatics‹ and ›killers‹ in the North, Ohanaeze leaders are interested in a joint future, though under conditions that have to be renegotiated. By proposing a looser form of (con)federation, they are offering their counterparts a deal that could profit both sides: The South would continue to transfer a part of the oil revenues to the impoverished North. In return, Igbo or Yoruba migrants would be granted the right to live there without religious harassment. Should violence against Christians escalate because politicians do not restrain their gangs, the South could suspend its cooperation, drain the Northern region financially and block the routes to the ports on the coast. However, the future will not be determined by a rational calculation of Igbo interests. MASSOB's call for secession has mobilized many young men who believe they have nothing to lose. Igbo elders try to profit from the militancy of their ›boys‹, but they also feel threatened by them: »Those of us who profess one Nigeria are in danger. The youths may eliminate us.«[182]

When Islamic politicians pushed through the Sharia legislation despite all protests, they may have acted out of equally pragmatic considerations. By threatening to allow the religious conflicts to escalate, they could push

---

181 *The News*, 17 April 2000, pp. 14–15; *Newswatch*, 29 May 2000, p. 13; *The Source*, 30 August 2004, p. 33.
182 Dr. Ezeife, in *Tell*, 11 October 2004, p. 21.

the Christian president and other politicians in the South to make compromises. However, the politicians are not the only actors in the religious
drama. The revival of political Islam has made it easier for ordinary Muslims to unite for a common cause. In the name of Allah, they can confront
all political authority, from the Christian president to their own corrupt
elite. Though the political class still has much influence on the masses,
Sharia enthusiasm has strengthened religious counter-elites who feed on
popular discontent.

Sharia as a Counter-Model to Democracy

> »Nigeria is the freest country in the world.
> You can get away with everything.«

Divine versus Human Law

Most Sharia supporters had hoped for a religious renewal that would liberate society from decades of moral and economic decay. But the Islamic upper class, now acting as the pioneer of a divine order, was no more concerned with the fate of its impoverished fellow believers than it had been before. Kano, the metropolis of the North, had a longstanding reputation as the ›capital of vices‹. The rich had made it their habit to fly to London to go shopping, while at home, before local audiences, they ranted about the decadence of the West. According to a former minister who had moved in these circles for a long time, there was no reason to take their pious assertions seriously: »Every one of these Sharia politicians is an adulterer. Why should these people fight to stone adulterers?«

The rich have always seen it as their privilege to defy the laws of the land.[1] Only the poor and weak have to endure harassment and humiliation by police officers and government employees, while those who arrive in luxury limousines, with bodyguards or police escorts, cannot be intimidated by anyone. Their wealth buys them the freedom to do what they like, without regard for the rules that apply to others. Nor were these people impressed by the new God-given laws. They saw to it that a cow thief had his right hand amputated, and they dragged some women into court to have them sentenced for adultery. But otherwise they assumed that they were safe from Sharia vigilantes behind the walls of their mansions or palaces. Everything they needed for their entertainment continued to be available, in private clubs and guest houses, in officers' messes and on the campuses of local universities. Students at Zamfara's polytechnic complained that wealthy men drove to the female students' dormitories and picked girls for their »one night shows«: »no male student in this polytech-

---

1 Achebe, *Trouble*, pp. 31–34.

nic can keep a girl friend. *Sharia* monitors are everywhere. We can't take a girl out of this campus. We will be caught. When car owners come here from Sokoto and Gusau to pick girls, the *Sharia* monitors often look the other way.«[2]

The majority of believers had no illusions about the debauchery of the ruling class. Preachers in mosques openly stated that Sharia only targeted the poor. Since the divine law was applied half-heartedly at best, disenchantment with the state-decreed Islamization grew. Governor Sani had promised his voters that the »spiritual upliftment« which leads to God, would also lead to »prosperity.«[3] Yet the state-imposed fight against immorality, against adulteresses and petty thieves, did nothing to change the fact that people continued getting poorer. This is not to say that the endeavor to Islamize state and society will flag. The Sharia campaign of corrupt politicians may be discredited, but not the idea of Sharia itself. Rather, the conviction was spreading among the faithful that in order to achieve peace and justice, the holy law had to be enforced against the hypocrisy of governors and emirs.

For radical Muslims, the attraction of Sharia lay in the fact that it authorized them to take the rulers to task. A university lecturer in Maiduguri canvassed for the new legislation with the argument: »Sharia is the rope with which these politicians will be hanged. The people will lynch them. All the big men who now recite godly phrases are the ones who have plunged this country into misery through their greed.« The great majority of the faithful lack this kind of revolutionary fervor. But many do hope that Sharia will help to keep the excesses of the rulers within tolerable bounds. The immutable law of God shall be the yardstick by which even the powerful must be judged. Thus the arrogant elite would be integrated into a moral community, in which rulers and ruled are united by a shared culture, as they had been in the mythical beginnings of Islam. A first step toward this goal is to find a common language by using the moral categories and imagery of the Koran. Thus they could initiate a process of communication between the social milieus which are otherwise drifting apart. So far, the ruling classes – shielded in their fortresses, behind concrete walls and barbed wire – have refused to assume responsibility for the plight of their subjects. The billion dollar profits from oil sales made it easy to isolate themselves from their country's fate. They could afford to let the

---

2 *Newswatch*, 17 September 2001, p. 24.

3 *Hotline*, 4 June 2000, p. 24.

economy and infrastructure deteriorate, because the oil rents continued to flow despite the general decline, guaranteeing them a life of luxury.[4]

Since Nigerians never found ways to control their ruling class, they could only hope that politicians would submit at least to the authority of God. The idea of a theocracy was regarded as an alternative to democracy; it derived its attraction from the experience that Western concepts of development had led to a dead end. For many decades Nigerians had striven to modernize themselves following European models, and the result was a disaster. Even under the new democratic system which, Western experts had praised as the way out of the crisis, the social and economic decay continued. Foreign companies withdrew from the country, as it was apparent that Nigeria was heading toward more violence.[5] During the election campaign in 1999, Obasanjo had promised that the transition to democracy would improve people's living conditions. Yet the promised ›dividend of democracy‹ did not reach the vast majority of Nigerians. What they needed most, namely work for the millions, who could not find employment in the de-industrialized cities and on the eroded, overpopulated land, was beyond the competency of a democratic government.[6]

The new democratic institutions did not even succeed in taming the highhandedness of government authorities. Just as in the times of military rule, some state governors left teachers and other civil servants for months without pay, and the citizens were unable to hold these governors accountable. The complicated web of democratic rules, with its separation of powers and reciprocal checks and balances, did not prevent politicians from looting public funds. It looked as if democratic institutions were open to all kinds of manipulations. The National Assembly, for example, made headlines because its members debated about their furniture allowances, the number of official cars and the president's private jet.[7] Or they discussed how to change the electoral laws to their advantage; and whatever they agreed upon was declared the law of the land. Against this farce, orthodox Muslims insisted that politicians were not allowed to pass this or

---

4 Herbst, *Nigeria*, pp. 158, 164.

5 According to the Economist Intelligence Unit, Nigeria ranked last in an assessment of investment risks in 60 countries (*Business Day*, 8 April 2002, p. 14).

6 No reliable figures about the unemployment rate are available. The federal government placed it at 10.8 percent in 2003, while the vice president put the rate at 50 percent (Economist Intelligence Unit, *Country Profile Nigeria 2005*, p. 29).

7 See the title story in *Africa Today*, May 2000: »Nigeria's Lawmakers: Fat Cats with Fast Cars.«

that law at their discretion: God as the sovereign had provided his people with a canon of basic laws which was beyond the politicians' scheming. Sharia reformers claimed that these divine instructions were clear and unequivocal, and that they regulated all social relations. If applied consistently, they would set all the things right that have gotten out of balance.

In conversations with Europeans, Muslims emphasized that Sharia was not just about mutilations and other cruel punishments. Much more important, so they suggested, was the fact that it completely reshaped people's everyday existence. It specified how the faithful should act in any situation of public and private life: »[Sharia] is not just about crime and punishment. This constitutes only about 10 per cent of the Sharia. Our way of life, that is, from the day you were born to the day you enter the grave is governed by Sharia. How you eat, walk, talk, [...] everything.«[8] This may be a depressing prospect for Europeans, but for many Nigerians it evoked the dream of a world which is no longer torn by strife, because everyone has found their place in an all-encompassing order. The only means to end the ruthless fight of everybody against everybody else is religious submission, the collective renunciation of sovereignty by all members of society. This submission does not necessarily mean a humiliation of the individual; after all, it turns all people into servants of God. Since society has proven incapable of balancing conflicting interests, it needs a law which is superimposed by an external force. Peace and harmony can only arise, if everyone does what has been prescribed since ancient times.

In this respect, the Islamic utopia presents itself once again as an alternative to the Western liberal concept of state. The fact that democracy does not instruct people on how to live, but encourages them to follow their own autonomous will is viewed as a deficiency. Instead of creating harmony, the game of democracy spurs strife and competition. Citizens are urged to pursue their selfish interests, instead of being reminded of their responsibility for each other. For many believers, this unleashed individualism is the inevitable result of a secular mindset that has eliminated religion from public life. By returning to the divine commandments, they want to limit that »excessive freedom« which benefits, above all, the rich and unscrupulous.[9]

Unlike Christianity, Islam offers its followers the model of a divinely sanctioned way of life. Each institution, each social obligation or transac-

---

8 The Emir of Gwandu, in *The News*, 24 April 2000, p. 18.
9 Last, *Charia*, p. 152.

tion is to be measured against the standards of the faith,[10] and these standards are set in stone: »Islam […] is universal. It is the same all over the world. And it has never changed from the beginning and will not change till the end.«[11] Sharia reformers are not traditionalists who set local Islamic customs against the corruption of the modern world. Indigenous forms of Islamic piety are not suitable as a source of religious renaissance, because they are always mixed with ›pagan‹ rites. If Muslims simply wanted to reclaim their precolonial past, they could debate openly and decide democratically which elements of tradition they want to adopt. For instance, believers who do not attach great importance to the Sharia injunctions could instead focus on the Sufi mysticism of the old, but still popular, brotherhoods. However, mystic traditions, which were inspired by Christian and Far Eastern religions and which became established in Islam as late as the eleventh century, were never entirely cleared of the suspicion of heresy. Sharia reformers who wish to transform their society according to the »model of the prophetic state«,[12] accept nothing but the holy texts (and their orthodox exegesis) as their guideline. Professor Sada, Director of the Institute for Islamic Legal Studies, which was commissioned to draft a uniform Sharia penal code, stressed the exclusive validity of the divine revelation. When asked whether his team of jurists would also draw on the penal codes of Egypt and Pakistan, where Sharia has been combined with elements of Western law, he explained that they would adhere exclusively to the »classical books of law.«[13] The only chance to avoid endless strife seems to rest in strict orthodoxy. Islamic scholars have to refer to something that is eternally valid, to a revelation that emanates directly from God so that it precedes all historical controversies among Muslims.[14] To the believer's mind, the divine instructions exist as unquestionable truths, beyond all personal opinions and interpretations. Advocates of Sharia who defended the rigorous punishments for adultery or blasphemy, sometimes told me that they merely adhered to what had been decreed: »It's not my personal view. It's not that I want to impose my view on others. We talk about a divine law.«[15]

---

10 Schacht, *Islamic Law*, p. 201.

11 Dr. Lateef Adegbite, in *Vanguard*, 24 March 2002, p. 21; Imam, *The Madinan Model*, p. 86.

12 Sanusi, *Islamisation*, p. 1; Imam, *The Madinan Model*, 77.

13 At the Sharia conference in Bayreuth, July 11–12, 2003.

14 The Koran, unlike the Bible, claims to be »literally the words of God« (Hodgson, *Islam*, p. 73).

15 A lecturer at the Department of Religious Studies, University of Jos.

From the perspective of Western Enlightenment, it is anachronistic that the laws by which people have to abide should not be based on their own free will. When Muslims claim to submit to God's law, they seem to succumb to a kind of self-mystification, as they ignore that Sharia, like any other written law, were compiled by jurists. Long after the holy texts were recorded, Muslim scholars combined individual passages in such a way that they coalesced into a comprehensive system:

»instead of taking *Shari'a* for what it is – a particular methodology for constructing a coherent system out of human understanding of divine sources in specific historical context – Muslims tend to completely identify that system with its sources. It is imperative to overcome this mistaken identification of *Shari'a* with Islam as a religion in order to realize the possibility of constructing an alternative system out of human understandings of Islamic sources in modern context.«[16]

Nigeria's Muslims, however, have little interest in demystifying divine law in the vein of Western Bible philology. The refusal to identify Sharia as a human creation is hard to comprehend for Europeans who are used to subjecting holy texts to a historical-critical analysis. Yet the recourse to a self-contained system of immutable laws is not as irrational as Western critics suggest. Seen as a direct expression of divine will, Sharia has the advantage of being exempt from human strife and manipulation. Human authority is not to be trusted. No legitimate law can emerge from the disputes of senators and congressmen who fight each other over money and political influence. The power to pass laws should be taken from humans and placed into God's hand: »government [...] laws are subject to changes, Islamic Laws are constant and not flexible to the wishes of the people.«[17]

---

16 Elnaiem, *Human Rights*, p. 6. – From this perspective, advocates of »Classical Sharia« (Abubakar D. Muhammad, *Muslim Responses*, p. 6) commit a grave mistake. What they are dealing with when reading the ancient law books, is a product of legal science, *fiqh*, but they take it to be the divine message itself, *sharia*, and they confuse the society of the Prophet with the stories told about it.

17 *Hotline*, 12 March 2000, p. 29. – Some Sharia advocates, like Prof. Sada (*Commentary*, p. 176) explicitly reject ›democracy‹, but political controversies do not revolve around this term. As the polls by Afrobarometer indicate, a majority of Muslims are in favor of some vaguely defined democracy. Nevertheless, reservations about individual autonomy and civil rights are clearly expressed. They are motivated not only by religious considerations, but also by a sense of hierarchy that is more developed among Hausa and Fulani than among the Igbo and other Southerners: »Egalitarianism and equality – the normative founts on which democratic, electoral politics is constructed – lack conceptual as well as linguistic currency in Hausaland« (Miles, *Elections*, p. 74). As a Hausa villager put it: »[In Democracy] men wander around like cattle, without any

While human players, who pursue their particular interests, use the instruments of the state to prevail against their competitors, God knows no enemies against whom he would have to defend himself. He does not need to take sides, but has everyone's welfare at heart: »Shari'a has come from God and is, therefore, not a product of selfish human interest, whether class, sectional or individual.«[18]

In times when institutions crumble, sacred texts that promise orientation become precious.[19] The faithful do not have to engage in political debates to find rules on which a just order can be built. Such rules were given long ago; they just need to be acknowledged and applied diligently. As in the early days of Islam, God's revelation can turn into a social force that transforms the world: »Soon after the founding of the faith, Muslims succeeded in building a new form of society, which in time carried with it its own distinctive institutions, its art and literature, its science and scholarship, its political and social forms, as well as its cult and creed, all bearing an unmistakable Islamic impress.«[20] However, Sharia can only prove its ability to transform the ruling structures, if it is not subject to the manipulations of politicians. As long as certain interest groups arbitrarily determine which rules shall and which shall not apply, they abuse the divine law for profane purposes. In this case, sovereignty is not with God, but with those who choose from among the divine rules what suits their interests. The danger of abuse can only be averted by insisting on a »total« and »uncompromising« application of Sharia.[21] For that reason, religious orthodoxy is attractive not only for legal scholars, but also for the mass of believers. In their effort to limit the lawlessness of the ruling class, it becomes important to defend pure Sharia against all attempts to adulterate it: »Shari'a [...] is a revealed law from the Almighty God and nobody can reduce it to suit his own whims.«[22]

---

direction. [...] Each goes his own way, lost, until there's no more herd« (quoted in Miles, *Elections*, p. 75).

18 Gumi, *Where I stand*, p. 79.

19 Ludwig, *Religion und Politik*, p. 12.

20 Hodgson, *Islam*, p. 71.

21 Yadudu, *Benefits of Shariah*, p. 2; Mohammed, *Muslim Intellectuals*, p. 8. – Prof. Yadudu was legal advisor to General Abacha.

22 Ado-Kurawa, *Shari'ah*, p. 306.

The Failure of Democracy

> »If God does not punish Nigeria in future,
> then He (God) certainly owes the people
> of Sodom and Gomorrah an apology.«[23]

During the transition to democracy, citizens hoped, above all, that their economic well-being would improve. A democratically renewed Nigeria, they had been told, would attract foreign donors and investors. But international companies, which had shut down their branches during military rule, dared not risk investing in Lagos or Kano a second time. Why should they build new production plants when the existing ones only ran at half capacity?[24] Apart from crude oil, Nigeria offered nothing of interest to large corporations. During his state visits abroad, President Obasanjo solicited direct investments, and his administration indeed created more favorable conditions for investors. Exchange restrictions were lifted, some import tariffs were lowered, and the government's monopoly on telecommunication and on the energy sector was eased. In other respects, however, Nigeria's Fourth Republic confirmed the experiences of other African states that a democratic regime can be as dysfunctional for economic development as an authoritarian one.[25] Managers of German companies reported that it had become more expensive to obtain government contracts or to get spare parts through the customs, because the circle of politicians and civil servants who demanded bribes had grown: »When dealing with military officers, the rules were straightforward. [...] Today all kinds of local politicians interfere: people who are completely out of control.«

The failure to curb corruption was often blamed on the president's weakness. Personal shortcomings, however, are not the source of the current crisis; the deciding factor is the failure of the democratic system and its representatives. Nigeria's elites make a living by plundering public resources. Each attempt to establish the rule of the law is a direct attack on their existence. Alongside this class of government profiteers, there has never evolved a stratum of independent businessmen with an interest in a transparent public administration. And there are few other interest groups that would support a reform of the state bureaucracy. The president met

23 Rev. (Dr.) James Ukaegbu, in *Champion*, 23 December 1996.
24 Economist Intelligence Unit, *Country Profile Nigeria 2005*, p. 37.
25 Herbst, *Nigeria*, p. 164.

central demands of the trade unions, when he drastically raised the salaries of civil servants. This was a prerequisite for any attempt to create a more efficient and less corrupt administration. By the end of the Abacha regime, police officers were earning less than 10 dollars a month, and the basic monthly salary for teachers had been less than 20 dollars. Two years later, incomes had increased almost tenfold. But when Obasanjo set out to privatize the ailing state enterprises and to streamline the inflated state bureaucracy, the Nigerian Labour Congress stood up against the government.[26]

It is unlikely that the fight against corruption would have yielded better results with a new generation of politicians and a reformed, more federal constitution. Muslim critics had good reason to question the whole ›democratic‹ system and look for alternatives. They were understandably bitter about the arrogance of Western critics who did not acknowledge any other ideas of law and morality apart from their own. Western governments and aid organizations tried to push Nigeria, by means of financial incentives and political pressure, to copy European models of development, as if the standard formula of human rights, multi-party elections and free market economy were suited for all societies: »It was readily assumed that where states evidently did not ›work‹, this was because they had failed to adopt the formula that had worked so well elsewhere.«[27]

For Muslims who fought the secular political order, there was no fundamental difference between the current civilian regime and its military predecessors: »Successive governments have failed the nation because the rulers have continued to wield power without the fear of God.«[28] Nigeria's politicians could not be held accountable, not even by democratic institutions, so there was nothing but the hope that God's authority would force them to assume responsibility for the people. The holy law, which is above political factionalism, is concerned with the well-being of all, while democracy, as a system of human self-determination, elevates self-interest to the status of a guiding principle. Democracy does not prescribe how a just order should evolve; it merely provides a set of formal rules to organize the competition for power. Yet Nigeria's politicians do not adhere to the rules, and there is no *demos* that could force them to. Citizens do not articulate common interests, but line up behind ethnic and religious leaders. Given

26 Economist Intelligence Unit, *Country Report Nigeria 2004*, pp. 7, 22–23.
27 Clapham, *Challenge*, p. 789.
28 Dr. Lateef Adegbite, in *Tell*, 21 October 2002, p. 71.

these deep divisions of ›civil society‹, politicians do not have to bow to any public interest or to the will of the people. They can decide among themselves, in a game of intrigues and shifting alliances, on how positions are shared: »Democracy in Nigeria is still very much about the struggle among the competing elite over who gets what.«[29] Soon after the transition to democracy, it was obvious that the newly created democratic institutions were as corrupt as other parts of the state apparatus. In both chambers of the National Assembly, members knew that they could disrupt government business, and they had no qualms about using this power to extort money: »Pushing reforms through Nigeria's parliament is like trying to roll a meatball through a cage of hyenas.«[30] It is said that even in the case of the anti-corruption law, the delegates had to be bribed before they passed the bill.[31] Incidentally, the law had little effect, because parliament watered it down two years later, overriding the president's veto.[32]

Personal greed alone does not explain why so many representatives of the people line their pockets. They have financial obligations, not only toward their own clients, but toward the powerful ›godfathers‹ who sponsored their careers. For a seat in parliament or a governor's office, the contenders had to invest a lot. The decision on who got which mandate or post was usually made in negotiations within the ruling party. The PDP convention, which nominated the presidential candidate, was reminiscent of a bazaar, with thousands of delegates offering their votes for sale. The primaries for the Senate and the House of Representatives left a similar impression: »It was cash-and-carry, and victory went to the highest bidder.«[33] Thus public offices turned into a benefice which had to pay off. As a local party leader explained: »Those who are in politics to make money […] must win elections by all means.«[34] The party official then added that he had had to take two of his private cars to a money lender in order to finance his election campaign. Often enough it was not their own possessions that candidates invested. Becoming a senator or governor was so expensive that aspirants turned to local power brokers, asking them to support their election. In return they promised their sponsors that they

---

29 *West Africa*, 16 September 2002, p. 8.
30 *Economist*, 6 April 2002, p. 39; Economist Intelligence Unit, *Country Report Nigeria 2005*, p. 18.
31 Bergstresser, *Zweite Wahl*, p. 47.
32 *Tell*, 26 May 2003, pp. 19–23.
33 *New African*, March 2003, p. 18.
34 *The News*, 27 March 2000, p. 30.

would supply them with government contracts or make monthly payments to them from the state account. The Governor of Anambra spoke openly about a written contract in which he had granted one of his sponsors the right to appoint two commissioners in the future cabinet, one for finance, the other for public works.[35]

It will hardly be possible to stop the trafficking in public offices. The rich and powerful cannot be kept from investing in politics, because there are few other investment opportunities. Oil rents are the main source of wealth, and the most direct access to it leads through government agencies. A newspaper report covering the 2003 election campaign in Southeast Nigeria stated that »almost every rich man in Igboland is involved in politics.«[36] The permeation of state power and economic power explains why the players fight so bitterly to oust each other from public offices: »power is overpriced in Nigeria so that the contest for it becomes a matter of life and death.«[37] There is simply too much at stake. A businessman who loses political influence must fear economic ruin as well. This is why it looks too risky, even under democratic institutions, to allow one's rivals to take over state power. »people [...] think that they can only make a living being in government and that if they are not in government, that government must not survive.«[38]

While senators and congressmen in remote Abuja can easily evade public control, one should expect democratic control mechanisms to work better at the local level. The federal provisions of the constitution, which transfer substantial powers to the state parliaments and local government councils, bring state decisions closer to the people. Observers, however, have the impression that corruption is just as prevalent here as it is at the federal level.[39] Take the example of Orji Kalu, the Governor of Abia, who claimed that he was richer than the entire state he ruled.[40] According to a report by the Economic and Financial Crimes Commission, Kalu embezzled one-third of all the money that flowed from the federation account into the state coffers.[41] Yet he blamed the poverty of his people

---

35 *Newswatch*, 14 May 2001, pp. 32–33.
36 *Tell*, 10 March 2003, p. 22.
37 Ake, *Democratic Agenda*, p. 34; cf. Hauck, *Konsolidierungschancen*, p. 193.
38 Yohana Madaki, a retired colonel and human rights lawyer, in *Tell*, 25 September 2000, p. 24.
39 *Tell*, 17 December 2001, p. 36 and 20 October 2003, p. 23.
40 *Tell*, 19 February 2001, p. 20.
41 *Tell*, 15 May 2006, p. 20.

on the Yoruba president who spurned the rights of the »Igbo race.«[42] Kalu's chauvinistic rhetoric made him a »folk hero«, particularly for the younger generation.[43] Thus he immunized himself against attacks from the capital. Federal authorities could not risk suing him for embezzlement of public funds. What happened in Abia was viewed as the internal affair of the Igbo, and the intervention by a Yoruba president would not be welcome. Yet Obasanjo had a further reason not to take on Orji Kalu and other PDP governors. He needed their support in order to prevail against his challenger Buhari in the 2003 presidential election. Elections are rigged and won at the local level. Only those who can win over the most powerful and unscrupulous elements in as many states as possible, will prevail in a democratic contest. At the end of his second term, when Obasanjo had consolidated his power, he instituted a more aggressive anti-corruption policy. By late 2006, the Economic and Financial Crimes Commission investigated more than 2,000 cases and had secured 88 convictions. As under former regimes, the purge was selective, »targeting expendable politicians or political rivals.«[44] However, Obasanjo took care not to provoke the Hausa-Fulani elite. His main aim was apparently to intimidate recalcitrant PDP governors into endorsing his hand-picked successor, Umaru Yar'adua.

Democracy seems to be just another way of incapacitating people. But the people are not merely cheated of their rights; they participate actively in destroying democratic institutions. Instead of forcing their leaders to comply with the laws, they encourage them to appropriate as much public money as possible. A minister or senator who comes home empty-handed is regarded as a loser, or worse: He will be suspected of feigning righteousness in order to dodge sharing his booty with his relatives. Since almost everyone tries to profit from corruption and nepotism, it is difficult to find a common platform from which the crimes of the ruling class could be criticized.[45] Ordinary citizens expressed outrage at Sani Abacha who embezzled billions of dollars for himself and his followers, but the general

---

42 *The Week*, 19 May 2003, p. 36; *Tell*, 5 February 2001, p. 24.

43 After eight years in office, his reputation had suffered. However, Ohanaeze (or one of its factions) endorsed him as the Igbo candidate for the 2007 presidential election. This gives a vivid idea about the contribution of ethnic self-determination groups to democracy.

44 Economist Intelligence Unit, *Country Profile Nigeria 2007*, p. 8 and *Country Report Nigeria 2006*, p. 21.

45 Daniel Jordan Smith, *Culture of Corruption*, p. 193.

was simply doing on a large scale what almost every Igbo or Yoruba expected of their own leaders:

»we, the ordinary people, will expect the man at the top to be corrupt and if the man is not corrupt, we say that the man has no senses. [...] if I'm standing for re-election [as governor – J.H.] and I come to you, you will expect me to give you money. From where do you think I'll get that money? [...] if you watch the society from top to ground floor every segment is corrupt! Every Nigerian who is a small man will tell you those at the top are corrupt. Put him in a position, any small position you will find him corrupt! [...] if you are in a position to take N[aira] 1 000, you will take! If you put him in a position to take a million, he will take.«[46]

Even in the villages and local government areas, people do not succeed in using the institutions of democracy to hold the ruling class accountable. The inability to organize themselves independently of their own corrupt leaders is closely linked to the predominant mode of social relations, namely clientelism. The poor, though they are numerically dominant, do not form a class which would pursue collective interests. They are not common victims of an aristocracy that would extract tribute, nor are they, but for a few exceptions, factory workers who might fight collectively against exploitation. The vast majority, who work as hoe cultivators or who seek odd jobs in the informal sector, eke out a living on their own. Without the support of relatives or other benefactors, who have become rich through government jobs or drug trafficking, many would not be able to maintain their livelihood. The villas of the rich are beleaguered by suppli-cants who beg for jobs, small benefits, or protection from enemies. Despite the resentment of the arrogant rich, it would be disastrous to stand up against those one needs. The poor do not demand collective rights but display servility and ask for individual favors. In competition with all the other poor, they make every effort to find influential sponsors who tie them to a network of patronage that provides a little security. For everyone knows that in a situation of distress, the solidarity of the poor will be less helpful than the generosity of the rich. The predominance of personal dependencies is one of the main reasons why no democratic culture has evolved: »horizontal networks of (more or less egalitarian) civic engage-ment and social exchange are largely absent or superficial, and social life is organized vertically into pyramids of patron-client relations, with material rewards flowing from the top down and support from the bottom up.«[47]

---

46 Achike Udenwa, Governor of Imo State, in *Tell*, 25 March 2002, p. 35.
47 Diamond, *Nigeria*, p. 418; Chabal/Daloz, *Africa Works*, pp. 20, 30.

There is not much chance that the poor and disenfranchised among the Igbo, Hausa and Kanuri will unite to stop their elites from looting public funds. Realism dictates that one should fight for one's immediate interests and support one's leaders, because a part of their stolen wealth will trickle down to the poor who gather loyally around them. Since all have to secure a share of the loot, they do not pay much attention to the moral qualities of their leaders. Ibrahim Babangida, the former president, referred to himself as an »evil genius.«[48] And the Igbo leader Ojukwu professed: »In politics, if you are feared, you will get everything.«[49] Right and wrong, good and evil have been hopelessly muddled, so the pious wrath of the Muslims is understandable. Sharia supporters are not the only people who are disgusted with the »collapse of moral values«[50], their Christian opponents also lament that society is »traumatized and sick.«[51] A just political order cannot evolve from a brutalized society. Both Christians and Muslims agree that a moral renewal must emerge from an external source, which is not contaminated by the general social decay. Only divine revelation, which exists independently of the corrupt present, has retained the idea of a better life. To pursue this idea, people have to disentangle themselves from a morally bankrupt world. Christians convey this demand for a break with a sinful life often as radically as Muslims, though in a different language: »every Nigerian right now is dangling on the edge of the valley of evil.« »we are the problem ourselves. The problem [...] is ingrained in us, and to resolve it will require a complete crushing [...] of our personality.«[52]

Politically active Christians may denounce the depravity of the ruling class with the radical zeal of Old Testament prophets, but they cannot offer a way out of the crisis apart from appealing to the integrity of every individual who must be willing to start a new life by being born again.[53] Unlike Muslims, Christians do not have a political vision with which to confront the present system. They lack a common goal that could inspire and motivate believers; this could be one of the reasons why they are losing ground to their Islamic rivals. In their disputes with Muslims, Christian churches find themselves in the thankless role of defending the irreligious political order. The Head of the Catholic Bishop's Conference argued for a

---

48 *Tell*, 24 July 1995, front page.
49 *Tell*, 18 September 2000, p. 30.
50 Abubakar D. Muhammad, *Muslim Responses*, p. 7.
51 Kalu, *Religious Dimension*, p. 671.
52 *Guardian*, 5 May 1996; *Tempo*, 5 December 1996.
53 Meyer, *Break with the Past*, p. 329; Ojo, *Pentecostal Movements*, p. 176.

strict separation of state and church: »When you are in a position of trust, forget about your religion because it is a private affair between you and your God. If you want to bring religion in, let it be after office hours.«[54] The churches fight for the existing secular institutions and thus for a European system of state order which is in decline. Only in a few cases do church leaders speak out against Western models: »›democracy‹ has failed. [...] I am not talking about just Nigeria, but the whole world. It has to fail because it is not God's arrangement. [...] democracy is the devil's alternative to God's kingdom.«[55] The kingdom of the Christian God, however, is not of this world, and Christian critics of democracy cannot develop an alternative that would be based on the message of Jesus.

Islam not only articulates the discontent with the economic and moral decline, it also promises to renew the political system. It provides the only political vision that can transform individual despair into a collective force and direct it toward a common goal. Thus it is unlikely that the faithful will turn away from Islam's political promises. Where else should they find a way out of their plight? Many Muslims who supported left-leaning populist parties, like the Northern Elements Progressive Union and the People's Redemption Party, are drawn to Sharia today.[56] The camp of the ›progressives‹ has discredited itself, at the latest under the rule of Sani Abacha. Shortly after the annulled elections in 1993, when the general staged a coup, some prominent Third-World-Marxists and human rights activists joined his cabinet to serve the military regime: »Abacha had used them to stabilise his government and has now thrown them into the dustbin of history.«[57] Today, socialist ideas play hardly a role in public debates. And what left-wing academics proposed to challenge the Obasanjo administration seemed strangely out of touch with reality: »We could have nationalized foreign-owned companies, stopped the exports of agricultural products, and put an end to the imports of manufactured goods from Europe and America.«[58] Not a word about foreign companies that were Africanized as early as the 1970s, when the government took over the majority stake of Shell, Peugeot and other corporations. Today the problem at hand is rather one of privatizing state-owned companies that have never been

---

54 Archbishop Okogie, in Kukah, *Religion*, p. 228.
55 Pastor John Ekong, in *The Week*, 15 April 2002, p. 32.
56 Sanusi, *Shari'a Debate*, p. 11.
57 *Tell*, 28 October 1996, p. 11.
58 Babalola, *Democracy*, p. 886.

profitable. For the Ajaokuta steel plant, which frittered away almost five billion dollars without producing a single ton of steel, it was difficult to find a buyer willing to invest.[59] The idea to stop food exports is equally absurd, since Nigeria has long since become a net importer of food.

A New Era of Justice

Islam, unlike Christianity, presents itself as a religion of law and order. Pilgrims returning from Saudi Arabia report that, thanks to the draconian punishments, the cities are completely safe. Public executions and lashings act as a deterrent and are thus an attractive aspect of Islamic law. Another advantage of Sharia, according to its proponents, is its clarity. Right and wrong are well-defined, comprehensible to all believers regardless of their level of education. While Sharia emphasizes the material aspect of the law, its European counterpart attaches much importance to complicated rules of litigation. The priority of procedural rationality is intended to give protection against arbitrary decisions, but secular courts in Nigeria, based on English common law, do not work predictably. Court cases often drag on for years, only to end in arbitrary judgments because the crucial agreements are made behind the scenes. Even within the courtrooms it remains obscure to the uninitiated observer, how the truth is established. Dismissing an action or ruling in favor of the accused, despite strong evidence, already undermined the reputation of the colonial jurisdiction. People were stunned when defendants were released, only because the judges had to observe rules that are often referred to, in Nigerian parlance, as ›technicalities‹ or ›legal niceties‹.

Another feature of the European legal system that does not make sense to most Nigerians, is the separation of judicial and executive powers. It is meant to safeguard citizens against infringements by the authorities. In Nigeria, however, the two branches of the state apparatus do not control, but obstruct each other. Police officers often refuse to hand over suspects to the courts, because they do not trust the judges. Again and again, they had to watch how criminal proceedings were closed upon payment of ›bail‹, i.e. bribes. Or they noticed that trials were not held because prosecutors had ›misplaced‹ the files. Police officers are therefore tempted to

---

59 Economist Intelligence Unit, *Country Profile Nigeria 2005*, p. 37.

pre-empt court officials and extort bribes themselves. In order to supplement their modest salaries, they arrest citizens, often under some pretext, and keep them like hostages, until they are ›bailed out‹. Another way of dealing with real or alleged criminals is to execute them without a trial: »Robbers kill innocent people. What is wrong with police killing them? It saves ou[r] time.«[60] According to a report by a government commission, illegal executions took place in all parts of the country.[61] Years ago, 400 bodies were discovered near a hospital in Lagos, apparently brought there from police cells.[62]

Police officers routinely explain that those executed were armed robbers – which is probably true in most cases. But it is no secret that normally police and criminals work closely together: »out of ten robberies in Lagos, seven are believed to be carried out either by soldiers and policemen or their relations living in the barracks.«[63] State power often appears like an evil, uncontrollable force. It is strange, therefore, that Nigerians continue to resort to the police to solve their disputes.[64] Why do they file charges and pursue lawsuits? Of course they cannot expect justice from either the police or the court system. Their aim is, rather, to turn the avarice and viciousness of the authorities against their enemies. Clients who want an adversary arrested, contact some police officers and, if a price is agreed, leave the victim's name and address. That person will then be detained, often on flimsy charges, until some relatives are notified, and ransom is paid. The game of having people arrested and bailed out is unpredictable, though. Thousands of detainees were not released but incarcerated for years without trial. According to a government commission which visited the overcrowded prisons, two-thirds of the inmates were never legally convicted. Some inmates sat in their cells for ten years without ever seeing a judge.[65] If they were brought to trial, they could not expect justice either. Money comes into play in many trials, and if the sums are substantial, judges may pronounce prison sentences against

---

60 A police officer, in *Newswatch*, 3 April 1995, p. 21.

61 *Guardian*, 17 March 2001; Human Rights Watch, *Political Shari'a?*, p. 6.

62 Civil Liberties Organisation, *Above the Law*, p. 34. – For police murders after the end of military rule, see *Tell*, 1 October 2001, pp. 24–32: »No End to the Bloodlust.«

63 *Tell*, 25 March 2002, p. 30.

64 Some German companies operating in Nigeria advised their employees not to turn to the police, if they were assaulted or robbed.

65 *Guardian*, 31 January 1995 and 12 February 1996; *Tell*, 5 January 2004, p. 46 and 11 October 2004, pp. 30–31; Human Rights Watch, *Political Shari'a?*, p. 6.

defendants who are obviously innocent.[66] Justice for sale favors the well-to-do. They can have their opponents put in prison over land disputes or personal feuds.

Since European forms of jurisdiction do not effect justice, it is not hard to dismiss them. Vigilantes such as the Bakassi Boys, who fought criminals far more effectively than the police, did not maintain the façade of proper legal proceedings. They investigated the truth in their interrogation cells, without public trials. Together with the rules of due process, they dismissed the principle that executive and judicial powers should be separated. Vigilante members who arrested and interrogated suspects also sentenced and executed them. In Anambra State alone, in the heart of Christian Nigeria, the Bakassi Boys are said to have killed more than 2000 citizens between April 2000 and January 2002.[67] In the marketplace of Onitsha (which I visited several times) public executions could be witnessed almost every week, staged more cruelly than the *hudud* punishments of Islamic law. The Bakassi fighters threw their tied victims to the ground and hacked at them with their dull machetes for minutes on end, poured gasoline over their mutilated bodies and set them on fire while some of them were still alive. Among the people who pushed and shoved to watch the gruesome scenes, I could not find anyone who expressed irritation or disgust. Even the governor, who supported the vigilante group with tax money, did not distance himself from the appalling executions. He maintained that critics had no right to condemn the Bakassi methods as long as they could not offer convincing alternatives. »You don't need to bother about what the human rights people, civil rights people and the lawyers say. [W]hen we were crying that armed robbers were killing us, innocent people, nobody did anything. [...] If you catch a confirmed armed robber and you kill him and the human rights [!] are shouting, is it fair?«[68] Western ideas of law are so thoroughly discredited that the majority of citizens view them as an obstacle in their quest for justice.

The Igbo, who more than other Nigerians appreciate Western ways of life, find it difficult to openly break with ›modern‹ ideas of law. No Igbo politician of repute has suggested a revival of precolonial traditions of jurisdiction. Although most push for severe punishments for robbers, they

---

66 Civil Liberties Organisation, *Justice for Sale*, pp. 120, 136–139.
67 Estimates by the Civil Liberties Organisation, in Amnesty International, *Vigilante Violence*, p. 9.
68 *Newswatch*, 18 September 2000, p. 14.

fear that the spread of »jungle justice«[69] will lead into a world of archaic violence. Islam, in contrast, makes it easy for citizens in the North to advocate torturous punishments. It offers a respectable, internationally recognized discourse, which its followers can use to express their resentment of the Western human rights culture. Insisting on the controversial *hudud* punishments thus had a highly symbolic meaning. It demonstrated that Muslims proudly turned their back on self-professed moral experts in the West who, with an almost colonial sense of mission, denounced other views of justice as barbaric. When the government of Zamfara proclaimed an uncensored form of Sharia, the occasion was celebrated as a joyous act of state. Governor Sani had previously received delegates from Saudi Arabia and Sudan, who had assured him of their support in implementing Sharia.[70] When the first amputation took place on March 22, 2000, the picture of the amputee with his mutilated and bandaged arm was offered for sale at all big markets. In the congress hall of Gusau, the amputation could be watched as a video clip, and the state's chief judge was so moved while watching it that he had tears in his eyes.[71] It is bewildering for Europeans that state-authorized torture is not only tolerated, but publicly staged and sanctified. They tend to forget that the »shame in punishing«[72] is a late achievement of European history. Even after the Enlightenment, the »desire for cruelty« was still so natural »that princely weddings or festivals on a grand scale were unimaginable without executions, torture or an auto-da-fé.«[73]

In a country that is plagued by violence it sounded appealing when the administration of Zamfara promised its citizens »instant justice.«[74] Litigants who turned to a Sharia court were often heard on the same day and received their judgment immediately after the trial. Since no importance was attached to written documents and time-consuming application procedures, the parties involved could present their cases themselves, without costly attorneys. The advantages of this instant justice were so obvious that even Christians were inclined to make use of it. Some Igbo merchants dragged their Muslim debtors to Sharia courts, because that was the easiest

---

69 *Newswatch*, 29 March 1999, p. 17.
70 Further offers of help came from Libya, Iran and Malaysia (Freedom House, *Talibanization*, pp. 5, 17, 24–25).
71 *Tell*, 1 May 2000, pp. 25–27.
72 Foucault, *Discipline and Punish*, p. 10.
73 Nietzsche, *Genealogie der Moral*, pp. 215, 214.
74 *Hotline*, 4 June 2000, p. 24.

way to collect their debts.[75] Even Nigeria's Justice Minister, who rejected the Sharia laws as unconstitutional, admitted that they offered an effective dispensation of justice: »if a man owes you money, you can get paid in the evening. Whereas in the regular courts, you can sit in court for ten years and get no justice.«[76] In principle, Sharia courts are bound to the same laws of procedure as the secular courts, because the procedural laws fall into the legislative competence of the federation, not the states. But Islamic judges often ignore them as they do not fit into the Sharia system.[77] In order to rid themselves of the burden of foreign law concepts, Muslims plead for a pure and simple form of Sharia which is sometimes imagined as a continuation of African traditions: »We have to go back to the roots where elders sit down under the tree and settle disputes and throw away technical rules of the whiteman sense of judgement. It is an entirely different system from ours.«[78]

Sharia judges, who used to handle only matters of personal law and who are now assigned to criminal cases, have not been trained in Nigerian procedural law. In order to become judges they did not have to complete a law course or take exams; the requirement for their employment was merely to be competent in Islamic law.[79] This is another reason why many refuse to adhere to formalities which are foreign to Islamic tradition. Sharia does not know many of the distinctions which European law applies to evaluate the intention of a perpetrator and the extent of his guilt: »The concepts of guilt and criminal responsibility are little developed, that of mitigating circumstances does not exist; any theory of attempt, of complicity, of concurrence is lacking.«[80] From a European point of view, the law of evidence is particularly problematic. In criminal trials, only two sorts of evidence are admitted: the testimony of at least two eyewitnesses or the perpetrator's confession. Only the Maliki school permits judgments based on circumstantial evidence, but just for two closely defined offenses: If an unmarried woman (or a woman who has been widowed or divorced for some time) gets pregnant, she cannot deny having had unlawful sexual

---

75 Ahmad, *Scharia*; Gaiya, *Shari'ah Debate*, p. 5; Last, *Charia*, p. 150.

76 Kanu Agabi, in *Economist*, 7 September 2002, p. 46.

77 For instance, »the testimony of women and non-Muslims usually was accorded less weight in Shari'a courts« (U.S. Department of State, *Nigeria 2006*, p. 8).

78 Ibrahim Buba, a Fulani attorney, in *The Week*, 19 November 2001, p. 15.

79 Even at the Sharia appeal courts, judges who had no university degree in Islamic law were appointed (Abun-Nasr, *Islamisches Recht*, pp. 218–220).

80 Schacht, *Islamic Law*, p. 187.

intercourse. And if a person smells strongly of alcohol, it is sufficient proof that he or she has been drinking. When it comes to other offences, the conviction of a defendant is more difficult. In cases of burglary or theft, there will often be no sufficiently qualified witnesses (i.e. witnesses who are male and Muslim and who have a spotless reputation). They are required to have observed the crime with their own eyes and to make identical statements at court.[81] Given these difficulties in securing a conviction, the perpetrators' confessions play an important role, which may tempt the authorities into obtaining them by force.[82] Nigeria's Sharia courts have acknowledged forced confessions as sufficient basis for a verdict. Researchers of Human Rights Watch were able to speak to 26 prisoners who had been sentenced to amputation of limbs and who were waiting for the execution of their punishment: »None of the defendants had legal representation in the lower or upper Shari'a courts which sentenced them. The majority of the defendants had had their statements extracted under torture.«[83] According to Islamic law, a convict can revoke his confession until the moment the punishment is executed. However, in doing so he risks, at least under Nigerian conditions, that he will be taken back to his cell and once more subjected to intense interrogations.[84]

Islamic jurisdiction provides little protection against unfair judgments. During colonial times, in 1933, Sharia courts were subordinated to the supervision of a British appellate court, the High Court in Kaduna. And in independent Nigeria, all constitutions since 1979 stipulated that the Sharia court system is not autonomous. Any decision of the highest Islamic courts, the Sharia Courts of Appeal in Kano, Sokoto, Zamfara and other states of the North, can be overruled by the Supreme Court, if one of the affected parties files a claim against it. This is one of the reasons why adulteresses have thus far not been stoned, though Sharia Courts of Appeal confirmed the death sentences. Muslims have long pushed for amending the constitution to ensure that Sharia judges are no longer subordinate to the Supreme Court, which is obliged to uphold Nigeria's West-

---

81 Peters, *Islamic Criminal Law*, pp. 3–4, 36; Schacht, *Islamic Law*, pp. 18–19, 193–194. – As an alternative to the two male witnesses, one man and two women are also accepted as witnesses.

82 Last, *Charia*, p. 151.

83 Human Rights Watch, *Political Shari'a?*, p. 41; cf. Finkel, *Crime*, p. 5.

84 Nigeria's police stations are known for »routinely« using torture (Civil Liberties Organisation, *Above the Law*, p. 22; Human Rights Watch, *Political Shari'a?*, pp. 3, 6). Forced confessions are therefore not a specifically Muslim problem.

ern-style constitution. Should the Islamic jurisdiction be withdrawn from secular control, it is difficult to predict whether it would develop its own control mechanisms. In the classic doctrine of Sharia, appellate courts were not envisaged: »there is no means of reversing an unjust judgment, because strict Islamic law does not recognize stages of appeal.«[85] Whoever felt treated unjustly could try to get the emir or a superior judge to take on the case and revoke the judgment. However, there was no right to a hearing. Like in precolonial times, today's judges strive to decide legal disputes irrevocably and to have the verdict executed on the spot. In the case of a thief in Gusau who was lashed and imprisoned for six months, instant justice meant that the crime, the arrest, the trial and the commencement of the punishment all occurred on the same day.[86] Since Sharia judges are used to ruling with a wide discretion, they have no interest in strengthening appeal mechanisms.[87] How arbitrarily judges can decide, is illustrated by a journalist who witnessed a number of trials in Katsina State, among them the case of a Hausa woman who wanted to divorce her husband:

»We don't talk, she says [...]. He doesn't eat what I cook, she goes on, and we haven't had sex in weeks. – I have two wives, the man answers, in his defense. – And maybe the judge notices how distraught the woman is when she says in a voice that sounds beaten down, ›I don't want to be married to him any longer‹, but what he's paying attention to is the sight of a man on bended knee, beseeching his wife not to divorce him. ›He loves you very much‹, the judge says. – ›God forgives this man on one knee. You must, too‹, adds one of the scholars. – Divorce denied. Next case.«[88]

The local Sharia courts that are now authorized to pass death sentences have long been notorious for their high-handedness. The extent of their abuse of office, according to a lawyer in Kano, is »unimaginable«: »They are the worst courts. Ninety percent of the area judges, if you were to apply the Sharia rules that witnesses must be upstanding citizens, would not even be competent to testify.«[89] With the introduction of a strict form of Sharia,

85 Schacht, *Islamic Law*, p. 189; Abun-Nasr, *Islamisches Recht*, p. 212.

86 Peters, *Islamic Criminal Law*, p. 60. – A sixteen-year old girl who became pregnant out of wedlock received a punishment of 100 lashes shortly after giving birth, although an appeal procedure was pending (Freedom House, *Talibanization*, pp. 22–23).

87 »[T]he appellate procedure is alien to Maliki law and resented as an intrusion by the Alkalis« (Sklar, *Political Parties*, p. 358).

88 Finkel, *Crime*, p. 3.

89 Dr. Kumo, in Maier, *This House*, p. 178; cf. Last, *Charia*, p. 149.

these courts were expected to give birth to a »new era of justice.«[90] There was a strong moral pressure on the judges to prove that they took their religious office seriously, and this pressure probably brought some improvements. In a time of religious fervor, when it is easy for militant preachers to mobilize large crowds, it can be dangerous for Sharia judges to defy basic rules of justice. But as soon as the religious enthusiasm abates, judicial authorities can easily evade public control, because Islamic law knows no institutions which check the dispensation of justice. It simply speaks of the judge's obligation to decide fairly and without bias. The prophet never tolerated corruption, as a Sharia supporter told me: When a female thief, to escape her just punishment, turned to one of Mohammed's daughters, asking her to speak on the thief's behalf, the prophet was incensed and reproached his own daughter.[91] Inspired by such models of religious righteousness, many believers dream of a God-fearing world in which the powerful tremble before the Sharia judges.[92] But in the past, the *alkalis* did not act as advocates of the disenfranchised masses; they were rather part of the corrupt upper class. Traditionally they were appointed by the emirs, and they often had personal relations to the aristocratic families, say, through marriage alliances.[93]

There is a further reason why the introduction of full Sharia will probably fail to curb judicial lawlessness. Islamic law gives the judges wide latitude to determine punishments. It prescribes specific punishments only for theft, fornication and a few other *hudud* offenses. In all other cases the Sharia Penal Code specifies a maximum penalty, but leaves it to the judges to choose an appropriate punishment. Some convicts may get away with a mere admonition, while others receive prison sentences, lashes or fines.[94] Furthermore, the judges are authorized to punish at their own discretion any conduct that they consider prohibited by the holy scriptures, even if it is not mentioned in the Sharia Penal Code.[95] As long as Sharia judges only handled private disputes, from 1960 to 2000, they could not impose *tazir* punishments. But before independence, when they could hear all cases,

90 Last, *Charia*, p. 149.

91 Cf. Ibraheem Sulaiman, *Revolution*, p. 70.

92 *Ibid.*, p. 143.

93 Abun-Nasr, *Islamisches Recht*, p. 208; Schacht, *Islam in Northern Nigeria*, p. 126.

94 Zamfara State of Nigeria 2000, *Sharia Penal Code*, Section 102; cf. Ostien, *Islamic Criminal Law*, p. 4.

95 Zamfara State of Nigeria 2000, *Sharia Penal Code*, Section 92; Peters, *Islamic Criminal Law*, pp. 3, 39; Schacht, *Islamic Law*, p. 207.

they made ample use of discretionary punishments: not to rein in corrupt rulers, but to squelch protests against them. Opposition politicians who ›insulted‹ emirs or government officials were repeatedly sentenced to prison or public flogging on the basis of such discretionary punishments.

One of the »archaic«[96] traits of Sharia, which links it to the old Arabic culture of blood vengeance, is that it views offenses such as murder, criminal assault or damage of property as a private affair between the parties involved. The authorities confine themselves to guaranteeing the injured party a right to revenge if it insists on it. The relatives of a murder victim are free to forgive the murderer or agree to the payment of blood money. The decision whether a murder is avenged or not, does not lie with the state authorities but with the victim's family. And what family would insist on the execution of an emir's son? Nigerians tend to view members of the upper class as ›untouchables‹. If Sharia were applied to the letter, society would lose its claim to see all lawbreakers being brought to book.

The Utopia of Just Rule

Muslims who view Sharia as an alternative to Western democracy interpret it as a »system of government«,[97] as a kind of Islamic »constitution.«[98] It is not just meant to lay down laws for the believers, but also to establish a political order that can enforce these laws. After all, Nigerians who do not care much about official regulations will not be impressed by new law books. The new penal code of Zamfara, for instance, proscribes bribery and stipulates a sentence of up to five years in prison. Bribery, however, was already punishable under the secular law, by a prison sentence of up to seven years, yet the law did not have any effect: »Punishing everyone who took bribes in the past would mean sacking virtually the entire civil ser-

---

96 Schacht, *Islamic Law*, p. 207.
97 Lateef Adegbite, in Williams/Falola, *Religious Impact*, p. 21; Doi, *Islam*, p. 210; Al-Zakzaky, *Shari'ah Part 1*, pp. 2, 3 (usually spelled El-Zakzaky or el Zak-Zaky). – Ali Mazrui (*Two Africas*, p. 156) stresses that the political pretensions of Sharia are a major aspect of the recent law reform: Sharia is »nothing new in Northern Nigeria. What is new is *Shariacracy* – the adoption of the Sharia as the foundation of governance.«
98 Gwandu, *Sokoto Caliphate*, p. 12; Opeloye, *Desecularizing*, p. 104; Bunzu, *Muslims*, p. 61; Wushishi, *Resurgence of Shari'ah*, p. 40.

vice.«[99] In contrast to hitherto existing law, Sharia was expected to force even the highest political authorities to act according to the principles of divine justice. The holy law, however, which is believed to have such a drastic effect, does not devise institutions to limit the power of the rulers, and so the vision of a theocratic order, for which millions of Muslims took to the streets, remains vague.[100] Instead of discussing alternative constitutional models, political imagination has focused on the idealized images of just rulers, as they appear in the stories about Mohammed and his immediate successors, the four rightly-guided caliphs. Usman dan Fodio and his companions, whose wars of conquest devastated much of today's Northern Nigeria, also serve as examples of »upright, honest and totally selfless leaders.«[101] It is said that they lived a modest life, close to the people, and that they gave audience to anybody who sought advice, even the poorest.[102] Similar reports circulate about the Caliph Umar, who with his own hands brought a sack of grain to a woman in need. The problem with these narratives is, however, that they do not tell us how to get caliphs and other rulers to tend to the wishes of the people. The claim by Sharia advocates that the holy scriptures contain the blueprint of a government system which is based on the rule of law, is fictitious. Neither the four rightly-guided caliphs nor their successors were legal rulers. In the heroic beginnings of Islam, the leaders of the *umma*, the community of believers, exercised either charismatic or traditionalist authority.[103] In Mohammed's lifetime, when God's will was immediately present in the words of the prophet, it was not necessary to devise a system of governance that was bound by legal limitations: »the Quran [...] provided directly for no government other than that of the Prophet himself.«[104] Mohammed was guided directly by God. He did not *follow* the law, he *proclaimed* it, and in doing so he took the liberty to modify parameters which he himself had earlier imposed as divine commandments.[105]

---

99 *Economist*, 15 January 2000, Nigeria Survey, p. 7.

100 This also applies to other countries where Muslims call for Sharia in order to achieve social justice: »In these contexts, the word is characteristically deprived of detail, of complexity, and of association with the intellectual tradition of *fikh*« (Calder, *Shari'ah*, p. 282).

101 Doi, *Islam*, p. 300.

102 Moumouni, *Uthman dan Fodio*, p. 118; Ado-Kurawa, *Shari'ah*, p. 282.

103 Tibi, *Fundamentalism*, p. 102.

104 Hodgson, *Islam*, p. 207; An-Na'im, *Islamic Reformation*, pp. 76–77.

105 After God had announced to him that no man shall have more than four wives, he learned in a later revelation that this rule did not apply to him: »O Prophet, We have

His immediate successors, though praised for their godly rule, did not see themselves as guardians of a social and political order warranted by divine law. Under their authority the old Bedouin customary law was widely in use, intertwined with Islamic prescripts, later with Roman and Persian traditions as well.[106] Attempts to create a unified law, deduced entirely from the holy scriptures, were not initiated by the caliphs, but by private legal scholars. Sharia did not reflect and codify the actual practice of Islamic rule, but was born out of an attempt to contain the despotism of Islamic authorities. The Prophet's successors had appropriated the power apparatus of the Persian Empire and of those Byzantine provinces which the jihadists had conquered. Against the imperial pretensions of Islamic monarchs, religiously-minded scholars set something entirely immaterial: the revealed word of God from which they derived since the late eighth century a self-contained legal system. Much later, the scholarly ideal of the rule of law was projected into the beginnings of Islam, but Sharia has never served as the constitution of an Islamic empire.[107] The classic caliphate of the eighth and ninth centuries guaranteed its citizens a high level of prosperity and peace, not because the monarchs obeyed the divine law, but because they boldly ignored it. The Abbasides, who led Islamic civilization to its zenith, were »masters in absolutism.«[108] In order to keep their vast empire together, they instructed judges to apply the unified law which had emerged in the law schools of Bagdad, Kufa and Medina. The monarchs, however, reserved the right to have a final say in legal as well as political affairs. They tortured and killed their opponents, without asking Sharia judges for their verdict. And they did not hide their absolutist claim: »as

---

made lawful for thee […] any woman believer, if she give herself to the Prophet and if the Prophet desire to take her in marriage, for thee exclusively, apart from the believers« (*Koran* 33: 50, pp. 432–433).

106 Endress, *Islamische Geschichte*, pp. 73–74; Schacht, *Islamic Law*, p. 15.

107 El-Affendi, *Rationality*, pp. 157–160; Tibi, *Fundamentalism*, pp. 160, 165. – »It is not meaningful to speak of the Prophet's rule in terms of constitutionalism. That term implies legal limitations on the powers of the ruler and his political accountability to a human entity other than himself, whereas the Prophet was to the Muslims the agent of God, and his words and deeds were the only criteria of validity and legality. […] the Prophet was the sole recipient and interpreter of divine revelation and the ultimate executive and judicial head of the community« (An-Na'im, *Islamic Reformation*, pp. 76–77).

108 Hodgson, *Islam*, p. 271.

symbol of [the caliph's] power, there stood beside him the executioner, ready to kill the most exalted personage at a word.«[109]

Even for devout, God-fearing monarchs it would not have been possible to rule according to the immutable laws of God, because the holy scriptures did not provide answers for many questions. The transition from a personal, charismatic form of rule to the administration of a world empire created an enormous demand for legal regulations, which could not be met by referring to laws that had emerged centuries ago in a tribal, largely segmentary society. The caliphs had to create new laws, yet they maintained the fiction that they did not redesign the legal system, but merely interpreted it according to changing circumstances. So their innovations were not called laws but administrative regulations or ordinances.[110] Furthermore, the new regulations had to be consistent with Sharia, at least nominally. All holy laws, which claim unlimited validity, are »compelled to resort to circumventing strategies in order de facto to annul normatively imperative regulations, or more accurately, to be able to tolerate their being disregarded.«[111] With the help of legal fictions and auxiliary constructions, divine orders such as the prohibition of usury could be circumvented. Yet the claim of Islamic law to regulate all aspects of life, obstructed processes of differentiation like the emergence of a constitutional and commercial law. Political religion did not tolerate that different spheres of society organized themselves autonomously, according to their own internal logic:

»The frequent ambivalence or silence of religious norms with respect to new problems and practices [...] results in the unmediated juxtaposition of the stereotypes' absolute unalterableness with the extraordinary capriciousness and utter unpredictability of the same stereotypes' validity in any particular application. Thus, in dealing with the Islamic *shar'iah* it is virtually impossible to assert what is the practice today in regard to any particular matter.«[112]

Since the holy scriptures do not provide reliable information on the political order Allah intended, their value as a guide for the future is limited. Full Sharia, when it was reintroduced in Northern Nigeria, de-emphasized disputes among Muslims for a while, but it could not settle them. Politicians, clerics and traditional rulers have interpreted God's will in completely different ways, and none of them can claim that his or her idea of an

---

109 *Ibid.*, p. 283.
110 Bernard Lewis, *Middle East*, p. 224; Schacht, *Islamic Law*, pp. 53–54, 87.
111 Schluchter, *Hindrances to Modernity*, p. 112.
112 Weber, *Economy and Society*, p. 578.

Islamic society is the genuine one. This also applies to radical Muslims who are disappointed with the state-decreed Islamization. As defenders of »true Sharia«,[113] they assert that Islam strives for »absolute justice«[114]: »So long as Islam is reduced to amputating the hands of goat thieves and stoning pregnant divorcees among rural women it is stripped of its revolutionary potential as a system that challenges corruption, injustice and extreme social and economic inequalities.«[115] Yet divine law is not so clearly on the side of the disenfranchised masses. Early Islam created an »aristocracy of conquerors« who lived by exploiting the subjugated peoples.[116] Caliph Usman, a son-in-law of the Prophet, is said to have accumulated an enormous private fortune, including 100,000 Roman gold coins and a million Persian silver coins.[117] Along with texts that praise the personal modesty of individual monarchs, the religious tradition contains passages which express the self-confidence of a proud caste of warriors:

> »The most pious adherents of the religion in its first generation became the wealthiest […]. The Muslim tradition depicts with pleasure the luxurious raiment, perfume, and meticulous beard-coiffure of the pious. The saying that »when god blesses a man with prosperity he likes to see the signs thereof visible upon him« – made by Muhammad, according to tradition, to well-circumstanced people who appeared before him in ragged attire – stands in extreme opposition to any puritan economic ethic and thoroughly corresponds with feudal conceptions of status.«[118]

Democratically-minded Muslims who want to dispense with the authoritarian traditions of Islam, invoke the original teachings of the Koran. Some claim that the holy law prescribes the creation of democratic institutions, but they can only adduce two verses in which *shura*, consultation, is mentioned rather casually.[119] In Sura 3: 159, the Prophet is exhorted, when quarrelling with his followers: »take counsel with them in the affair.« And in Sura 42: 38 it is reported that the believers »counsel between them.«[120] Tradition has it that Mohammed took advice from his closest confidants, Abu Bakr and Umar in particular. One of his successors, Caliph Umar,

---

113 Gaiya, *Shari'ah Debate*, p. 5.

114 Adegbite, *Political Agenda*, p. 2.

115 Sanusi, *Shari'ah Debate*, p. 10.

116 Bernard Lewis, *Middle East*, p. 58; Hodgson, *Islam*, p. 208; Weber, *Economy and Society*, pp. 444, 474.

117 Bernard Lewis, *Middle East*, p. 59; Sanusi, *Islam, Probity*, p. 3.

118 Weber, *Economy and Society*, p. 624.

119 Adegbite, *Political Agenda*, p. 2.

120 *Koran*, pp. 65, 502.

expanded the circle of advisers to five or six people, all of them relatives or in-laws of the Prophet who were well-versed in his teachings.[121] Naturally, a people's representation that passes laws was never envisioned. Islamic scholars agreed that all laws which the *umma* needed had been entirely revealed, so the only issue was to apply them correctly. For that purpose it made sense to consult a small group of experts who knew how to interpret the word of God. It would have been fallacious to insist on equality when establishing an advisory committee, and to grant all believers, even the uneducated ones, a say or even voting rights: »In traditional Islam, only those Muslims with intimate knowledge of Islamic sources, that is, the *ulema* and the *faqih*, are the appropriate class for interpreting the will of God, the one and only legislator.«[122]

There is another aspect of Sharia that makes it difficult to subject the rulers to public control: its tendency not to draw a distinction between a public office and the person who holds it. Islamic law did not develop concepts such as institution, corporation, or juristic person, not even that of a public treasury.[123] Money which is handled by political authorities does not really belong to somebody, so it is not property in the true sense and cannot be stolen. In accordance with this orthodox understanding, Governor Sani stated: »If a civil servant takes government money, he is not a thief.«[124] A minister or governor who lines his pockets, has done nothing more than abuse the citizens' »trust«, and in this case he must resign from office. While petty thieves, who have stolen the equivalent of eight dollars, face amputation,[125] large-scale criminals, such as former President Babangida, do not have to worry about losing a hand.

According to divine law, the poor have at least a right to alms. It is the responsibility of Islamic authorities to collect *zakat*, alms' tax, and to distribute it among those in need.[126] Thus the administration of some Sharia states tried to establish public *zakat* funds with regular contributions by business people. But the wealthy preferred to decide by themselves to

---

121 Bosworth, *Shura*, pp. 504–505; Bernard Lewis, *Middle East*, pp. 142–145; Tibi, *Fundamentalism*, pp. 30, 174–176.
122 Tibi, *Fundamentalism*, p. 176; An-Na'im, *Islamic Reformation*, pp. 78–79.
123 Schacht, *Islamic Law*, pp. 125, 155, 206.
124 Ahmed Sani, in *Tell*, 8 September 2003, p. 40; Oloyede, *Commentary*, p. 297; Peters, *Islamic Criminal Law*, p. 3.
125 This is the minimum value of the stolen item, as fixed by a Sharia court in Sokoto State (Peters, *Islamic Criminal Law*, p. 22).
126 Sanusi, *Zakat*, pp. 1–2.

whom they gave charitable gifts.[127] Like other big men in Nigeria, they are accustomed to redistributing a part of their wealth in order to gain prestige through their generosity and to establish personal dependencies. At the beginning of the Sharia era, Zamfara's commissioner of justice declared that the new government would strive for »wealth redistribution.«[128] The administration gave out bicycles to their poorest employees and distributed hundreds of motorcycles among unemployed youths. It doled out food at Ramadan and granted interest-free loans to some of its citizens.[129] However, further reform efforts have stalled.

The Sharia campaign has raised expectations which are impossible for the state governments to meet. Whether popular anger will turn against the political elite, depends, among others, on the political choices and loyalties of the *ulama*. Preachers and scholars who have profited from their association with emirs and politicians may remind the mass of believers that the Koran urges them to submit to Islamic authorities: »obey God, and obey the Messenger and those in authority among you.«[130] The term Islam means »submission«, »complete devotion to the will of God.«[131] The believers are considered servants of God and not, like in Christianity, children of God. Obedience is demanded of the caliphs as well, they have to profess allegiance to Islam, but in return they can claim to be acknowledged as legitimate rulers by their subjects. This kind of trade-off does not make strong demands on their morality, because Sunni Islam usually judges the rulers pragmatically. In order to be seen as legitimate, they do not have to enforce Sharia laws rigorously. What is essential is to confirm the Islamic identity of the polity and to defend the cause of Islam in conflict with unbelievers.[132] Since the renaissance of political Islam in the late twen-

---

127 Last, *Charia*, p. 145. – In Sokoto State, the *zakat* authority collected the equivalent of 4,000 Euro within the first three years of the introduction of Sharia (Adamu, *Haushaltsstrategien*, p. 300).

128 Ahmed Bello Mahmud, *Shari'ah*, p. 8.

129 *Newswatch*, 10 September 2001, p. 42; Civil Liberties Organisation, *Sharia*, p. 2. – The chairman of Governor Sani's 2003 re-election campaign diverted 300 motorcycles meant for the Poverty Reduction Programme. Some civil servants stole food intended for the students of Zamfara's secondary schools, and the »kingpin of the syndicate« used his share of the booty »to finance his current pilgrimage to Mecca« (*Tell*, 16 February 2004, pp. 22–23).

130 *Koran*, 4: 59, p. 81.

131 Watt/Welch, *Islam*, p. 263; Schimmel, *Islam*, p. 17.

132 An-Na'im, *Islamic Reformation*, p. 93; Eisenstadt, *Öffentlichkeit*, p. 316; Schacht, *Islamic Law*, p. 84.

tieth century, the possibility of gaining legitimacy through the proclamation of Sharia was used particularly by autocratic regimes: in Libya under Colonel Gaddafi, in Pakistan under General Zia-ul-Haq and in Sudan under Colonel Numeiri.

Politicians who borrow God's authority are playing a dangerous game. When religion is to guide public affairs, then imams in the Friday mosques are empowered to comment on daily political issues and to challenge the authorities. Since the rulers draw their legitimacy from their obedience to God, there is no obligation to be loyal to a »pseudo-Muslim government.«[133] »obedience to God is absolute [...] obedience to those in authority is conditional.«[134] »It is not reprehensible to kill unjust miscreants and their helpers – even if they pray and pay *zakat* and perform pilgrimage.«[135] Believers have the right to rise against a government that turns away from God. However, there is no church or any other institution that would be authorized to decide on behalf of the *umma*, when a fight against the rulers is justified. Any preacher or scholar who gathers enough followers can call for a revolt against pseudo-Islamic rulers. The history of Northern Nigeria is shaped by a long tradition of religious violence and Mahdi rebellions. Usman dan Fodio, who called the despotic Hausa kings unbelievers and declared a jihad on them, is still viewed by most Muslims in the North as the role model of a religious reformer. In 1980 a preacher like Maitatsine, who addressed the urban poor, could unleash a series of uprisings against the Islamic establishment which cost almost 10,000 lives. The agitation for full Sharia, two decades later, revived the resentment against the depraved, hypocritical authorities, one of the targets being the Emir of Kano who was pelted with stones in his Rolls Royce.[136]

Protests against the established powers often erupt in a destructive way, because opposition is not integrated by institutional means.[137] In European societies a network of associations and intermediary powers emerged as early as the Middle Ages, creating its own forms of law and administration, while in the caliphates, a similar system of separation of powers never evolved. Whoever propagated political-religious reforms had to appeal to the collectivity of believers in order to mobilize supporters and confront

---

133 Sulaiman, *Revolution*, pp. 105.
134 Yahya, *Shari'ah*, p. 3.
135 Sulaiman (*Revolution*, pp. 105, 3) quoting al-Maghili.
136 *Tell*, 16 June 2003, p. 36.
137 Eisenstadt, *Öffentlichkeit*, p. 319.

the authorities, if necessary, by force: »military venture with wholesale revolt continued to pose an ideal for reformers.«[138] In the absence of institutional separation, government critics sought a spatial-geographical separation, modeled after the Prophet's *hijra*, his flight from Mecca, where the authorities did not tolerate him, to Medina, where he established his own political community as a power base to wage war on his former hometown.[139] Like Mohammed and his followers, militant Muslims in Northern Nigeria, usually children of the upper class, fled their home and sought refuge in the borderland to Cameroon and Niger, from where they have attacked several border towns since the end of 2003. The group that burned down the local police stations and flew the Afghan flag was referred to as Taliban in the media, yet they called themselves *hijra*. In order to dislodge them from their lairs in a mountainous area, the army deployed heavy artillery.[140]

The mass of believers who drift between powerlessness and revolt find no reliable, sustainable means to influence government policy. Instead of institutionalizing control over the ruling class, Sharia supporters focused on replacing the corrupt rulers by fair and God-fearing leaders: »the ultimate source of restraint for a ruler in the face of enormous power at his disposal is his inner self, his conscience, his consciousness of Allah.«[141] One of the few Sharia politicians who had a reputation for being principled and incorruptible was Muhammad Buhari, the former military ruler, who ran as presidential candidate of the oppositional ANPP in the 2003 and 2007 elections. From January 1984 to August 1985, Buhari had ruled Nigeria with an iron fist. In order to cleanse the country of crime and corruption he decreed that each citizen could be incarcerated indefinitely without a court hearing:

»Torture, arbitrary and unlimited arrests were widely practiced. The punishments were severe: a minimum of 21 years imprisonment for economic crimes, death

---

138 Hodgson, in Laitin, *Hegemony*, p. 33.

139 Laitin, *Hegemony*, p. 33.

140 *Tell*, 12 January 2004, p. 26 and 26 April 2004, pp. 22–26; *Newswatch*, 11 October 2004, pp. 22–25. – When in April 2007 a police station in metropolitan Kano was stormed, the media spoke of a Taliban attack (*BBC News*, http://news.bbc.co.uk/go/pr/fr/-/2/hi/af rica/6564629.stm). The police who arrested two alleged Taliban leaders accused them of cooperating with al-Qaeda and recruiting Nigerians for military training in Mauritania (*Tell*, 1 March 2007, http://tellng.com/news/articles/070222-2/news/Sprep_terrornort h.html; cf. Chalk, *Islam*, p. 428).

141 Sulaiman, *Revolution*, p. 145.

penalty for drug trafficking, willful destruction of public property, crude oil smuggling and the like, public executions of muggers«, and in addition a »campaign against the immorality of women.«[142]

Journalists who criticized his administration were jailed, based on Decree Number 4 which »forbade the publication or broadcast of anything [...] that might bring government officials into ridicule or disrepute.«[143] The retired general has never distanced himself from his brutal human rights violations.[144] Up until his candidacy in the presidential election, he had never had a friendly word for democracy; at least the ruling PDP posted a reward for any citizen who could submit a quote in which Buhari made a positive statement about democracy.[145] Despite his contempt for a civilian government bound by the rule of law, he found strong support in the Muslim North, not so much among the elite, who considered him too unbending, but among the common people. Many recalled how the general had thousands of corrupt civil servants thrown out of office without trial. Even high-ranking politicians of the unpopular previous government were arrested; thus it seemed as if Buhari was promptly and uncompromisingly enforcing the will of the people. But he was probably not in office long enough to become as unpopular as the succeeding military rulers. Toward the end of his incumbency it became evident that his War against Indiscipline was a convenient means of ridding himself of political opponents. In any case, backers of his administration, such as the Emir of Gwandu, got away unscathed.[146]

---

142 Hauck, *Demokratisierung*, pp. 74–75.
143 Diamond, *Nigeria*, p. 441; *Tell*, 21 April 2003, p. 16; Soyinka, *Open Sore*, p. 91.
144 He also refused to testify before the human rights commission (Bergstresser, *Nigeria 2001*, p. 151; *Economist*, 1 September 2001, p. 37).
145 Jockers/Peters/Rohde, *Wahlen*, p. 86.
146 Hauck, *Demokratisierung*, p. 75; Soyinka, *Open Sore*, pp. 81–92; Diamond, *Nigeria*, p. 441.

Sharia Controversies among Muslims

The Political Players

Some Christian critics claimed that the Sharia conflict had been planned well in advance: »Zamfara and other states of the North are acting out a script written by some political interest (groups) in the North, aimed at destabilizing the Obasanjo administration.«[1] The idea of a conspiracy looked plausible, because the Muslim elite in the North had backed the demand for Sharia almost unanimously. Even left-wing politicians like Balarabe Musa, who had always spoken out against the Islamic establishment, made politically correct statements: »Any opposition against Sharia is opposition against Islam.«[2] But behind this façade of religious unity, Sharia created much controversy and resentment. Most governors resisted having to rule according to divine law; yet they joined the pro-Sharia lobby under pressure from religious zealots. It is more difficult to assess the attitudes of other Islamic politicians toward Sharia. When they spoke with Western diplomats or business people, some of them claimed that they had only reluctantly joined the Sharia movement. Even the Sultan of Sokoto, I was assured, was deeply unhappy about the religious campaign. The fact that Sharia had split the whole country was allegedly due to an unfortunate concurrence of circumstances. Even Governor Sani, who initiated the process, had not expected the campaign to cause such a stir. He was said to be appalled at the consequences of his actions, but could no longer shake off his role as a redeemer.

Yet he seemed to enjoy his role as a religious leader. Despite the protests in Nigerian and international media, he appeared most confident at public meetings: »Allah has made me the commander of Muslims in Nigeria as a whole .... I call on all Nigerian Muslims that if they hear that

---

1 Richard Akinnola, Center for Free Speech, in *Tell*, 10 April 2000, p. 25.
2 *Tell*, 26 June 2000, p. 18.

Yerima [Sani] has started, they should come out to demonstrate their love for me.«[3] He went on to say that he was prepared to die and that his government would pay for the medical care for those who were wounded in the coming conflicts, even if they had to be taken to Saudi Arabia for treatment.[4] Like Sani, the Sultan of Sokoto also contributed actively to the religious polarization. When a violent confrontation loomed in February 2000, because the strong Christian minority in Kaduna was unwilling to accept the proposed Sharia law, the sultan and his delegation of 18 emirs went to see the governor and insisted on the passage of the bill.[5] When Islamic authorities insisted nevertheless in private conversations that they regretted the introduction of Sharia, their statements should be taken with a pinch of salt. As a German diplomat explained: »Northern politicians consistently give us the impression that they do not want religious fanaticism. But we also know they like telling people from the West what we want to hear.«

All the same, it is probably true that Ahmed Sani was not acting on behalf of the Islamic elite, when he began his struggle for Sharia. Most likely he simply wanted to court the support of local Islamic groups in order to win the gubernatorial elections. His opponent Aliyu Gusau, the PDP candidate, was a man with excellent political connections. As the National Security Adviser, General Gusau had coordinated the state security services. After he lost the election, he was confirmed in his office as National Security Adviser by President Obasanjo. Thus he had huge resources at his disposal with which to destabilize the government of Ahmed Sani. The governor's position was precarious for yet another reason. When he joined the race for the governor's election in late 1998, he did so at the instigation of Colonel Yakubu, Zamfara's military governor, in whose government Ahmed Sani had headed the Department of Lands and Housing. As Nigeria's military governors had embezzled the state's resources and left substantial debts, most of their successors launched investigations against them, yet Governor Sani refused to harass his patron. Colonel Yakubu got into trouble nonetheless, because the federal government put him on trial for attempting to murder the editor of the Guardian, a liberal newspaper, which had clashed with the Abacha government.[6]

---

3 *Insider Weekly*, 22 October 2001, p. 18; *Tell*, 29 October 2001, pp. 33–34.
4 *Insider Weekly*, 22 October 2001, p. 18.
5 Danfulani, *Sharia Issue*, p 16; Odey, *Sharia*, p. 99.
6 Maier, *This House*, p. 187.

Diplomats who had known Ahmed Sani at earlier stages of his career had the impression that he was not guided by religious motives. As they recalled, he had been a sociable, good-humored man who liked his beer and amused himself with his mistresses. Sani himself admitted that he had not taken the tenets of his faith seriously. Only on a pilgrimage to Saudi Arabia did he realize that he was not a good Muslim, and he suddenly started crying.[7] With the transition to democracy he changed his appearance, grew a full beard and adhered to a strict Islamic dress code. Gold-framed photos of the governor and audiocassettes of his speeches or sermons were on sale in markets all over Northern Nigeria. Many Muslims believed that he had morally purged himself, and this conviction was probably backed by the fact that Sani openly admitted some of his past transgressions: »When I was at the Central Bank, in the foreign exchange (department), I would take $800,000 to the (presidential) villa for the ECOMOG operations and sometimes the officer would dash me $10,000 or $5,000.«[8]

Like Ahmed Sani, most Northern leaders, including Buhari and Shagari, had been discredited by their complicity with the Abacha regime. Turning to divine law was one of the few ways »to cleanse themselves of association with a now illegitimate past.«[9] Virtually everyone who later emerged as a champion of divine justice had stayed loyal to the military regime to the end. Though General Abacha had broken his promise to restore democracy, Hausa-Fulani politicians backed him and his campaign to become a democratically ›elected‹ civilian president. When military rule suddenly ended, they had maneuvered themselves into moral bankruptcy. The transition to democracy with its phony elections did not provide them with new legitimacy. So the religious renewal was an attractive option, especially for members of the opposition All People's Party, which was commonly referred to as Abacha's People's Party. They found that cloaking themselves in religion was a good way to protect themselves from possible government assaults.

Once the Sharia campaign got under way, individual politicians were powerless to stop it. Kaduna's governor, Ahmed Makarfi, initially resisted the return to Islamic law by arguing that »the state shall not profess any

---

7 *Ibid.*, p. 185.
8 *Ibid.*, p. 186.
9 Reno, *Sectarian Violence*, p. 229; Paden, *Islam*, 2.

particular religion.«[10] In Gombe State, which also has a strong minority of Christian ›indigenes‹, the governor sought to block the legislative initiative too. Yet his resistance to Sharia was not motivated by a commitment to protect the rights of religious minorities. Governor Hashidu had no reservations about using state power to advance his religious agenda. Among ethnic groups in the south of his state, which are predominantly Christian, he appointed Muslim chiefs and sought to transform their territories into emirates.[11] Likewise, Governor Makarfi strengthened Muslim enclaves in the Christian-dominated south of Kaduna State, while trying to split the umbrella organization of the Christian minorities, the Southern Kaduna Peoples' Union.[12] The violent protests, triggered by the Sharia campaign, jeopardized this strategy. In addition, Hashidu, Makarfi and other governors had no interest in having religious considerations curtail their freedom of action.

However, open resistance to the law reform did not last long. The Governor of Gombe, nicknamed ›bishop‹ by Muslim zealots, had stones thrown at him by angry youths. In Kano, imams threatened to declare the governor an apostate, and in Kaduna, they instructed all mosques to curse the governor every day.[13] The fact that state governments bowed to religious pressure was interpreted by some Sharia activists as a »triumph of people's power over elite dominance.«[14] But popular rage alone would not have sufficed. It only worked because the anti-Sharia governors found no support in the Islamic public sphere. No religious authority opposed the declaration of the Supreme Council for Islamic Affairs that every Muslim is obliged to support Sharia. Even the political elite no longer tried to keep religious claims at bay, as they had done in the 1980s and 1990s. As long as Hausa-Fulani politicians had dominated civilian and military regimes, they had not heeded the demand for full Sharia. The transition to democracy in early 1999 did not temper this reluctance. During the election campaign, all candidates apart from Ahmed Sani simply ignored the Sharia issue. The decision to rally behind Sharia and confront Southern politicians was only made in February 2000, following the Sharia clashes in Kaduna. In view of the many fatalities, the federal government had entered into negotiations

---

10 *Tell*, 3 December 2001, p. 36.

11 Harnischfeger, *Control over Territory*, pp. 448–451.

12 *The Week*, 19 November 2001, p. 13; *Newswatch*, 29 May 2000, p. 46.

13 Abubakar D. Muhammad, *Muslim Responses*, p. 6; *Tell*, 31 July 2000, p. 37; personal information in Kano and Gombe.

14 Yadudu, *Benefits of Shariah*, p. 12.

with the 19 Northern governors and some elder statesmen. Vice President Atiku Abubakar, himself a Northerner, pushed for the suspension of the Sharia legislation. However, among Hausa-Fulani leaders, who held intensive consultations, the pro-Sharia line prevailed. By committing themselves to obey the will of God, they established a new paradigm for political debates: Political action had to be justified in terms of religious obligations. When the Hausa-Fulani elite insisted that theft and adultery must incur draconian penalties, they did not base their argument on pragmatic secular reasons, but on their religious duty: the submission to God. Needless to say, most did not take their obligations seriously, but weighed the advantages and disadvantages of Sharia. Yet they could not do so openly, as it would have been frivolous to debate whether observing the divine commands was politically expedient or not.

By declaring their commitment to Sharia, politicians competed with each other to appear as guardians of religious laws. Some young, aspiring talents, who felt that their ambitions were thwarted, acted particularly rigorously in order to oust the old, morally discredited generation.[15] Those under assault sought to defend themselves by also appearing to advocate a religious renewal. As a means to extort loyalty, the Sharia campaign was aimed especially at politicians of the ruling PDP who were tempted to betray Northern interests, like Vice President Abubakar, Foreign Minister Sule Lamido and others who filled the quotas for Northerners in the cabinet. These potential traitors were compelled to take sides: either to join their fellow Muslims or to turn into a tool of the Christian president. At the height of the religious mobilization, even the vice president, who had been labeled a »stooge of Christians«, had to abandon his resistance to Sharia.[16]

While the Islamic establishment in the North joined the Sharia campaign, Muslim politicians in Yorubaland rejected it. The Governor of Lagos, Ahmed Tinubu, said that he was under pressure to introduce Islamic law.[17] Religious authorities in the North had called on their fellow Muslims in the South to adopt the legal reform, and some Yoruba had embraced the demand for Sharia. In Oyo State, in which Muslims form a clear majority, Islamic associations set up a Sharia court, which heard per-

---

15 Fayemi, *Religion*, p. 150.
16 *The News*, 25 September 2000, p. 54; *Tell*, 31 July 2000, p. 36.
17 *Tell*, 23 September 2002, p. 46.

sonal disputes and occasionally a criminal case like adultery.[18] However, the governor, himself a Muslim, was unwilling to support this initiative. The Muslim governors of Kwara and Osun felt the same, but none of them put forward a religious justification for rejecting Sharia.[19] They simply ignored the political claims of their religion, not so much out of a concern for human rights and the constitution, but due to ethnic considerations: Introducing Sharia would have threatened Yoruba unity.[20]

Religious authorities in the North accused their Yoruba co-religionists of not taking their faith seriously. However, a religious confrontation would be disastrous for the Yoruba.[21] Both Christians and Muslims were aware that the call by Northern Muslims to join the Sharia campaign and establish Islamic courts in Yorubaland was not meant to bring peace. After decades of religious conflicts in the North, Hausa-Fulani politicians would benefit if the »Sharia virus«[22] spread to other parts of the country. A Northern journal, in favour of Sharia, hinted that the Sharia controversy should fall upon their enemies like a curse: »Yoruba have enough Muslim population to adopt their own mode of Sharia and create their own fratricide.«[23] So far, ethnic solidarity has proven stronger than religious loyalty. As one Muslim chief put it: »I'm a Yorubaman first and foremost. [...] I have a duty to my race.«[24] Yoruba still recall the devastations of the nineteenth century, when Hausa and Fulani jihadists used Islam as a means of political subjugation. Since the invaders destroyed the old Oyo Empire, the northern parts of Yorubaland have been Islamized, but the foreign conquerors never acknowledged Yoruba Muslims as equals. Even today, the Emir of Ilorin is a member of a royal Fulani family who refuses to address his subjects, most of whom are Yoruba, in their mother tongue.

Mistrust of Northern Muslims had hardened in 1993, when the Sultan of Sokoto and other Hausa-Fulani leaders supported the annulment of the

---

18 Bergstresser, *Nigeria 2002*, p. 158; Human Rights Watch, *Political Shari'a?*, p. 14; Yakubu, *Sharia Imbroglio*, pp. 54–55.

19 Sklar, *Unity or Regionalism*, p. 48.

20 Gaiya, *Shari'ah Debate*, p. 5; Ado-Kurawa, *Shari'ah*, pp. 184–185, 188.

21 In Lagos, where an equal number of Muslims and Christians have to coexist, Sharia clashes could be far more destructive than in the cities of the North: »I can see the blood flowing in southern and northern Sudan being chickenfeed, compared to what will happen in this country« (Brigadier Benjamin Adekunle, in *Tell*, 27 March 2000, p. 17).

22 *Tell*, 17 April 2000, p. 48.

23 *Hotline*, 9 April 2000, p. 37.

24 Quoted in Ado-Kurawa, *Shari'ah*, p. 194; cf. Aguwa, *Religious Conflict*, p. 347.

presidential election. Its winner, Moshood Abiola, had been treated by the Northern elites not as a fellow Muslim who deserved their support, but as a Yoruba who should be kept out of power.[25] Ethnic considerations had eclipsed religious ones, and it appeared to Yoruba patriots that the call to introduce Sharia in Southwest Nigeria had similar motives. The attempt to deepen antagonisms between Christians and Muslims was obviously aimed at splitting Yoruba society, so as to break its resistance to Hausa-Fulani supremacy:

»such a move is bound to be read, sooner than later, as a declaration of war on Yoruba land, a continuation of Fulani conquest by the same means and a subterfuge to re-launch the jihad [...] The idea obviously is to trigger another round of in-fighting [...] having reflected deeply on what became of MKO Abiola in the hands of his Muslim brothers, more and more Yoruba Muslims now seem to have determined never again to be used by people who never fully accept them either as fellow Muslims or even as human beings.«[26]

There is another reason why Muslim governors in Yorubaland hesitated to heed the Sharia demands. Politicians who introduced religious law could hardly get rid of it again. At a conference on Sharia in Nigeria, held in Bayreuth in July 2003, experts doubted that Islamic governors had the power to abolish the divine law.[27] Any governor who renounced the laws of God, would be regarded by orthodox Muslims as an apostate who might be cursed by a *fatwa*. Militant Sharia supporters had already made it clear that Muslims who refused to identify with the cause of Islam did so at great risk: »The Holy Qur'an has unambiguously classed all such people with the kafirs (infidels) [...] [T]he position they so wish to protect is as ephemeral as their lives.«[28] Despite such threats, reservations about Sharia have been expressed more openly in recent years. Yet it remains difficult to formulate basic criticism. What principles could politicians invoke if they wished to renounce their religious obligations? Progress, modernity, or human rights? As long as there are no credible alternatives to Sharia, Muslims in the North will probably be caught up in the religious discourse.

---

25 Adesina, *Christian-Muslim Relations*, pp. 114–115.

26 *Vanguard*, 7 December 2001, p. 16; cf. Ransome-Kuti, *Sharia*, pp. 1–2.

27 Cf. Sklar, *Unity or Regionalism*, p. 48; Suberu, *Democratizing Nigeria*, p. 77.

28 *Hotline*, 19 March 2000, p. 26. – Shehu Sani, chairman of the Civil Rights Congress and »one of the very few Northerners who openly opposed the Islamic legal system«, received a parcel with »leaflets denouncing ›enemies of the North and Islam‹ and a movement chart which meticulously spelt out in detail [his] daily movement schedule« (*The News*, 5 March 2001, p. 28).

The religious zeal of Sharia supporters could force the rulers to feign piety. At Friday prayers they mingled with the ordinary faithful, but they did not feel obliged to take the people's interests seriously. Even the most godly governors shirked their religious obligations as soon as their privileges were at stake. When Governor Sani was asked by a journalist whether he was prepared to refund the money he had misappropriated, his blunt answer was no. He would hold on to his possessions because »I allow relatives and other people to stay in my houses.«[29] In addition, he claimed that as the scion of a royal Fulani family, he had always been blessed with wealth.[30]

In view of the arbitrary way in which Sharia courts prosecuted theft and adultery, outsiders had the impression that Sharia was an instrument of oppression used by the ruling class: »it was a move by the political elite to tighten power over a population variously described as Nigeria's poorest, most marginalized, most vulnerable to oppression.«[31] However, Sharia as a political instrument lends itself to many sides. In Jigawa State, *hisba* members arrested a son of the Emir of Dutse and caned him for drinking alcohol; as a result, an emirate official dissolved the vigilante group.[32] But not every emir or governor could deal with the Sharia enforcers so boldly. In Kano, Governor Kwankwaso overestimated his power when he announced that no cleric could tell him what to do, »no matter how long his beard is.«[33] Kwankwaso was voted out of office in April 2003 after just one term. However, his defeat was not merely attributable to protests by the faithful. The governor had antagonized influential members of the local establish-

---

29 Maier, *This House*, p. 186. – When Sani declared his assets in October 1999, he possessed »nine houses, seven farms, [...] and shares in two private companies« (*ibid.*). In 2006, when he launched his presidential campaign, he had the means to set up 112 campaign offices all over Nigeria (*Guardian*, 22 January 2007, p. 15).

30 Maier, *This House*, p. 187.

31 Finkel (*Crime*, p. 3), summing up what Sharia critics claimed; cf. Gwamna, *Christian Reactions*, p. 4. – According to Ruud Peters (*Enforcement*, p 125), »Islamic criminal law [is] an attractive option for political elites in the Muslim world. [...] it provides an effective instrument of control and repression. [...] The spectacle of public executions, amputations and floggings symbolizes the supreme power of the regime and the futility of resistance against it.«

32 Fwatshak, *Shari'a Enforcement*, p. 19; *Tell*, 16 February 2004, p. 24.

33 *Economist*, 10 January 2004, p. 32.

ment, and these rivals used the religious resentment against this brash politician to bring him down.[34]

Many members of the elite found playing the role of pious zealots a nuisance. But as it was not opportune to express their resistance openly, they defied the divine commandments in silence. Senior officials in Yobe State looking for amusement would spend their weekends in neighboring Maiduguri, where Sharia was more lax: »They come in hordes to have [...] the best things of life which are abundant in town.«[35] Islamic societies, not only in Africa, have a strong tolerance for double standards. However, the amount of hypocrisy people will acquiesce in depends on what else the political caste has to offer them besides pious phrases. In Saudi Arabia, the ruling families have sufficient resources to provide the majority of their subjects with a secure livelihood. In Northern Nigeria, where there are only a few enclaves of wealth, the gap between rich and poor is far wider. In the early 1990s, one-third of Nigerians were believed to live on less than one dollar a day. By 1998 this figure had grown to 48 percent, and today, despite record earnings from the sale of oil, it is 70 percent.[36] More than 100 million Nigerians are mired in poverty. Even if under favorable conditions the economy grew at 6 percent a year, it would take 30 to 40 years for the average income to return to 1970 levels.[37] The present economic growth is fuelled by high oil prices, not by industrial investments, so Nigerians have little reason to chase the chimera of Western progress.

Islamic politicians have good reason to fear the people's wrath. Their claim to be recognized as religious authorities is condemned as arrogant by many devout Muslims. Sacred tradition does not envisage elected governors or parliamentarians, so these offices do not bestow religious legitimacy. Only through their personal piety and knowledge of Islam could politicians qualify as leaders of the *umma*. But who among them has taken the trouble to read the classical works of jurisprudence, according to which they claim to rule? As soon as they enter theological terrain and debate with the *ulama* on the correct interpretation of the scriptures, they lose out to their rivals. The call to base public life on divine principles gives Islamic

---

34 The election campaign of his successor Shekarau was funded by Bashir Magashi, a retired major-general, and other big men in Kano (*Tell*, 22 January 2007, p. 31; *National Review*, September 2003, pp. 22–23).

35 *Newswatch*, 17 September 2001, p. 27.

36 *Newswatch*, 12 March 2001, p. 42; Economist Intelligence Unit, *Country Profile Nigeria 2007*, p. 16.

37 Kappel, *Nigeria*, p. 10.

scholars and preachers the right to meddle in political matters. As the Koran's message is available to anybody, it cannot be constrained to serve only the interests of a particular group. All sorts of people may enter the competition for religious expertise. Intellectuals, who used to have little interest in theological disputes, are now keen to cite the word of God, as the masses are far more receptive to a religious language than to the theories of Karl Marx or Franz Fanon.[38] While the political authorities assume an Islamic identity, opposition against them is Islamized too. Government critics who reject the state-driven Islamization do not take offence at Sharia itself. Their anger is reserved for the professional politicians who act as guardians of divine virtue, despite their moral turpitude: »How can society purge itself if the propagators of renewal are rotten to the core? No one can clean himself with a filthy sponge.«[39]

Religious Authorities

The office of the sultan and the emirs is more in line with classical concepts of Islamic rulers. In precolonial times, the Fulani aristocracy could rule autocratically, as their decisions were not supervised by a parliament or a group of scholars. Their right to rule was based on a mandate from God, which the initiator of the jihad, Usman dan Fodio, handed down to his successors. As Sokoto's rulers modeled their empire on the Arab Medina, they referred to themselves as caliphs: deputies of the Prophet. Their power was first curtailed by the colonial administration, and it hit rock bottom under the rule of the military, who robbed them of their most significant privileges – the right to distribute land and to hold court over their subjects. Despite forfeiting these powers, they have weathered the storms of modern politics surprisingly well. While civilian and military regimes came and went in quick succession, the throne of Sokoto is still

---

38 Like Marxism, political Islam promises a privileged role to intellectuals. As the »conscience of society« they are destined to lead the political transformation, following the paradigm of Usman dan Fodio and al-Maghili, a fifteenth-century scholar, active in Kano and Katsina, who demonstrated how an individual »could effect a lasting change in the life of nations and set their history, almost single-handedly, upon a totally different course, by the sheer force of his intellect, his moral authority and his absolute reliance on Allah« (Sulaiman, *Revolution*, pp. 15, 9, 144).

39 A lecturer at the University of Maiduguri, 26 January 2002.

occupied by a direct descendant of Usman dan Fodio, and most emirate leaders also trace their lineage to the early jihadists.

Since all forms of secular rule have failed, the traditional dignitaries are claiming political power once again. Under military rule, they had demanded the chairmanship of local government councils,[40] but the generals confidently thwarted the ambitions of the religious establishment. When the sultan died in 1988 and a successor was elected, General Babangida refused to recognize the kingmakers' will and appointed a business associate, Ibrahim Dasuki, as the highest Muslim authority. The new sultan, though of royal blood, was so unpopular that when he attended Friday prayers at a mosque he often required a police escort. Only protection from the military kept him in power. When he fell out of favor, his career came to an end. General Abacha declared Dasuki's son Sambo a conspirator, had wanted posters put up on the walls of the sultan's palace and sent the sultan himself into exile in April 1996.[41]

With the transition to democracy, the power of the ›feudal‹ authorities was paradoxically reinforced. Governors who prepared for reelection sought to buy the support of local bigwigs. Emirs as well as non-Islamic kings and chiefs received new official cars and had their palaces renovated or extended. Yet the governors and other elected politicians were reluctant to transfer genuine authority to their opponents. In the contest between modern and traditional elites, the emirs only have a chance if they pose as guardians of Islam and emphasize the piety that binds them to the mass of the believers. This does not mean that they are enamored of Sharia. The Emir of Gwandu, who ranks just below the sultan in the hierarchy of traditional rulers, demonstrated his religious zeal by forcing Christians to move their churches to the suburbs, yet he showed little enthusiasm for full Sharia: »Sharia has always been with us, the world did not come to an end because some aspects of it were not implemented.«[42] As with civilian politicians, it is not an enticing prospect for the emirs to be subject to the rigors of Islamic law, but they cannot afford to oppose it in principle. Of course, it is common knowledge that they are more interested in Western luxury goods than in the wisdom of the Koran. Virtues such as piety,

---

40 *Newswatch*, 24 October 1994, p. 23.

41 *The Week*, 25 March 1996, pp. 13–15; *Tell*, 6 May 1996, pp. 10–20; Maier, *This House*, pp. 157–158. – The new sultan, Muhammadu Maccido, endorsed Abacha's plan to be elected civilian president (Sanusi, *Islamisation*, p. 2).

42 *The News*, 24 April 2000, p. 19; *Newswatch*, 17 September 2001, p. 29.

which they are supposed to embody outwardly, only play a subordinate role internally. They do not gain access to the highest offices due to their religious expertise but rather their ethnic and social background. Sultan Ibrahim Dasuki, who led the *umma* until 1996, did not even speak Arabic, the language of the Koran.[43] The scion of a royal family, he had studied at Oxford, and his son majored in political science at Harvard. Yet he warned his subjects against acquiring alien, non-Islamic knowledge: »Western education destroys our culture.«[44]

The return of religion into politics provides an opportunity for the emirs to play a major role beyond their own courtly circles. All the same, their attitude to Sharia is ambivalent, as they have to fear religious rivals who use Islamic orthodoxy to push aside the arrogant aristocrats. Islamic preachers and scholars, whose authority is not based on a hereditary office, show a more tenacious interest in enforcing God's laws. All Muslim organizations that T. H. Gwarzo investigated in Kano backed the reform movement in principle: »at no time did any group in Kano state ever criticize the need to return to Shariah.«[45] The return to religious orthodoxy provides them with a dual benefit:

1. As the canon of divine laws is recognized by all currents of Islam, the joint struggle to enact these commandments may overcome internal disputes, at least temporarily: »You can see the solidarity among the Muslims today. It was never so since independence […]. You don't hear [about] crisis between Izala and others anymore. They are all united by Sharia.«[46]

2. Those jurists and imams who are not born into families of the upper class possess little more than their knowledge of holy scriptures. It is precisely this knowledge that gains in value, when Muslim societies strive to regulate all areas of life in accordance with God's instructions. The authority of scholars and preachers extends with the scope of the religious laws they interpret. This creates a counter-elite, which challenges the politicians' monopoly on decision making. The chance to transform their religious authority into power only arose because politicians like Sani, Shagari and Buhari resorted to religious mobilization: »These politicians have shot themselves in the feet by the introduction of Sharia.«[47]

43 *Tell*, 10 October 1994, p. 11.
44 *Guardian*, 24 May 1994; König, *Zivilgesellschaft*, pp. 82–83.
45 Gwarzo, *Civic Associations*, pp. 311–312.
46 Ahmed Lemu, former Grand Khadi of Niger State, in *Vanguard*, 24 March 2002, p. 20.
47 *Tell*, 5 February 2001, p. 39.

Under the largely secular regime, which the colonial power had imposed on Africans, Islamic scholarship was considered either antiquated or reactionary. Only the decline of the postcolonial order imbued religious experts with new significance. But competition among them is fierce. In the last three decades, increasing numbers of the most talented young people have turned to studying Islam. And as many of them have to use this qualification to make a living, they are pushing for Islamic culture to take center stage in society: »With so many Muslim school-leavers and university graduates with little chance for employment, Islamic activism could provide the means of achieving influence and economic advancement.«[48] One way of exploiting their religious authority is to be co-opted by politicians and accept government offices with pay. The parliaments of the Sharia states created Councils of Ulama to advise judges and *hisba* groups. Of course, the ambitions of the *ulama* went far beyond what the governors were willing to concede to them. However, Nigeria's Sunnis are not as well organized as the clergy in Shiite Iran. Religious experts do not have any professional representation apart from the government-controlled councils, thus it is difficult to articulate common interests. In principle, they all agree on the necessity of Sharia, but this common goal does not preclude fierce infighting. Some *ulama* joined the courtly circles of the emirs in order to acquire money and prestige, while others stood up as spokesmen for the oppressed masses. Preachers who agitated against the corrupt political class launched tirades of hatred against any authorities the country still had: »We as Muslims, we don't recognize the authority of the federal government, state government, local government and any form of authority [...]. What is between us and them is enmity, eternal enmity, fight, war, forever until the day they will come to the book of Allah.«[49]

Most organizations are prepared to work with governors and parliamentarians who are committed to the Islamic cause. The long-established

---

48 *Quinn*, Pride, p. 62. – More than 60 percent of university graduates in the North are believed to be unemployed (*Economist*, 28 April 2007, p. 46). Arab countries face a similar problem: The demand to reorganize all social and economic life according to religious law is propagated mainly by those who have little other qualifications than their knowledge of sacred texts. Their number has been growing, as schools and universities teach more courses in Islamic Studies than ever, so the demand to Islamize state and society will not subside. In Saudi Arabia, two out of every three Ph.D. theses are submitted in Islamic studies (Baer, *Fall*, p. 58).

49 Yakubu Yahaya, a faction leader of the Muslim Brothers, in *Tell*, 30 September 1996, p. 16; cf. Kalu, *Religious Dimension*, p. 680.

Sufi fraternities, which dominated religious life until well into the 1970s, had always allied with the established Islamic authorities. The Qadiriyya was closely connected with the Caliphate of Sokoto and later with the governing Northern Peoples' Congress, whereas the Tijaniyya supported the Emir of Kano and his local allies. A pragmatic relationship to the rich and powerful is also characteristic of the Izala, which appeared as the vanguard of the Sharia movement.[50] Its spiritual leader, Abubakar Gumi (1924-1992), had never shied away from confronting individual representatives of the political establishment. He had even issued a *fatwa* against the Sultan of Sokoto during the colonial era. It stated that it was un-Islamic for the sultan to accept the title ›Knight of the British Empire‹.[51] But Gumi did not see himself as a people's advocate striving to bring down the feudal authorities. As a member of the Fulani elite he was a close confidant of the political establishment and especially of Ahmadu Bello, the Premier of the Northern Region: »I became his principal adviser on all judicial and religious matters.«[52] Under the premier's tutelage he rose to become the country's most senior Islamic judge in 1962. In his autobiography he also described how his benefactors provided him with further privileges, such as the house which the son of an emir gave him as a present.[53] However, he insisted that these tokens of acknowledgment did not corrupt him. He continued to censure politicians who disobeyed God's laws, and he praised pious-minded leaders who were prepared to accept the advice of Islamic scholars. As long as members of the elite were guided by divine principles in their decision-making, there was no reason to object to their privileges. In this, Sheikh Gumi adhered to the Wahabi ideas he had become familiar with in Saudi Arabia. The rulers did not need to be monitored by the people, they only had to listen to the scholars' advice.

Political opposition in Nigeria is often not committed to a reform of the political system, but is used by marginalized groups to challenge their

---

50 »The Izala were [...] always willing to tolerate Northern Nigeria's ›conservative‹ political status and were prepared to support the consolidation of the modernist Northern elites« (Loimeier, *Playing*, p. 361). Studies on the Izala came to very divergent results. Roman Loimeier (*ibid.*) emphasized »Izala's apolitical stance«, while Ousmane Kane (*Muslim Modernity*, p. 242) characterized them as a »political organization of the most sophisticated type.« Peter Chalk (*Islam*, pp. 422–425) described them, oddly enough, as non-violent, moderate and democratic.

51 Loimeier, *Islamische Erneuerung*, p. 123.

52 Gumi, *Where I Stand*, p. 100.

53 *Ibid.*, p. 63.

exclusion and force their way into being co-opted into the ruling circles.[54] Even radical religious leaders allowed themselves to be bought by Sharia governors – with government offices, cars and free flights to Mecca: »It is little wonder that these leaders are referred to in the community as ›Malaman Gwamnati‹ i.e. government spokesmen.«[55] But there were also prominent Muslims, who steadfastly refused to collaborate. The best known is Ibrahim El-Zakzaky, leader of the Shiite-inspired Islamic Movement, also known as the Muslim Brothers. Under civilian and military regimes he spent a total of nine years in prison. When released after the end of the Abacha dictatorship, he became one of the harshest critics of democratically ›elected‹ politicians. More than others he lived up to the ideal of the European intellectual: unswerving in his convictions, unimpressed by the temptations of high political offices, urbane and with relaxed, agreeable manners. Instead of studying theology, he read economics at Zaria, the North's best university. His closest staff were also mostly academics; yet their radical, ›progressive‹ positions attracted mainly the urban poor. In Kano they were able to put half a million supporters on the street, more than any party politician could hope for.[56]

In Northern Nigeria, El-Zakzaky was the only significant »Islamic cleric« who openly rejected the Sharia campaign as a political maneuver of the ruling class. Whether governors introduced secular or religious laws was immaterial to him: »I don't think they are interested in implementing any law.«[57] His criticism was of course not aimed at Sharia itself. On the contrary, he viewed the divine law as too precious to be left to politicians who used it in their election campaigns. In the hands of the corrupt elite, which applied religious law arbitrarily, it became an »instrument of oppression« to subdue the impoverished masses.[58] For him, before true Sharia could be established, it was necessary to bring down these oppressors and replace them with a new generation of God-fearing rulers.

The struggle against despotism and social injustice was associated, in the case of Sheikh El-Zakzaky and his followers, with a religious fervor that sought to eliminate anything un-Islamic. Their political ideal was an Islamic Republic based on the Iranian model. Nonetheless, after visiting

---

54 Chabal/Daloz, *Africa Works*, p. 26.

55 Gwarzo, *Civic Associations*, p. 301.

56 Maier, *This House*, p. 166.

57 *The News*, 12 June 2000, p. 25. – »only the Muslim Brothers have not come out to support states that have adopted the Shariah« (Gwarzo, *Civic Associations*, p. 313).

58 El-Zakzaky, in Maier, *This House*, p. 178.

Iran in 1990, one of their leaders complained that morals there had become too lax and that women were taking too many liberties.[59] Among the liberties, which the Islamic Movement was not willing to tolerate, were disrespectful statements by journalists: »The punishment for anyone who ridicules or abuses Prophet Mohammed is death.«[60] The charge of insulting the Prophet was leveled at Muslims as well as Christians, and this provoked a series of clashes. In Kano, the Muslim Brothers stormed a police station in order to snatch an Igbo merchant who had been arrested for blasphemy. The charge against him was that he (or his wife) had torn several pages out of a Koran and used them as toilet paper. The mob beheaded the accused man, stuck his head on a pike and marched with it for several hours through the city.[61]

As the Muslim Brothers repeatedly clashed with the police and other opponents, one of their leaders was instructed to set up a paramilitary group in 1991: »I designed it along the lines of the Revolutionary Guards in Iran, and I had also read about the Hitler youth movement.«[62] The young militants with their yearning for martyrdom declared quite candidly that they would resist any orders of the authorities.[63] With this uncompromising attitude they could not expect to be integrated into government-funded *hisbas*. The recruitment of official *hisba* groups was supervised in all Sharia states by committees in which the majority of members was appointed by government. These committees often filtered out volunteers who seemed to be hostile to the state authorities. Immediately after the introduction of Sharia laws, Muslim activists had formed independent *hisbas* who moved against anti-Islamic activities without a government mandate. When arresting criminals and other »anti-social elements«[64] they often did not hand them over to the police, but pronounced judgments themselves and executed them on the spot. Police officers and other critics sometimes described them as terror gangs who raped and extorted money, while the *hisba* volunteers accused the police of sabotaging

59 Maier, *This House*, p. 171.
60 Malam Yakubu Yahaya, leader of the Muslim Brothers in Katsina, in *African Guardian*, 22 April 1991, p. 25; cf. Muhammad Dahiru Sulaiman, *Shiaism*, p. 191.
61 *Newswatch*, 6 February 1995, p. 25; *Le Monde*, 15 March 1995. They subsequently published a photo of this trophy in their magazine Al Tajdil (Best, *Challenge*, p. 348).
62 Abubakar Mujahid, leader of the Muslim Brothers in Kano, in Maier, *This House*, p. 168.
63 Muhammad Dahiru Sulaiman, *Shiaism*, pp. 188, 194; *Tell*, 26 August 1996, p. 11.
64 Gwarzo, *Civic Associations*, p. 306.

Sharia, as the officers often released suspects brought to them by Sharia monitors.[65]

Independent *hisba* groups are said to have opened offices »in thousands of communities«, so it is virtually impossible to monitor their activities.[66] This is one of the reasons why no one could assess how often Sharia penalties have been imposed.[67] Supervising the activities of independent and official *hisba* groups should have been the task of the »Islamic civil society«[68], but its organizations are ill-suited to exercise democratic control, as they themselves are not structured democratically. The traditional Sufi groups are dominated by sheikhs, who keep their position for life and are eager to appoint their sons as successors. The more radical or reformist organizations, which are often led by former members of the Muslim Students' Society, have a more modern structure with committees and board members. Nevertheless, they are held together less by democratic procedures than by the authority or charisma of their leaders.[69] In case of internal disputes, when leaders of (local) factions clash, they are not inclined to submit to majority decisions, but break away and form rival organizations. This inner weakness and fragmentation makes it difficult to negotiate and enforce agreements with representatives of the Islamic reform movement. In order to overcome their internal divisions, they have to mobilize their followers for a common goal, such as the struggle for Sharia. But what helps them to unite, brings them into conflict with non-Muslims. When rival factions managed to contain their hostilities, »the confrontation between Muslims and Christians began to harden.«[70]

---

65 Fwatshak, *Shari'a Enforcement*, pp. 16–19; Olaniyi, *Vigilantes*, p. 66.

66 Gwarzo, *Civic Associations*, p. 306.

67 A popular form of Sharia was practiced by Lamido Sada, a Fulani leader in Gombe State, with good contacts to the political establishment. He instructed his militiamen to chop off the hands of armed robbers. In his court, he conducted »trial by ordeal after reading verses from the Holy Quran« (*Tell*, 30 May 2005, pp. 66–67).

68 Gwarzo, *Civic Associations*, p. 290.

69 *Ibid.*, pp. 309, 314–315.

70 Kane, *Muslim Modernity*, p. 211; Loimeier, *Nigeria*, pp. 61–62.

A Liberal or Progressive Sharia

Observers in the South of Nigeria were dismayed that virtually no Muslims in the North protested against the Sharia campaign. Even the ›progressives‹, who had been considered critics of the political establishment, did not pick a fight with Governor Sani and other Sharia authorities: »The silence of Nigerian socialists of northern extraction in the matter is chillingly eloquent.«[71] Intellectuals in the North and South no longer had the impression of being part of the same public sphere. This feeling of alienation even applied to the small group of Hausa-Fulani Muslims who did speak out against the Sharia project, because their criticism was not based on principles which they might share with Sharia critics in the South. Constitutional provisions such as the rejection of a state religion, equality before the law, religious freedom and other human rights played just a minor role for Muslim critics in the North, as they avoided contradicting Sharia on behalf of principles which derived from secular, non-religious sources. Most of them acknowledged the necessity of organizing public and private life in accordance with divine laws and argued from within the Islamic tradition. This self-restriction left Sharia critics in the North with two strategies of reasoning: 1. They could cite reasons why the introduction of Sharia under the present circumstances should be postponed. 2. They could reject the letter of the law and emphasize its spirit, which allowed a more moderate, progressive, or ›anti-feudal‹ form of Sharia to be conceived.

There were several reasons why Muslims submitted to these restrictions of the debate. Criticizing Sharia in principle was difficult, because the sacred texts did not contain arguments one could adduce in order to reject the implementation of Sharia. Muslims who still wished to disavow the ancient rules attracted the suspicion that they were guided by irreligious considerations. A senator in Abuja, who preferred to remain anonymous, described how difficult it was to oppose the religious project: »I am a Muslim and I know what they are doing is not proper but I cannot speak against the implementation of Sharia. It would mean political suicide.«[72] Some Muslims feared violent retaliation if they criticized the new laws: »It may be mistaken for antagonism towards Islam. In the process, these jobless street

---

71 Williams, *Lugard*, p. 24.
72 *The News*, 10 April 2000, p. 19.

beggars called almajiris can be mobilized to burn down your property.«[73] However, external pressure alone cannot explain why the Sharia project gained such widespread support. Another reason is that advocates of full Sharia could present their case with clear and plausible arguments. They had the additional advantage that the rules of the political discourse had changed. Political claims were only valid, if they were derived from the will of God or, at least, if they did not contradict his will. This favored political actors whose reasoning was as close as possible to God's word.

Given these constraints on the political discourse, it is no coincidence that the most radical criticism of the new Sharia legislation came from a religious authority whose godly disposition was beyond doubt: Ibrahim El-Zakzaky, leader of the Islamic Movement or Muslim Brothers. He viewed the Sharia project as premature: As long as Muslims had not seized power in Nigeria, but still faced Christian resistance, they could only introduce a corrupt form of Sharia: »the total application of shari'ah is only possible where the system of government is purely Islamic.«[74] Other Sharia critics, who were less militant than El-Zakzaky, also argued that the introduction of Sharia should be postponed, but they gave different reasons. They maintained that as long as people in their present squalor were unable to live in decency and dignity, it would be unreasonable to act against petty criminals with the rigor of divine laws: »Islam requires social justice and when all the conditions for social justice are established, then any person who takes any person's property ought to pay.«[75] One of the leading intellectuals in Northern Nigeria, Abubakar Umar, pointed out that the history of Islam provided the role model of a pious ruler who temporarily dispensed with the *hudud* punishments: »Khalif Umar […] found a man guilty of theft but he did not cut his hand off. Why? Because at that time, there was so much economic distress, there was famine in the land.«[76] Measured by the rules of orthodox Islamic jurisprudence, this was a weak argument, as it was based only on one episode in the *hadith*, i.e. the accounts of the early period of the *umma*. In the Koran, there is no mention that God's instructions to mankind can be suspended under certain circumstances. But even irrespective of such scholarly casuistry, the argument that a just social order would have to be created before Sharia laws

---

73 Anonymous source, in *Tell*, 10 April 2000, p. 27.

74 Al-Zakzaky, *Shari'ah Part 2*, p. 3.

75 Bala Bello Maru, Zamfara State PDP Secretary, in *Newswatch*, 17 September 2001, p. 23.

76 *Tell*, 13 November 2000, p. 30.

can come into effect, is not convincing. How is society expected to transform itself if not by following divine commandments? Deterrent punishments that compel people to observe God-given rules are supposed to lead mankind on the path of moral betterment. For devout Muslims, the amputation of limbs is not the purpose of their religious efforts, but just a means of freeing themselves from vice. It is said that when the Prophet decreed divine laws, the Arab world was in a state of godlessness and moral turpitude; only with the help of Sharia did he manage to »clean« society.[77]

A second strategy of Sharia critics, besides calling for a postponement of full Sharia, was to propose »alternate interpretations«[78] of the sacred law. Again, the validity of Sharia was acknowledged in principle, only its literal application was questioned: »We get the distinct impression from many of the current advocates of the Shari'ah that it is essentially a punitive, political arrangement dealing with beverages and dress codes, the amputation of limbs and the refurbishment of mosques.«[79] Such changes only created a façade of piety; society appeared Islamized but its unjust social order remained unaffected: »Neo-fundamentalism neither challenges the class-character of the state nor shows any interest in altering the underlying social relations. It is consistent with the most retrogressive and feudal systems and thus exists in harmony with backward structures like the monarchy in Saudi Arabia and the Nigerian state.«[80]

Instead of blindly copying the precepts of the Koran and the *hadith*, it seemed necessary to adapt them to present-day requirements:

»This is a different age, a different society and a different world. A different legal process responsive to the peculiarities and unique characteristics of this age, this society and this strange world is an absolute and inescapable necessity. […] Sharia is first and foremost an idea, even before it is law.«[81]

But how does one arrive at the ›idea‹ that is hidden behind the wording of the law? Sanusi Lamido Sanusi, the most eloquent proponent of a

---

77 Abdulkadir Orire, General Secretary of Jama'atu Nasril Islam, in *Vanguard*, 24 March 2002, p. 21.

78 Sanusi, *Shari'a Debate*, p. 10.

79 Mohammed/Adamu/Abba, *Talakawa*, pp. 8–9.

80 Sanusi, *Shari'a Debate*, p. 7. – At the Sharia conference in Bayreuth, July 11–12, 2003, Sanusi summarized his assessment of the present Sharia law in two sentences: »Northern elites chop off the hands of goat thieves. That's all.«

81 Ibraheem Sulaiman, *Sharia Restoration*, p. 4.

(post)modern interpretation of Sharia, suggested a philosophical approach. Whatever God's purpose was, when he decreed Sharia, it could only be understood if attention was paid to the essence of God, to the attributes ascribed to him in the Koran: »A proper apprehension of Allah, His Beautiful Names (*al-asma' al-husna*) and His Exalted Attributes (*as-sifat al-'ula*) must necessarily transform our ethic.« »A Muslim who believes in Allah the Just cannot stand injustice.«[82] If God is praised as the just one, his law must also serve justice. Sanusi concluded from this premise that Sharia demanded the eradication of exploitation and oppression. Of course, other interpreters may see divine justice in completely different terms, more in keeping with the patriarchal traditions of Islam. By invoking the ›idea‹ of Sharia, virtually any political position can be taken. If Muslims followed Sanusi's advice when drafting the laws of the state, they would be as free as the citizens of a Western democracy. Despite the ancient injunctions, they could promulgate any law they felt was just.

Orthodox critics of this liberal theology pointed out that it leads to arbitrary interpretations of the holy scriptures. If the tenets of Islam were reduced to abstract values such as justice, the divine message would evaporate and the ›Islamic‹ label could be applied to all kinds of political stances. For intellectuals like Sanusi, whose ideas of class struggle found little favor among the common people, religion seemed to be just an instrument of popularizing his own ideologies. That he was less concerned with God's revelation than with secular matters was clear from the thoroughly irreligious authors he invoked: Gramsci, Althusser, Poulantzas, Foucault, Chomsky and Said.[83] Thus, with his reinterpretation of Islam, alien Western ideas intruded in the Sharia debate: »Sanusi […] draws his motivation from Western intellectual tradition and not from the Islamic tradition.«[84] His preference for »kafir philosophers« (i.e. infidels) was seen to be consistent with the good contacts he maintained with Western aid organizations and the secular-oriented press in Southern Nigeria: »Everything that he writes is published by all the papers he sends [it] to, without any censor. He is also very much patronized by the NGO's.«[85]

Like intellectuals in the West, Sanusi assumed that the purpose of the state was to serve the people's welfare. Hence, when making laws, the

---

82 Sanusi, *Islam, Probity*, p. 5.
83 Sanusi, *Shari'a Debate*, p. 9.
84 Mohammed, *Muslim Intellectuals*, p. 15.
85 *Ibid.*, pp. 6, 14.

interests of the citizens should be paramount. This model of self-determination, which united leftist and liberal critics of Sharia, was rejected by orthodox Muslims, as it seemed to be based on a materialistic, irreligious attitude, which saw the purpose of mankind in its material well-being: »Where did they get that idea that the society will be alright, [when you] give everybody what he should eat, everybody has his house, everybody has everything«?[86] A focus on material concerns was a form of idolatry. With this verdict, devout Muslims rejected the shameless addiction to pleasure which seemed to be characteristic of Western societies. By discarding all theories that made people's self-interest the basis of legal relationships, they clung to their religious conviction, but they also reacted to the present realities of Nigeria with its rampant, self-destructive individualism. All the dilapidated institutions, the factories and hospitals standing empty, testified that the unbridled pursuit of material interests led not to affluence but to disaster. Without moral and religious principles that might remedy the lack of consideration for others, people were swept up in the maelstrom of a predatory economy, in which everyone was out to fleece everyone else. Muslims who sought a way out turned to a transcendent force which could break the principle of self-interest, and this required obedience to God. When waiving personal liberties and submitting to divine demands, the letter of the law was decisive, because a law that could be interpreted in any way had no binding force on people.

One could argue that scholars, preachers and kadhis had self-serving motives for urging obedience to the letter of the law. Their influence grew when religious norms were strictly enforced in all spheres of life. Thus they claimed that the sacred law, written more than a millennium ago, contained all knowledge that was essential to run society: »there is not an aspect of life which Almighty Allah has neglected in the Book.« Sharia »can provide answers to all the problems of mankind.«[87] There was no need to borrow from other cultures and religions, so all alien ideas should be renounced: »purify society of all un-Islamic practices and [...] live solely according to the way laid down by Allah, the Sharia.«[88] European observers tend to assume that such statements reflect the social interests of their authors. But the willingness to submit to divine laws was also born out of genuinely

86 Abdulkadir Orire, General Secretary of Jama'atu Nasril Islam, in *Vanguard*, 24 March 2002, p. 21; Mohammed, *Muslim Intellectuals*, p. 8.

87 Sambo, *Shari'a*, p. 41.

88 Philip Ostien on Usman dan Fodio, in Abubakar D. Muhammad, *Muslim Responses*, p. 4.

religious motives. When human beings have failed at all attempts to improve the conditions under which they live, they are more inclined to surrender to God's providence. God, who created mankind, knows best by which rules it is to operate. A leader of the Muslim Brothers explained that running a society was similar to servicing a car. If you want to do things right, stick to the manufacturer's manual.[89] The present social decline was explained by the disobedience of man who turned away from the instructions of his creator: »for a Muslim community to operate without shari'ah [...] is not pleasing to Allah, therefore, misfortunes and sufferings may follow that community as a punishment from Allah.«[90] If mankind's fate lay in the hands of God, it was important to win back his favor, and this could only be done by submitting to his will. God was prepared to lead men out of their misery, if only they followed him: »So fear not men, but fear you Me; and sell not My signs for a little price. Whoso judges not according to what God has sent down – they are the unbelievers.«[91]

The Letter of the Law

The idea that it should be left to the discretion of the faithful to modify Koranic precepts, is alien to this orthodox way of thinking. If God had willed that some institution was authorized to create new rules, why is it not mentioned in the Koran? The sacred text emphasizes instead that God has revealed his will to mankind conclusively and comprehensively through Mohammed, the last of the prophets: »Today I have perfected your religion for you.«[92] As the Koran does not empower the Muslim community to abrogate laws from the time of Mohammed, it is understandable that orthodox scholars warned against such arbitrary acts: »A Muslim must worship God not as he desires, but only in the manner specified by God Himself.« »It is not possible to arbitrarily select which [laws] to accept or not.«[93] From a Muslim perspective it is a typical feature of Christianity that

89 Muhammad Mahmud Turi, in *Tell*, 30 September 1996, p. 20.
90 Abubakar D. Muhammad, *Muslim Responses*, p. 7; Last, *Charia*, p. 147; Moumouni, *Uthman dan Fodio*, p. 119.
91 *Koran* 5: 44, p. 107.
92 *Koran* 5: 3, p. 100.
93 Gumi, *Where I Stand*, pp. 142, 92; cf. *Koran* 2: 79, p. 10 and 2: 85, p. 10–11: »woe to those who write the Book with their hands, then say: ›This is from God‹.« »do you believe in

it deliberately discarded parts of the divine revelation: »Some other religions are lucky. They are able to revise their scriptures. [...] We don't have that choice in Islam. We cannot for example, say in Islam, we would pray twice daily instead of five times.«[94] Unlike Islam, in its Sunni form, Christianity has institutions like the papacy, the episcopal councils and synods, which are authorized to sanction doctrinal changes. The Roman church discussed the validity of divine dictates right from its beginning. Yet this relative freedom from irrevocable laws is seen, by devout Muslims, as a failing: »Christianity is nothing [...], if you are saying I follow Jesus, in what way? There are no rules, no regulations, no anything. [...] on Sundays, you only go to listen to songs.«[95] The books of the Old Testament do contain divine commandments that match the strict provisions of Sharia in great detail – one only has to consider the many dietary and purity taboos. But these rules were already abolished in the early Christian era. The crucial event was the egregious deed of St. Paul who »made the sacred book of the Jews into one of the sacred books of the Christians«, but tore out its »tabooistic norms.«[96] As the doctrines of the Old and New Testaments contain such divergent ideas of law and morality, Christian authorities were compelled to depart from the wording of the laws. This breach with literalism did not constitute a betrayal of the original Christian message. Rejecting the letter of God's revelation and elevating its inner meaning was not a sacrilege, as the founders of the religion had already practiced it: »for the letter killeth, but the spirit giveth life.«[97]

---

part of the Book, and disbelieve in part? What shall be the recompense of those of you who do that, but degradation in the present life, and on the Day of Resurrection to be returned unto the most terrible chastisement?«

94 Dr. Lateef Adegbite, in *Vanguard*, 24 March 2002, p. 21; Gumi, *Where I Stand*, p. 58; Oloyede, *Shari'ah*, p. 297.

95 Abubakar Gumi, in Odey, *Sharia*, pp. 54–55; Ibrahim Sulaiman, *Shari'ah and Constitution*, pp. 64–65.

96 Weber, *Economy and Society*, p. 622.

97 The Second Letter of Paul to the Corinthians (3: 6). Similarly in Romans (7: 6): »But now we are delivered from the law, that being dead wherein we were held; that we should serve in newness of spirit, and not *in* the oldness of the letter.« This disengagement from the Mosaic tradition was contested between Paul and the congregation in Jerusalem, yet it prevailed because Jesus had made similar statements: »Ye have heard that it hath been said, An eye for an eye, and a tooth for a tooth: But I say unto you, That ye resist not evil: but whosoever shall smite thee on thy right cheek, turn to him the other also« (Matt. 5: 38–39). From a Muslim perspective, such passages of the New Testament are falsifications of the original Biblical message. Why should Jesus, if he were sent by God, give instructions that contradict God's previous pronouncements? »a

Muslims regard the fact that the Christian message encompasses so many varied texts as proof that it cannot be authentic. Why should God have given man contradictory commandments? The different books of the Bible seem to represent the opinions of very divergent authors, not the will of the one, unwavering God. The conclusion which already Mohammed had drawn from these inconsistencies was that Jews and Christians had falsified the early manifestations of God's revelation. Moses, David and Jesus had been Muslim prophets, but their teachings were refuted and distorted by their unworthy followers:

»We gave to Moses the Book, and after him sent succeeding Messengers; and We gave Jesus son of Mary the clear signs, and confirmed him with the Holy Spirit; and whensoever there came to you [Jews] a Messenger with what your souls had no desire for, did you become arrogant, and some cry lies to, and some slay? And they say, ›Our hearts are uncircumcised.‹ Nay, but God has cursed them for their unbelief.«[98]

The Koran also accuses Christians of having willfully discarded parts of God's teachings and made up others, such as the claim that Jesus was the son of God. Against this relapse into polytheism, the Koran argues that only Mohammed's message has preserved or reestablished in its pristine purity the age-old prophecy, from Adam via Moses to Jesus. Islam's right to exist, compared with that of the two older Abrahamitic religions, is based on this claim that the suras of the Koran express the will of God unaltered, word for word: »all the messages which Almighty Allah sent through various messengers to various nations up to the last Prophet [...] are all messages of Islam. [...] the Holy Quran is today the only Holy Book which is still as it was revealed.«[99]

One could argue that the Koran also comprises inconsistencies and contradictions, especially between suras that originated in Mecca and those

---

Christian should sit down for a while [...] to ponder over the possibility of God to have suddenly changed His mind and rendered the law ineffectual as if He is also a creature like us who progress by trials and error« (Saleh Dogara Muhammad, *Qur'an*, p. 8).

98 *Koran* 2: 87–88, p. 11.

99 Sambo, *Shari'a*, pp. 36, 420. – »Judaism and Christianity had been true religions at the time of their advent [...]. These revelations were, however, rendered obsolete by the apostolate of Muhammad. Whatever truth they contained was incorporated in his message. What was not incorporated was not true, and was the result of the distortion and corruption of these earlier scriptures by their unworthy custodians« (Bernard Lewis, *Middle East*, pp. 219–220). »Muslims have historically seen Christianity as a truncated or perverted Islam« (Hodgson, *Islam*, pp. 28, 365–366).

later revealed in Medina. When its verses were compiled, many were taken out of context and listed one after the other, often with no relation between them, so their meaning only becomes clear after meticulous interpretation. The Koran's early exegetes were aware of these problems, but they applied all their reasoning to resolve inherent contradictions, as they were convinced that the 6,346 verses of the Koran were spoken by only one divine voice: »The Qur'ân [...] has been accepted as literally the words of God«,[100] and it is indeed far more consistent than the Bible. While the Old and New Testaments consist of texts that emerged over a thousand years, the message of the Koran was revealed by only one prophet and recorded while he was still alive. As a statesman »with unlimited power«,[101] Mohammed had given explicit and unmistakable instructions, which referred directly to socio-political matters. Some legal matters, like the proper rules of inheritance, are dealt with in such detail that it seems the divine legislator wanted to regulate all contingencies of human life.[102]

Nonetheless, many legal issues remain unresolved in the Koran, so Islamic kadhis relied initially on local traditions of law. However, the scholars of the great law schools succeeded in officially abolishing the ancient Arab common law and the legal traditions of the subdued Roman and Iranian provinces. Only sacred knowledge was to be permitted as a source of law, and this knowledge included not only the prophetic revelation in a narrow sense (i.e. the teachings of Koran). The Prophet was divinely inspired in everything he did and said, so his personal way of life and his actions as a statesman could also serve as a paradigm.[103] In order to draw up a legal system that was in all its details derived from Islamic principles, scholars referred to what was reported from the time of the Prophet. These accounts, which had been handed down orally, were of course more diverse than the original divine revelation, but when selecting suitable reports, jurists considered only those as authentic, which were consistent with the Koran. Thus a fairly homogeneous corpus of texts emerged: six

---

100 Hodgson, *Islam*, p. 73.

101 Hartmann, *Kalifat*, p. 235; An-Na'im, *Islamic Reformation*, p. 77.

102 »If a man perishes having no children, but he has a sister, she shall receive a half of what he leaves; and he is her heir if she has no children. If there be two sisters, they shall receive two-thirds of what he leaves; if there be brothers and sisters, the male shall receive the portion of two females. God makes clear to you, lest you go astray; God has knowledge of everything« (*Koran* 4: 176, pp. 97–98).

103 Hodgson, *Islam*, pp. 327–328; Bernard Lewis, *Middle East*, p. 222.

major collections of *hadith* with thousands of pages, also deemed sacred,
though to a lesser degree than the Koran.[104]

Creating a system of law that derived solely from the Koran and the
hadith, offered several advantages. It was supposed to end controversies
over God's demands, contain factionalism, and avert the risk of fratricidal
religious wars. Moreover, it could make the judiciary's behavior more predictable. Of course, for cases that were not stipulated in the Koran and
hadith, new rules had to be invented. The great law schools not only systematized laws that already existed, they also complemented Sharia. This
implied taking autonomous decisions in order to produce additional
›divine‹ laws. But even this limited form of law creation, *ijtihad*, was organized in a way that eliminated as far as possible independent reasoning and
human discretion. Some jurists had suggested that cases on which the
divine legislator kept silent should be decided according to principles of
justice, common welfare or the interest of the state. However, such noble
principles that allowed judges a wide margin to decide according to their
own preference would not have led to legal security but to endless disputes
about the welfare of the people or the state. Therefore, legal scholars
developed a largely mechanical process of establishing new laws, which
was meant to exclude human arbitrariness. In order to decide controversial
cases in accordance with divine standards, they looked for similar cases in
the Koran or *hadith*, inferred a general rule from them and applied it to the
disputes at hand.[105] With this procedure, known as *qiyas*, the four great
Sunni law schools arrived at very similar conclusions: a »coherent« system
of laws that only differed from each other in details.[106] Even Sunni and
Shia jurists shared a wide consensus, so that Sharia, as the irrevocable law
of God, has been acknowledged far beyond orthodox circles: »The supremacy, or at least the crucial importance, of the Shari'ah has been accepted
not only in most Islamic currents, but even by most sorts of opinion
within each current – whether mystic or literalist.«[107]

Modernizers who wished to replace the ›outdated‹ Sharia laws with new
ones could scarcely invoke a divine mandate. Instead, they introduced
philosophical reasoning and other non-religious ways of thinking in order

---

104 Davutoglu, Secularisation, pp. 184–185; Hodgson, Islam, pp. 324–325.
105 El-Affendi, *Rationality*, p. 156; Hodgson, *Islam*, pp. 327–332; Schacht, *Islamic Law*, pp. 34–35, 202, 211.
106 Schacht, *Islamic Law*, pp. 201, 3, 16, 29; Hodgson, *Islam*, pp. 336–337.
107 Hodgson, *Islam*, pp. 351, 278, 326.

to tackle orthodoxy: »The greatest tragedy in Sunni thought is its hatred of philosophy and philosophers and its enthronement of the legalistic rulings of jurists over all facets of our life.«[108] In order to shake off these constraints, Ibraheem Sulaiman of the Ahmadu Bello University claimed that Sharia laws only had temporary validity: »The founders of the [law] schools [...] never intended to solve the problems of generations yet to come, of which they kn[e]w nothing, neither did they ever claim that the results of their output were valid for all time.«[109] But this is merely an arbitrary assertion. The jurists of the eighth and ninth centuries were certainly convinced that the divine instructions they systematized were not only intended for their own time. When they availed themselves of the right to create new laws by *ijtihad*, they did not wish to abolish Koranic regulations and replace them with more modern ideas. Their intention was simply to plug legal gaps by applying Islamic principles to areas for which no explicit rules existed in the holy scriptures. After generations of jurists had debated and finally decided most open legal issues, the idea took hold in Sunni Islam from around 900 that the »gate of ijtihad« and thus the way to new laws were closed.[110]

Today, many if not most jurists no longer feel bound to this consensus, though Abubakar Gumi, Nigeria's most prominent Sharia expert, warned:

»No aspect of our lives is left to human judgment. Everything we do must be according to the laws of God. For example, no less than seventeen regulations in Islam govern how one should carry out such a private and routine habit as visiting the toilet. Other aspects of life with greater complexity or social consequence attract far more rules, and it is not possible to arbitrarily select which ones to accept or not.«[111]

But even Gumi believed that it was legitimate to complement Sharia law in order to adapt it to modern needs.[112] How far these changes may go and what direction they should take cannot be determined in advance. Sunni Islam knows no official body that is authorized to decide theological disputes, thus fierce arguments are bound to occur. Yet these debates cannot be held freely. Even *ijtihad* does not give the Islamic public sphere permis-

---

108 Sanusi, *Islam, Probity*, p. 5.
109 Ibraheem Sulaiman, *Sharia Restoration*, p. 4.
110 Anderson, *Law Reform*, p. 7; Bernard Lewis, *Middle East*, p. 226; Tetzlaff, *Islamisches Erbe*, pp. 41–46.
111 Gumi, *Where I Stand*, p. 92.
112 Loimeier, *Islamische Erneuerung*, p. 143.

sion to disengage from religious constraints and change past laws at will. Resolute modernizers may claim that a contemporary form of Sharia will not be a »replica« of the old laws, but »may almost amount to a new invention.«[113] But what entitles them to call such an invention ›Sharia‹? If everything were up for revision, people would rise to being masters of their religion, and God's commands would be debased. Devout Muslims will resist such a process that could lead – as in Europe – to a ›godless‹ society. What their rivals, the Sharia modernizers, are calling for looks like the »Pauline abrogation of Jewish law«, which opened the path to secularism: »Sanusi and the modernists before him wanted to change the rules so that Islam will be totally reformed as Christianity leading to complete secularization and the abolishing of Islam just as Christianity was abolished.«[114]

As already mentioned above (p. 161), there were not only religious reasons why the devout stuck to the letter of the law. In order to counteract social decay, Nigerians had to form a moral community. Only if they regained a common understanding of good and evil, right or wrong could they stand up to the corrupt elite and exert public pressure on it. In a society that was deeply divided by ethnicity and class distinctions, religion provided a precious source of universal legal and moral concepts. Nigeria's Muslims did not turn to the holy scriptures merely to be told that they could renounce God's rules at will. On the contrary, their religion was supposed to give them guidance so that moral and political debates could be based on common principles. Disputes would still be allowed; only the number of possible arguments was to be restricted drastically. Nobody would present claims that were incompatible with the will of God. Islam would thus become a kind of arena, in which the legitimacy of political demands was to be negotiated.

Intellectuals who did not wish to pay heed to the letter of the law undermined the consensus which Sharia activists wished to establish. Invoking the »spirit of Sharia«[115] could not create unity; it only opened the floodgates to all possible interpretations of God's message. If the modernizers had their way, the debate about law and morality would relapse into the same arbitrariness as before the introduction of Sharia. How divergently the sacred texts could be interpreted when the wording of the law no longer mattered shall be illustrated in the remaining pages of this

---

113 Ibraheem Sulaiman, *Sharia Restoration*, p. 4.
114 Mohammed, *Muslim Intellectuals*, pp. 5, 6.
115 Ladan, *Legal Pluralism*, pp. 35, 33; Mahdi, *Shari'a*, p. 4.

chapter by looking at the debates about women's rights. Zaynab Alkali, a professor at the University of Maiduguri, argued, based on her historical-critical reading of the Koran, that polygamy should be abolished:[116] When the Prophet allowed men to marry up to four wives, his society was at war with its neighbors, and there were many widows who needed to be provided for. Today, a man was available for every woman, so the original reason for polygamy no longer applied. This inventive interpretation did not impress the Islamic establishment. Muslim males saw the benefits of polygamy in a different light, and they had the power to enforce their point of view. The official guidelines for Sharia vigilantes in Kano stated: »Hisbah must embark on re-orientation of women on virtues of polygamy … they should counter western tendency and propaganda that view polygamy as outdated.«[117]

There are many reasons why women are not happy with the current gender relations. Khadiya Umar, a lecturer at the University of Jos, gave a bitter account of old men with wealth and influence who saw it as their privilege to marry young girls: never more than four simultaneously but in swift succession. Following this principle, a man in her hometown had married 24 wives without damaging his reputation.[118] Sharia will do nothing to change such practices, as it gives men the right to spurn their wives by making a simple declaration of intent. It suffices to say three times in the presence of witnesses: ›I divorce you‹, and the marriage is annulled. Women, in contrast, are only divorced if a court gives its consent, though many wives had not chosen their husbands. According to the rules of the Maliki school, a father may give his underage daughter in marriage even against her will; among the Hausa this often happens to young children. By the age of twelve, the majority of girls are already married.[119] The proposal to set a minimum age for marriage was rejected by the parliaments, as even the Prophet, who married a nine-year old, did not specify one. Among the Hausa, a newly wedded girl moves into her husband's home immediately, but the marriage is not usually consummated before the onset of puberty; if it does occur, it was until recently illegal. Under the old penal code, the

---

116 Lecture at the University of Frankfurt, 9 December 2002.
117 Hisba Guidelines Kano, in Gwarzo, *Civic Associations*, p. 308.
118 Kahdiya Umar at the Sharia conference in Bayreuth, July 11–12, 2003.
119 Callaway/Creevey, *Islam*, pp. 34, 36.

rape of a minor in marriage was a criminal offence. However, this felony was abolished when Sharia law was introduced.[120]

About a third of all the regulations which the Koran imposes on the faithful apply to marital and family matters.[121] These include many precepts that restrict women's freedom of movement and social contacts. As men are given the task of overseeing their wives, they are expressly permitted to beat them. Men are also favored in legal matters: when dividing an inheritance, claiming custody of children or giving evidence in court.[122] However, feminists in Northern Nigeria do not appreciate it when women from abroad highlight these discriminatory provisions. At a conference of the Heinrich-Böll Foundation in Lagos on Sharia and Women's Human Rights, only one of the delegates mentioned the many restrictive regulations: Codou Bop from Senegal, a country with a mainly Islamic population but without state-enforced Sharia law. Her summary: »I do not believe there are Islamic foundations to support women's human rights.«[123] This statement unleashed vehement protest. She was accused of quoting passages of the Koran out of their historic context; her lecture was said to be »poorly researched« and »misleading.«[124] If »correctly understood«, Sharia was totally compatible with human rights: »all the guaranteed human rights under the modern international instruments [Universal Declaration of Human Rights etc. – J.H.] are within the purview of the general human rights that Quran has made available to all human beings regardless of orientation, belief, gender.«[125] The Koran, which stated that man and woman were created from a single being, namely Adam, thus acknowl-

---

120 Ostien, *Islamic Criminal Law*, p. 4; compare section 282 of the old Penal Code with section 128 of the Sharia Penal Code in Zamfara; also Anderson, *Islamic Law*, p. 177. – In cases of extra-marital rape, the legal position of women is also very precarious now. If they bring a complaint of rape, they risk being condemned for pre-marital or extra-marital sexual intercourse: »If a woman reports to the police that she is a victim of rape, this can easily be construed as a confession to unlawful intercourse which makes her liable to the *hadd* punishment, unless she can prove that intercourse took place without her consent. The burden of proof in that case is hers. Moreover, if her attacker does not confess, her accusations against him amount to defamation […], for which she can be punished by an additional eighty lashes« (Peters, *Islamic Criminal Law*, p. 19).

121 Callaway/Creevey, *Islam*, p. 29.

122 Hodgson, *Islam*, pp. 180–182, 341–342; Schacht, *Islamic Law*, pp. 161–168.

123 Bop, *Women's Rights*, p. 97.

124 Haruna, *Women's Rights*, p. 107; Aliyu, *Development*, p. 124.

125 Haruna, *Women's Rights*, p. 104; Aliyu, *Development*, p. 124; Ladan, *Women's Rights*, pp. 47, 49; Khadijah Abdullahi Umar, *Muslim Women*, p. 18.

edged that they had equal rights in principle.[126] Compared with the way of life of pre-Islamic Bedouins, the social status of women had improved thanks to the Koran. Women had gained the right to dispose of their own property without their husband's interference. Some Muslim feminists argued that the Prophet must have been guided by the intention of strengthening the legal position of women. Therefore, in order to carry on his intentions, other restrictions should also be abolished.[127]

Efforts to defend the progressive tendencies of Sharia against Western-oriented, secular critics sound strange when expressed by feminists. But how else should they deal with Sharia? A lecture by Khadijah Umar began with the blunt statement: »Sharia in Northern Nigeria has come to stay.«[128] Anything women can achieve has to be claimed or asked for within a religiously defined framework, on the platform of Islam. A poor basis on which to negotiate better conditions for women. In order to be heard, they are forced to refer to texts that were written 1,400 years ago: »Northern Nigerian women discuss their political goals in terms of a reinterpretation of Muslim law. [...] public rejection of the Sharia would be unthinkable.«[129] Since women appeared as Sharia supporters before a domestic audience, they also had to play this role when attending discussions abroad. They even affirmed that Islam was in principle very accommodating to the rights of women. Zaynab Alkali, who was announced as an African feminist, when she gave a lecture at the University of Frankfurt, surprised her audience by professing: »We women have nothing against Sharia.«[130] As a sign that she acknowledged the dictates of her religion, she had put on a head-scarf, just like other Muslim feminists who came to Germany to take part in Sharia debates. If they were to dress and argue differently in front of Europeans than at home, they would risk forfeiting their credibility in Nigeria. Muslims would accuse them that their pious garb at home was

---

126 Ladan, *Women's Rights*, pp. 49, 59; Nasir, *Women's Rights*, p. 24; Khadijah Abdullahi Umar, *Muslim Women*, p. 7; Audi, *Secularism*, p. 121; Hauwa Mustapha, *Islamic Legal System*, p. 110.

127 Khadijah Abdullahi Umar, *Muslim Women*, p. 9; Anonymous, *Supreme Council*, p. 15; Nasir, *Women's Rights*, pp. 25–26.

128 At the Sharia conference in Bayreuth, in Khadijah Abdullahi Umar, *Muslim Women*, p. 1.

129 Callaway/Creevey, *Islam*, p. 194.

130 Women in the Arab world argue in a similar fashion. Based on their testimony, the idea is spreading in Western media that Islam is in principle favorably disposed to the rights of women: »Muslim feminists argue that there is nothing in Islam properly understood that requires the subordination of women« (Carens/Williams, *Muslim Minorities*, p. 143).

nothing but a masquerade to conceal their pursuit of Western, secular interests.

Being compelled to base their claims on quotes from the Koran and *hadith* does not allow a free debate. Yet it would be wrong to assume that commitments to Sharia, when made by Western-educated women, are not meant seriously. Embracing their Islamic tradition is important to many, as it enables them to set themselves apart from unwanted cultural influences.[131] Western individualism seems to lead to a permissive, irresponsible society, which flouts the rules of decency and shame, and destroys the »African woman's dignity.«[132] The rejection of legal and ethical concepts originating in the West is also noticeable among Sharia modernizers such as S. L. Sanusi: Human rights, as Europeans and Americans understand them, cannot be the norm for Muslims.[133] When Ruud Peters reminded him at the conference in Bayreuth that the human rights to which Europeans referred were acknowledged in the statutes of the United Nations, he replied: »And who pays for the United Nations?« For progressives like Sanusi who deconstruct the sacred traditions of Islam, it is certainly not advisable to invoke Western secular tenets. However, Sanusi was not only bowing to external pressure. In discussions with him and other opponents of the state-enforced Sharia, I had the impression that they cherished their Islamic identity, not least because of their antipathy toward Western modernity.[134]

---

131 O'Brien, *Charia*, p. 56.

132 Khadijah Abdullahi Umar, *Muslim Women*, p. 17. – The Islamic idea that men and women should play different, complementary roles is acceptable to many female Muslim activists, which is why they reject Western demands for equal rights. In their view it is more important to strengthen marital bonds and protect women against arbitrary divorce. This could secure their social status, improve their material welfare, and guarantee access to their children (Khadijah Abdullahi Umar, *Muslim Women*, p. 6; Callaway/Creevey, *Islam*, p. 194; Westerlund, *Islamism*, pp. 315–316).

133 Sanusi, *Class, Gender*, p. 6.

134 Shehu Sani, chairman of the Civil Rights Congress, whose organization was sponsored by the Friedrich Ebert Foundation, Germany, told me: »People in the West are vultures.« In order to roll back Western cultural influence, he approved the government policy in Iran, where tuning into TV stations such as CNN was prohibited (personal communication, Kaduna, 8 March 2001). Muhammed Ladan, another modernizer, regards concessions to Christians only as a temporary device: »We must for now content ourselves with legal pluralism.« But in the long term, Nigeria needed a unified law based on Islam. So the introduction of Sharia in the North is only a first step, though a significant one: »the Sokoto Caliphate [...] has been reborn as the nucleus of a new, powerful nation« (Ladan, *Legal Pluralism*, pp. 35, 5, 32, 25).

Debates between Muslims and Christians

Secularism

From a Christian point of view, Sharia politicians have broken a religious compromise that had held the multi-faith country together since independence. This compromise could not prevent religious clashes which had claimed approximately 20,000 lives in the 1980s and 1990s (if one includes the victims of the Maitatsine riots). But these conflicts could be quelled, as the ruling military were more or less intent on keeping a neutral stance. With the transition to democracy, the rulers in the North openly took the side of the Muslim majority. When Governor Sani announced a far-reaching Islamization of his state and other governors followed suit, everyone anticipated an escalation of religious violence. Sunday Mbang, the president of the Christian Association of Nigeria (CAN), an umbrella organization of all churches, called the introduction of full Sharia »irresponsible madness.«[1] Wole Soyinka even feared it would be the »prelude to civil war.«[2]

Sharia prompted Muslims and Christians to fight for control of the state, with dire consequences for the unity of Nigeria. In order to prevent a religious confrontation, the Christian Association of Nigeria called on state authorities in the North to suspend their new Sharia laws and assume a position of religious neutrality. Most Christians were willing to accept that Muslims continued to decide family disputes with the help of Sharia courts and that these courts were funded with taxpayers' money. Yet they did not want the state to take on further religious obligations. The rival faiths should not try to gain influence by using the coercive instruments of the

---

1 *Tell*, 6 March 2000, p. 20.
2 Quoted in Metan, *Dilemmas*, p. 290. – According to Toyin Falola, Sharia »pushed the country to the brink of a religious war and sharpened the religious divide beyond the point of healing« (quoted in Korieh, *Islam*, p. 118).

state, but should restrain their competition by relying solely on religious means: the attraction of their gospel. Christians pointed out that a secular state was not anti-religious; it only committed itself not to favor either of the two great faiths.[3] From a Christian perspective, this was a fair compromise, as it guaranteed that both sides would be treated equally. For Sharia supporters, it was an unacceptable proposal, because the separation of religion and politics, imposed by the British, was alien to Islam.[4] What Christians proposed as the basis for a mutually beneficial coexistence originated in the political and religious traditions of Europe: »this secular legal system [i]s essentially Christian.«[5] Though the British had left in 1960, the British system remained in force, and this privileged Nigeria's Christians. They could live under a constitutional arrangement that suited them, while Muslims were not allowed to revive their own legal traditions. For Dr. Datti Ahmed, the president of the Supreme Council for Sharia, it was perfectly legitimate that the people in Kano, Borno and Zamfara freed themselves from this paternalism: »Why do we have to continue to follow the common law which is based originally on Christian doctrines«?[6]

Defenders of Western constitutional principles might object that secular law is not Christian, because it developed by overriding the claims of religious authorities. In the course of Europe's religious wars, when it became clear that none of the warring parties could permanently defeat their opponents, Catholics and Protestants had to learn to coexist. And this was only possible if they based their coexistence on legal principles, which were »independent of confessional allegiance.«[7] State laws must not be determined by the doctrines of any of the faiths, otherwise they could not be recognized by all citizens. So the validity of divine commands was largely restricted to the private sphere, and the citizens became free to determine the laws of the state as they wished. In the realm of politics, the holy scriptures were replaced by the social contract: the free agreement between autonomous citizens. As the secular state acknowledged the sovereignty of men, it was not bound by biblical precepts. Adulterers were not

---

3 Committee, *Report*, p. 35; Ilesanmi, *Constitutional Treatment*, pp. 549–550; Nwabueze, *Unconstitutionality of Sharia*, p. 3.

4 Lateef Adegbite in Clarke/Linden, *Islam*, p. 171; Gumi, *Where I Stand*, p. 127; Falola, *Violence in Nigeria*, p. 76; Ilesanmi, *Religious Pluralism*, p. 180.

5 Birai, *Tajdid*, p. 193; Ahmed Bello Mahmud, *Shari'ah*, p. 9; Westerlund, *Secularism*, pp. 83–84.

6 *The News*, 15 May 2000, p. 23.

7 Taylor, *Modes of Secularism*, p. 32.

stoned, although the Mosaic law calls on Christians to do so. Rejecting such religious demands was relatively easy in Europe, because the early Roman church had distanced itself from these archaic Biblical injunctions since its beginnings. Moreover, the New Testament did not oblige Christians to run the state on the basis of religious law: »Render therefore unto Caesar the things which are Caesar's; and unto God the things that are God's.«[8] Based on this dualism of religious life and the realm of politics, which was determined by its own secular laws, Christianity in modern Europe turned into a faith that focused on the inner, personal bond with God. The faithful should follow their religious convictions; so the clergy urged them not to commit adultery and other sins, but the churches did not borrow the authority of the state and its instruments of coercion to enforce a pious life.

A religion that is largely restricted to personal piety and congregational life within the churches is not acceptable to orthodox Muslims. The *umma*, as it was conceived in the canonical texts, is a politically-constituted community. Sunni jurists never justified in principle the separation of state and religion. The main role of the state was to be the »Custodian of the Sharia.«[9] State pressure to ensure religious conformity seemed necessary because a life pleasing to God could not be led individually, but only in a community that established a divine order:[10] »in Islam, its core is neither an inner spiritual experience nor cognitive assent to a body of doctrine. It is acceptance of the law.«[11] If Muslims rejected the letter of the law and embraced secular authorities, their religion would turn into a more private faith and approximate Christianity. Thus it would lose a central element of its self-legitimation: to be the true guardian of Mosaic laws. Moreover, the faithful would have to fear that a non-binding, liberal Islam would suffer a similar decline as Christianity has in Europe.[12] Many suspected that the call by Christians to make religion a matter of personal piety was calculated to

---

8 Matthew 22: 21.

9 Ladan, *Legal Pluralism*, p. 24; cf. Black, *Religion*, p. 372; Bernard Lewis, *Middle East*, p. 224.

10 Hodgson, *Islam*, pp. 71, 74; Alkhateeb, *Islamic Unity*, p. 13.

11 Bruce, *Fundamentalism*, p. 107. – Islam's strict and unequivocal monotheism does not demand complex dogmas to be considered true, only a clear commitment to Allah and his Prophet (von Grunebaum, *Studien*, p. 27; Weber, *Economy and Society*, pp. 564, 570, 625).

12 Ado-Kurawa, *Conference*, p. 22.

weaken Islam. Secularization was therefore seen as a strategy of religious confrontation and a continuation of the crusades by other means.[13]

Even intellectuals who would welcome the adoption of Western, secular attitudes could hardly imagine Islam undertaking such a radical departure from its main doctrines: »Secularism, is unlikely to succeed [...] [A]dvocates of secularism will appear to be calling on their own societies to abandon their Islamic cultural and religious foundations.«[14] Religious authorities had never renounced Islam's claim to shape the public sphere; this claim was just relegated to the background by secular ideologies like nationalism and socialism, which dominated political debates for some decades. With the failure of these ideologies, the political aspirations of religion have again taken center-stage, and the laws of God can no longer be banished from public life: »Not only fundamentalists but all Muslims, when they take their faith seriously, must reject the idea of a secular, pluralist state in which non-Muslim parties can compete openly for power.«[15]

As long as state and religion are kept apart, Muslims cannot live the way they are instructed to by their holy scriptures. Therefore, Sharia supporters had good reason to complain that the Western-style constitution prevented them from practicing their faith freely. A constitution that promised them religious freedom and insisted at the same time on secularism contradicted itself, as the two constitutional principles were mutually exclusive.[16] While Christians praised secular law as a safeguard of religious tolerance, Muslims saw it as a means of oppression: »Christian leaders have remained [...] intolerant.« »The rights of Muslims and Muslim organizations are trampled upon.«[17]

Dialogue on Human Rights

For Christians it may have sounded cynical that Sharia supporters campaigned on behalf of tolerance and religious freedom. After all, Sharia

---

13 Mohammed, *Muslim Intellectuals*, p. 13; Mu'azzam/Ibrahim, *Religious Identity*, p. 77; Sakpe, *Terrorist*, pp. 19–21, 44.

14 An-Na'im, *Political Islam*, p. 119.

15 Black, *Religion*, pp. 383, 381.

16 Bashir Sambo, Zamfara State Chief Justice, in Abd al-Masih/Ibn Salam, *Sharia*, p. 11; Ilesanmi, *Constitutional Treatment*, p. 542.

17 Ado-Kurawa, *Shari'ah*, pp. 285, 275; Balewa, *Common Law*, p. 10.

aimed at a strict regimentation of religious life. By employing the instruments of the state to enforce compliance with religious laws, orthodox Muslims prevented their co-religionists from deciding how to worship God: They disregarded »the ultimate right and duty of the individual conscience to make moral decisions.«[18] Sharia activists did not deny that they wished to exert religious pressure on their fellow-Muslims, yet they did not see this as a breach of democracy and human rights: »The adoption of Shari'ah by any person or State that professes the Islamic faith is not a question of choice. It is compulsory especially with the advent of democracy [...]. [T]he people of Zamfara State have [...] insisted on their fundamental right to observe their religion as decreed by Allah.«[19] With the transition to democracy, the Muslim majority in Kano, Zamfara and Sokoto acquired the right to live in accordance with the dictates of their faith. This right is not the same as the constitutional principle that grants freedom of religion and conscience to each citizen. For Sharia supporters, freedom of religion was not a right that individuals could assert vis-à-vis the authorities, but a collective right. It authorized the Islamic community to compel its members to practice their faith correctly. What the *umma* called for in terms of rights, were duties from an individual's perspective: duties owed to God and all those who exercised authority in his name. Thus, when Christians and Muslims argued about human rights, they referred to very different concepts. Governor Sani found it incomprehensible that Christians accused him of violating human rights: »Islam as a religion and a complete way of life, has made respect for human rights central to all its adherents [...] this was why Allah prohibited undue interaction between men and women.«[20] »In Sharia, there are human rights for everything.«[21]

Islam's emphasis on accepting God-given rules was not the only reason for the rejection of secular principles; Muslims had other, non-religious reasons as well. If they followed the example of European societies and confined their faith to the private sphere, a vacuum would be created: »The

---

18 Obadare (*Religious NGOs*, p. 149), quoting Casanova, Public Religions.
19 Ahmed Bello Mahmud, *Shari'ah*, p. 9. – Cf. Juergensmeyer, *Terror in the Mind of God*, p. 216: »freedom of religion means freedom to live under religious law.«
20 *Tell*, 14 October 2002, p. 66. – »in the charter of human rights granted by Islam [...] a woman's chastity must be respected and protected at all times« (Al-Khamis, *Religious Leaders*, p. 98).
21 Abdulkdir Orire, General Secretary of Jama'atu Nasril Islam, in *Vanguard*, 24 March 2002, p. 21.

desire to live in an ethical world, where [...] people share and realize a common understanding of the good life, remains unfulfilled.«[22] The lack of a common moral orientation posed a serious threat in a state that was incapable of halting the social and economic decline. State bureaucracies, which ought to manage social and economic progress, had become so dysfunctional that Nigerians had to look for alternatives. Even European societies have largely given up efforts to transform themselves by state-driven social engineering.[23] Once secular ideologies had lost their appeal, only religion remained as a means to regulate people's behavior and change the social and political conditions under which they lived. In order to fulfill this function, religion had to be freed from secular constraints. It could cause a fundamental renewal, but only if it was allowed to penetrate all spheres of society.

Christian churches sought to improve men from the inside by inducing a change of heart. Thus they relied on moral appeals, not on state coercion. Protestants and Evangelicals in particular pointed out that external constraints did not lead to a religious renewal but to hypocrisy: »purity originates from the heart [...] [P]iety will remove the need for external structures that still leave the heart dirty.«[24] By urging their followers to internalize Christian moral precepts, the churches wished to encourage personal virtues. But in a thoroughly corrupt world, individual efforts to behave honestly were constantly discouraged and abused.[25] Only concerted political action could overcome the system of violence and corruption that held people captive. Islam's willingness to employ compulsion and extend it into all areas of life, was an advantage in this reform project. If society could only be transformed by unanimous, collective efforts, it made sense to hold all community members accountable and force them to meet their obligations.

Christians who insisted on secular principles sabotaged the project of a social renewal and hindered Muslims from liberating themselves from the burden of social decay. As Christians defended the existing irreligious order, they were blamed for all sorts of immorality. Muslim resentment was directed, above all, against migrants from the South, who had vehe-

---

22 Bubner, *Studien*, p. 48.

23 Ellis/ter Haar, *Worlds of Power*, p. 187.

24 Committee, *Report*, p. 38.

25 Unflinching adherence to Christian morality can be a recipe for disaster. I read in a Kenyan newspaper that a born-again Christian who steadfastly refused to pay bribes failed his driving test seven times.

mently denounced Sharia: »these people [Southerners] have lowered our moral standards, debased our value system and introduced vices that were hitherto unknown to us, such as armed robbery.«[26] The fight against social decline was entwined with the rejection of foreign, un-Islamic influences. Muslims strengthened their religious identity to set themselves apart from infidels: »the clamour for Shari'a [...] is a result of sustained resist[a]nce to the reign of looting, injustice, greed and promiscuity which southerners have taught and imposed on the North.«[27]

Despite their resentment, Muslims and Christians are aware that they will have to get along, since none of them wants to split the federation. Most politicians have lost interest in a religious confrontation, but they have not made any serious attempts to negotiate a constitutional settlement or some other treaty that would regulate the rights and duties of the religious groups. Representatives of the Christian Association of Nigeria told me they had no idea how security could be achieved in the long run. Both Muslim and Christian leaders have appealed to their followers to maintain peace, and sometimes they have issued joint declarations, for instance a press release by CAN and the Supreme Council for Islamic Affairs that called upon Nigerians to work toward free and fair elections in April 2007. However, the talks in various dialogue forums did not bring a consensus on how the relations between the major faiths should be organized:

»dialogue [...] has tended to focus on Christian leaders teaming up with Muslim leaders, holding hands and smiling while the cameras click and click around the corridors of the powerful. These pictures are then sent out through the media and they are supposed to send out signals to the effect that if ordinary Christians and Muslims see that their leaders are working together in peace and harmony, they would follow suit. These cycles of dialogue have been going on in Nigeria for many years and yet, as it is clear, the violence has not relented.«[28]

It is difficult to tell how seriously Muslims and Christians take the pronouncements of their leaders. When Nigeria's media reported on the Mohammed caricatures in the Danish press, CAN was the first to condemn this insult to Islam, even before Muslim organizations spoke out against it. Yet two weeks later, on 18 February 2006, violent protests against the blasphemy in Danish media turned against the Christian minority in Northern Nigeria, first in Maiduguri where Muslim youths

---

26 *Hotline*, 3 April 2000, p. 17.
27 *Hotline*, 26 March 2000, p. 32.
28 Kukah, *Managing Christian-Muslim Relations*, pp. 397–398.

burnt 30 churches and killed some dozen Christians. From here, the riots spread to other Northern towns, and on 21 February, Christian Igbo retaliated, killing hundreds of Hausa in Onitsha. Muslim authorities like the sultan had fueled the protests by calling for the Danish embassy to be closed. In Kano, parliamentarians burnt Danish flags and declared a boycott of Danish goods.[29]

The government of Kano State had declared its commitment to interreligious dialogue, yet as its 2006 Ramadan Message it chose a verse from the Koran that urged Muslims not to consider Christians as friends: »He among you who taketh them (Christians) for friends is one of them.«[30] At the same time, the government pressured Christian schools to adopt the Islamic dress code. A representative of the Catholic diocese in Kano told me that he and his colleagues had withdrawn from the dialogue, as they had the impression that their Muslim counterparts were mainly interested in publicity. Muslims organized common press conferences in order to make the world believe that Muslims and Christians got along well under Sharia. Yet they evaded discussions about Islamic law and declined to sign a communiqué which contained the sentence: »There should be continuous dialogue between both Christians and Muslims for a better understanding of Shari'a in Islam.«[31]

Muslims did not want infidels lecturing them on how to understand their religion, and they resented being taught the advantages of a critical historical reading of their holy scriptures: »whether or not Qur'an was the word of Allah or the word of Muhammed, is entirely the business of the Muslim.«[32] Christians and Muslims could not expect to reach a common understanding of religious freedom and the political role of religion. When they met at conferences, they assured each other that they were committed to peace, but such declarations expressed, at best, a shallow consensus. At a series of lectures and seminars, sponsored by the European Union, the

---

29 *Africa Research Bulletin. Political, Social and Cultural Series*, 1–28 February 2006, p. 16549; *Daily Trust*, 2 February, 9 February and 15 February 2006. – According to the Christian Association of Nigeria, Borno State (*Religious Disturbances*, p. 1), 56 churches were destroyed and 60 persons killed.

30 *Tell*, 30 October 2006, p. 52; cf. *Koran* 5: 51, p. 108: »O believers, take not Jews and Christians as friends; they are friends of each other. Whoso of you makes them his friends is one of them. God guides not the people of the evildoers.«

31 Communiqué of Kaduna Provincial Interreligious Dialogue Seminar, in Salihu, *Interreligious Dialogue*, p. 86.

32 Omotosho, *Religious Violence*, p. 29.

chief imam of a mosque in Jos pointed out that the term ›Islam‹ »is derived from the word ›As-salam‹ meaning peace.« But interpreting Islam as an »embodiment of peace« does not mean that the author waived the political claims of his religion: »peace is achievable only through the divine natural laws of Allah.«[33] This is the orthodox position, which has grave implications for unbelievers.

Reverend Matthew Hassan Kukah, who has participated in many dialogues on peace and religious tolerance, described them as an »exercise in futility.«

»The idea here is to create the impression that the violence that societies experience can be averted if only Muslims come to a greater understanding and appreciation of what Christians believe in and vice versa. […] But […] is it really the case that understanding one another's faith is enough condition for ensuring tolerance among believers?«[34]

Talks between Muslims and Christians were more productive when they focused on practical political issues. In Kaduna State, Governor Makarfi brokered a compromise that allowed Christians to preserve their freedoms.[35] This success was not based on a deeper understanding of each other's religious convictions. As a bishop in Kaduna explained: Muslims were forced to negotiate, because the Sharia clashes had shown that Christians could stand their ground. A representative of Jama'atu Nasril Islam (JNI), an organization close to the emirs, put it more diplomatically: You cannot simply implement Sharia, when you have a majority. You must be cautious not to antagonize people. Christians in Kaduna city feel relatively secure, but only when living in their own quarters. Since the Sharia clashes in February and May 2000 the city has been segregated. Areas south of the Kaduna River are largely Christian, while the north is dominated by Muslims. In Zamfara, the governor did not open negotiations on how to contain Sharia, yet he claimed to have good personal relations with Christians:

---

33 Khalid Aliyu Abubakar, *Islamic Perspective on Peace*, pp. 11, 10. – In order to highlight the importance of peace in Islam, the author mentioned that a Muslim, when praying, had »to send peace to his prophet, himself and to the righteous servants of Allah« (*ibid.*, 12). However, the author did not suggest that the faithful should extend these wishes to unbelievers. Muslims in many parts of the Middle Belt no longer greet their Christian neighbours with »Salam.« Christians told me that the way they were greeted changed, after Izala preachers had lectured local Muslims on the religiously correct behavior (cf. Committee, *Report*, p. 21).

34 Kukah, *Managing Christian-Muslim Relations*, p. 400; cf. Kukah, *Sub-Saharan Africa*, p. 163.

35 Marshall, *Nigeria*, pp. 124–125; Yusuf, *Managing Muslim-Christian Conflicts*, pp. 253–255.

»We have Christians in this state, and they've been very happy with us. They have been co-operating and they're satisfied that th[is] law does not affect them at all.«[36] At the end of his tenure as governor, Ahmed Sani Yerima founded a Yerima Christian Alliance (YCA) which supported him in his 2007 presidential campaign.[37] However, when I talked to officials of several churches in the capital Gusau, in December 2006, they complained that the state government did not protect them.

Identification with Global Communities

The settlement of local conflicts was difficult, because Muslims and Christians identified with their world-wide communities and saw themselves as actors in a global confrontation: »Whatever happens to Muslims in Afghanistan, Bosnia Herzegovina, Chechnya, China, Iran, Iraq, Kashmir or Philippines is not a distant event, but a living reality, which attracts the prayers of the Nigerian Muslim in private and in public.«[38] In their domestic affairs, they faced a similar enemy. Christians who resisted Sharia sought to prevent Islam from regaining its strength, so they were implicated in a global conspiracy: »it is a Christian agenda of a gang-up against the Muslims. [...] Nigerian Christians are also doing their own part of work as stipulated by the American New World Order that targets Islam as its archenemy.«[39] The accusation against Igbo and Yoruba Christians that they allowed themselves to be misused by Western imperialists contained an implicit appeal to switch sides, join the process of social renewal which Muslims have initiated, and repel the malign influence of the West. Some Muslims argued that Nigeria's Christians had nothing to fear from living under Islamic authorities, saying that Sharia was not directed against African Christians, let alone against Christianity in general, but against the decadent, permissive culture of the West, which threatened all forms of religion: »I would be the last person to argue that adopting Sharia will have no effect whatsoever on the lifestyle of non-Muslims. It will. [...] [How-

36 *The News*, 10 April 2000, p. 16.

37 *Guardian*, 22 January 2007, p. 15.

38 Dahiru Yahya, *Shari'ah*, p. 7. – »At the news of the New York bombings, Muslims danced in the streets of Palestine and Gusau« (Kenny, *Islam*, p. 1).

39 *Hotline*, 12 March 2000, p. 31.

ever] what is at risk is not true Christian life, but the more tolerant attitude of Westernized Christians and Muslims to many of the vices all criminal codes are meant to check.«[40] Vices such as adultery or theft, which Islamic law seeks to eradicate, are also condemned in the Bible and incur harsh punishment.[41] European societies that ignore these prohibitions and give free rein to moral decay are thus seen to be misguided by irreligious, godless ideas. To get out of their aberration, they should emulate the example of Muslims: »If [...] the West puts the two (i.e. politics and religion) together again, it may have a better chance of solving its own problem [...] of moral decadence, exemplified by widespread drug abuse, pedophil[ia], gay priesthood and gay weddings.«[42]

The appeal to join their Muslim brothers and reject alien Western influences may have been contrived to appease Christian critics and weaken the front of Sharia opponents. However, this is not to say that Sharia supporters were not serious when they called for »resistance to Westernization.«[43] Many Muslims blamed their misery on the machinations of hostile forces, especially in Europe and North America, which used their economic hegemony to turn the Northern states of Nigeria into »industrial deserts.«[44] In order to understand the global forces that bore upon their lives, Muslims tended to read »the classical history of Islamic jihad and the Christian crusades into contemporary politics.«[45] According to this pattern, the desire to destroy Islam was already a major motif of the British colonial conquest: »the British imperialists were infidels and grandsons of the crusaders whose aims and objectives were to wipe out Islam from the face of the earth.«[46] This assault on the core of their identity left Muslims defenseless. Sharia had fortified their society; without it, alien ideas could take possession of them:

»Our culture has in the recent past been [...] polluted by foreign ideas that end up destabilizing our society and making it difficult for us to define our identity. The

---

40 Mohammed Haruna, in *Hotline*, 9 April 2000, pp. 24–25.

41 *Hotline*, 12 March 2000, p. 14, and 9 April 2000, p. 25; cf. Leviticus, 20: 10.

42 *Hotline*, 9 April 2000, p. 25.

43 Mazrui, *Shariacracy*, p. 4.

44 Ado-Kurawa, *Muslim Secularists*, p. 1.

45 Tibi, *Fundamentalism*, p. 16; cf. Ellis/ter Haar, *Worlds of Power*, pp. 185–187.

46 *Hotline*, 7 May 2000, p. 33. – Ali Mazrui (*Islam*, p. 16) claims that European colonialism »arrested the spread of Islam.« However, not all Sharia advocates share this view: »The jihad of 1800s and the British intervention of 1900s made possible greater expansion of Islam into non-Hausa areas« (Dahiru Yahya, *Shari'ah*, p. 8).

result is confusion in thought and action, which has given rise to a general state of frustration and restlessness, manifested in deviant behavior among the generality [of] our people such as armed robbery, drug abuse, large scale fraud, break-up of marriages.«[47]

The present social decay, which appears as the result of a hybrid, multi-cultural way of life, is confronted with the just, well-ordered world of the past. In the days of the jihad, devout Muslims were only guided by Allah's instructions, so they could establish Islam in its »pristine purity«:[48] »after the Jihad, shari'ah was fully implemented and very effective at all sections of Muslims' life in the north.«[49] It was only with the British conquest that Sharia could no longer be applied unrestrictedly and that the corruption of Islamic courts set in: »the more these Courts have been ›secularized‹ the more they failed to adjudicate fairly and justly.«[50] The foreign conquerors who undermined the moral and legal basis of the caliphate, also destroyed the harmony that had existed among its many peoples: »ethnicity, either as thought or deed, was unheard of in the region.« »Centuries of social and political interaction had led to unity and mutual respect among the various communities.«[51] The torment caused by slave hunts and the destruction of non-Islamic societies are matters Hausa-Fulani intellectuals usually stay silent about.[52] Islam, which was imposed on large parts of the population by jihad, is stylized as the »authentic«[53] culture of the country, whereas Western, secular culture, which put an end to the Fulani caliphate, is seen as a foreign, destructive force. Some Muslims claim that the legitimate authority of the old established religion could only be broken because the colonial administration systematically discriminated against Muslims: »Christianity was made the State religion in Nigeria and all official policies

---

47 Okunnu, *Women*, p. 5.

48 Doi, *Islam*, p. 44.

49 Abubakar D. Muhammad, *Muslim Responses*, p. 2; Khan, *Mirath*, p. 181; Tabi'u/Rashid, *Islamic Law*, p. 48; Gwandu, *Sokoto Caliphate*, pp. 11–12; cf. Harneit-Sievers, *Jihad vs. Miss World*, pp. 7–8.

50 Tabi'u/Rashid, *Islamic Law*, p. 37; Ado-Kurawa, *Shari'ah*, pp. 290, 292, 307.

51 Gumi, *Where I Stand*, pp. 125, 119; Doi, *Islam*, p. 44.

52 Abubakar Gumi (*Where I Stand*, p. 191) does mention reports of slave raids: »Minority Christian groups […] take liberty with history so that all fault was visited on the Hausa/Fulani. Their grandfathers were said to have hunted for and sold the grand-fathers of the minority groups as slaves.« But according to Gumi, there was no »delibe-rate policy to enslave any nations«.

53 Mazrui, *Shariacracy*, p. 4.

by government were deliberately arranged to support Christians.«[54] Even for the Sharia crisis, decades later, the Europeans were ultimately to blame, because Christian resistance to Islamic law was »the result of European indoctrination«: »The Europeans trained the African Christians in such a way that they hate Islam and everything associated with it including the *Shari'ah*.«[55]

While Muslims tend to see themselves as victims of Western aggression, their religion promises victory over their enemies, as Dahiru Yahya, Professor of History in Kano, explains:

»Since the beginning of its history, Islam has been in perpetual conflict on all its territorial and intellectual frontiers on account of the broadness of its claims. For almost one thousand and four hundred years, Islam is locked in war with Hinduism in the Indian sub continent, with Chinese in Western China and South-east Asia, with the Slavic world in Russia and the Balkans, with Latin Christendom in Western Europe and North Africa, with animistic tribalism in sub-Saharan Africa and with secularism at its home base. […] At the beginning of its history Islam expelled and confined the Roman Empire to a corner of Europe and destroyed and replaced with itself the Byzantine and Persian empires and earned for itself permanent enmity from the Latin and Hellenist successors. It up-rooted Christianity from its home base in the Middle East and pushed it to an alien environment in secular Europe where it was finally destroyed with now less than 5% church attendance where marketing strategy was not applied. Islam has recently pushed France out of Algeria, Russia out of Afghanistan and the Caucasus and the USA out of Iran.«[56]

Seen from this perspective, Nigeria's Muslims can only gain strength if they guard themselves against the corrupting influence of the West. In the ceaseless struggle against moral laxity and decadence, Sharia has the

---

54 Gumi, *Where I Stand*, p. 188.
55 Ibrahim Sulaiman, *Shari'ah and Constitution*, pp. 63, 62. – While Muslims accused the Europeans of having fought against Islam, Nigerian Christians assumed the opposite: In order to prevent power falling into the hands of Christian Igbo or Yoruba, the British rigged the 1952/53 census, so that the Northerners obtained a majority of seats in the national assembly (Benjamin Adekunle, in *Tell*, 27 March 2000, p. 15). According to prominent Igbo and Yoruba politicians, the British government is still in alliance with the Muslim North and made covert arrangements in favor of the Sharia campaign: »It is in the British interest to support Sharia in the North because Britain has a lot to do with Muslim states« (*Tell*, 31 July 2000, pp. 27, 28).
56 Dahiru Yahya, *Shari'ah*, p. 1. – »Islam itself is an unconquerable force which, in spite of all oppositions, subversions and attacks from its enemies everywhere, must express its domineering will and assert its authority over all other systems« (Ibrahim Sulaiman, *Shari'ah and Constitution*, p. 53).

advantage of making deviant behavior obvious to everyone. Individuals who do not adhere to the dress code or who do not join in common prayers stand out from the crowd of devout Muslims. By punishing or ostracizing them, the *umma* constitutes itself as a moral community and strengthens its cohesion. Unity is achieved not by balancing and institutionalizing different interests, but by mobilizing the faithful against common enemies. Sharia supporters try to eliminate evil in their midst and attribute it to the world of infidels. In this drama of asserting their identity, the West plays an indispensable role. As an embodiment of everything that threatens the harmony and well-being of Muslims, it becomes an object of bizarre suspicions. In Kano, the Council of Ulama expressed concern at the activities of Western development agencies and issued an ultimatum to all international aid organizations to leave the state.[57] Criticism focused for a while on the polio vaccinations by UNICEF. It was said that the vaccination program was part of an American conspiracy to depopulate the country. Dr. Datti Ahmed, president of the Supreme Council for Sharia, warned: »We believe that modern-day Hitlers have deliberately adulterated the oral polio vaccines with anti-fertility drugs and contaminated it with certain viruses which are known to cause HIV and AIDS.«[58] In order to protect their citizens, four Northern states stopped the vaccination program in July 2003. Kano's governor explained that it was »a lesser of two evils, to sacrifice two, three, four, five even 10 children (to polio) than allow hundreds of thousands or possibly millions of girl-children likely to be rendered infertile.«[59] The number of polio infections rose indeed, and the virus spread to neighboring countries, so UN officials urged the authorities to end their boycott. In June 2004, a solution was reached: The polio eradication program was resumed, but with a vaccine made in the Muslim country of Indonesia.

The rejection of Western influences and the attempted concentration on »pristine Islam«[60] does not mean that Sharia supporters were turning away from modernity. Rather, they were looking for an »alternative modernity«[61] that was more in line with Arab paradigms: with glittering sky-

---

57 *Tell*, 5 February 2001, p. 40; Ibrahim, *Democracy*, p. 16.

58 Quoted in Maryam Yahya, *Polio Vaccines*, p. 188.

59 *Ibid.*, p. 188; cf. Ibrahim, *Polio Paranoia*, pp. 32–33; *Economist*, 10 January 2004, p. 32; *Tell*, 8 March 2004, pp. 56–57; *Newswatch*, 16 August 2004, pp. 54–55.

60 Kane, *Muslim Modernity*, p. 88.

61 *Ibid.*, p. 246.

scrapers as in Saudi Arabia, but without the decadence of the West.[62] This vision had no place for a renaissance of traditional ›African‹ values. Sharia supporters seemed to be more interested in »de-Africanizing«[63] their culture and renouncing those traditions which they shared with their Christian fellow-citizens. This further eroded trust and diminished the common ground on which negotiations could be based.

A Changing Christianity

Christians are less militant in their opposition to ›pagan‹ practices, yet the Pentecostal and other charismatic churches also tend to demonize their ›heathen‹ past.[64] Most would agree that a social renewal cannot be achieved by reviving ideals and institutions of precolonial times. This does not mean that African Christians embrace the moral and political concepts of European societies. Their relationship with the Western world is rather ambivalent. It is their opponents who have identified them with the West. When American forces attacked Afghanistan and Iraq, Muslim protesters marched through Kano, shouted anti-US slogans and burnt down the churches and stores of Christians.[65] Matthew Hassan Kukah warned Muslims and Christians not to engage in »proxy wars«, and he lamented that Muslim scholars »mistakenly use the words West and Christianity synonymously.«[66] European societies which had entered a »post-Christian era« could no longer be a paradigm for African Christians.[67]

A Sharia study by Freedom House, which sought to raise sympathy for the Christian minority, pointed out that Muslims on their protest marches

62 Pilgrims returning from Mecca and Medina reported on the wealth which they often interpreted as the result of a strict Islamic way of life: »the United States of America […] have the largest investments [in] Saudi Arabia. […] They have not treated the kingdom of Saudi Arabia as a pariah state and their investments are the most secured […] because Islam is against dishonesty« (Dr. Lateef Adegbite, in *Vanguard*, 24 March 2002, p. 21). »only one murder case was reported in 1997 in Saudi Arabia where Shari'ah is being practised« *(Hotline*, 23 April 2000, p. 31; cf. Nouhou, *Wahhabisme*, p. 78).

63 *Miles*, Shari'a, p. 65. – »L'ennemi n'est pas la modernité mais la tradition, ou plutôt […] tout ce qui n'est pas la tradition du Prophète« (Olivier Roy, in Kane, *Réformisme*, p. 118).

64 Meyer, *Break with the Past*, p. 329; Gifford, *African Christianity*, pp. 333–334.

65 *Tell*, 29 October 2001, pp. 32–33.

66 Kukah, *Managing Christian-Muslim Relations*, pp. 393, 408.

67 *Ibid.*, p. 403.

carried posters of Osama bin Laden, while Christian demonstrators waved American flags.[68] However, enthusiasm for Western societies is usually lukewarm. Church representatives have distanced themselves from the West's moral decay and from a liberal Christianity that accepted such profanity:

>the primate of [the] Anglican Church, Archbishop Jasper Akinola had said the minds of all Nigerian Christians [...]. [Homosexuality] is a perversion of Christianity and Christian Culture. [...] Anytime, we see a self confessed Gay bishop or reverend we'll withdraw. We will withdraw from World Council of Churches. It is incompatible with Christianity especially African Christianity and time has come now when we should go and re-Christianize the white people.«[69]

Nigeria's Christians do not want to defend Western permissiveness, and they can hardly afford it when competing with a law-centered religion like Islam: »Muslims have tried to make converts by arguing that the Christian West is decadent and sexually irresponsible – a belief that finds daily confirmation in Western films and television. If the Anglican Communion accepted gay bishops or approved gay unions, Muslims would gain an enormous propaganda victory.«[70] Apart from accommodating Muslims, the fact that Nigerian Christians criticize the liberal attitudes of their coreligionists in Europe is also an expression of a fundamental change in African Christianity. Liberating themselves from Western dominance, African churches re-orientate their doctrines, and this also affects their relationship with the state. Most still call for secularism,[71] but less out of conviction than out of pragmatism, namely to prevent religious polarization. Separating religion and politics looks like a relic of colonial times that has never taken root among Africans. At a Sharia conference in Jos in January 2004, secularism found few defenders.[72] Black theologians stress that religion in Africa has always been an all-embracing force that permeates all aspects of life.[73] As African Christians reflect worldly affairs in religious terms, they tend to apply the Bible's message directly to political matters.[74] Many pas-

---

68 Freedom House, *Talibanization*, pp. 4, 16, 32; Metan, *Dilemmas*, p. 289.

69 Ola Makinde, Methodist Archbishop of Lagos, in *Newswatch*, 3 May 2004, p. 45.

70 Jenkins, *Defender of the Faith*, p. 49.

71 Obadare, *Religious NGOs*, p. 141.

72 Harneit-Sievers, *Debate about Sharia*, p. 3. – An increasing number of theologians and church officials believe that in an intensely religious country like Nigeria secularism is »impracticable« (Gaiya, *Christianity*, p. 370).

73 Aderibigbe, *African Religion*, p. 41.

74 Gifford, *African Christianity*, pp. 42–43.

sages of the Old Testament depict a warlike God who is intensely interested in political affairs and who brings death and destruction to his enemies. In these parts of the Bible, Nigeria's Christians may find a sort of
truth that is better suited to their present conflicts than the ideals of an
enlightened, tolerant Christianity.

In a lecture for the Muslim-Christian Dialogue on Peace in Jos, Pastor
Charles Dah stated that the Old and New Testaments gave contradictory
messages. Christians, however, had no choice; they had to abide by the
doctrine of Jesus, who did not allow any form of violence: »Ye have heard
that it hath been said, Thou shalt love thy neighbour, and hate thine
enemy. But I say unto you, Love your enemy, bless them that curse you, do
good to them that hate you.«[75] Pastors of the Evangelical Church of West
Africa (ECWA) and the Church of Christ in Nigeria (COCIN) told me that
they urged church members not to retaliate as this was the only way to
break the cycle of violence.[76] However, they were losing influence over
Christian youths who did not want to stand idly by when they saw their
communities being threatened. Young Tarok and Goemai did not admit
pastors into their confidence when they planned their revenge attack on
Muslims in Yelwa. Some militants even announced they would kill Christian elders who tried to sabotage their fight.

In their competition with Islam, many Christians see it as a handicap
that the New Testament does not allow them to fight back: With »our non-
aggressive posture, we gradually, but steadily lose vantage grounds to those
whose faith is in no way superior to ours, but whose heart is grafted in
conquest by force.«[77] After the religious unrest in Maiduguri, prompted by
protests against the Mohammed caricatures, the President of the Christian
Association declared that Christians had a right to defend themselves:

»From all indications, it is very clear now that the sacrifices of the Christians in this
country for peaceful co-existence with people of other faiths ha[ve] been sadly
misunderstood to be weakness. We have for a long time now watched helplessly
the killing, maiming and destruction of Christians and their property by Muslim
fanatics and fundamentalists at the slightest or no provocation at all. We are not

---

75 Matthew 5: 43–44; cf. Dah, *Christian Perspective on Violence*, pp. 63–64; Okezie, *Christian
    Perspective on Peace*, pp. 4–7. – The Apostle Paul restated this non-retaliation principle:
    »Recompense to no man evil for evil« (Romans 12: 17).

76 As part of their de-escalation strategy, CAN in Northern Nigeria circulated a flyer that
    called on Christians not to consider the religious affiliation of politicians when voting in
    the April 2007 elections.

77 Abiola Babatope, in Mu'azzam/Ibrahim, *Religious Identity*, p. 66.

unaware of the fact that these religious extremists have the full backup and support of some influential Muslims who are yet to appreciate the value of peaceful co-existence. That an incident in far away Denmark which does not claim to be representing Christianity could elicit such an unfortunate reaction here in Nigeria, leading to the destruction of Christian Churches, is not only embarrassing, but also disturbing and unfortunate. It is no longer a hidden fact that a long standing agenda to make this Nigeria an Islamic nation is being surreptitiously pursued. […] May we at this stage remind our Muslim brothers that they do not have the monopoly of violence in this nation.«[78]

As in other parts of Africa where Muslims and Christians were living closely together, much of the new charismatic Christianity spreading in Nigeria has assumed a »combative anti-Islamic stance«.[79] Some politicians such as the Igbo leader Ojukwu picked up on this mood and posed as defenders of their faith: »we are tired of being threatened. No religion has a monopoly of violence. If […] you tell me about the Jihad, know that we had our Crusades too, and you did not fare better.«[80] In this confrontational mood, Christianity and Islam came to resemble each other.[81] As Muslims fought for control of the state in order to enforce their ideas of law and justice, Christians also asserted political claims. There are, of course, many other fields where Islam and Christianity have influenced each other. Muslims, for example, have copied Christian missionary techniques by building schools and hospitals with funds from Saudi Arabia. They also set up healing centers, based on Pentecostal paradigms, where Muslims seek spiritual rebirth and faith healing.[82] But such efforts to break into the realm of the other religion have reinforced their rivalry.

---

78 Peter J. Akinola, Anglican Primate of the Church of Nigeria, http://anglican-nig.org/CAN_reaction.htm, 13. 9. 2007.

79 Gifford, *African Christianity*, pp. 317, 347; Ojo, *Pentecostal Movements*, pp. 175, 186; Maduagwu, *Religion*, p. 17; Falola, *Christian Radicalism*, pp. 267–270, 277.

80 *Tell*, 6 March 2000, p. 25. – Such vindictiveness can also be found among clerics. The bishop of an independent church in Igboland, Alexander Ekewuba, warned Muslims: »Let them thank God that I am not a politician, otherwise any time they kill one Igbo man in Kano or Kaduna, I will order that 10 Moslems be killed here« (*The Source*, 25 February 2002, p. 12).

81 Christian reactions to political Islam are analyzed in Hock, *Islam-Komplex*.

82 Cf. *Tell* (8 December 2003, p. 51) on the Nasrul-Lahi-Il-Fathi Society (NASFAT).

Prospects

The Sharia movement has lost political momentum. Spectacular punishments are not carried out, and the *hisba* vigilantes keep a low profile, yet the religious revival has entrenched the Islamic identity of most Sharia states. Sharia regulations are an effective means of staking claims over territory and to assert political dominance. Religious minorities have to accept discrimination or risk violence and expulsion. A new constitution that would circumscribe the scope of Islamic law and create legal security is not in sight. The extent to which Sharia regulations affect the lives of Muslims and non-Muslims depends on local circumstances. In Zamfara, the enthusiasm of Sharia monitors has been dampened, while the Sharia campaign in Kano has received a new impetus through Governor Shekarau, who was reelected in 2007.

The potential for violence in Northern Nigeria is likely to increase, and religion will play a prominent role in future conflicts. In the Middle Belt, where land is getting scarce, Muslim ›settlers‹ and Christian ›indigenes‹ are fighting for control over territory and political offices. In this context, religion is attractive not as a resource for peace, but as a means of mobilizing for violent conflict. Political Islam, with its claim to enforce religious laws, is well suited to mobilize for the defense of land and to assert political dominance.[1] Since the rival groups have not negotiated a treaty or a constitutional settlement, the question arises as to whether future massacres can be averted. International debates have focused on strategies to defuse the crisis, and in this context, the possibilities of outside intervention have been discussed.

None of the parties to the conflict has called upon international organizations to intervene in the Sharia dispute. The general public in Europe and North America, however, was disquieted by the human rights violations, in particular when the news broke that Safiyya Hussaini, a widow

---

1 Harnischfeger, *Control over Territory*, pp. 439–452; Hastings, *Holy Lands*, pp. 34, 47–51.

who had taken a lover, had been sentenced to death. In Spain, 600,000 people signed an Amnesty International petition; Pope John Paul II called on the faithful to pray for Safiyya, and the mayors of Rome and Naples declared the accused an honorary citizen of their cities.[2] However, once the death sentence was rescinded, interest in Sharia dissipated. Nigerians sometimes told me that the West should play a more active role in the conflict, but this opinion was only voiced by Christians. In their view, the West had a moral obligation to intervene, because Sharia threatened the freedom of religion and other human rights. The equanimity of Europeans and Americans embittered many Christians in Northern Nigeria, because they believed that their backs were to the wall: »We know, Muslims run to England and Germany and get help. Why don't Europeans help us to survive in Nigeria?«[3] Yet the restraint of Europeans is understandable. If they intervened in the name of human rights, they would be siding with one of the parties to the conflict, and this would deepen the divide between the two camps. However, if one explores possibilities for intervention, one can choose among several options, only one of which is defending human rights. International organizations could also act as intermediaries in the conflict, or they could try to help Muslims find a more moderate form of Sharia. A closer look at these three options shows that none of them would have much of a positive impact:

1. Those who want to interfere in Nigeria on behalf of human rights can cite good reasons for doing so. Nigeria obligated itself to uphold these rights when it signed international treaties, such as the United Nations Convention against Torture and other Cruel, Inhuman and Degrading Punishments. Moreover, since May 1999 a democratic constitution has been in force, so the political actors should be reminded to adhere to the rules. The Obasanjo administration has made no attempt to defend the sanctity of the constitution, because it assumed that there was no consensus in the population on constitutional principles. Some jurists, however, pointed out that the president and his minister of justice were bound to protect the constitution, even if they did not find it politically opportune.[4] Moreover, according to international law, Obasanjo's government was responsible for all human rights violations committed by state agencies,

2 Kalu, *Safiyya*, p. 399; *Tell*, 8 April 2002, p. 40.

3 A member of the ECWA Church in Zonkwa, Kaduna State, 5 March 2001.

4 Iwobi, *Sharia Controversy*, p. 156.

including Sharia courts in the North.[5] Therefore, a US-based human rights organization, Freedom House, demanded that Nigeria's government be pressured to sue the Sharia governors at the Supreme Court:

»The U.S. government should [...] urge the government of Nigeria to take the following steps. [...] seek constitutional rulings on the new Sharia to ensure the rights of all Nigerians under international human rights standards and the Nigerian Constitution. [...] All private groups that try to enforce Sharia should be disbanded and those who attack their fellow citizens should be arrested and charged with assault.«[6]

The question is, however, whether diplomatic pressure would achieve what the experts of Freedom House hope for: constraining »extremist Islamic movements« and promoting a »moderate Islam.«[7] As soon as Europeans or Americans took the stage as advocates of human rights and of a largely secular constitution, they would be perceived to be hostile to Islam. Their commitment would only widen the gap between the conflicting parties, and confirm the perception of many Sharia activists that their struggle against Christian Igbo or Yoruba is also a struggle against Western influence. The Sharia dispute would look like a confrontation between Islam and the West, with grave consequences for the local actors. It would be more difficult for Christians and Muslims to discuss compromises, and it would stifle debates among Muslims. Sharia critics within the Muslim camp, such as S. L. Sanusi, who are suspected of sympathizing with the West anyway, would find it harder to plead for a milder form of Sharia: »Western interference on the basis of human rights will be absolutely counter-productive.«[8] Insisting that the democratic constitution be recognized by all actors would be futile for various reasons, not the least because the constitution does not enjoy much respect among Christians either. Nigeria's Christians defend the freedom of speech and religion and, to some extent, equality before the law, but otherwise they similarly ignore human rights. When fighting crime or defending their territory against ›non-indigenes‹, Christians are no less violent than Muslims. It would be erroneous to assume that the Sharia controversy divides Nigerians between opponents and supporters of human rights.

---

5 The International Commission of Jurists attested this responsibility of the federal government in a letter to President Obasanjo (Iwobi, *Sharia Controversy*, p. 162).

6 Freedom House, *Talibanization*, pp. 11–12.

7 *Ibid.*, p. 10.

8 S. L. Sanusi at the Sharia Conference in Bayreuth, July 11–12, 2003.

2. Instead of siding with Nigeria's Christians, Western organizations could act as neutral go-betweens. There are several good reasons for doing so. Christians and Muslims have to find a new modus vivendi, because the present constitutional arrangements are so dysfunctional that most politicians flagrantly ignore them. Nigeria's Fourth Republic, like its predecessors, cannot cope with ethnic and religious antagonisms. Its institutions simply were not designed to organise the relationships between communities that keep vigilantes and militias to control their territory. Therefore, community leaders will have to look for new rules that may secure a peaceful coexistence. So far, they have not entered any serious negotiations: »The opposing camps now appear to have battled each other to a standstill and retreated to their respective bunkers.«[9] Needless to say, both sides meet in various institutions, such as the Muslim-Christian Dialogue Forum, but the »[c]ontestation of power and space has generated an atmosphere of mutual distrust and suspicion, thus hampering inter-faith dialogue and peaceful coexistence.«[10] Whether Europeans or Americans would be able to overcome this mistrust is more than questionable, as the Muslim side would not consider them impartial arbiters.

A further problem is what solution Western mediators should propose. A fair compromise could only emerge if both sides accorded each other the same rights. State institutions would then have to act neutrally in religious matters. However, such a solution is unacceptable to orthodox Muslims because the »principal function« of the state is to enforce Islamic laws.[11] Muslim politicians are aware that shaping state authorities according to their divine commands goes against the principle of equality. But what is objectionable about it? The Koran says that God raised the Muslims above all other communities and gave them responsibility for society at large.[12] Christians are not forced to convert, but they have to give themselves over to the care of God-guided authorities. From a Western perspective, this political dominance of a religious group violates the principle of self-determination. But many Muslims will not consider this an injustice. When I tried to explain why Christian minorities are afraid of losing their autonomy, a lecturer of Islamic Studies at the University of Jos assured me »you have nothing to fear. We will take good care of you.«

---

9 Iwobi, *Sharia Controversy*, p. 122.

10 Adogame, *Politicization of Religion*, p. 136.

11 Bernard Lewis, *Middle East*, p. 224; von Grunebaum, *Studien*, p. 26.

12 *Koran* 3: 110, p. 59; Hodgson, *Islam*, p. 322.

Even if both sides signed a treaty, this would not give religious minorities much security. Nobody can force the rival parties to abide by their agreements, and there are no inner convictions that would urge them to respect the interests of the other side. Sharia supporters may call for a »constant dialogue« with Christians,[13] and profess their commitment to »freedom« and »democracy« in a »united Nigeria«, but in the same breath they say that Islamic principles are non-negotiable, because the »supremacy of Allah« does not allow this: »Muslims [...] cannot compromise on the law of God.«[14] As long as Muslims live together with about 60 million Christians, they must of course make concessions. Sharia in its current form is full of half-measures and compromises. Yet such concessions are only valid until revoked. Nothing that Christians and Muslims agree upon could be binding upon politicians like Ahmed Sani, if it is not in line with God's commandments: »Sharia is superior to the Constitution of Nigeria.«[15] Even if Muslim politicians are sincere in looking for a lasting solution that considers the interests of Christians, their compromises will be questioned by orthodox Muslims. What counts from an orthodox point of view are God's instructions, which offer little protection to Christians: in the worst case the *dhimmi* status which is meant to humiliate infidels.[16] The forms of discrimination that the sacred law holds in store for infidels are still known from colonial times. Back then, a Muslim accused of murdering a Christian could be set free by the court if he swore his innocence on the Koran.[17]

The difficulty of reaching a reliable agreement that could generate trust is not only due to political Islam. Politicians all over Nigeria do not care about treatises, mutual obligation, and laws of reciprocity: »Part of the African tragedy is that refined and civil manners [...] have been eroded.«[18] Nobody can expect his rivals to play by the rules, so legal relationships are being replaced by clientelism and other personal dependencies which are

---

13 Ahmed Bello Mahmud (*Shari'ah*, p. 9), Justice Minister of Zamfara.

14 Dr. Lateef Adegbite (*Political Agenda*, pp. 1, 2, 3), Secretary General of the Supreme Council for Islamic Affairs.

15 Gouverneur Sani, in Civil Liberties Organisation, *Sharia*, p. 5.

16 »Fight those who believe not in God and the Last Day and do not forbid what God and His Messenger have forbidden – such men as practise not the religion of truth, being of those who have been given the Book [Christian and Jews – J.H.] – until they pay the tribute out of hand and have been humbled« (*Koran* 9: 29, p. 182; cf. Firestone, *Jihad*, pp. 53, 63–64).

17 Willink Commission, *Fears of Minorities*, p. 126.

18 Ibrahim, *Democracy*, p. 3.

not subject to public control.[19] Moreover, political elites prefer to settle things by informal arrangements, so that written constitutions, parliamentary laws and bureaucratic rules are losing their relevance.[20]

A contract between Christians and Muslims would have little validity for yet another reason. Nigeria is not growing into a cohesive nation. Political deals brokered in Abuja matter little in the 36 states where hundreds of ethnic groups (or their elites) decide largely among themselves how to settle their conflicts. In the case of the Sharia controversy, a central solution is not feasible because there is not just one national Sharia conflict, but dozens of local conflicts, each of which involves different actors. Christians and Muslims will reach at best tenuous local compromises that are not based on mutually recognized legal principles, but on changing power relationships.

3. If the transition to an Islamic legal order is an »irreversible process«, then the main task, from a European perspective, will be »damage control.«[21] Western politicians or non-governmental organizations could try to persuade religious and political authorities in Northern Nigeria to be less stringent in applying Sharia. Talking to Muslims about how to design a moderate Islamic law, presupposes that Europeans and Americans suspend their own notions of law and justice. They have to grant that freedom of religion, equality before the law and other Western constitutional principles no longer apply. Interest could then focus on improving the legal security of Muslim citizens, for example by promoting a uniform Sharia code and by training Sharia judges and *hisba* vigilantes.[22] In addition, one could support Muslim intellectuals who advocate a liberal interpretation of the divine commandments. However, Muslims who renounce the letter of the law are already accused of being »agents of the West.«[23] Support from Europe or the United States would discredit them further, as the revival of religion is meant to keep Western influences at bay: »the recent re-introduction of

---

19 Chabal/Daloz, *Africa Works*, pp. 16, 30; Osaghae, *Amoral Politics*, p. 74.

20 Cf. Ellis/ter Haar, *Worlds of Power*, p. 184. – In the absence of public control, politicians seal their deals by secretly swearing at ancient shrines to the old deities.

21 Peters, *Islamic Criminal Law*, p. 44.

22 Fwatshak, *Shari'a Enforcement*, p. 19. – According to Prof. Sada, the Volkswagen Foundation co-funded the compilation of a standardized Sharia penal code (personal communication, Zaria, 29 December 2006). The Heinrich Böll Foundation in Lagos was approached to support the training of Sharia judges, but declined.

23 Sanusi, *The West*, p. 254.

shari'ah in Nigeria is [...] because of [...] the collapse of moral values, and the influence of western culture.«[24]

Western influence is part of the problem, not the solution. For this reason, the potential for European experts to influence the development of Sharia is very limited. They may present their arguments in an Islamic garb by quoting the Koran, but Nigerian Muslims do not like to take advice from unbelievers when religious matters are at stake: »Nobody should tell us how to go about our religious obligations.«[25] How can someone who does not believe in the teachings of Islam be so presumptuous as to interpret them for the faithful? In one of his many television chats, President Obasanjo raised the question whether the Prophet, were he to live in the twenty-first century, would have issued laws like those introduced by Governor Sani. Sharia supporters were indignant that a Christian was meddling in their affairs, and the magazine Hotline reminded the president that blasphemy was punishable by death.[26]

Some outside observers have exaggerated expectations in an inter-faith dialogue. John S. Pobee of the World Council of Churches assumes that Muslims and Christians are ultimately guided by the same ideas of justice. In order to create a more humane society, each religion just has to follow its own divine commandments: »build [...] communities that are guided by the values of God's rule, namely sacrificial love, truth, righteousness and justice, freedom, reconciliation, and peace. Religious human rights can be fostered when the unique claims of each and every religion are taken seriously.«[27] However, Muslims who take their religious doctrines seriously have to adopt legal principles that hinder the development of freedom and human rights. Since the cruel punishments for theft, fornication and blasphemy were ordained by God, they are unlikely to be abolished. As an Islamic High Court judge declared: »The law of *hudûd* is a no go area.«[28] Nigeria's Muslims will of course find ways of skirting the Sharia monitors. They take the liberty of manipulating the sacred law and picking those elements that suit them. Yet this freedom in dealing with religious doctrines is not used as human rights advocates in the West would like. How God's will is implemented depends on power structures, so the weak and

---

24 Abubakar D. Muhammad, *Muslim Responses*, p. 7.
25 *Hotline*, 12 March 2000, pp. 29–30.
26 *Hotline*, 19 March 2000, p. 26.
27 Pobee, *Religious Human Rights*, p. 5.
28 Peters, *Islamic Criminal Law*, pp. 44, 38.

disenfranchised have little prospect of improving their fate. The Director of the Institute for Islamic Legal Studies, who represents religious orthodoxy is not averse to modernizing Sharia, but he stated clearly what type of modernity he did not wish to see: paternity tests based on DNA tests, which would strengthen the legal position of women and contribute to some gender equality.[29] Advocates of women's rights have argued that the laws of the Maliki School unduly discriminate against females. An unmarried woman or a widow who becomes pregnant can be sentenced for fornication, while the man whom she names as the father of the child can deny any involvement, unless four male Muslim witnesses come forth who observed him commit the unlawful act.[30]

Women's rights activists and other Sharia critics who counter this biased form of justice are a small and largely isolated minority in the Islamic public sphere. In Western media they are quoted extensively, and this may give rise to the impression that the Sharia debate fosters the emergence of an Islamic civil society. Yet the public sphere is dominated by religious organizations that permit no open debate among their members. Their central message is that sincere Muslims have to bow to religious commands. T. H. Gwarzo, a Sharia advocate who knows Islamic organizations from the inside, offered a sobering account in his study on Kano:

»Islamic civic associations irrespective of their principles or objectives are completely male dominated associations. [...] internal democratic structures [...] of almost all Islamic civic associations in Kano are suspect. [...] The member [...] is not taught to think freely [...]. Most groups think that an immediate, totally perfect and a purified version of Islam is achievable on demand. [...] Almost all Islamic civic associations appear to stifle ideological dialogue. This is done on three levels, internally among its members, with other Islamic organizations and finally with non-Islamic groups, religious or secular. This resulted in nurturing utopian and idealistic concepts among its members and allowed theoretical and puritan ideas to remain untested.«[31]

---

29 Prof. Sada of the Ahmadu Bello University at the Sharia Conference in Bayreuth, 2003.

30 Danfulani, *Women*, pp. 2–3, 11, 13.

31 Gwarzo, *Civic Associations*, pp. 314–315. – For a similar argument see Jibrin Ibrahim (*Democracy*, p. 3): »most of civil society in Africa is located within the religious sphere. [...] What has not been sufficiently emphasised is that many active religious movements have an even more effective capacity and record of inculcating intolerance, an ideology of contempt and exclusion and indeed, incitement to annihilate the other.« Susan O'Brien gives a more positive account of Kano's »civil society« and of Sharia, which she sees as the »product of a democratic process« (O'Brien, *Charia*, p. 49).

Western experts, who seek a dialog with Muslims in order to help them formulate a moderate form of Sharia, will learn that their intervention has a very limited impact on the legal situation. This raises the question whether it is worthwhile accepting the validity of a divine legal order and giving it international legitimacy. Why should Western politicians and NGOs (or the United Nations) recognize holy texts as a legitimate basis for state legislation, when these texts call for the discrimination of women and unbelievers? When it is granted that Nigeria's Muslims may live in keeping with their sacred law, then Muslims elsewhere, in Kenya, Tanzania or South Africa, will also be encouraged to claim Sharia. This would make it difficult for international organizations to denounce human rights violations. And it would have serious consequences for the peaceful coexistence of Muslims and Christians. Even a restricted form of Sharia that waived amputations and stonings rejects the principle of equality before the law. Muslims who organize their public life by their own exclusive laws segregate themselves from their fellow citizens. At the same time they open a religious contest for state power, since they need the state apparatus to enforce their laws.

The Sharia controversy overlaps with conflicts over scarce resources, especially over land. This is an additional reason why outside intervention, in whatever form, will yield little results. Assuming responsibility for solving a crisis is not reasonable, when there is no long-term solution in sight. In former times, landless farmers could hope to find work by migrating into the cities. Yet industries have declined, especially in the North of Nigeria. At the beginning of the 1990s, Kano still had 500 factories: a decade later 300 of them had closed.[32] Since the fast-growing population no longer has the opportunity to integrate into a modern, industrializing sector of society, people will fight more desperately for the few scraps of arable land that have not yet been cultivated.

Rules to settle these conflicts could only work if the contending parties agreed on them. Members of ethnic and religious groups would have to share moral and legal convictions that commit them to seek amicable solutions. Such convictions cannot be imposed or created by outside intervention. In Yorubaland, where Muslims and Christians want to preserve their unity, there is a wide consensus to interact on the basis of secular rules,

---

32 *Tell*, 16 December 2002, pp. 55–56. – Kano's Minister of Trade rejected the imputation that the introduction of Sharia accelerated the disinvestment of foreign capital: »Are industries not collapsing all over Nigeria?« (*ibid.*, p. 57).

whereas in the North, Muslims have discarded secular principles, so the religious groups have no more rules to settle their conflicts. It is unlikely that constitutional models imported from the West will be revived, since Muslims have good reasons to regard them as foreign and neocolonial. Given the failure of democracy, it is also understandable that they seek alternatives in their own religious traditions. Both Muslims and Christians want to combat a »moral meltdown.«[33] In such a setting, the institutions of the secular state are of little help. Where state administrations decay, the spiritual force of religion is the most effective means of enforcing conformity and compliance with rules. Many Muslims hope that the divine law will help them to discipline themselves and to restore a moral order. On this basis, state institutions would have a better chance to function. It is my impression, however, that the recourse to Sharia will not achieve this aim. As the analysis of the current conflicts suggests, the struggle for religious (and ethnic) self-determination will not promote peace and justice, neither within the Islamic society nor in Muslims' relationships with non-Muslims:

1. Within Islamic society, the legitimacy of state authorities will probably continue to erode. The political elites of the North, discredited by their alliance with the military, gained at best some temporary legitimacy when they turned into advocates of an Islamic order. Measured against the ideals of the caliphate, the powers-that-be hardly have a chance to establish their religious authority. The call for divine justice discredits the corrupt rulers, but it does not show a way of replacing the existing political system with a new one. The holy law can neither be consistently applied nor formally abrogated. Thus, legal insecurity increases:

»It is wrong for society to maintain a law it does not intend to enforce because people can no longer take the law as a reliable guide to permissible and impermissible conduct. To maintain a law without intending to enforce it is dangerous because it leaves too much discretion in the hands of those charged with enforcing the law, enabling them to select cases for enforcement based on selfish and other corrupt purposes.«[34]

What is permissible or forbidden depends on shifting power structures, on the influence of local politicians and emirs, on *hisba* groups and militant preachers.

2. The introduction of full Sharia has made it difficult to reach a lasting agreement with non-Muslims. Observers in the South of the country are

---

33 Kukah, *Human Rights*, p. 25.
34 An-Na'im, *Islamic Reformation*, p. 88.

under the impression that the rejection of common constitutional principles marked the »end of an epoch.«[35] The Muslim North has bidden farewell to the project of nation building. By organizing ›their‹ states along their own religious laws, Muslims demonstrated that they wished to go their own ways in moral, legal and political matters. Of course, no one wants to pass up the oil revenues, so they have to maintain the common state as a means of redistributing resources from the South to the North. However, material interests alone will not suffice to keep Nigeria united. What may help to avert disintegration is the awareness that all segments of the country would suffer. Muslims and Christians, Igbo, Yoruba and Hausa-Fulani could not sever their links peacefully.[36] They would probably resort to large-scale expulsions, and the successor states, defined in ethnic or religious terms, would become ensnared in boundary wars and conflicts over natural resources and trade routes. The problem of finding rules that allow for a peaceful coexistence would persist. Negotiating compromises might even be harder if the institutional framework of the federation fell away and the joint army were dissolved.

---

35 Williams, *Lugard*, p. 22.
36 Sklar, *Unity or Regionalism*, p. 46.

Bibliography

Abd al-Masih, K. O./Ibn Salam, M. J., *What You Have not Heard about the Sharia Question*, Published by JPC, Inc. [n.p.] 2000.

Abubakar, Khalid Aliyu, »Islamic Perspective on Peace«, in: Dennis Ityavyar/Zacharys Gundu (eds.), *Muslim/Christian Dialogue on Peace in Jos*, Jos 2004, 9–12.

Abubakar, Sa'ad, »The Northern Provinces under Colonial Rule: 1900–1959«, in: Obaro Ikime (ed.), *Groundwork of Nigerian History*, 2nd Edition, Ibadan 1984, 447–481.

Abun-Nasr, Jamil M., »Islamisches Recht im nigerianischen Rechtssystem«, in: Jamil M. Abun-Nasr (ed.), *Muslime in Nigeria*, Münster/Hamburg 1993, 201–225.

Achebe, Chinua, *The Trouble with Nigeria*, 2nd Edition, Enugu 1985.

Adamu, Fatima L., »Haushaltsstrategien, Frauen und Sharia-Gerichtshöfe in Sokoto/Nordnigeria«, *Peripherie*, 24 (2004), 284–305.

Adegbite, Lateef, »The Role of Muslim Leaders in the Government of Nigeria«, [Paper] Presented at the 12th Religious Studies Conference, Held at the University of Ibadan, April 4–7, 1978, in: Peter B. Clarke/Ian Linden, *Islam in Modern Nigeria. A Study of a Muslim Community in a Post-Independence State 1960–1983*, Mainz/München 1984, 169–174.

— Political Agenda for Muslims, Paper Delivered at the ›Conference on Islam in Nigeria‹, Ilorin, Kwara State, http://thisdayonline.com/archive/2001/04/15/2 0010415po105, 7. 12. 2004.

Adekson, Adedayo Oluwakayode, *The ›Civil Society‹ Problematique. Deconstructing Civility and Southern Nigeria's Ethnic Radicalization*, New York/London 2004.

Adeleke, Ademola, »Islam and Hausa Culture«, *Lagos Historical Review*, 5 (2005), 99–110.

Aderibigbe, Gbola, »African Religion and Christianity in Dialogue. An Appraisal from the African Perspective«, *Africana Marburgensia*, 32, 1/2 (1999), 39–56.

Adesina, Abdur-Razaq B., »Christian-Muslim Relations in Contemporary Northern Nigeria between 1980–2002«, *Islamochristiana*, 29 (2003), 111–120.

Adogame, Afe, »Politicization of Religion and Religionization of Politics in Nigeria«, in: Chima J. Korieh/G. Ugo Nwokeji (eds.), *Religion, History, and Politics in Nigeria. Essays in Honor of Ogbu U. Kalu*, Lanham [et al.] 2005, 125–139.

Ado-Kurawa, Ibrahim, *Shari'ah and the Press in Nigeria. Islam versus Western Christian Civilization*, Kano 2000.

— *Muslim Secularists' Rationalisations against Shari'ah*, Kano 2001, http://kanoonline. com/publications/pr_articles0001.html, 5. 8. 2006.

— *Jos International Conference on Comparative Perspectives on the Shari'ah in Nigeria*, Published by Trans West Africa Limited [n.p.] 2004.

Agbakoba, Olisa/Obeagu, Obiora, *Sharia. Death Penalty and the Constitution*, http:// thisdayonline.com/archive/2002/09/17/20020917law01, 7. 12. 2004.

Agbese, Pita Ogaba/Kieh, George Klay, »Military Disengagement from African Politics. The Nigerian Experience«, *Afrika Spectrum*, 27, 1 (1992), 5–23.

Agbu, Osita, *Ethnic Militias and the Threat to Democracy in Post-Transition Nigeria*, Uppsala 2004.

— »Re-inventing Federalism in Post-Transition Nigeria. Problems and Prospects«, *Africa Development*, 29, 2 (2004), 26–52.

Aguwa, Jude C., »Religious Conflict in Nigeria. Impact on Nation Building«, Dialectical Anthropology, 22 (1997), 335–351.

Ahmad, Ali, »Die Scharia aus nigerianischer Sicht«, Die Welt [Hamburg], 24 August 2002.

Ajayi, J. F. Ade/Smith, Robert, Yoruba Warfare in the Nineteenth Century, 2nd Edition, Ibadan 1971.

Ajetunmobi, Musa A., »Reorganisation of Legal System in Northern Nigeria – Appraisal of 1958 Recommendations«, Islamic and Comparative Law Quarterly, 10/11 (1990/1991), 96–108.

Ake, Claude, »Time for a Democratic Agenda«, Tell [Lagos], 22 August 1994, 33–34.

Akinyele, R. T., »Ethnic Militancy and National Stability in Nigeria. A Case Study of the Oodua People's Congress«, *African Affairs*, 100 (2001), 623–640.

Albert, Isaac O., »The Sociocultural Politics of Ethnic and Religious Conflicts«, in: Ernest E. Uwazie [et al.] (eds.), *Inter-Ethnic and Religious Conflict Resolution in Nigeria*, Lanham 1999, 69–87.

Aliyu, Amina Adamu, »Development in Northern Nigeria and Islam«, Paper Presented at a Conference on *Islamic Legal System and Women's Rights in Northern Nigeria*, Organised by WARDC, Lagos, and WACOL, Enugu, with Support of Heinrich Böll Foundation, at Abuja, October 27–30, 2002, http://boellnigeria. org/documents/Sharia%20and%20Women's%20Human%Rights, 23. 11. 2004, 123–126.

Al-Khamis, Muhammad, »The Role of Religious Leaders in Peace Building and Sustenance«, in: Dennis Ityavyar/Zacharys Gundu (eds.), *Muslim/Christian Dialogue on Peace in Jos*, Jos 2004, 93–102.

Alkhateeb, Fouad, »Islamic Unity«, *Nigerian Journal of Islam*, 1, 1 (1970), 11–14.

Alli, Warisu O., »Commentary« [to Abdulkader Tayob, The Demand for Shari'ah in African Democratisation Processes], in: Philip Ostien [et al.] (eds.), *Comparative Perspectives on Shari'ah in Nigeria*, Ibadan 2005, 57–66.

Almond, Gabriel A./Appleby, R. Scott/Sivan, Emmanuel, *Strong Religion. The Rise of Fundamentalisms around the World*, Chicago/London 2003.

Al-Zakzaky, Ibraheem Yaqoub, *Application of the Shari'ah in the Contemporary World. Lessons from some Muslim Countries. Part 1*, Paper Presented at the ›Conference on Nature and Application of the Shari'ah‹, Bayero University Kano, 1999, http://muslimedia.com/archives/features00/shariah1.htm, 6. 12. 2004.

— *Application of the Shari'ah in the Contemporary World. Lessons from some Muslim Countries. Part 2*, Paper Presented at the ›Conference on Nature and Application of the Shari'ah‹, Bayero University Kano, 1999, http://muslimedia.com/archives/features00/shariah2.htm, 6. 12. 2004.

Amnesty International, *Nigeria. Vigilante Violence in the South and South-east*, AI Index: AFR 44/014/2002.

Anderson, J. N. D., *Islamic Law in Africa*, London 1954.

— *Law Reform in the Muslim World*, London 1976.

Aniagolu-Tribunal, »Report on the Maitatsine Riot«, *New Nigerian* [Kaduna], 23 November 1981 – 2 January 1982.

An-Na'im, Abdullahi Ahmed, *Toward an Islamic Reformation. Civil Liberties, Human Rights, and International Law*, New York 1990.

— »Political Islam in National Politics and International Relations«, in: Peter L. Berger (ed.), *The Desecularization of the World. Resurgent Religion and World Politics*, Washington 1999, 103–121.

— »The Future of Shari'ah and the Debate in Northern Nigeria«, in: Philip Ostien [et al.] (eds.), *Comparative Perspectives on Shari'ah in Nigeria*, Ibadan 2005, 327–357.

[Anonym.], *The Supreme Council for Sharia in Nigeria [SCSN] Advertorial: Islam or [His]-lam* [An early version circulated by e-mail in November 2001. The text I used dates 4 December 2003. I received it from Dr. Isaac Laudarji, Kano].

Audi, Jummai, »On the Issue of Secularism«, Paper Presented at a Conference on *Islamic Legal System und Women's Rights in Northern Nigeria*, Organised by WARDC, Lagos, and WACOL, Enugu, with Support of Heinrich Böll Foundation, at Abuja, October 27–30, 2002, http://boellnigeria.org/documents/Sharia%20and%20Women's%20Human%Rights, 23. 11. 2004, 116–122.

Awofeso, Niyi/Ritchie, Jan/Degeling, Pieter, »The Almajiri Heritage and the Threat of Non-State Terrorism in Northern Nigeria. Lessons from Central Asia and Pakistan«, *Studies in Conflict & Terrorism*, 26 (2003), 311–325.

Ayu, Iyorchia D., »Towards a Revolutionary Solution of the Mafia Problem«, in: Bala J. Takaya/Sonni Gwanle Tyoden (eds.), *The Kaduna Mafia. A Study of the Rise, Development and Consolidation of a Nigerian Power Elite*, Jos 1987, 125–146.

Babalola, Ademola, »Democracy and National Development«, in: Toyin Falola (ed.), *Nigeria in the Twentieth Century*, Durham, North Carolina 2002, 881–887.

Bach, Daniel C., »Managing a Plural Society. The Boomerang Effects of Nigerian Federalism«, *Journal of Commonwealth and Comparative Politics*, 27, 1/2 (1989), 218–245.

— »Indigeneity, Ethnicity, and Federalism«, in: Larry Diamond [et al.] (eds.), *Transition without End. Nigerian Politics and Civil Society under Babangida*, Boulder/London 1997, 333–349.

— »Application et implications de la charia. Fin de partie au Nigeria«, *Pouvoirs*, 104 (2003), 117–127.

— »Inching towards a Country without a State. Prebandalism, Violence and State Betrayal in Nigeria«, in: Christopher Clapham [et al.] (eds.), *Big African States*, Johannesburg 2006, 63–96.

Baer, Robert, »The Fall of the House of Saud«, *Atlantic Monthly*, May 2003, 53–62.

Balewa, B. A. T., *Common Law and Sharia in Nigeria. An Unresolved Problem of Coexistence*, Enugu 2002.

Ballard, J. A., »»Pagan Administration‹ and Political Development in Northern Nigeria«, *Savanna*, 1, 1 (1972), 1–14.

Barnes, Andrew E., »»Evangelization Where it Is not Wanted‹. Colonial Administrators and Missionaries in Northern Nigeria during the First Third of the Twentieth Century«, *Journal of Religion in Africa*, 25, 4 (1995), 412–441.

— »Christianity and the Colonial State in Northern Nigeria, 1900–1960«, in: Toyin Falola (ed.), *Nigeria in the Twentieth Century*, Durham, North Carolina 2002, 281–292.

Barnhart, Michael G., »An Overlapping Consensus. A Critique of Two Approaches«, *Review of Politics*, 66, 2 (2004), 257–283.

Barrett, David B./Kurian, George T./Johnson, Todd M., *World Christian Encyclopedia. A Comparative Survey of Churches and Religions in the Modern World*, 2nd Edition, Vol. 1, Oxford 2001.

Barry, Brian, *A Treatise on Social Justice*, Vol. 2, Justice as Impartiality, Oxford 1995.

Bello, Ahmadu, *My Life*, Cambridge 1962.

Berger, Peter L., »The Desecularization of the World. A Global Overview«, in: Peter L. Berger (ed.), *The Desecularization of the World. Resurgent Religion and World Politics*, Washington 1999, 1–18.

Bergstresser, Heinrich, »Nigeria. Militärherrschaft ohne Ende?«, in: Joachim Betz/Stefan Brüne (eds.), *Jahrbuch Dritte Welt 1995. Daten. Übersichten. Analysen*, München 1994, 75–87.

— »Nigeria«, in: Rolf Hofmeier/Cord Jacobeit (eds.), *Afrika Jahrbuch 1999. Politik, Wirtschaft und Gesellschaft in Afrika südlich der Sahara*, Opladen 2000, 145–161.

— »Überzogene Demokratiehoffnungen? Nigeria am Scheideweg«, in: Joachim Betz/Stefan Brüne (eds.), *Jahrbuch Dritte Welt 2000. Daten. Übersichten. Analysen*, München 2000, 132–144.

— »Nigeria«, in: Rolf Hofmeier/Cord Jacobeit (eds.), *Afrika Jahrbuch 2000. Politik, Wirtschaft und Gesellschaft in Afrika südlich der Sahara*, Opladen 2001, 138–153.

— »Nigeria«, in: Rolf Hofmeier/Andreas Mehler (eds.), *Afrika Jahrbuch 2001. Politik, Wirtschaft und Gesellschaft in Afrika südlich der Sahara*, Opladen 2002, 141–157.

— »Nigeria«, in: Rolf Hofmeier/Andres Mehler (eds.), *Afrika Jahrbuch 2002. Politik, Wirtschaft und Gesellschaft in Afrika südlich der Sahara*, Opladen 2003, 155–171.

— »Zweite Wahl. Nigeria zwischen Wählerwillen, Gebetsorgien und Benzinknappheit«, *Der Überblick*, 39, 3 (2003), 45–47.

Berman, Bruce, »Ethnicity, Bureaucracy & Democracy. The Politics of Trust«, in: Bruce Berman [et al.] (eds.), *Ethnicity & Democracy in Africa*, Oxford/Athens 2004, 38–53.

Best, Shedrack, »The Islamist Challenge. The Nigerian ›Shiite‹ Movement«, in: Monique Mekenkamp [et al.] (eds.), *Searching for Peace in Africa. An Overview of Conflict Prevention and Management Activities*, Utrecht 1999, 345–352.

Birai, Umar M., »Islamic Tajdid and the Political Process in Nigeria«, in: Martin E. Marty/R. Scott Appleby, (eds.), *Fundamentalisms and the State. Remaking Polities, Economies, and Militance*, Chicago/London 1993, 184–203.

Black, Antony, »Religion and Politics in Islam. Fundamentalism in Historical Perspective«, in: Manfred Walther (ed.), *Religion und Politik. Zu Theorie und Praxis des theologisch-politischen Komplexes*, Baden-Baden 2004, 371–385.

Boer, Jan H., *Nigeria's Decades of Blood*, Belleville, Ontario 2003.

Bop, Codou, »Women's Human Rights in Muslim Societies in Africa«, Paper Presented at a Conference on *Islamic Legal System and Women's Rights in Northern Nigeria*, Organised by WARDC, Lagos, and WACOL, Enugu, with Support of Heinrich Böll Foundation, at Abuja, October 27–30, 2002, http://boellnigeria. org/documents/Sharia%20and%20Women's%20Human%Rights, 23. 11. 2004, 89–98.

Bosworth, C. E., »Shura«, in: C. E. Bosworth [et al.] (eds.), *The Encyclopaedia of Islam*, 2nd Edition, Vol. 9, Fascicules 155–156, Leiden 1996, 504–505.

— »Siyasa«, in: C. E. Bosworth [et al.] (eds.), *The Encyclopaedia of Islam*, 2nd Edition, Vol. 9, Fascicules 159–160, Leiden 1997, S. 693–694.

Bratton, Michael, »Briefing. Islam, Democracy and Public Opinion in Africa«, *African Affairs*, 102 (2003), 493–501.

Bratton, Michael/Lewis, Peter, *The Durability of Political Goods? Evidence from Nigeria's New Democracy* (= Afrobarometer. Working Paper No. 48), Cape Town/Legon-Accra/East Lansing, Michigan 2005.

Bratton, Michael/Mattes, Robert/Gyimah-Boadi, E., *Public Opinion, Democracy, and Market Reform in Africa*, Cambridge/New York/Melbourne 2005.

Bruce, Steve, *Fundamentalism*, Cambridge 2000.

— *Politics and Religion*, Cambridge 2003.

Brumberg, Daniel, »Islam Is Not the Solution (or the Problem)«, *Washington Quarterly*, 29, 1 (2006), 97–116.

Brunner, Markus, *The Unfinished State. Demokratie und Ethnizität in Nigeria*, Hamburg 2002.

Bubner, Rüdiger, *Drei Studien zur politischen Philosophie*, Heidelberg 1999.

Byang, Danjuma, *Sharia in Nigeria. A Christian Perspective*, Jos 1988.

Byman, Daniel, »Constructing a Democratic Iraq. Challenges and Opportunities«, *International Security*, 28, 1 (2003), 47–78.

Cahen, Cl., »Dhimma«, in: B. Lewis [et al.] (eds.), *The Encyclopaedia of Islam*, 2nd Edition, Vol. 2, Leiden/London 1965, 227–231.

Calder, N., »Shari'a«, in: C. E. Bosworth [et al.] (eds.), *The Encyclopaedia of Islam*, 2nd Edition, Vol. 9, Fascicules 153–154, Leiden 1996, 321–326.

Callaway, Barbara/Creevey, Lucy, *The Heritage of Islam. Women, Religion, and Politics in West Africa*, Boulder/London 1994.

Carens, Joseph H./Williams, Melissa S., »Muslim Minorities in Liberal Democracies. The Politics of Misrecognition«, in: Rajeev Bhargava (ed.), *Secularism and Its Critics*, 2nd Edition, New Delhi 1999, 137–173.

Chabal, Patrick/Daloz, Jean-Pascal, *Africa Works. Disorder as Political Instrument*, Oxford 1999.

Chalk, Peter, »Islam in West Africa. The Case of Nigeria«, in: Angel M. Rabasa [et al.], *The Muslim World after 9/11*, Santa Monica 2004, 413–432.

Christelow, Allan, »Islamic Law in Africa«, in: Nehemia Levtzion/Randall Pouwels (eds.), *The History of Islam in Africa*, Athens/Oxford/Cape Town 2000, 373–396.

— »Islamic Law and Judicial Practice in Nigeria. An Historical Perspective«, *Journal of Muslim Minority Affairs*, 22, 1 (2002), 185–204.

Christian Association of Nigeria, Borno State, *Religious Disturbances in Borno State. A Demand for Intervention of Federal Government and Setting up a Judicial Commission of Inquiry* [Letter to President Obasanjo, unpublished].

Christian Association of Nigeria, Zamfara State, *Peace and Democracy in Nigeria, Being a Text Presented by the Christian Association of Nigeria (CAN) Zamfara State on behalf of All Christians in the State to the National Orientation Agency*, December 2001 [unpublished].

Christian Association of Nigeria, Zamfara State, [Protocol of a] *Meeting on 14th January, 2002 with Gusau Local Government CAN Pastors and Commissioner of Lands and Housing, Zamfara State in the Commissioner's Office* [unpublished].

Chukkol, Kharisu Sufiyan, »Application & Limitation of Penal Code«, Paper Presented at the National Conference on Shari'a, *Hotline* [Kaduna], April 9, 2000, 27–30.

Civil Liberties Organisation, *Above the Law. A Report on Torture and Extra-Judicial Killings by the Police in Lagos State, Nigeria*, Researched and Written by Chukwuma Innocent, Surulere, Lagos 1994.

— *Justice for Sale. A Report on the Administration of Justice in the Magistrates and Customary Courts of Southern Nigeria*, by Eze Onyekpere, Surulere, Lagos 1996.

— *Sharia and the Future of Nigeria. Report of the Trip by the Civil Liberties Organisation, CLO, Hurilaws and Other NGO's to Zamfara State (11th–13th February 2000)* [unpublished].

— *Clear and Present Danger. The State of Human Rights and Governance. Year 2004*, [Lagos?] 2005.

Clapham, Christopher, »The Challenge to the State in a Globalized World«, *Development and Change*, 33, 5 (2002), 775–795.

— *The Decay and Attempted Reconstruction of African Territorial Statehood* (= University of Leipzig Papers on Africa No. 69), Leipzig 2004.

Clarke, Peter B./Linden, Ian, *Islam in Modern Nigeria. A Study of a Muslim Community in a Post-Independence State 1960–1983*, Mainz/München 1984.

Coleman, James S., »Nationalism in Tropical Africa«, *American Political Science Review*, 48, 2 (1954), 404–426.

— *Nigeria. Background to Nationalism*, 2nd Edition, Benin City/Katrineholm 1986.

[Committee], *Report of the Committee to Consider the Implications of the Introduction of Sharia Legal Code on Christians and Other Non-Muslims in Gombe State*, Vol. 1, Findings, Observations and Recommendations, November 2000 [unpublished].

Crampton, E. P. T., *Christianity in Northern Nigeria*, 2nd Edition, London 1979.

Crone, Patricia, *Medieval Islamic Political Thought*, Edinburgh 2004.

Crowder, Michael, *The Story of Nigeria*, 4th Edition, London 1978.

Crozier, D. H./Blench, R. M. (eds.), *An Index of African Languages*, 2nd Edition, Abuja/Ilorin/Dallas 1992.

Dah, Charles, »The Christian Perspective on Violence«, in: Dennis Ityavyar/Zacharys Gundu (eds.), *Muslim/Christian Dialogue on Peace in Jos*, Jos 2004, 59–65.

Danfulani, Umar Habila Dadem, *Women under Shari'a in Northern Nigeria. The Issue of Zina, Adultery. Who Will Cast the First Stone?*, Paper Presented at the Conference on ›The Sharia Debate and the Shaping of Muslim and Christian Identities in Northern Nigeria‹, Held at the University of Bayreuth, July 11–12, 2003 [unpublished].

— »Commentary« [to Sanusi Lamido Sanusi, The West and the Rest], in: Philip Ostien [et al.] (eds.), *Comparative Perspectives on Shari'ah in Nigeria*, Ibadan 2005, 275–292.

— *The Sharia Issue and Christian-Muslim Relations in Contemporary Nigeria*, Stockholm 2005.

Danfulani, Umar Habila Dadem/Fwatshak, Sati U., »Briefing. The September 2001 Events in Jos, Nigeria«, *African Affairs*, 101 (2002), 243–255.

Danfulani, Umar/Ludwig, Frieder/Ostien, Philip, »›The Sharia Controversy and Christian-Muslim Relations in Nigeria«, *Jahrbuch für kontextuelle Theologien* (2002), 70–95.

David, Peter, »In the Name of Islam«, *Economist* [London], *A Survey of Islam and the West*, 13 September 2003, 3–16.

Davutoglu, Ahmet, »Philosophical and Institutional Dimensions of Secularisation. A Comparative Analysis«, in: Azzam Tamimi/John L. Esposito (eds.), *Islam and Secularism in the Middle East*, London 2000, 170–208.

Diamond, Larry, *Class, Ethnicity and Democracy in Nigeria. The Failure of the First Republic*, Houndsmill, Basingstoke, Hampshire 1988.

— »Nigeria. The Uncivic Society and the Descent into Praetorianism«, in: Larry Diamond [et al.] (eds.), *Politics in Developing Countries. Comparing Experiences with Democracy*, 2nd Edition, Boulder 1995, 416–491.

Dibua, J. I., »Citizenship and Resource Control in Nigeria. The Case of Minority Communities in the Niger Delta«, *Afrika Spectrum*, 39, 1 (2005), 5–28.

Doi, Abdurrahman I., *Islam in Nigeria*, Zaria 1984.

Douglas, Oronto/Ola, Doifie, »Defending Nature, Protecting Human Dignity – Conflicts in the Niger Delta«, in: Monique Mekenkamp, [et al.] (eds.), *Searching for Peace in Africa. An Overview of Conflict Prevention and Management Activities*, Utrecht 1999, 334–338.

— Nourishing Democracy, Nurturing Diversity. Ethnic Militancy as Resistance Politics in Nigeria, in: Tunde Babawale (ed.), *Urban Violence, Ethnic Militias and the Challenge of Democratic Consolidation in Nigeria*, Lagos 2003, 41–47.

Dudley, B. J., *Parties and Politics in Northern Nigeria*, London 1968.

Durham, W. Cole, »Nigeria's ›State Religion‹ Question in Comparative Perspective«, in: Philip Ostien [et al.] (eds.), *Comparative Perspectives on Shari'ah in Nigeria*, Ibadan 2005, 144–167.

Ebeku, Kaniye S. A., »Constitutional and Human Rights Issues in the Implementation of Islamic Law in the Northern States of Nigeria – a Critical Appraisal«, *Recht in Afrika*, 7 (2004), 155–176.

Ebo, Adedeji, »Small Arms Proliferation in Nigeria. A Preliminary Overview«, in Okechukwu Ibeanu/Fatima Kyari Mohammed (eds.), *Oiling Violence. The Proliferation of Small Arms and Light Weapons in the Niger Delta*, Lagos 2005, 1–35.

Economist Intelligence Unit, *Country Profile 2003. Nigeria*, London 2003.

— *Country Report, February 2004. Nigeria*, London 2004.

— *Country Report, August 2005. Nigeria*, London 2005.

— *Country Profile 2005. Nigeria*, London 2005.

— *Country Report, November 2006. Nigeria*, London 2006.

— *Country Profile 2007. Nigeria*, London 2007.

Eisenstadt, Shmuel N., »Die Öffentlichkeit in muslimischen Gesellschaften«, in: Nilüfer Göle/Ludwig Ammann (eds.), *Islam in Sicht. Der Auftritt von Muslimen im öffentlichen Raum*, Bielefeld 2004, 311–325.

Ejobowah, John Boye, »Who Owns the Oil? The Politics of Ethnicity in the Niger Delta of Nigeria«, *Africa Today*, 47, 1 (2000), 29–47.

Ekeh, Peter P., »The Structure and Meaning of Federal Character in the Nigerian Political System«, in: Peter P. Ekeh/Eghosa E. Osaghae (eds.), *Federal Character and Federalism in Nigeria*, Ibadan 1989, 19–44.

El-Affendi, Abdelwahab, »Rationality of Politics and Politics of Rationality. Democratisation and the Influence of Islamic Religious Traditions«, in: Azzam Tamimi/John L. Esposito (eds.), *Islam and Secularism in the Middle East*, London 2000, 151–169.

Ellis, Stephen/ter Haar, Gerrie, *Worlds of Power. Religious Thought and Political Practice in Africa*, London 2004.

Elnaiem, Buthaina Ahmed, »Human Rights of Women and Islamic Identity in Africa«, *Recht in Afrika*, 5 (2002), 1–15.

Emmer, Pieter C., »Lieber Sklave als tot?«, *Der Überblick*, 38, 1 (2002), 12–18.

Endress, Gerhard, *Einführung in die islamische Geschichte*, München 1982.

Enwerem, Iheanyi M., *A Dangerous Awakening. The Politicization of Religion in Nigeria*, Ibadan 1995.

Essien, Victor L. K., »The Northern Nigerian Penal Code. A Reflection of Diverse Values in Penal Legislation«, *New York Law School Journal of International and Comparative Law*, 5, 1 (1983), 87–102.

Falola, Toyin, »Christian Radicalism and Nigerian Politics«, in: Paul A. Beckett/Crawford Young (eds.), *Dilemmas of Democracy in Nigeria*, Rochester 1997, 265–282.

— *Violence in Nigeria. The Crisis of Religious Politics and Secular Ideologies*, Rochester 1998.

Falola, Toyin/Adebayo, A., »Pre-Colonial Nigeria. North of the Niger-Benue«, in: Richard Olaniyan (ed.), *Nigerian History and Culture*, Burnt Mill, Harlow, Essex 1985, 56–96.

Fani-Kayode, Femi, »This Virus Called Sharia«, *Tell* [Lagos], 17 April 2000, 48–49.

Fawole, W. Alade, »Voting without Choosing. Interrogating the Crisis of ›Electoral Democracy‹ in Nigeria«, in: Tukumbi Lumumba-Kasongo (ed.), *Liberal Democracy and Its Critics in Africa. Political Dysfunction and the Struggle for Social Progress*, Dakar 2005, 149–171.

Fayemi, J. Kayode, »The Place of Religion in Constitutional Reform in Nigeria«, in: Otive Igbuzor/Ololade Bamidele (eds.), *Contentious Issues in the Review of the 1999 Constitution*, Lagos 2002, 143–158.

Fearon, James D., »Commitment Problems and the Spread of Ethnic Conflict«, in: David A. Lake/Donald Rothchild (eds.), *The International Spread of Ethnic Conflict. Fear, Diffusion, and Escalation*, Princeton, New Jersey 1998, 107–126.

Federal Republic of Nigeria, *Constitution of the Federal Republic of Nigeria 1999*, Lagos 1999.

Finkel, David, »Crime and Holy Punishment«, *Washington Post*, 24 November 2002, http://washingtonpost.com/wp-srv/resetcookie/front.htm, 10. 4. 2003.

Firestone, Reuven, *Jihad. The Origin of Holy War in Islam*, New York/Oxford 1999.

Fisher, Humphrey J., *Slavery in the History of Muslim Black Africa*, London 2001.

Flint, John, »Planned Decolonization and its Failure in British Africa«, *African Affairs*, 82 (1983), 389–411.

Foucault, Michel, *Discipline and Punish. The Birth of the Prison*. 2nd Edition, Harmondsworth, Middlesex, England 1991.

Fourchard, Laurent, »Violence et ordre politique au Nigeria«, *Politique africaine* 106 (2007), 5–27.

Freedom House, *The Talibanization of Nigeria. Radical Islam, Extremist Sharia Law and Religious Freedom*, 2002, http://freedomhouse.org/religion/pdfdocs/Nigeria%2 0Report.pdf, 12. 11. 2004.

Fricke, Werner/Malchau, Gilbert, »Die Volkszählung in Nigeria 1991 – Geographische Aspekte eines politischen Pokers«, *Zeitschrift für Wirtschaftsgeographie*, 38, 3 (1994), 163–178.

Froelich, J. C., »Essai sur les causes et méthodes de l'islamisation de l'afrique de l'ouest du XIe siècle au XXe siècle«, in: I. M. Lewis (ed.), *Islam in Tropical Africa*. Studies Presented and Discussed at the Fifth International African Seminar, Ahmadu Bello University, Zaria, January 1964, Oxford 1966, 160–173.

Fuller, Graham E., »The Future of Political Islam«, *Foreign Affairs*, 81, 2 (2002), 48–60.

Fwatshak, Sati U., *Shari'a Enforcement in Northern Nigeria. The Hisba and the Publics*, Paper Presented at the Conference on ›The Sharia Debate and the Shaping of Muslim and Christian Identities in Northern Nigeria‹, Held at the University of Bayreuth, July 11–12, 2003 [unpublished].

Gaiya, Musa A. B., *Complexity of the Shari'ah Debate in Nigeria*, Paper Presented at the Conference on ›The Sharia Debate and the Shaping of Muslim and Christian Identities in Northern Nigeria‹, Held at the University of Bayreuth, July 11–12, 2003 [unpublished].

— »Christianity in Northern Nigeria, 1975–2000«, *Exchange*, 33, 3 (2004), 354–371.

Gausset, Quentin, »Islam or Christianity? The Choices of the Wawa and the Kwanja of Cameroon«, *Africa*, 69, 2 (1999), 257–278.

— »The Spread of Islam in Adamawa (Cameroon)«, in: Thomas Bierschenk/Georg Stauth (eds.), *Islam in Africa*, Münster 2002, 167–185.

Gellner, Ernest, *Postmodernism, Reason and Religion*, London/New York 1992.

Gifford, Paul, *African Christianity. Its Public Role*, Bloomington/Indianapolis 1998.

Gilliland, Dean S., *African Religion Meets Islam. Religious Change in Northern Nigeria*, Boston/London 1986.

Gleave, M. B./Prothero, R. M., »Population Density and ›Slave Raiding‹ – a Comment«, *Journal of African History*, 12, 2 (1971), 319–327.

Greiter, Susanne/Jockers, Heinz/Rohde, Eckart, »Wahlbeobachtung in Nigeria. Eindrücke einer EU/UN-Beobachtergruppe in den Bundesstaaten Benue, Taraba und Bornu, Februar 1999«, *Afrika Spectrum*, 33, 3 (1998), 339–349.

Grunebaum, Gustav E. von, *Studien zum Kulturbild und Selbstverständnis des Islams*, Zürich/Stuttgart 1969.

Gumi, Abubakar, *Where I Stand*, 3rd Edition, Ibadan 2001.

Gwamna, Je'adayibe Dogara, *An Assessment of Christian Reactions to Shariah ›Introduction‹ in Northern Nigeria*, Paper Presented at the Conference on ›The Sharia Debate and the Shaping of Muslim and Christian Identities in Northern Nigeria‹, Held at the University of Bayreuth, July 11–12, 2003 [unpublished].

— »Commentary« [to Gerrie ter Haar, Religion: Source of Conflict or Resource for Peace?], in: Philip Ostien [et al.] (eds.), *Comparative Perspectives on Shari'ah in Nigeria*, Ibadan 2005, 320–326.

Gwandu, A. A., »Aspects of the Administration of Justice in the Sokoto Caliphate and Shaykh Abdullahi Ibn Fodio's Contribution to it«, in: S. Khalid Rashid (ed.), *Islamic Law in Nigeria. Application and Teaching*, Lagos 1986, 10–27.

Gwarzo, Tahir Haliru, »Activities of Islamic Civic Associations in the Northwest of Nigeria. With Particular Reference to Kano State«, *Afrika Spectrum*, 38, 3 (2003), 289–318.

Habermas, Jürgen, »Equal Treatment of Cultures and Limits of Postmodern Liberalism«, *Journal of Political Philosophy*, 13, 1 (2005), 1–28.

— »Religion in the Public Sphere«, *Philosophia Africana*, 8 (2005), 99–109.

Hackett, Rosalind I. J., »Rethinking the Role of Religion in the Public Sphere. Local and Global Perspectives«, in: Philip Ostien [et al.] (eds.), *Comparative Perspectives on Shari'ah in Nigeria*, Ibadan 2005, 7–26.

Hamza, Ibrahim, »Amirul Inglis?«. Lugard and the Transformation of the Northern Nigerian Aristocracy, c. 1903–1918«, in: Toyin Falola (ed.), *Nigeria in the Twentieth Century*, Durham, North Carolina 2002, 119–131.

Harneit-Sievers, Axel, *Jihad vs. Miss World. Politik, Religion und Geschichte in Nigeria*, Vortrag am Zentrum Moderner Orient, Berlin, 22 September 2003, http://uni-kassel.de/fb5/frieden/regionen/Nigeria/harneit.html, 21. 11. 2005.

— *Encounters and No-Go Areas in the Nigerian Debate about Sharia. Report on the Conference ›Comparative Perspectives on Sharia in Nigeria‹, Jos (Nigeria)*, January 15–17, 2004, http://gamji.com/NEWS3276.htm, 27. 5. 2004 [in: Afrika Spectrum, 38, 3 (2003), 415–420].

— *Constructions of Belonging. Igbo Communities and the Nigerian State in the Twentieth Century*, Rochester 2006.

Harnischfeger, Johannes, »The Bakassi Boys. Fighting Crime in Nigeria«, *Journal of Modern African Studies*, 41, 1 (2003), 23–49.

— »Sharia and Control over Territory. Conflicts between ›Settlers‹ and ›Indigenes‹ in Nigeria«, *African Affairs*, 103 (2004), 431–452.

— »Islamisation and Ethnic Conversion in Nigeria«, *Anthropos*, 101 (2006), 37–53.

Hartmann, Angelika, »Kalifat und Herrschaft im Islam. Erinnerung an Vergangenes und Zukünftiges«, in: Angelika Hartmann (ed.), *Geschichte und Erinnerung im Islam*, Göttingen 2004, 223–242.

Haruna, Balarabe A., »Women's Human Rights under Islam«, Paper Presented at a Conference on *Islamic Legal System und Women's Rights in Northern Nigeria*, Organised by WARDC, Lagos, and WACOL, Enugu, with Support of Heinrich Böll Foundation, at Abuja, October 27–30, 2002, http.//boellnigeria.org/documents/Sharia%20and%20Women's%20Human%20Rights, 23. 11. 2004, 99–107.

Hasenclever, Andreas/Rittberger, Volker, »Does Religion Make a Difference? Theoretical Approaches to the Impact of Faith on Political Conflict«, in: Pavlos Hatzopoulos/Fabio Petito (eds.), *Religion in International Relations. The Return from Exile*, Houndsmill, Basingstoke, Hampshire/New York 2003, 107–145.

Hastings, Adrian, »Holy Lands and their Political Consequences«, *Nations and Nationalism*, 9, 1 (2003), 29–54.

Hatzopoulos, Pavlos/Petito, Fabio, »The Return from Exile. An Introduction«, in: Pavlos Hatzopoulos/Fabio Petito (eds.), *Religion in International Relations. The Return from Exile*, Houndsmill, Basingstoke, Hampshire/New York 2003, 1–20.

Hauck, Gerhard, »Demokratisierung und Entwicklung – Testfall Nigeria«, *Peripherie*, 45 (1992), 67–76.

— »Die Konsolidierungschancen der afrikanischen Demokratie am Beispiel Nigerias. Zum Verhältnis von Staat, Ethnoparteien und konfliktfähigen Gruppen«, in: Rainer Tetzlaff [et al.] (eds.), *Afrika zwischen Dekolonisation, Staatsversagen und Demokratisierung*, Hamburg 1995, 189–200.

Herbst, Jeffrey, »Is Nigeria a Viable State?«, *Washington Quarterly*, 19, 2 (1996), 151–172.

Herskovits, Jean, »Nigeria's Rigged Democracy«, *Foreign Affairs*, 86, 4 (2007), 115–130.

Higazi, Adam, »Violence urbaine et politique à Jos (Nigeria), de la période coloniale aux élections de 2007«, *Politique africaine*, 106 (2007), 69–91.

Hiskett, Mervyn, *The Sword of Truth. The Life and Times of the Shehu Usuman dan Fodio*, New York 1973.

— »The Nineteenth-Century Jihads in West Africa«, in: John E. Flint (ed.), *The Cambridge History of Africa*, Vol. 5, From c. 1790 to c. 1870, Cambridge 1976, 125–169.

— *The Course of Islam in Africa*, Edinburgh 1994.

Hitti, Philip K., *History of the Arabs from the Earliest Times to the Present*, 10th Edition, London/Basingstoke 1981.

Hock, Klaus, *Der Islam-Komplex. Zur christlichen Wahrnehmung des Islams und der christlich-islamischen Beziehungen in Nordnigeria während der Militärherrschaft Babangidas*, Hamburg 1996.

— »Die Kraft der Prophezeiung und die Macht der Geister. Anmerkungen zur religiösen Dimension gewaltsamer Konflikte im westafrikanischen Kontext«, *Zeitschrift für Missionswissenschaft und Religionswissenschaft*, 83, 3 (1999), 210–230.

Hodgson, Marshall G. S., *The Venture of Islam. Conscience and History in a World Civilization*, Vol. 1, The Classical Age of Islam, Chicago/London 1977.

Hogben, S. J., *An Introduction to the History of the Islamic States of Northern Nigeria*, Ibadan 1967.

Horowitz, Donald L., *Ethnic Groups in Conflict*, Berkeley/Los Angeles/London 1985.

Human Rights Watch, *Nigeria. The Bakassi Boys. The Legitimization of Murder and Torture*, http://hrw.org/reports/2002/nigeria2index.htm, 11. 6. 2002.

— *The O'odua People's Congress. Fighting Violence with Violence*, http://hrw.org/reports/2003/nigeria0203/nigeria0203.pdf, 12. 10. 2005.

— ›Political Shari'a‹ Human Rights and Islamic Law in Northern Nigeria, http://hrw.org/english/docs/2004/09/21/nigeri9364_txt.htm, 18. 5. 2005.

— *Revenge in the Name of God. The Cycle of Violence in Plateau and Kano States*, http://hrw.org/reports/2005/nigeria0505/nigeria0505text.pdf, 12. 10. 2005.

Hunwick, John, »Sub-Saharan Africa and the Wider World of Islam. Historical and Contemporary Perspectives«, in: Eva Evers Rosander/David Westerlund (eds.), *African Islam and Islam in Africa. Encounters between Sufis and Islamists*, Athens, Ohio 1997, 28–54.

Hyden, Goran, »Conjunctures and Democratisation«, in: Dele Olowu [et al.] (eds.), *Governance and Democratisation in Nigeria*, Ibadan 1995, 49–64.

— »Governance and the Reconstitution of Political Order«, in: Richard Joseph (ed.), *State, Conflict, and Democracy in Africa*, Boulder/London 1999, 179–195.

Ibrahim, Jibrin, »Ethno-Religious Mobilisation and the Sapping of Democracy in Nigeria«, in: Jonathan Hyslop (ed.), *African Democracy in the Era of Globalisation*, Johannesburg 1999, 93–111.

— »Whither the Dividends of Democracy in Nigeria?«, *News from the Nordic Africa Institute*, 3 (2001), 2–5.

— *Democracy and Minority Rights in Nigeria. Religion, Shari'a and the 1999 Constitution*, Paper for the Conference on ›Globalisation, State Capacity and Self-Determination in Muslim Contexts‹, University of California, Santa Cruz, March 7–10, 2002, http://2.ucsc.edu/cgirs/conferences/Carnegie/papers/ibrahim. pdf, 18. 1. 2005.

— »The National Conference and the Challenge of Developing Democratic Federalism in Nigeria«, in: Otive Igbuzor/Ololade Bamidele (eds.), *Contentious Issues in the Review of the 1999 Constitution*, Lagos 2002, 159–222.

— »Polio Paranoia«, *BBC Focus on Africa*, April–June 2004, 32–33.

Idowu-Fearon, Josiah, »The Shari'a Debate in the Northern States of Nigeria and its Implications for West Africa Sub-Region«, in: Johnson Mbillah/John Chesworth (eds.), *From the Cross to the Crescent*, Nairobi 2004, 15–24.

Ikelegbe, Augustine, »The Perverse Manifestation of Civil Society. Evidence from Nigeria«, *Jounal of Modern African Studies*, 39, 1 (2001), 1–24.

— »State, Ethnic Militias, and Conflict in Nigeria«, *Canadian Journal of African Studies*, 39 (2005), 490–516.

Ilesanmi, Simeon O., *Religious Pluralism and the Nigerian State*, Athens, Ohio 1997.

— »Constitutional Treatment of Religion and the Politics of Human Rights in Nigeria«, *African Affairs*, 100 (2001), 529–554.

Iliffe, John, *Africans. The History of a Continent*, Cambridge 1995.

Imam, Yahya Oyewole, »Towards a Viable Constitutional Arrangement in Nigeria. The Madinan Model«, *Hamdard Islamicus*, 23, 3 (2000), 77–88.

Isichei, Elizabeth, *A History of Nigeria*, 2nd Edition, London/Lagos/New York 1984.

— »The Maitatsine Risings in Nigeria 1980–85. A Revolt of the Disinherited«, *Journal of Religion in Africa*, 17, 3 (1987), 194–208.

Iwobi, Andrew Ubaka, »Tiptoeing through a Constitutional Minefield. The Great Sharia Controversy in Nigeria«, *Journal of African Law*, 48, 2 (2004), 111–164.

Jama'atu Nasril Islam, »Memorandum«, in: Ghazali Basri, *Nigeria and Shari'ah. Aspirations and Apprehensions*, Leicester 1994, 80–82 [first in New Nigerian, 24 December 1986].

Jenkins, Philip, *The Next Christendom. The Coming of Global Christianity*, Oxford 2002.

— »Defender of the Faith. Why all Anglican Eyes in London are Nervously Fixed on a Powerful African Archbishop«, *Atlantic Monthly*, November 2003, 46–49.

Jinadu, L. Adele, »Explaining and Managing Ethnic Conflict in Africa. Towards a Cultural Theory of Democracy«, *African Journal of Political Science*, 9, 1 (2004), 1–26.

Jockers, Heinz/Peters, Ralph-Michael/Rohde, Eckart 2003, »Wahlen und Wahlbeobachtung in Nigeria, März – Mai 2003«, *Afrika Spectrum*, 38, 1 (2003), 79–97.

Johnson, James Turner, *The Holy War Idea in Western and Islamic Traditions*, University Park, Pennsylvania 1997.

Joseph, Richard, »Autocracy, Violence, and Ethnomilitary Rule in Nigeria«, in: Richard Joseph (ed.), *State, Conflict, and Democracy in Africa*, Boulder/London 1999, 359–373.

Juergensmeyer, Mark, *Terror in the Mind of God. The Global Rise of Religious Violence*, 3rd Edition, Berkeley/Los Angeles/London 2003.

Kalu, Ogbu U., »The Religious Dimension of the Legitimacy Crisis, 1993–1998«, in: Toyin Falola (ed.), *Nigeria in the Twentieth Century*, Durham, North Carolina 2002, 667–685.

— »Safiyya and Adamah. Punishing Adultery with Sharia Stones in Twenty-First-Century Nigeria«, *African Affairs*, 102 (2003), 389–408.

Kane, Ousmane, »Le réformisme musulman au Nigeria du Nord«, in: Ousmane Kane/Jean-Louis Triaud (eds.), *Islam et islamisme au sud du Sahara*, Aix-en-Province/Paris 1998, 117–135.

— *Muslim Modernity in Postcolonial Nigeria. A Study of the Society for the Removal of Innovation and Reinstatement of Tradition*, Leiden/Boston 2003.

Kappel, Robert, *Nigeria. Mangelnder Reformwille zementiert politische Instabilität*, 2nd Edition (= University of Leipzig Papers on Africa. Politics and Economics Series No. 57), Leipzig 2001.

Kastfelt, Niels, »Christianity, Colonial Legitimacy and the Rise of Nationalist Politics in Northern Nigeria«, in: Terence Ranger/Olufemi Vaughan (eds.), *Legitimacy and the State in Twentieth-Century Africa. Essays in Honour of A. H. M. Kirk-Greene*, Houndsmill, Basingstoke/London 1993, 191–209.

Keane, John, »The Limits of Secularism«, in: Azzam Tamimi/John L. Esposito (eds.), *Islam and Secularism in the Middle East*, London 2000, 29–37.

Keay, E. A./Richardson, S. S., *The Native and Customary Courts of Nigeria*, London/Lagos 1966.

Kenny, Joseph, »Sharia and Christianity in Nigeria. Islam and a ›Secular‹ State«, *Journal of Religion in Africa*, 26, 4 (1996), 338–364.

— »Islam. ›Authentic‹ or ›Fanatical‹, *Shalom. A Spiritual/Pastoral Quarterly* [of the Catholic Church, Ikeja, Lagos], 17, 1 (2002),1–6.

— »Commentary« [to Ruud Peters, The Enforcement of God's Law. The Shari'ah in the Present World of Islam], in: Philip Ostien [et al.] (eds.), *Comparative Perspectives on Shari'ah in Nigeria*, Ibadan 2005, 135–139.

Kepel, Gilles, *The Revenge of God. The Resurgence of Islam, Christianity and Judaism in the Modern World*, Cambridge 1994.

Kew, Darren, »Democrazy – Dem Go Craze, O‹. Monitoring the 1999 Nigerian Elections«, *Issue. A Journal of Opinion*, 27, 1 (1999), 29–33.

Khan, Mohammad Mustafa Ali, »A Case for Teaching Mirath as an Independent Course in Nigeria«, in: S. Khalid Rashid (ed.), *Islamic Law in Nigeria. Application and Teaching*, Lagos 1986, 181–194.

King, Lamont Dehaven, »State and Ethnicity in Precolonial Northern Nigeria«, in: Maghan Keita (ed.), *Conceptualizing/Re-Conceptualizing Africa. The Construction of African Historical Identity*, Leiden/Boston/Köln 2002, 9–30.

Kogelmann, Franz, *Islamisches Recht und Scharia-Debatten in Nigeria*, http://uni-kassel.de/fb5/frieden/regionen/Nigeria/islam.html, 21. 11. 2005.

— »The ›Sharia Factor‹ in Nigeria's 2003 Elections«, in: Benjamin F. Soares (ed.), *Muslim-Christian Encounters in Africa*, Leiden/Boston 2006, 256-274.

König, Claus-Dieter, *Zivilgesellschaft und Demokratisierung in Nigeria*, Münster/Hamburg 1994.

Kohlhammer, Siegfried, »Islam und Toleranz. Duldung, Ausbeutung, Demütigung«, *Merkur*, 56, 7 (2002), 589–600.

[Koran]: *The Koran Interpreted,* Translated with an Introduction by Arthur J. Arberry, Oxford 1998 [Since the suras are not numbered, I used the numeration given in Ahmed Ali, *Al-Qur'an. A Contemporary Translation*, 2nd Edition, Princeton 1986].

Korieh, Chima J., »Islam and Politics in Nigeria. Historical Perspectives«, in Chima J. Korieh/G. Ugo Nwokeji (eds.), *Religion, History, and Politics in Nigeria. Essays in Honor of Ogbu U. Kalu*, Lanham [et al.] 2005, 109–124.

Kukah, Matthew Hassan, *Religion, Politics and Power in Northern Nigeria*, 2nd Edition, Ibadan 1994.

— »Sharia Law, National Integration and Pastoral Challenges«, *Shalom. A Spiritual/Pastoral Quarterly* [of the Catholic Church, Ikeja, Lagos], 17, 1 (2002), 23–29.

— *Human Rights in Nigeria. Hopes and Hindrances*, Aachen 2003.

— [»Paper«, Presented at a Conference by] Centre for Democracy & Development, *Beyond Sharia. Interpreting Recent Religious and Ethnic Clashes in Nigeria* [n.d.], http://cdd.org.uk/sharia.htm, 5. 1. 2005.

— »Managing Christian-Muslim Relations in Africa«, in: Chima J. Korieh/G. Ugo Nwokeji (eds.), *Religion, History, and Politics in Nigeria. Essays in Honor of Ogbu U. Kalu*, Lanham [et al.] 2005, 391–411.

— »Christian-Muslim Relations in Sub-Saharan Africa. Problems and Prospects«, *Islam and Christian-Muslim Relations*, 18, 2 (2007), 155–164.

Kukah, Matthew Hassan/Falola, Toyin, *Religious Militancy and Self-Assertion. Islam and Politics in Nigeria*, Aldershot 1996.

Küng, Hans, *Der Islam. Geschichte, Gegenwart, Zukunft*, München/Zürich 2004.

Ladan, Muhammed Tawfiq, »Women's Rights and Access to Justice under the Sharia in Northern Nigeria«, Paper Presented at a Conference on *Islamic Legal System und Women's Rights in Northern Nigeria*, Organised by WARDC, Lagos, and WACOL, Enugu, with Support of Heinrich Böll Foundation, at Abuja, October 27–30, 2002, http://boellnigeria.org/documents/Sharia%20and%20 Women's%20Human%Rights, 23. 11. 2004, 37–88.

— *Legal Pluralism and the Development of the Rule of Law in Nigeria. Issues and Challenges in the Development and Application of the Sharia*, Paper Presented at the ›International Conference on Sharia, Penal and Family Laws in Nigeria and in the Muslim World‹, Organised by the International Human Rights Law Group, Abuja 2003, http://nigerianewsnow.com/News/November03/231103sharia.htm, 6. 12. 2004.

Laitin, David D., *Hegemony and Culture. Politics and Religious Change among the Yoruba*, Chicago/London 1977.

— »The Sharia Debate and the Origins of Nigeria's Second Republic«, *Journal of Modern African Studies*, 20, 3 (1982), 411–430.

Last, Murray, *The Sokoto Caliphate*, London 1967.

— »La charia dans le Nord-Nigeria«, *Politique africaine*, 79 (2000), 141–152.

— »Towards a Political History of Youth in Muslim Northern Nigeria, 1750–2000«, in: Jon Abbink/Ineke van Kessel (eds.), *Vanguard or Vandals. Youth, Politics and Conflict in Africa*, Leiden/Boston 2005, 37–54.

Levtzion, Nehemia, »Islam in the Bilad al-Sudan to 1800«, in: Nehemia Levtzion/Randall L. Pouwels (eds.), *The History of Islam in Africa*, Athens/Oxford/Cape Town 2000, 63–91.

Levtzion, N./Hopkins, J. F. P. (eds.), *Corpus of Early Arabic Sources for West African History*, 2nd Edition, Princeton 2000.

Levtzion, Nehemia/Pouwels, Randall L., »Patterns of Islamization and Varieties of Religious Experience among Muslims of Africa«, in: Nehemia Levtzion/Randall L. Pouwels (eds.), *The History of Islam in Africa*, Athens/Oxford/Cape Town 2000, 1–18.

Lewis, Bernard, *The Middle East. A Brief History of the Last 2,000 Years*, 2nd Edition, New York 1997.

Lewis, I. M., »Introduction«, in: I. M. Lewis (ed.), *Islam in Tropical Africa*, 3rd Edition, London 1980, 1–98.

Lewis, Peter M., »Endgame in Nigeria? The Politics of a Failed Democratic Transition«, *African Affairs*, 93 (1994), 323–340.

Lewis, Peter/Alemika, Etannibi/Bratton, Michael, *Down to Earth. Changes in Attitudes toward Democracy and Markets in Nigeria* (= Afrobarometer Paper No. 20), Cape Town/Legon-Accra/East Lansing, Michigan 2002.

Logams, P. Chunun, »Traditional and Colonial Forces and the Emergence of the Kaduna Mafia«, in: Bala J. Takaya/Sonni Gwanle Tyoden (eds.), *The Kaduna Mafia. A Study of the Rise, Development and Consolidation of a Nigerian Power Elite*, Jos 1987, 46–59.

Loimeier, Roman, »Das ›Nigerian Pilgrimage Scheme‹. Zum Versuch, den Hagg in Nigeria zu organisieren«, *Afrika Spectrum*, 23 (1988), 201–214.

— »Die Dynamik religiöser Unruhen in Nord-Nigeria«, *Afrika Spectrum*, 27, 1 (1992), 59–80.

— *Islamische Erneuerung und politischer Wandel in Nordnigeria. Die Auseinandersetzungen zwischen den Sufi-Bruderschaften und ihren Gegnern seit Ende der 50er Jahre*, Münster/Hamburg 1993.

— »Islamic Reform and Political Change. The Example of Abubakar Gumi and the Yan Izala Movement in Northern Nigeria«, in: Eva Evers Rosander/David Westerlund (eds.), *African Islam and Islam in Africa. Encounters between Sufis and Islamists*, London 1997, 286–307.

— »Playing with Affiliations. Muslims in Northern Nigeria in the 20th Century«, in: Laurent Fourchard [et al.] (eds.), *Entreprise religieuses transnational en Afrique de l'Ouest*, Paris/Ibadan 2005, 349–371.

— »Nigeria. The Quest for a Viable Religious Option«, in: William F. S. Miles (ed.), *Political Islam in West Africa. State–Society Relations Transformed*, Boulder/London 2007, 43–72.

Loimeier, Roman/Reichmuth, Stefan, »Bemühungen der Muslime um Einheit und politische Geltung«, in: Jamil M. Abun-Nasr (ed.), *Muslime in Nigeria. Religion und Gesellschaft im politischen Wandel seit den 50er Jahren*, Münster/Hamburg 1993, 41–81.

Lovejoy, Paul E., »Problems of Slave Control in the Sokoto Caliphate«, in: Paul E. Lovejoy (ed.), *Africans in Bondage. Studies in Slavery and the Slave Trade*, Wisconsin 1986, 235–272.

Lovejoy, Paul E./Hogendorn, Jan S., *Slow Death for Slavery. The Course of Abolition in Northern Nigeria*, 1897–1936, Cambridge 1993.

Low, Victor N., *Three Nigerian Emirates. A Study in Oral History*, Evanston, Illinois 1972.

Lubeck, Paul M., »Islamic Protest under Semi-Industrial Capitalism. 'Yan Tatsine Explained«, *Africa*, 55, 4 (1985), 369–389.

Ludwig, Frieder, *Religion und Politik im Kontext multireligiöser afrikanischer Staaten am Beispiel Nigerias* [n.d.] [unpublished].

— *The Sharia Controversy and Christian-Muslim Relations in Northern Nigeria*, Paper Presented at the Conference on ›The Sharia Debate and the Shaping of Muslim and Christian Identities in Northern Nigeria‹, Held at the University of Bayreuth, July 11–12, 2003 [unpublished].

Lugard, Frederick D., »Northern Nigeria«, *Geographical Journal*, 23, 1 (1904), 1–27.

Maduagwu, Michael O., »Religion and National Security. The Challenge for Nigeria in the 21st Century«, in: Chidi Ikonné/Ima O. Williams/Eucharia N. Nwagbara (eds.), *Security, Social Services, and Sustainable Development in Nigeria*, Port Harcourt 2005, 8–27.

Magbadelo, John Olushola, »The Politics of Religion in Nigeria«, *World Affairs*, 7, 2 (2203), 70–94.

Mahdi, Saudatu M. S., *Shari'a Implementation in Nigeria. Implications for Women's Rights*, Paper Presented at the Conference on ›The Sharia Debate and the Shaping of Muslim and Christian Identities in Northern Nigeria‹, Held at the University of Bayreuth, July 11–12, 2003 [unpublished].

— »Women's Rights in Shari'ah. A Case for Codification of Islamic Personal Law in Nigeria«, in: Philip Ostien [et al.] (eds.), *Comparative Perspectives on Shari'ah in Nigeria*, Ibadan 2005, 1–6.

Mahmud, Ahmed Bello, *Paper on the Adoption and Implementation of Shari'ah Legal System in Zamfara State*, Presented at the JNI-Sponsored Seminar on Shari'ah in Jigawa State, by Alh. Ahmed Bello Mahmud, Hon. Attorney-General & Commissioner for Justice, Zamfara State, July 6, 2000 [unpublished].

Mahmud, Sakah Saidu, »Islamism in West Africa«, *African Studies Review*, 47, 2 (2004), 83–95.

Maier, Karl, *This House Has Fallen. Midnight in Nigeria*, New York 2000.

Malchau, Gilbert, *Einkommensstruktur kleinbäuerlicher Haushalte und gesamtwirtschaftlicher Strukturwandel in Südost-Nigeria. Untersuchung im Rahmen eines erweiterten Tragfähigkeitsansatzes im dichtbesiedelten Hinterland von Uyo*, Hamburg 1998.

Malik, Sayed H. A., »The Shari'ah in the Life of a Muslim«, in: I. A. B. Balogun (ed.), *Islamic Tenets and the Shari'ah*, Ibadan 2000, 155–165.

Manz, Beatrice F., »Multi-Ethnic Empires and the Formulation of Identity«, *Ethnic and Racial Studies*, 26, 1 (2003), 70–101.

Marshall, Paul, »Nigeria. Shari'a in a Fragmented Country«, in: Paul Marshall, *Radical Islam's Rule. The Worldwide Spread of Extreme Shari'a Law*, Lanham [et al.] 2005, 113–133.

Mason, Michael, »Population Density and ›Slave Raiding‹ – the Case of the Middle Belt of Nigeria«, *Journal of African History*, 10, 4 (1969), 551–564.

Mazrui, Ali A., »Islam between Ethnicity and Economics. The Dialectics of Africa's Experience«, in: Thomas Salter/Kenneth King (eds.), *Africa, Islam and Development. Islam and Development in Africa – African Islam, African Development*, Edinburgh 2000, 15–54.

— *Shariacracy and Federal Models in the Era of Globalization. Nigeria in Comparative Perspective*, [Paper Presented] at the Conference on ›Restoration of Shariah in Nigeria. Challenges and Benefits‹, Sponsored by the Nigeria Muslim Forum, and Held in London, on April 14, 2001, http://sharia2001.nmnonline. net/ma zrui paper.htm, 30. 4. 2004.

— *A Tale of Two Africas. Nigeria and South Africa as Contrasting Visions*, London 2006.

McCain, Danny, »Which Road Leads beyond the Shari'ah Controversy? A Christian Perspective on Shari'ah in Nigeria«, in: Philip Ostien [et al.] (eds.), *Comparative Perspectives on Shari'ah in Nigeria*, Ibadan 2005, 7–26.

Meagher, Kate, »Hijacking Civil Society. The Inside Story of the Bakassi Boys Vigilante Group of South-eastern Nigeria, in: *Journal of Modern African Studies*, 45, 1 (2007), 89–115.

Meek, C. K., *The Northern Tribes of Nigeria. An Ethnographical Account of the Northern Provinces of Nigeria together with a Report on the 1921 Decennial Census*, 2nd Edition, London 1971.

Merkel, Wolfgang, »Religion, Fundamentalismus und Demokratie«, in: Hans-Bernhard Petermann (ed.), *Islam. Erbe und Herausforderung. 5. Heidelberger Dienstagsseminar*, Heidelberg 2004, 97–117.

Merkel, Wolfgang/Croissant, Aurel, »Formale und informale Institutionen in defekten Demokratien«, *Politische Vierteljahresschrift*, 41, 1 (2000), 3–30.

Meyer, Birgit, »›Make a Complete Break with the Past.‹ Memory and Post-Colonial Modernity in Ghanaian Pentecostalist Discourse«, *Journal of Religion in Africa*, 28, 3 (1998), 316–349.

Miles, William F. S., *Elections in Nigeria. A Grassroots Perspective*, Boulder/London 1988.

— »Religious Pluralism in Northern Nigeria«, in: Nehemia Levtzion/Randall Pouwels (eds.), *The History of Islam in Africa*, Athens/Oxford/Cape Town 2000, 209–224.

— *African Islamism, from Below*, http://worldandihomeschool.com/public/2003/december/mtpub1print.asp, 14. 12. 2003.

— »Shari'a as De-Africanization. Evidence from Hausaland«, *Africa Today*, 50, 1 (2003), 51–75.

Milner, Alan, »Sentencing Patterns in Nigeria«, in: Alan Milner (ed.), *African Penal Systems*, London 1969, 263–292.

Mohammed, Abubakar Siddique/Adamu, Sa'idu Hassan/Abba, Alkasum, *The Living Conditions of the Talakawa and the Shari'ah in Contemporary Nigeria*, Zaria 2000.

Mohammed, Danladi Adamu, *Muslim Intellectuals and the Sharia Debate in Nigeria*, http://nigerdeltacongress.com/...slim_intellectuals_and_the_sha.htm, 10. 4. 2003.

Moumouni, Seyni, »›Actualité du cheikh 'Uthman dan Fodio (1754–1817). Un héritage convoité‹. Essai d'une analyse des discours religieux et historiques relatifs au concept de la bonne gouvernance«, *L'Afrique politique* (2002), 111–120.

Mu'azzam, Ibrahim/Ibrahim, Jibrin, »Religious Identity in the Context of Structural Adjustment in Nigeria«, in: Attahiru Jega (ed.), *Identity Transformation and Identity Politics under Structural Adjustment in Nigeria*, Uppsala 2000, 62–85.

Muhammad, Abubakar D., *Muslim Responses to the Re-Implementation of Sharia in Northern Nigeria*, Paper Presented at the Conference on ›The Sharia Debate and the Shaping of Muslim and Christian Identities in Northern Nigeria‹, Held at the University of Bayreuth, July 11–12, 2003 [unpublished].

Muhammad, Saleh Dogara, *The Qur'an and the Bible on Shari'ah Law. A Brief Comparative Approach on the Issue of Shari'ah Law from the Divine Books*, Kaduna [n.d.].

Muhibbu-Din, M. A., »Principles of Islamic Polity towards ›Ahl al-Kitab‹ and Religious Minorities«, *Journal of Muslim Affairs*, 24, 1 (2004), 163–174.

Muslim Students' Society, Ahmadu Bello University, Zaria, »Press Release« [1978?], in: Peter B. Clarke/Ian Linden, *Islam in Modern Nigeria. A Study of a Muslim Community in a Post-Independence State 1960–1983*, Mainz/München 1984, 167–168.

Mustapha, Abdul Raufu, »Transformation of Minority Identities in Post-Colonial Nigeria«, in: Attahiru Jega (ed.), *Identity Transformation and Identity Politics under Structural Adjustment in Nigeria*, Uppsala 2000, 86–108.

— »Ethnicity & the Politics of Democratization in Nigeria«, in: Bruce Berman [et al.] (eds.), *Ethnicity & Democracy in Africa*, Oxford/Athens 2004, 257–275.

Mustapha, Hauwa, »Islamic Legal System, Women's Rights and Development in Northern Nigeria«, Paper Presented at a Conference on *Islamic Legal System and Women's Rights in Northern Nigeria*, Organised by WARDC, Lagos, and WACOL, Enugu, with Support of Heinrich Böll Foundation, at Abuja, October 27–30, 2002, http://boellnigeria.org/documents/Sharia%20and%20Women's%20Human%Rights, 23. 11. 2004, 108–115.

Nadel, S. F., *A Black Byzantium. The Kingdom of Nupe in Nigeria*, London/New York/Toronto 1942.

Nasir, Jemila, »Women's Human Rights in Secular and Religious Legal System«, Paper Presented at a Conference on *Islamic Legal System and Women's Rights in Northern Nigeria*, Organised by WARDC, Lagos, and WACOL, Enugu, with Support of Heinrich Böll Foundation, at Abuja, October 27–30, 2002, http:// boellnigeria.org/documents/Sharia%20and%20Women's%20Human%Rights, 23. 11. 2004, 1–36.

National Institute for Policy and Strategic Studies, *Religious Disturbances in Nigeria*, Jos 1986.

Ngou, C. M., »The 1959 Elections and Formation of the Independence Government«, in: Peter P. Ekeh/Patrick Dele Cole/Gabriel O. Olusanya (eds.), *Nigeria since Independence. The First Twenty-Five Years*, Vol. 5, Politics and Constitutions, Ibadan 1989, 80–105.

Ngowke, I. B., *Islam, the O.I.C. and Nigerian Unity*, Enugu 1986.

Nietzsche, Friedrich, »Zur Genealogie der Moral. Eine Streitschrift«, in: Friedrich Nietzsche, *Werke in zwei Bänden*, Vol. 2, München 1973, 175–288.

Nnoli, Okwudiba, *Ethnic Politics in Nigeria*, 2nd Edition, Enugu 1980.

Nolte, Paul, »Die Rückkehr der Religion«, *Handelsblatt* [Düsseldorf], 22 September 2004, 10.

Nouhou, Alhadji Bouba, »Islam et politique au Nigeria. Du malikisme au wahhabisme«, *Afrique contemporaine*, 201 (2002), 72–82.

— *Islam et politique au Nigeria. Genèse et évolution de la chari'a*, Paris 2005.

Nwabueze, Ben, *The Unconstitutionality of the State Enforcement of Sharia Law*, Excerpts from a Paper Delivered at a Symposium in Owerri, Imo State, by the Knights of St. Christopher, 2000, http://ogbaru.org/buezeon%20sharia.html, 7. 12. 2004.

Nwachukwu, Ijeoma, »The Challenge of Local Citizenship for Human Rights in Nigeria«, *African Journal of International and Comparative Law*, 13, 2 (2005), 235–261.

Nwanaju, Isidore Uchechukwu Chibuzo, *Christian-Muslim Relations in Nigeria. A Historical-Theological Reflection upon the Mutual Co-Existence of Christians and Muslims*, Nijmegen 2004.

Nwobi, Simeon Okezuo, *Sharia Law in Nigeria. What a Christian Must Know*, Abuja 2000.

Nzeh, Casimir Chinedu O., *From Clash to Dialogue of Religions. A Socio-Ethical Analysis of the Christian-Islamic Tension in a Pluralistic Nigeria*, Frankfurt/M. 2004.

Obadare, Ebenezer, »Religious NGOs, Civil Society and the Quest for a Public Sphere in Nigeria«, *African Identities*, 5, 1 (2007), 135–153.

O'Brien, Susan M., »La charia contestée. Démocratie, débat et diversité musulmane dans les ›états charia‹ du Nigeria«, *Politique africaine*, 106 (2007), 46–68.

Odey, John Okwoeze, *The Sharia and the Rest of Us*, Enugu 2000.

Oduyoye, Modupe, *The Shariy'ah Debate in Nigeria. October 1999 – October 2000*, Ibadan 2000.

Ojo, Matthews A., »Pentecostal Movements, Islam and the Contest for Public Space in Northern Nigeria«, *Islam and Christian-Muslim Relations*, 18, 2, (2007), 175–188.

Okeke, Okechukwu, *Hausa-Fulani Hegemony. The Dominance of the Muslim North in Contemporary Nigerian Politics*, Enugu/Lagos/Los Angeles 1992.

Okezie, G., »Christian Perspective on Peace«, in: Dennis Ityavyar/Zacharys Gundu (eds.), *Muslim/Christian Dialogue on Peace in Jos*, Jos 2004, 1–7.

Okunnu, Lateefah, *Women, Secularism and Democracy. Women's Role in the Regeneration of Society*, Paper Delivered at the Conference on Sharia, Held at the Commonwealth Centre, Kensington, London, http://shariah2001.nmnonline.net/okunnu_paper.htm, 30. 4. 2004.

Olaniyi, Rasheed, *Community Vigilantes in Metropolitan Kano, 1985–2005*, Ibadan 2005.

Olorunfemi, Akin, »The Fulani Jihad and the Sokoto Caliphate in the Nineteenth Century«, in: Richard Olaniyan (ed.), *Nigerian History and Culture*, Burnt Mill, Harlow, Essex 1985, 123–137.

Oloyede, Is-haq O., »Shari'ah in the North, Concerns of the South. Renewed Controversy over Shari'ah Law in Nigeria«, in: I. A. B. Balogun (ed.), *Islamic Tenets and the Shari'ah*, Ibadan 2000, 129–153.

— »Commentary« [to Sanusi Lamido Sanusi, The West and the Rest], in: Philip Ostien [et al.] (eds.), *Comparative Perspectives on Shari'ah in Nigeria*, Ibadan 2005, 292–302.

Omeje, Kenneth, »Military Rule and the Destabilisation of Nigeria Political Culture. The Politics of De-Democratisation«, *African Political Science Review*, 1, 1 (2000), 115–129.

Omolewa, Michael, »Myth and Reality of the Colonial Legacy in Nigerian Education, 1951–84«, in: Tekena N. Tamuno/J. A. Atanda (eds.), *Nigeria since Independence. The First Twenty-Five Years*, Vol. 3, Education, Ibadan 1989, 9–34.

Omotosho, A. O., »Religious Violence in Nigeria – the Causes and Solutions. An Islamic Perspective«, *Swedish Missiological Themes*, 91, 1 (2003), 15–31.

Onagoruwa, Olu, »Sharia. Declare State of Emergency in Zamfara«, in: Olu Onagoruwa, *Law and Contemporary Nigeria. Reflections*, Lagos 2004, 315–319 [first in Vanguard, 12 November 1999].

Opeloye, M. O., »Problems of Desecularizing Nigeria's Political Order«, *Islamic Quarterly*, 32 (1988), 101–113.

Osaghae, Eghosa E., *Trends in Migrant Political Organizations in Nigeria. The Igbo in Kano*, Ibadan 1994.

— »Amoral Politics and Democratic Instability in Africa. A Theoretical Exploration«, *Nordic Journal of African Studies*, 4, 1 (1995), 62–79.

— *Crippled Giant. Nigeria since Independence*, London 1998.

Osswald, Rainer, *Das Sokoto-Kalifat und seine ethnischen Grundlagen. Eine Untersuchung zum Aufstand des 'Abd As-Salam*, Beirut/Wiesbaden 1986.

Ostien, Philip, *A Study of the Court Systems of Northern Nigeria with a Proposal for the Creation of Lower Sharia Courts in Some Northern States*, Jos 1999.

— »Ten Good Things about the Implementation of Shari'a Taking Place in Some States of Northern Nigeria«, *Swedish Missiological Themes*, 90, 2 (2002), 163–174.

— »An Opportunity Missed by Nigeria's Christians. The 1976–78 Sharia Debate Revisited«, in: Benjamin F. Soares (ed.), *Muslim-Christian Encounters in Africa*, Leiden/Bosten 2006, 221–255.

— *Islamic Criminal Law. What It Means in Zamfara and Niger States*, Nigeria [n.d.] [unpublished].

Ottaway, Marina, »Ethnic Politics in Africa. Change and Continuity«, in: Richard Joseph (ed.), *State, Conflict, and Democracy in Africa*, Boulder/London 1999, 299–317.

Oyelade, E. O., »The Shari'a and National Unity in Nigeria«, in: Johnson Mbillah/John Chesworth (eds.), *From the Cross to the Crescent*, Nairobi 2004, 25–47.

Paden, John N., *Religion and Political Culture in Kano*, Berkeley/Los Angeles/London 1973.

— *Ahmadu Bello. Sardauna of Sokoto. Values and Leadership in Nigeria*, Zaria 1986.

— »Islam and Democratric Federalism in Nigeria«, *Africa Notes*, 8 (2002), 1–10.

— »Unity with Diversity. Toward Democratic Federalism«, in: Robert I. Rotberg (ed.), *Crafting the New Nigeria. Confronting the Challenges*, Boulder/London 2004, 17–37.

Park, A. E. W., *The Sources of Nigerian Law*, Lagos/London 1963.

Patriots, The, *A Bill for an Act to Make Provisions for Convening a National Conference of the Peoples of Nigeria for Purposes of Preparing a Constitution for Consideration and Adoption by the People of Nigeria at a Referendum and Matters Ancillary Thereto*, Prepared and Submitted by The Patriots [n.p.] [2001].

Peel, J. D. Y, *Religious Encounter and the Making of the Yoruba*, Bloomington/Indianapolis 2000.

Peel, Michael, *Crisis in the Niger Delta. How Failures of Transparency and Accountability are Destroying the Region*, Chatham House, Africa Programme, AFP BP 05/02, July 2005, http://riia.org/pdf/research/africa/BPnigerdelta.pdf, 25. 10. 2005.

Perham, Margery, *Native Administration in Nigeria*, 2nd Edition, London/New York/Toronto 1962.

Pérouse de Montclos, Marc-Antoine, »Le Nigeria à l'épreuve de la ›sharia‹«, *Ètudes*, 394, 2 (2001), 153–164.

— »Vertus et malheurs de l'islam politique au Nigeria depuis 1803«, in: Muriel Gomez-Perez (ed.), *L'islam politique au sud du Sahara. Identités, discours et enjeux*, Paris 2005, 529–555.

Peters, Ruud, *Islamic Criminal Law in Nigeria*, Ibadan 2003.

— »The Enforcement of God's Law. The Shari'ah in the Present World of Islam«, in: Philip Ostien [et al.] (eds.), *Comparative Perspectives on Shari'ah in Nigeria*, Ibadan 2005, 107–134.

Pobee, John S., *Religious Human Rights in Africa*, http://law.emory.edu/EILR/volumes/spring96/pobee.html, 6. 12. 2004 [in: Emory International Law Review, 10 (1996)].

Post, Kenneth/Vickers, Michael, *Structure and Conflict in Nigeria 1960–1966*, London/Ibadan/Nairobi 1973.

Quinn, Charlotte A./Quinn, Frederick, *Pride, Faith, and Fear. Islam in Sub-Saharan Africa*, Oxford 2003.

Ransome-Kuti, Beko, *The Sharia in South-Western Nigeria?*, http://nigerdeltacongress.com/sarticles/sharia_in_south.htm, 12. 10. 2005.

Rasmussen, Lissi, *Christian-Muslim Relations in Africa. The Cases of Northern Nigeria and Tanzania Compared*, London/New York 1993.

Rawls, John, *Political Liberalism*, New York 1993.

Reno, William, *Warlord Politics and African States*, Boulder/London 1998.

— »Gier gegen Groll. Nigeria«, in: Werner Ruf (ed.): *Politische Ökonomie der Gewalt. Staatszerfall und die Privatisierung von Gewalt und Krieg*, Opladen 2003, 291–298

— »The Roots of Sectarian Violence, and its Cure«, in: Robert I. Rotberg (ed.), *Crafting the New Nigeria. Confronting the Challenges*, Boulder/London 2004, 219–238.

Reynolds, Jonathan T., »The Politics of History. The Legacy of the Sokoto Caliphate in Nigeria«, in: Paul E. Lovejoy/Pat Ama Tokunbo Williams (eds.), *Displacement and the Politics of Violence in Nigeria*, Leiden/New York/Köln 1997, 50–65.

— *The Time of Politics (Zamanin Siyasa). Islam and the Politics of Legitimacy in Northern Nigeria 1950–1966*, San Francisco/London/Bethesda 1999.

Rothchild, Donald, »Ethnic Insecurity, Peace Agreements, and State Building«, in: Richard Joseph (ed.), *State, Conflict, and Democracy in Africa*, Boulder/London 1999, 319–337.

— »Assessing Africa's Two-Phase Peace Implementation Process. Power-Sharing and Democratization«, in: Patrick Chabal [et al.] (eds.), *Is Violence Inevitable in Africa? Theories of Conflict and Approaches to Conflict Prevention*, Leiden/Boston 2005, 147–169.

Roy, Olivier, *Globalised Islam. The Search for a New Ummah*, London 2004.

Sada, I. N., *Sharia in Nigeria. A Historical and Constitutional Brief*, Paper Presented at the Conference on ›The Sharia Debate and the Shaping of Muslim and Christian Identities in Northern Nigeria‹, Held at the University of Bayreuth, July 11–12, 2003 [unpublished].

— »Commentary« [to W. Cole Durham, Nigeria's ›State Religion‹ Question in Comparative Perspective], in: Philip Ostien [et al.] (eds.), *Comparative Perspectives on Shari'ah in Nigeria*, Ibadan 2005, 175–177.

Sagay, Itse E., »Reordering Nigerian Federalism. Making it More Confederal«, in: Robert I. Rotberg, (ed.), *Crafting the New Nigeria. Confronting the Challenges*, Boulder/London 2004, 85–98.

Sakpe, Abu Yakub Yunus, *Who is a Terrorist?*, [n.p.] 2001.

Salamone, Frank A., »Ethnic Identities and Religion«, in: Jacob K. Olupona/Toyin Falola (eds.), *Religion and Society in Nigeria. Historical and Sociological Perspectives*, Ibadan/Owerri/Kaduna 1991, 45–65.

Salihu, Joseph (ed.), *Interreligious Dialogue and the Shari'a Question*, Kano 2005.

Sambo, Bashir, *Shari'a and Justice. Lectures and Speeches*, Kaduna 2003.

Sandel, Michael J., »Religious Liberty. Freedom of Choice or Freedom of Conscience«, in: Rajeev Bhargava (ed.), *Secularism and Its Critics*, 2nd Edition, New Delhi 1999, 73–93.

Sanneh, Lamin, *Piety and Power. Muslims and Christians in West Africa*, Maryknoll, New York 1996.

— »Sacred Truth and Secular Agency. Separate Immunity or Double Jeopardy? Shari'ah, Nigeria, and Interfaith Prospects«, *Studies in World Christianity*, 8, 1 (2002), 31–62.

— »Shari'ah Sanctions as Secular Grace? A Nigerian Islamic Debate and an Intellectual Response«, *Transformation*, 20, 4 (2003), 232–244.

Sanusi, Sanusi Lamido, *Institutional Framework of Zakat. Dimension and Implications*, Lecture Delivered at a Symposium on ›Essentials for Building an Islamic

Ummah«, Held at Katuru Road Mosque, Ungwar Sarki, Kaduna, on Saturday 2/12/2000, http://gamji.com/sanusi18.htm, 30. 4. 2004.

— *Islam, Probity and Accountability. A Critical Essay in History, Philosophy & Law*, Text of the ›N.T.A. Channel 10 Annual Ramadhan Public Lecture‹ at the Auditorium of the Nigerian Law School, Victoria Island, Lagos. December 3, 2000, http://gamji.com/sanusi17.htm, 30. 4. 2004.

— *On the Islamisation of Politics & the Politicisation of Islam* (Revised) [n.d.], http://gamji.com/sanusi14.htm, 30. 4. 2004.

— *Class, Gender and a Political Economy of ›Sharia‹* [n.d.], http://nigerdeltacongress.com/carticles/class%20gender%20and%20the%20political%20economy%20of%20shar.htm, 27. 1. 2005.

— *The Shari'a Debate and the Construction of a ›Muslim‹ Identity in Northern Nigeria. A Critical Perspective*, Paper Presented at the Conference on ›The Sharia Debate and the Shaping of Muslim and Christian Identities in Northern Nigeria‹, Held at the University of Bayreuth, July 11–12, 2003 [unpublished].

— »The West and the Rest. Reflections on the Intercultural Dialogue about Shari'ah«, in: Philip Ostien [et al.] (eds.), *Comparative Perspectives on Shari'ah in Nigeria*, Ibadan 2005, 251–274.

Saro-Wiwa, Ken, »We Will Defend Our Oil with Our Blood«, in: Abdul-Rasheed Na'Allah (ed.), *Ogoni's Agonies. Ken Saro-Wiwa and the Crisis in Nigeria*, Trenton, NJ/Asmara 1998, 343–359 [first in Tell, 8 February 1993].

Schacht, Joseph, »Islam in Northern Nigeria«, *Studia Islamica*, 8 (1957), 123–146.

— *An Introduction to Islamic Law*, 2nd Edition, Oxford 1966.

Schimmel, Annemarie, *Der Islam. Eine Einführung*, 2nd Edition, Stuttgart 1995.

Schluchter, Wolfgang, »Hindrances to Modernity. Max Weber on Islam«, in: Toby E. Huff/Wolfgang Schluchter (eds.), *Max Weber & Islam*, New Brunswick/London 1999, 53–138.

— »Kampf der Kulturen?«, in: Wolfgang Schluchter (ed.), *Fundamentalismus, Terrorismus, Krieg*, Weilerswist 2003, 25–43.

Sklar, Richard L., *Nigerian Political Parties. Power in an Emergent African Nation*, 2nd Edition, New York/London/Lagos/Enugu 1983.

— »Unity or Regionalism. The Nationalities Question«, in: Robert I. Rotberg (ed.), *Crafting the New Nigeria. Confronting the Challenges*, Boulder/London 2004, 39–59.

Smith, Daniel Jordan, *A Culture of Corruption. Everyday Deception and Popular Discontent in Nigeria*, Princeton/Oxford 2007.

Smith, M. G., »The Jihad of Shehu Dan Fodio. Some Problems«, in: I. M. Lewis (ed.), *Islam in Tropical Africa*, 3rd Edition, London 1980, 213–225.

Sodiq, Yushau, »A History of Islamic Law in Nigeria. Past and Present«, *Islamic Studies*, 31, 1 (1992), 85–108.

Soyinka, Wole, *The Open Sore of a Continent. A Personal Narrative of the Nigerian Crisis*, New York/Oxford 1996.

Staudinger, Paul, *Im Herzen der Haussaländer. Reise im westlichen Sudan nebst Bericht über den Verlauf der Deutschen Niger-Benue-Expedition* [...], Oldenburg/Leipzig 1891.

Stewart, C. C., »Islam«, in: A. D. Roberts (ed.), *The Cambridge History of Africa*, Vol. 7, From 1905 to 1940, Cambridge 1986, 191–222.

Suberu, Rotimi T., »Religion and Politics. A View from the South«, in: Larry Diamond [et al.] (eds.), *Transition without End. Nigerian Politics and Civil Society under Babangida*, Boulder/London 1997, 401–425.

— *Federalism and Ethnic Conflict in Nigeria*, Washington 2001.

— »Democratizing Nigeria's Federal Experiment«, in: Robert I. Rotberg (ed.), *Crafting the New Nigeria. Confronting the Challenges*, Boulder/London 2004, 61–83.

— »Continuity and Change in Nigeria's Shari'a Debates«, in: Muriel Gomez-Perez (ed.), *L'islam politique au sud du Sahara. Identités, discours et enjeux*, Paris 2005, 209–226.

Sulaiman, Ibraheem, »Islam and Secularism in Nigeria. An Encounter of Two Civilisations«, *Impact International* [London], 24 Oct. – 13 Nov. 1986, 11–12.

— *A Revolution in History. The Jihad of Usman dan Fodio*, London/New York 1986.

— »The Shari'ah and the 1979 Constitution«, in: S. Khalid Rashid (ed.), *Islamic Law in Nigeria. Application and Teaching*, Lagos 1986, 52–74.

— *Sharia Restoration in Nigeria. The Dynamics and the Process*, Paper Delivered at the International Conference on Sharia at the Commonwealth Institute, London, April 14, 2001, Organised by the Nigerian Muslim Forum UK, http://shariah 2001.nmnonline.net/ibrahim_paper.htm, 30. 4. 2004.

Sulaiman, Muhammad Dahiru, »Shiaism and the Islamic Movement in Nigeria – 1979–1991«, in: Ousmane Kane/Jean-Louis Triaud (ed.), *Islam et islamismes au sud du Sahara*, Aix-en-Province/Paris 1998, 183–195.

Supreme Council for Shariah in Nigeria, »Revisiting the Plot to Destabilise Nigeria Using the United Nations (UN) Covert Campaign against Islam«, in: Jibrin Ibrahim, »Democracy and Minority Rights in Nigeria. Religion, Shari'a and the 1999 Constitution«, Paper for the Conference on *Globalisation, State Capacity and Self-Determination in Muslim Contexts*, University of California, Santa Cruz, March 7–10, 2002, http://2.ucsc.edu/cgirs/conferences/carnegie/papers/ibrahim.pd f, 18. 1. 2005, 24–27 [first in Daily Trust, 22–28 February 2002].

Tabiu, Muhammed, *Sharia, Federalism and Nigerian Constitution*, Paper Presented at the Conference on ›Restoration of Shariah in Nigeria. Challenges and Benefits‹, Sponsored by the Nigeria Muslim Forum, and Held in London, April 14, 2001, http://shariah2001.nmnonline.net/tabiu paper.htm, 30. 4. 2004.

Tabi'u, Mohammad/Rashid, S. Khalid, »The Administration of Islamic Law in Nigeria«, *Islamic & Comparative Law Quarterly*, 6, 1 (1986), 27–49.

Taheri, Amir, »Iran and Saudi Arabia. Two Zealots of Islamism«, *African Geopolitics*, 5 (2001/2002), 59–66.

Taylor, Charles, »Modes of Secularism«, in: Rajeev Bhargava (ed.), *Secularism and Its Critics*, 2nd Edition, New Delhi 1999, 31–53.

— »Democracy, Inclusive and Exclusive«, in: Richard Madsen [et al.] (eds.), *Meaning and Modernity. Religion, Polity, and Self*, Berkeley/Los Angeles/London 2002, 181–194.

— »Die Religion und die Identitätskämpfe der Moderne«, in: Nilüfer Göle/Ludwig Ammann (eds.), *Islam in Sicht. Der Auftritt von Muslimen im öffentlichen Raum*, Bielefeld 2004, 342–378.

ter Haar, Gerrie, »Religion. Source of Conflict or Resource for Peace?«, in: Philip Ostien [et al.] (eds.), *Comparative Perspectives on Shari'ah in Nigeria*, Ibadan 2005, 303–320.

Tetzlaff, Rainer, *Europas islamisches Erbe. Orient und Okzident zwischen Kooperation und Konkurrenz* (= Hamburger Beiträge zur Friedensforschung und Sicherheitspolitik, Heft 138), Hamburg 2005.

Thagirisa, Pavani, »A Historical Perspective of the Sharia Project & a Cross-Cultural and Self-Determination Approach to Resolving the Sharia Project in Nigeria«, *Brooklyn Journal of International Law*, 29, 1 (2003), 459–510.

Thomas, Scott M., »Taking Religious and Cultural Pluralism Seriously. The Global Resurgence of Religion and the Transformation of International Society«, in: Pavlos Hatzopoulos/Fabio Petito (eds.), *Religion in International Relations. The Return from Exile*, Houndsmill, Basingstoke, Hampshire/New York 2003, 21–53.

Tibi, Bassam, *The Challenge of Fundamentalism. Political Islam and the New World Disorder*, Berkeley/Los Angeles/London 1998.

Trimingham, J. Spencer, *The Influence of Islam upon Africa*, New York/Washington 1968.

Turaki, Yusufu, *The British Colonial Legacy in Northern Nigeria. A Social Ethical Analysis of the Colonial and Post-Colonial Society and Politics in Nigeria*, Jos 1993.

— *The Shari'a Debate in the Northern States of Nigeria. Implications for Muslims, Christians and Democracy in Nigeria*, Paper Presented at the Conference on ›The Sharia Debate and the Shaping of Muslim and Christian Identities in Northern Nigeria‹, Held at the University of Bayreuth, July 11–12, 2003 [unpublished].

Tyoden, Sonni Gwanle, *The Middle Belt in Nigerian Politics*, Jos 1993.

Ujo, C. A., »The Organizational and Social Manipulation Strategies of the Kaduna Mafia«, in: Bala J. Takaya/Sonni Gwanle Tyoden (eds.), *The Kaduna Mafia. A Study of the Rise, Development and Consolidation of a Nigerian Power Elite*, Jos 1987, 95–112.

Ukiwo, Ukoha, »Politics, Ethno-Religious Conflicts and Democratic Consolidation in Nigeria«, *Journal of Modern African Studies*, 41, 1 (2003), 115–138.

Umar, Khadijah Abdullahi, *The Northern Muslim Women under Sharia*, Paper Presented at the Conference on ›The Sharia Debate and the Shaping of Muslim and Christian Identities in Northern Nigeria‹, Held at the University of Bayreuth, July 11–12, 2003 [unpublished].

Umar, Muhammad Sani, »Changing Islamic Identity in Nigeria from the 1960s to the 1980s. From Sufism to Anti-Sufism«, in: Louis Brenner (ed.), *Muslim Identity and Social Change in Sub-Saharan Africa*, London 1993, 154–178.

— *Islam and Colonialism. Intellectual Responses of Muslims of Northern Nigeria to British Colonial Rule*, Leiden/Boston 2006.

U.S. Department of State, *Nigeria. Country Reports on Human Rights Practices. 2006*, Released March 6, 2007, http://state.gov/g/drl/rls/hrrpt/2006/78751.htm, 9. 3. 2007.

Usman, Yusufu Bala, *The Manipulation of Religion in Nigeria 1977–1987*, Kaduna 1987.

Vereecke, Catherine, »Ethnic Change and Continuity among the Fulbe of Aadamaawa Nigeria. The View from the Household«, in: Victor Azarya [et al.] (eds.), *Pastoralists under Pressure? Fulbe Societies Confronting Change in West Africa*, Leiden/Bosten/Köln 1999, 91–112.

Volkmann, Uwe, »Risse in der Rechtsordnung«, *Frankfurter Allgemeine Zeitung*, 11 March 2004, 8.

Waldmann, Peter, »Revenge without Rules. On the Renaissance of an Archaic Motif of Violence«, *Studies in Conflict & Terrorism*, 24 (2001), 435–450.

Walles, Kirsten V., »Shari'a and Politics since 1999«, in: Toyin Falola (ed.), *Nigeria in the Twentieth Century*, Durham, North Carolina 2002, 655–665.

Walls, Andrew F., »Africa as the Theatre of Christian Engagement with Islam in the Nineteenth Century«, in: David Maxwell (ed.), *Christianity and the African Imagination. Essays in Honour of Adrian Hastings*, Leiden/Boston/Köln 2002, 41–62.

Wan-Tatah, Victor F., »The Shari'ah Issue in Nigerian Politics«, *Studies in Contemporary Islam*, 2, 1 (2000), 28–37.

Watt, Montgomery W./Welch, Alford T., *Der Islam*, Vol. 1, Mohammed und die Frühzeit – Islamisches Recht – Religiöses Leben, Stuttgart/Berlin/Köln/Mainz 1980.

Weber, Max, *Economy and Society. An Outline of Interpretive Sociology*, Vol. 1, 2nd Edition, Berkeley/Los Angeles/London 1978.

Weiss, Holger, *Banga-Banga. Streß und Krisen im Hausaland (Nord-Nigeria) im 19. Jahrhundert*, Münster 1995.

Westerlund, David, »Secularism, Civil Religion, or Islam? Islamic Revivalism and the National Question in Nigeria«, in: Austin Metumara Ahanotu (ed.), *Religion, State and Society in Contemporary Africa. Nigeria, Sudan, South Africa, Zaire and Mozambique*, New York/San Francisco/Bern 1992, 71–101.

— »Reaction and Action. Accounting for the Rise of Islamism«, in: Eva Evers Rosander/David Westerlund (eds.), *African Islam and Islam in Africa. Encounters between Sufis and Islamists*, Athens, Ohio 1997, 308–333.

Whitaker, C. S., *The Politics of Tradition. Continuity and Change in Northern Nigeria 1946–1966*, Princeton, New Jersey 1970.

Williams, Adebayo, »Lord Lugard and the End of an Epoch«, *Africa Today*, May 2000, 22–24.

Williams, Pat/Falola, Toyin, *Religious Impact on the Nation State. The Nigerian Predicament*, Aldershot/Brookfield, USA 1995.

[Willink Commission], *Nigeria. Report of the Commission Appointed to Enquire into the Fears of Minorities and the Means of Allaying Them. Presented to Parliament by the Sec-*

retary of State for the Colonies by Command of Her Majesty, July 1958, London: Her Majesty's Stationary Office, Researched, Reviewed and Reproduced by League for Human Rights [n.p.] [n.d.].

Wushishi, Dantani Ibrahim, *Reasons for the Resurgence of Shari'ah in Nigeria*, Lagos 2004.

Yadudu, Auwalu Hamisu, *Benefits of Shariah and Challenges of Reclaiming a Heritage*, Paper Presented at the Conference on ›Restoration of Shariah in Nigeria: Challenges and Benefits‹. Sponsored by the Nigeria Muslim Forum, and Held in London, April 14, 2001, http://shariah2001.nmonline.net/yadudu_paper.ht m, 30. 4. 2004.

— *Sharia Implementation in a Democratic Nigeria. Between Deference to Popular Will and Libertarian Challenges*, Paper Submitted to the 3rd Annual Conference of the Center for the Study of Islam and Democracy, Held at Arlington, Virginia, USA, April 6–7, 2002, http://gamji.com/NEWS1284.htm, 6. 12. 2004.

Yahya, Dahiru, The Shari'ah and the Future of Nigeria, Kano 2001, http://kanoon line.com/publications/pr_articles0002.html, 5. 8. 2006.

Yahya, Maryam, »Polio Vaccines – ›No Thank You!‹ Barriers to Polio Eradication in Northern Nigeria«, *African Affairs*, 106 (2007), 185–204.

Yakubu, John Ademola, *The Dialectics of the Sharia Imbroglio in Nigeria*, Ibadan 2003.

Yoruba Agenda, The, Produced by Ad-hoc Planning Committee, [n.p.] 2005.

Yusuf, Hajiya Bilkisu, »Managing Muslim-Christian Conflicts in Northern Nigeria. A Case Study of Kaduna State«, *Islam and Christian-Muslim Relations*, 18, 2, (2007), 237–256.

Zabadi, I. S., »The Kaduna Mafia's Philosophy of the State and its Implications for Nigeria«, in: Bala J. Takaya/Sonni Gwanle Tyoden (eds.), *The Kaduna Mafia. A Study of the Rise, Development and Consolidation of a Nigerian Power Elite*, Jos 1987, 113–124.

Zamfara State of Nigeria, *Gazette. No.1. 15th June, 2000. Vol. 3. Law No. 10. Shariah Penal Code Law*, Gusau, Zamfara State: Ministry of Justice.

Newspapers und Journals

The African Guardian, Lagos
Africa Research Bulletin, Oxford
Africa Today, London
BBC. Focus on Africa, London
Business Day, Lagos
The Champion, Lagos
Daily Trust, Abuja
The Economist, London
Financial Times, London
The Guardian, Lagos
Hotline, Kaduna
Insider Weekly, Lagos
Le Monde, Paris
National Review, Kano
New African, London
New Impression, Kaduna
New Nigerian, Kaduna
The News, Lagos
News Service, Enugu
Newswatch, Lagos
Our Vision, Kaduna
The Source, Lagos
Der Spiegel, Hamburg
Tell, Lagos
Tempo, Lagos
This Day, Lagos
TSM. The Sunday Magazine, Lagos
Vanguard, Lagos
The Week, Lagos
Weekly Trust, Abuja
West Africa, London
Die Zeit, Hamburg

Index

Social Science

Stefani Scherer, Reinhard Pollak, Gunnar Otte, Markus Gangl (Hg.)
▶ **FROM ORIGIN TO DESTINATION**
Trends and Mechanisms in Social Stratification Research
2007 · 323 p. · ISBN 978-3-593-38411-5

Johannes Harnischfeger
▶ **DEMOCRATIZATION AND ISLAMIC LAW**
The Sharia Conflict in Nigeria
2007 · 260 p. · ISBN 978-3-593-38256-2

Helmut Willke
▶ **SMART GOVERNANCE**
Governing the Global Knowledge Society
2007 · 206 p. · ISBN 978-3-593-38253-1

Michael Dauderstädt, Arne Schildberg (eds.)
▶ **DEAD ENDS OF TRANSITION**
Rentier Economies and Protectorate
2006 · 249 p. · ISBN 978-3-593-38154-1

Magdalena Nowicka
▶ **TRANSNATIONAL PROFESSIONALS**
AND THEIR COSMOPOLITAN UNIVERSES
2006 · 280 p. · ISBN 978-3-593-38155-8

Sonja Puntscher Riekmann, Monika Mokre, Michael Latzer (eds.)
▶ **THE STATE OF EUROPE**
Transformations of Statehood from a European Perspective
2004 · 358 p. · ISBN 978-3-593-37632-5

campus
Frankfurt · New York